STATLIB

A Statistical Computing Library

William M. Brelsford
Bell Laboratories

Daniel A. Relles
The Rand Corporation

PRENTICE-HALL, INC. Englewood Cliffs, New Jersey 07632

Library of Congress Cataloging in Publication Data

Brelsford, William M.
    STATLIB: a statistical computing library.

    Includes index.
    1. STATLIB (Computer programs) I. Relles,
Daniel A., (date) II. Title.
QA276.4.B73   001.64'24   80-26701
ISBN 0-13-846220-8

Printed in the United States of America

10   9   8   7   6   5   4   3   2   1

Editorial/production supervision: Nancy Milnamow
Cover design: **Mark Binn**
Manufacturing buyer: Joyce Levatino

Prentice-Hall International, Inc., *London*
Prentice-Hall of Australia Pty. Limited, *Sydney*
Prentice-Hall of Canada, Ltd., *Toronto*
Prentice-Hall of India Private Limited, *New Delhi*
Prentice-Hall of Japan, Inc., *Tokyo*
Prentice-Hall of Southeast Asia Pte. Ltd., *Singapore*
Whitehall Books Limited, *Wellington, New Zealand*

PREFACE

This manual contains documentation for STATLIB, a statistical computing library. STATLIB contains FORTRAN-callable routines and a command language for executing many of them. The routines and commands are building blocks for statistical analyses; when properly linked, they provide many standard as well as nonstandard types of procedures.

STATLIB has been in use for many years at Bell Laboratories, elsewhere in the Bell System, and at the Rand Corporation. Inquiries from outside the Bell System concerning software availability should be directed to: Computing Information Service, Bell Telephone Laboratories, 600 Mountain Avenue, Murray Hill, New Jersey 07974.

The manual is organized in four parts. Part I is an introduction to the library. It indicates the various programming levels available and introduces by example some of the library's principal packages. Part II describes the library's high-level routines, all available in the STATLIB command language. Part III describes the library's low-level FORTRAN routines, used themselves as building blocks for the command language and of general interest to FORTRAN programmers. Part IV describes the various implementations of STATLIB and shows the operating system commands required to invoke parts of it.

To simplify exposition, the documentation omits details about what statistical models to apply and when; it assumes that the user is knowledgeable in that regard.

We are grateful to many statisticians for their contributions to STATLIB. David Preston developed the SPPAK software and wrote Chapter 7 of the manual. Robert Bassett wrote several routines for the TABLE package and re-wrote Chapter 8. Both Dave and Bob also contributed to other parts of the library's software and documentation and, along with William Lisowski and James Inglis, reviewed the manual, exercised the revised version of the software, and provided an endless stream of useful comments and suggestions. Earlier assistance was provided by Marsha Hopkins on TRIPAK and Linda Slade on TABLE. Min-Te Chao wrote the SIMPSN subroutine and Anne Robrock wrote XORDST. Phyllis Groll provided assistance in numerous areas.

Continuous feedback in the form of comments and suggestions from Bell System and Rand users has been invaluable and is gratefully acknowledged.

William M. Brelsford
Daniel A. Relles

CONTENTS

PART II

CHAPTER 4

CHAPTER 5

CHAPTER 6

CHAPTER 7

CHAPTER 8

CHAPTER 9

CHAPTER 10

PART III

CHAPTER 11

CHAPTER 12

CHAPTER 13

CHAPTER 16

PART I

INTRODUCTION

This manual contains documentation for subroutines in STATLIB, a statistical computing library. The library contains FORTRAN-callable subroutines and a command system for executing many of them in a language-level environment. The subroutines provide building blocks for statistical analysis rather than complete analyses themselves. The user links them together as required; depending upon how nonstandard the application, anywhere from a few to several statements may be needed apart from the data recoding. This orientation results in software that is flexible and powerful enough for the trained statistician, though in some cases difficult for the novice to use.

Part I of the manual provides an introduction to STATLIB. Chapter 1 acquaints the reader with design considerations that shaped the library. Chapters 2 and 3 introduce two of the library's principal packages: STPAK, for analyzing two-way matrices, and TSPAK, for analyzing time series data. These chapters expose the reader to the kinds of problems the library can handle and illustrate the level of programming required for standard as well as nonstandard jobs.

CHAPTER 1

INTRODUCTION TO STATLIB

STATLIB (pronounced stat'-libe) is a statistical computing system which provides a flexible and powerful means for analyzing data. It consists of a library of FORTRAN-callable subroutines and a command system (ISX) for executing them. The subroutines may be thought of as macro instructions that serve as building blocks for statistical analysis: e.g., read, print, plot, accumulate, regress, predict, etc. Some subroutines perform high-level functions, such as a sequence of multiple linear regression computations, or calculations associated with fitting a logistic regression function. And, for performing still higher-level functions, facilities exist that enable users to write new commands composed of sets of the standard STATLIB ones.

In designing STATLIB, we have tried to side-step the usual trade-off between versatility and ease of use by offering the user several levels of macro instructions. The examples below illustrate this point in a simple regression problem relating wages to experience. Each program reads a data matrix, computes the logarithms of wages, regresses the logarithms of wages on experience, and plots residuals versus predictions.

Program 1 - FORTRAN	
dimension data matrix	REAL*8 X(4,200)
independent, dependent vbls	INTEGER KV(2)/1,2/
read data matrix	READ(5,91)((X(I,J),I=1,2),J=1,200)
transform wages	DO 20 J=1,200
	20 X(2,J)=DLOG(X(2,J))
residuals	CALL REGPAR('RSID',3)
predictions [1]	CALL REGPAR('PRDN',4)
regress wages on experience	CALL REGX(2,4,200,X,2,KV)
plot resids vs predictions	CALL PPLOT(4,X,4,1,3,0,200)
	STOP
format for read	91 FORMAT(2F6.0)
	END
[1] Throughout this text, "predictions" is used as a synonym for "fitted values".	

```
                    Program 2 - FORTRAN
dimension data matrix      | CALL STDIM('SLRY',2,'EXP     WAGE     ')
read data matrix           | CALL STREAD('SLRY',5,'(2F6.0)',200)
transform wages            | CALL STFN1('SLRY','WAGE    ','LOG',
                           |   'WAGE    ')
residuals, predictions     | CALL STENL('SLRY',2,'RSID    PRDN    ')
regress wages on experience| CALL STREG('SLRY','WAGE    ',1,
                           |   'EXP     ')
plot resids vs predictions | CALL STPLT('SLRY','PRDN    ',1,
                           |   'RSID    ')
                           | STOP
                           | END
```

```
                  Program 3 - Command System
dimension data matrix      | STDIM SLRY 2 EXP WAGE
read data matrix           | STREAD SLRY 5 (2F6.0) 200
transform wages            | STFN1 SLRY WAGE LOG WAGE
residuals, predictions     | STENL SLRY 2 RSID PRDN
regress wages on experience| STREG SLRY WAGE 1 EXP
plot resids vs predictions | STPLT SLRY PRDN 1 RSID
```

```
             Program 4 - Command System Procedures
dimension, input matrix    | INPUT SLRY 2 EXP WAGE 5 (2F6.0) 200
transform wages            | STFN1 SLRY WAGE LOG WAGE
regress wages on experience| REGRESS WAGE ON EXP
plot resids vs predictions | PLOT RSID VS PRDN
```

Program 1 operates directly in FORTRAN, providing perhaps the
greatest latitude in data manipulation, but posing the greatest
programming difficulties.   It calls subroutines in REGPAK (Ch. 11),
STATLIB's regression package. The regression routine REGX itself
calls lower-level REGPAK routines, each of which performs one step in
the regression (e.g., accumulation, inversion, prediction, etc.).
When greater flexibility is required, the user may call these
routines directly.

Program 2 illustrates the use of a high level package of FORTRAN
routines, STPAK (Ch. 5). The code is simplified considerably and is
more understandable than Program 1; yet the user is still operating
in a FORTRAN mode. This level of programming is made possible by an
in-core data manager, DYNCOR (Ch. 9).   STPAK operates on two-way data
matrices (observations by variables) stored in DYNCOR blocks. The
user passes the names of the data blocks (e.g., SLRY) to STPAK
subroutines, which in turn use DYNCOR to create, access, rename, copy
and delete blocks as required.

Program 3 is written in ISX (Ch. 4), the STATLIB interactive command
system.   Subroutine names are used as commands and calling sequences
are retained for compatability with FORTRAN use, but FORTRAN's rigid
syntax is replaced by free-form input with punctuation removed. ISX
interprets each line and executes the proper subroutine call.   The
cost of interpretation is more than outweighed by removing the need
for compilation and for loading library subroutines separately.

Furthermore, when used on a time-sharing system, ISX provides true interactive computing.

Program 4 is also written in ISX, but makes use of several commands written themselves in ISX. A command language provides the capability of decoding variable-length argument lists, performing conditional branches, looping over groups of statements, as well as executing calls to subroutines. These features enable powerful commands to be written easily for general use or for specific applications.

In addition to STPAK, STATLIB contains high-level subroutine packages which deal with two other kinds of data structures: TSPAK (Ch. 6) and SPPAK (Ch. 7), for time series analysis, and TABLE (Ch. 8), for multi-way table analysis. The time series is a one-dimensional array containing one variable measured at a number of points in time (or space). An example is a series of maximum daily temperatures over a two-year period. The multi-way table is an array of arbitrarily high dimensionality: for example, a five-way table in which the entries are numbers of employees classified by race, sex, job level, salary range, and state. These packages use the same low-level computational routines as STPAK, including DYNCOR to store data and data description information. Furthermore, they contain routines which simplify the transfer of data between packages.

The scientist or engineer performing a standard analysis will usually want to use the simplest high-level commands available (such as Programs 3 and 4) but the statistical research worker developing new methodology will often require lower-level macros (Programs 1 and 2, or lower). While he could augment ISX with his own code, in some situations he might prefer to access STATLIB routines directly: for example, when the statistical analysis is part of a larger FORTRAN program or system, or when maximum efficiency in core storage or execution time is required. STATLIB's multi-level design enables him to do this easily.

Chapters 2 and 3 contain introductions to STPAK (Statistical Analysis of Two-Way Matrices) and TSPAK (Time Series Analysis) respectively. They are intended to acquaint the reader with the philosophy and structure of the packages, and of STATLIB generally. Each contains sample programs with discussions, progressing from very simple calculations to more complex procedures. The reader should work his way through one of these, pausing as necessary to peruse the appropriate documentation in Part II and perhaps to try similar analyses on the computer. Part II contains reference sections documenting ISX, the high-level packages, and the service routines that may be called from ISX. After assimilating parts of Chapters 2 and/or 3, the reader should be able to read and use these reference chapters. However, we stress the importance of actually using the system as one learns it; one can become "fluent" in the use of STATLIB only through practice. Part III documents the library's low-level routines (collected into packages themselves) which carry out the actual statistical computations for the high level packages and which may be called directly by the user, if necessary. Finally, Part IV contains information on STATLIB availability and current

implementations.   It   also   shows   the   system-dependent   commands
required to invoke the ISX program.

CHAPTER 2

STATISTICAL ANALYSIS OF TWO-WAY MATRICES

This chapter discusses the analysis of two-way matrices using STATLIB. STPAK (Ch. 5) is the principal package for handling this type of data structure; it performs such operations as loading the data into core, plotting, printing, distribution fitting, regression, cross-tabulation, logit maximum likelihood, and many more.

The two-way matrix is perhaps the most common of all statistical data structures. One dimension consists of observations or cases; the other contains variables or measurements on these observations. Frequently, in social science research, the observations correspond to people and the variables are personal attributes (e.g., age, race, sex, income). But observations can reference time, location, experimental conditions, or any other dimension that identifies units on which a given set of measurements may be taken.

In illustrating the application of STATLIB to analyzing such data, we consider an example which poses typical statistical and computing problems, focusing on the computing aspects of the problem. The example arises in a basic statistics course which emphasizes acquiring the tools of exploratory data analysis and modeling through experience. In one case each student receives a data set consisting of 250 observations on health expenditures from the 1970 CHAS-NORC Medical Expenditures Survey [1]; using this data, he constructs a health expenditures regression model. In producing his model, he utilizes his prior knowledge of how medical expenditures occur as well as his knowledge of relevant statistical methodology. Students' models are ultimately cross-validated on other students' data sets as well as on the entire data base of 11,155 observations.

1. INTRODUCTION TO STPAK

Analysis of data of this type typically involves (1) performing an initial exploration of the data, identifying spurious observations, and recognizing the variables correlated with expenditures; (2) developing some theory to focus the regression analysis on meaningful relationships; and (3) fitting and checking models. Below we describe how STPAK could be used to perform such an analysis. Examples are presented in the language of ISX (Ch. 4) -- the STATLIB command system.

1.1 Data Input

The first step is to bring the data matrix into the computer. The table below describes the data matrix and identifies the specific data to be used here.

CHAS-NORC 1970 HEALTH EXPENDITURES SURVEY

Variable	Cols	Description
INC	1-6	Family income (thousands)
EDUC	7-12	Education of head - (code:years) (1:0),(2:1-4),(3:5-6),(4:7-8), (5:9-11),(6:12),(7:13-15),(8:16+)
NONW	13-18	Nonwhite indicator
AGE	19-24	Age
FEM	25-30	Female indicator
HLTH	31-36	Health status - (0:exc or good), (1:fair),(2:poor)
EMP	37-42	Employment indicator
HEAD	43-48	Head of household indicator
INS	49-54	Insured indicator
EXPEND	55-60	1969 health expenditures
SIZE	61-66	Family size

For our purposes, there are four essential points to note:

the data matrix must have a name;

it must have a list of variables;

it must have a specific number of observations;

the actual data values must be stored in the computer.

In STPAK, the most common form of data matrix entry is as follows:

Defining a Data Matrix	
dimension [1]	STDIM HEXP 11 INC EDUC NONW AGE $ FEM HLTH EMP HEAD INS EXPEND SIZE
read	STREAD HEXP 10 (11F6.0) 250
[1] "$" as the last word on a line signifies a continuation line in ISX.	

STDIM: HEXP, 11 VBLS:
          INC EDUC NONW AGE FEM HLTH EMP HEAD INS EXPEND
          SIZE

STREAD: HEXP (11 BY 250), UNIT=10, 11 VBLS READ

The dimensioning command STDIM (p. 91) identifies the matrix (HEXP), the number of variables (11), and their names (income, education, etc.). The read command STREAD (p. 91) causes the data to be brought into core. Arguments of this command identify the input data file as FORTRAN unit 10, the record layout format as 11F6.0, and the number of observations as 250.

Data for STATLIB's high-level packages, such as STPAK, are stored internally in blocks managed by the STATLIB in-core data manager DYNCOR (Ch. 9). The space in which the blocks are stored is normally obtained by DYNCOR from the computer's operating system. In the above calls, DYNCOR block <DATA HEXP>, structured as an array with dimensions 11 by 250, is created and filled with data. The 11 variable names, right-padded with blanks and eight characters long, are stored in a separate DYNCOR block <*DAT HEXP>.

Numerous other ways are available for entering data. STSAMP (p. 119) and STUSER (p. 121) pass the data matrix into dummy FORTRAN subroutines, which the user may replace with his own. DYNCOR provides several other alternatives that are discussed later.

1.2 Preliminary Analysis

One could now call on the regression routine by prescribing the dependent and independent variables. But it is essential to carry out an exploratory analysis first, making sure the data were entered properly, checking whether the dependent or independent variables contain outliers, checking whether the dependent variable is excessively skewed, observing whether scatterplots exhibit unexpected patterns, etc. Below, we indicate how this might be done for the health expenditures data.

The first step is to organize the data into displays that can easily be understood. We begin by sorting them on expenditures and printing them.

Sort and Print	
reduce page width [1]	OPTION * PAGSIZ 65
sort	STSORT HEXP 1 EXPEND A
print	STPRT HEXP 0 F5.0

[1] Reduction of page width to 65 characters (and later of plot height to 20 lines) is done here to save space. Such reduction is often useful (or necessary) for terminal output, whereas full-page printout, with greater resolution, is usually desired on high-speed line printers. OPTION (p. 285) controls output for specific subroutines, groups of subroutines, or the entire library ("*").

```
STSORT: HEXP, DIR=A, VBLS:
        EXPEND
```

```
STPAK / STPRT                               07/09/80   PAGE  1

MATRIX=HEXP    OBS    1- 250

INC  EDUC NONW AGE   FEM  HLTH EMP  HEAD INS  EXPE SIZE

  7.   1.   1.  10.   1.   0.   0.   0.   1.   0.   11.
  6.   4.   1.   8.   0.   0.   0.   0.   0.   0.   10.
  6.   4.   1.  18.   0.   0.   0.   0.   0.   0.    5.
 11.   6.   0.  11.   1.   0.   0.   0.   1.   0.    6.
  5.   6.   1.  15.   0.   0.   0.   0.   0.   0.    6.
                        .  .  .  .  .

  5.   4.   0.  36.   1.   1.   0.   0.   1. 127.    5.
  9.   6.   0.  55.   0.   0.   1.   1.   1. 131.    3.
 10.   5.   0.  52.   0.   1.   1.   1.   0. 131.    4.
 18.   8.   0.  44.   0.   0.   1.   1.   1. 133.    5.
                        .  .  .  .  .

  5.   6.   0.  64.   1.   0.   0.   1.   1.1201.    1.
  7.   7.   0.   0.   0.   0.   0.   0.   1.1384.    8.
  3.   2.   0.  55.   0.   1.   0.   0.   0.1660.    3.
 12.   7.   0.  77.   0.   2.   0.   1.   1.1798.    2.
  1.   4.   0.  71.   1.   0.   0.   1.   0.2129.    1.
 11.   5.   0.  36.   1.   1.   1.   0.   1.2206.    4.
```

We can see that the data have been read in properly. But
expenditures appear to be highly skewed; e.g., more then 80 percent
of them are less than $300, whereas two people had expenditures over
$2000. Unless the demographic and household characteristics of the
people with large expenditures differ from the others, and the
printout indicates that they do not, we would expect similarly skewed
residuals from a regression fit, and should probably transform the
data first to reduce the length of their upper tail.

While there exist numerous skewness-reducing transformations to pick
from, and well-defined procedures for simultaneously estimating the
transformation parameters and regression coefficients that are most
compatible with given model assumptions, we side-step this sort of
analysis to simplify exposition. Our approach instead is to pick a
specific transformation -- the logarithm of [expenditures+1], carry
out an analysis with it, and ultimately validate that the residuals
from our analysis are roughly normal. The logarithmic transformation
is chosen partly because it yields such a set of residuals and partly
because the resulting model's coefficients are easy to interpret
(i.e., as percentage changes in expenditures per unit of the
independent variable).

The coding below obtains the desired transformation of expenditures.

Transforming the Dependent Variable	
add constant	STFN1 HEXP LEXP ADD EXPEND 1
logarithms	STFN1 HEXP LEXP LOG LEXP

STENL: HEXP, 1 VBLS:
         LEXP

STFN1:   HEXP, LEXP=ADD(EXPEND,1)

STFN1:   HEXP, LEXP=LOG(LEXP)

The transformed variable LEXP is then plotted against income and
size, two candidates for independent variables in the regression.

Plotting	
reduce plot height [1]	PPLOTP LINES 20
plot	STPLT HEXP AGE 1 LEXP
	STPLT HEXP INC 1 LEXP
[1] Often desirable for terminal output; the default plot height is 45 lines for high-speed printers. PPLOTP (p. 287) controls numerous other plot settings as well.	

STPAK / STPLT   07/09/80 PAGE 2

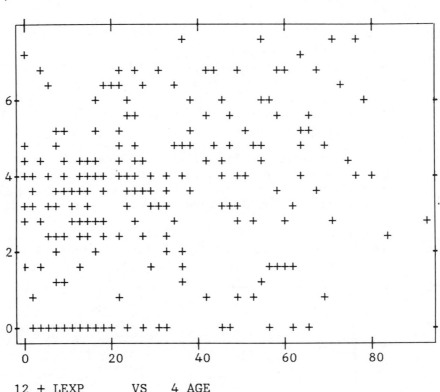

12 + LEXP   VS   4 AGE
MATRIX=HEXP

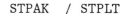

STPAK / STPLT   07/09/80   PAGE 3

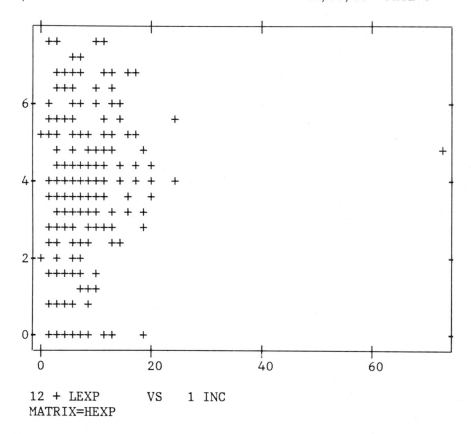

12 + LEXP   VS   1 INC
MATRIX=HEXP

We see immediately the presence of an outlier in income -- one person
with family income $73,000 per year. In any regression equation
containing untransformed income, this person might strongly affect
the coefficients of income and other variables correlated with it.

Another way to gain insight into trends is to compute "grouped" means
of the dependent variable for various levels of independent
variables.

Grouped Means	
age levels	STXRGN HEXP AGE 0 80 5
sums	STXTAB HEXP CM 1 2 AGE LEXP TOTAL
means	STFN2 CM LEXP DIV LEXP TOTAL
print	STPRT CM 0 0
plot	STPLT CM AGE 1 LEXP

STXRGN (p. 113) defines age levels centered at 0,5,10,...,80. STXTAB
(p. 114) then computes grouped sums of LEXP (a variable in the
matrix) and TOTAL (a variable not in the matrix, assumed by STXTAB to
represent a row of ones), storing these in a new matrix CM that also
contains their corresponding age levels. After average log
expenditures (LEXP divided by TOTAL) are computed, the new matrix is
printed, and average log expenditures are plotted against age. The
plot shows a monotone trend in expenditures with age, although the
relationship portrays a young/middle-aged/old effect rather than a
linear one.

STXRGN: HEXP, VBL=AGE, 17 CELLS: 0 TO 80 BY 5

STXTAB: HEXP TO CM, 1 GROUPING VBLS, 2 SUM VBLS:
        AGE LEXP TOTAL

STFN2: CM, LEXP=DIV(LEXP,TOTAL)

STPAK / STPRT   07/09/80   PAGE 4

 MATRIX=CM   OBS   1- 17

 AGE   LEXP   TOTAL

    0.0   3.20   20.00
    5.00   2.80   18.00
   10.00   2.45   29.00
   15.00   2.54   33.00
   20.00   3.82   20.00
   25.00   4.26   18.00
   30.00   2.59   14.00
   35.00   3.88   17.00
   40.00   4.77   10.00
   45.00   4.20   9.00
   50.00   3.77   15.00
   55.00   3.93   8.00
   60.00   3.97   12.00
   65.00   4.52   10.00
   70.00   4.73   7.00
   75.00   5.19   5.00
   80.00   5.41   3.00

STPAK / STPLT   07/09/80 PAGE 5

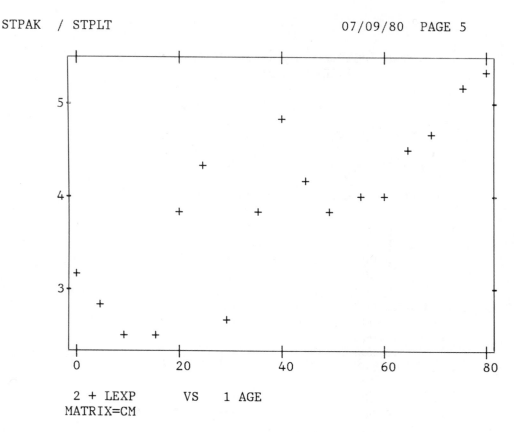

2 + LEXP   VS   1 AGE
MATRIX=CM

Note that the printout of matrix CM includes counts of persons by age
as variable TOTAL. This introduces the notion of a "cross-tab"
matrix, which in STPAK is simply a matrix of indicator variable sums
given one or more "grouping" variables. Note that this matrix no
longer describes people, but rather groups of people who share common
characteristics.

While minor variants of the above statements could be inserted
in-line for other choices of independent variables, it is much easier
to define an ISX command, or procedure, for executing them
separately.

Grouped Means Procedure	
define procedure [1]	/PROC GMEAN V1 V0 LOWER UPPER INCR
variable levels	STXRGN HEXP V0 LOWER UPPER INCR
sums	STXTAB HEXP CM 1 2 V0 V1 TOTAL
means	STFN2 CM V1 DIV V1 TOTAL
print	STPRT CM 0 0
plot	STPLT CM V0 1 V1
end procedure	/PROCEND

[1] Arguments are the sum (V1) and grouping variable (V0) names
and numbers defining the grouping intervals.

The GMEAN procedure is now stored in core and can be executed by
giving its name. When the procedure is called, the arguments in the
/PROC statement (p. 76) are replaced wherever they appear by the
arguments supplied. The statements below would produce plots of
average log expenditures by income (0,1,2,...,20) and health status

(0,1,2) groupings.

Executing the Grouped Means Procedure	
by income levels	GMEAN LEXP INC 0 20 1
by health status levels	GMEAN LEXP HLTH 0 2 1

1.3 Transforming the Independent Variables

A final step before calling on the regression routine is to transform the independent variables as prescribed by theory. As an example, one student's model contained dummy variables (employment status, race, head of household, and level of education) and transformed continuous variables (income and age) multiplied by some of these dummies.

Transforming Variables	
suppress STPAK messages	OPTION STMSG PRINT OFF
health status indicators	STCODE HEXP HLTH 0 2 1 EXGD FAIR $ POOR
recode education	STRCOD HEXP DUM EDUC 1 1 0 2 4 1 $ 5 6 2 7 8 3
education level indicators	STCODE HEXP DUM 0 3 1 ED0 EDNHS $ EDHS EDCL
recode age	STRCOD HEXP DUM AGE 0 15 0 $ 16 37 1 38 100 2
age level indicators	STCODE HEXP DUM 0 2 1 A1 A2 A3
bound income	STFN1 HEXP INC MIN INC 20
log(income+$1000)	STFN1 HEXP LINC ADD INC 1
	STFN1 HEXP LINC LOG LINC
low income indicator	STFN1 HEXP INTLOW LT INC 7
low income * log(income)	STFN2 HEXP LOWINC MLT INTLOW LINC
log(expenditures+1)	STFN1 HEXP LEXP ADD EXPEND 1
	STFN1 HEXP LEXP LOG LEXP
health status * insured	STFN2 HEXP EGINS MLT EXGD INS
young age	STFN2 HEXP A1 MLT A1 AGE
young adult female	STFN2 HEXP A2F MLT A2 FEM
employed * log(income)	STFN2 HEXP EMPINC MLT EMP LINC

A call to OPTION turns STPAK messages (printed by STMSG) off. Subroutine STCODE (p. 93) creates a series of dummy variables; in its first call, health status variables EXGD (excellent or good), FAIR, and POOR are defined according to whether HLTH is 0, 1, or 2. STRCOD (p. 99) recodes a given variable, creating in its first call the variable DUM which is 0, 1, 2, or 3 according to EDUC being in the intervals 1-1, 2-4, 5-6, or 7-8. STFN1 and STFN2 (p. 94) provide various functions of one or two variables: ADD (addition), LOG (logarithm), LT (the "less than" indicator function), and MLT (multiplication).

1.4 Regression and Residual Analysis

The program below calls STREG (p. 108) for multiple linear regression, resulting in the means and standard deviations being printed first, followed by a standard summary of the regression coefficients and an analysis of variance table. Fitted values ("predictions") and residuals PRDN and RSID are inserted into the matrix as variables for subsequent analysis.

Regression Computations	
rows for resids, predictions	STENL HEXP 2 RSID PRDN
regress	STREG HEXP LEXP 15 LOWINC INTLOW $
	EMPINC EMP NONW HEAD SIZE EXGD $
	EGINS A1 A2 A2F EDO EDNHS EDHS

REGPAK / REGMSD   07/09/80   PAGE 6

```
SAMPLE SIZE  . . . .  250
SUM OF WEIGHTS . . .  2.5000D+02
AVERAGE WEIGHT . . .  1.0000D+00
```

VARIABLE	MEAN	VARIANCE	STD DEV
1 INC	7.3595D+00	2.1982D+01	4.6885D+00
2 EDUC	5.0400D+00	2.5767D+00	1.6052D+00
3 NONW	3.2400D-01	2.1990D-01	4.6894D-01
4 AGE	2.9600D+01	4.9378D+02	2.2221D+01
5 FEM	5.4000D-01	2.4940D-01	4.9940D-01
6 HLTH	2.3600D-01	2.6938D-01	5.1902D-01
7 EMP	3.1200D-01	2.1552D-01	4.6424D-01
8 HEAD	3.2400D-01	2.1990D-01	4.6894D-01
9 INS	5.9600D-01	2.4175D-01	4.9168D-01
10 EXPEND	1.6548D+02	1.1056D+05	3.3251D+02
11 SIZE	4.5520D+00	6.1680D+00	2.4835D+00
12 LEXP	3.4856D+00	4.3083D+00	2.0757D+00
13 EXGD	8.0800D-01	1.5576D-01	3.9466D-01
14 FAIR	1.4800D-01	1.2660D-01	3.5581D-01
15 POOR	4.4000D-02	4.2233D-02	2.0551D-01
16 DUM	9.7200D-01	6.7793D-01	8.2336D-01
17 EDO	2.0000D-02	1.9679D-02	1.4028D-01
18 EDNHS	3.2800D-01	2.2130D-01	4.7043D-01
19 EDHS	4.9600D-01	2.5099D-01	5.0099D-01
20 EDCL	1.5600D-01	1.3219D-01	3.6358D-01
21 A1	2.7760D+00	2.3403D+01	4.8377D+00
22 A2	3.2400D-01	2.1990D-01	4.6894D-01
23 A3	3.2400D-01	2.1990D-01	4.6894D-01
24 LINC	1.9598D+00	3.5416D-01	5.9511D-01
25 INTLOW	5.8000D-01	2.4458D-01	4.9455D-01
26 LOWINC	9.0408D-01	6.9448D-01	8.3336D-01
27 EGINS	4.8400D-01	2.5075D-01	5.0075D-01
28 A2F	1.8400D-01	1.5075D-01	3.8826D-01
29 EMPINC	6.8831D-01	1.1488D+00	1.0718D+00

REGPAK / REGANL   07/09/80   PAGE 7


```
        SAMPLE SIZE  . . . . . . . .  250
        SUM OF WEIGHTS . . . . . . .  2.5000D+02
        ESTIMATED STD DEV . . . . .  1.7184D+00
        R SQUARED . . . . . . . . .  0.3559
```

VARIABLE		COEFFICIENT	ESTD STD DEV	T
0		5.5625D+00	5.0546D-01	11.0049
26	LOWINC	-6.6353D-01	3.8398D-01	-1.7281
25	INTLOW	7.7515D-01	7.4431D-01	1.0414
29	EMPINC	6.3192D-01	4.0643D-01	1.5548
7	EMP	-2.0612D+00	9.2101D-01	-2.2380
3	NONW	-6.2608D-01	2.6049D-01	-2.4035
8	HEAD	9.7085D-01	3.2391D-01	2.9973
11	SIZE	-5.5378D-02	5.2382D-02	-1.0572
13	EXGD	-1.1961D+00	3.5618D-01	-3.3583
27	EGINS	6.6233D-01	3.0840D-01	2.1476
21	A1	-6.9306D-02	3.0568D-02	-2.2673
22	A2	-8.6182D-01	3.6197D-01	-2.3809
28	A2F	1.3219D+00	4.2232D-01	3.1301
17	ED0	-1.8858D+00	8.4862D-01	-2.2221
18	EDNHS	-1.2522D+00	3.8014D-01	-3.2941
19	EDHS	-5.1478D-01	3.2990D-01	-1.5604

```
        12  LEXP      DEPENDENT VARIABLE
```


ANALYSIS OF VARIANCE

SOURCE	DF	SS	MS	F
REGRESSION	15	3.8182D+02	2.5454D+01	8.620
ERROR	234	6.9096D+02	2.9528D+00	
TOTAL	249	1.0728D+03		

To verify that the basic regression assumptions are not seriously violated, we display the residuals from this regression in various ways: in a conventional scatterplot with fitted values, in a smoothed grouped means plot (using the above procedure GMEAN), and in a normal probability plot. The first of these has no observations in the lower left portion, in part due to the lack of negative expenditures; otherwise, the plots reveal no serious departures from expected patterns.

Residual Plots	
residuals versus predictions	STPLT HEXP PRDN 1 RSID
grouped means	GMEAN RSID PRDN 1 6 1
fit normal quantiles	STFITD HEXP RSID NORMAL
normal probability plot	STPLT HEXP NORMAL 1 RSID

STPAK / STPLT   07/09/80   PAGE 8

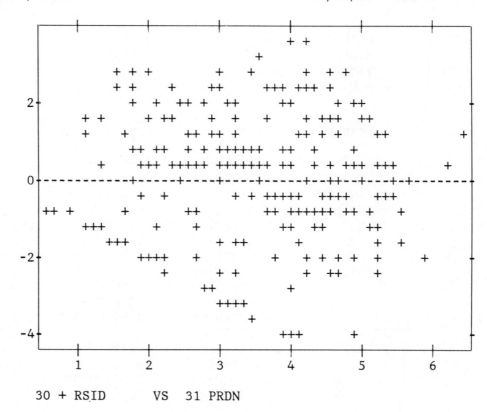

30 + RSID   VS   31 PRDN

STPAK / STPRT   07/09/80   PAGE 9

MATRIX=CM   OBS   1-   6

PRDN	RSID	TOTAL
1.00	-0.56	16.00
2.00	0.30	44.00
3.00	-0.13	63.00
4.00	-0.03	66.00
5.00	0.15	55.00
6.00	-0.43	6.00

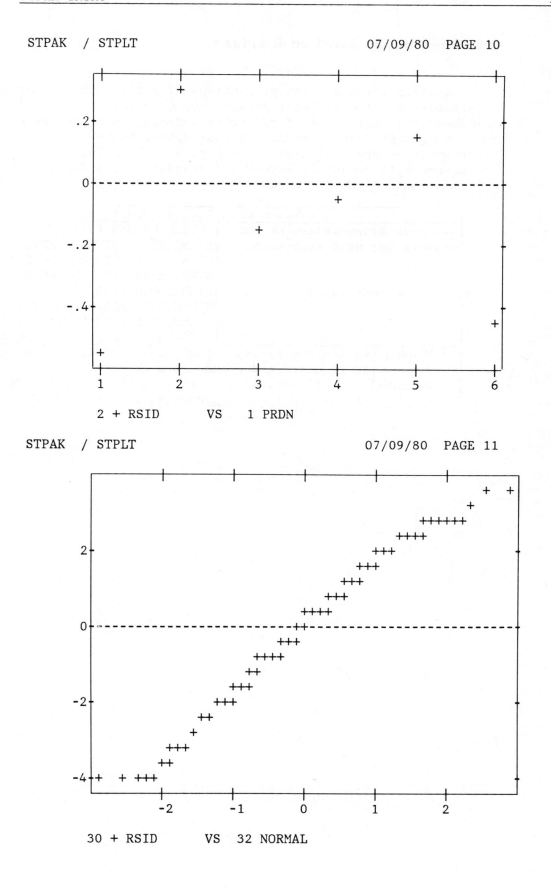

STPAK / STPLT   07/09/80 PAGE 10

2 + RSID   VS   1 PRDN

STPAK / STPLT   07/09/80 PAGE 11

30 + RSID   VS   32 NORMAL

1.5 Re-weighting Based on Residuals

Inserting residuals and predictions directly into the matrix not only
enables one to use the standard plot or print routines for residual
analyses, but also facilitates running iterative regressions which
reweight or trim observations that appear to be outliers. If, for
example, one wished to apply a Huber influence function to
down-weight residuals beyond two standard deviations, the following
statements might be coded.

Regession with Outlier Modification	
suppress means/stdevs output	OPTION REGMSD PRINT OFF
weights for next regression	STFN1 HEXP WGTS ABS RSID
	STFN1 HEXP WGTS MAX WGTS 3.4376
	STFN1 HEXP WGTS INV WGTS
force reaccumulation [1]	DYNDEL REG HEXP
regress	STREG HEXP LEXP 15 LOWINC INTLOW $
	EMPINC EMP NONW HEAD SIZE EXGD $
	EGINS A1 A2 A2F EDO EDNHS EDHS

[1] Needed because the earlier STREG call anticipated additional
regression requests and accumulated cross-products (without
weights) for all variables. Deleting DYNCOR block <REG HEXP>,
which contains these cross-products, forces reaccumulation.

REGPAK / REGANL   07/09/80   PAGE 12

    SAMPLE SIZE   250
    SUM OF WEIGHTS . . . .   7.2491D+01
    ESTIMATED STD DEV . . . . .   1.7041D+00
    R SQUARED 0.3632

    VARIABLE   COEFFICIENT   ESTD STD DEV   T

     0   5.5879D+00   5.0090D-01   11.1556
    26 LOWINC   -6.7395D-01   3.8061D-01   -1.7707
    25 INTLOW   7.6460D-01   7.3812D-01   1.0359
    29 EMPINC   6.2526D-01   4.0295D-01   1.5517
     7 EMP   -2.0443D+00   9.1307D-01   -2.2389
     3 NONW   -6.3946D-01   2.5801D-01   -2.4784
     8 HEAD   9.7784D-01   3.2156D-01   3.0409
    11 SIZE   -5.7773D-02   5.1893D-02   -1.1133
    13 EXGD   -1.1915D+00   3.5357D-01   -3.3699
    27 EGINS   6.5060D-01   3.0566D-01   2.1285
    21 A1   -6.9939D-02   3.0283D-02   -2.3095
    22 A2   -8.6345D-01   3.5927D-01   -2.4033
    28 A2F   1.3044D+00   4.1889D-01   3.1139
    17 ED0   -1.8743D+00   8.4031D-01   -2.2305
    18 EDNHS   -1.2340D+00   3.7678D-01   -3.2750
    19 EDHS   -4.8101D-01   3.2704D-01   -1.4708

    12 LEXP   DEPENDENT VARIABLE

ANALYSIS OF VARIANCE

    SOURCE   DF   SS   MS   F

    REGRESSION   15   3.8760D+02   2.5840D+01   8.898
    ERROR   234   6.7955D+02   2.9041D+00

    TOTAL   249   1.0671D+03

These regression coefficients do not differ significantly from those
of the earlier run. Setting aside the question of whether the right
variables are in the model, this would confirm at least that outliers
are not contaminating the estimates.

2. ADVANCED EXAMPLES

In this subsection, we assume that each student has obtained and
reported a model that he is happy with, and we evaluate his model on
several data sets: his own, those of other students, and the entire
data base of 11,155 observations. Although the examples show a
nonstandard application of the software, and therefore are of

limitted general interest, they do demonstrate certain advanced
features of STATLIB, including the usefulness of augmenting
statistical analyses with command system (ISX) and data management
(DYNCOR) statements. We use the ISX macro definition capability to
iterate procedures over data, and demonstrate how DYNCOR may be used
to save accumulation results.

2.1 Defining Models

Each student supplies an ISX procedure that produces his independent
and dependent variables and specifies the form of his final
regression equation. For the student whose commands appear above,
such a procedure might be as follows.

AA's Model Definition Procedure	
define procedure	/PROC AAMODL NAME
health status indicators	STCODE NAME HLTH 0 2 1 EXGD FAIR $
	POOR
recode education	STRCOD NAME DUM EDUC 1 1 0 2 4 1 $
	5 6 2 7 8 3
education level indicators	STCODE NAME DUM 0 3 1 EDO EDNHS $
	EDHS EDCL
recode age	STRCOD NAME DUM AGE 0 15 0 $
	16 37 1 38 100 2
age level indicators	STCODE NAME DUM 0 2 1 A1 A2 A3
bound income	STFN1 NAME INC MIN INC 20
log(income+$1000)	STFN1 NAME LINC ADD INC 1
	STFN1 NAME LINC LOG LINC
low income indicator	STFN1 NAME INTLOW LT INC 7
low income * log(income)	STFN2 NAME LOWINC MLT INTLOW LINC
log(expenditures+1)	STFN1 NAME LEXP ADD EXPEND 1
	STFN1 NAME LEXP LOG LEXP
health status * insured	STFN2 NAME EGINS MLT EXGD INS
young age	STFN2 NAME A1 MLT A1 AGE
young adult female	STFN2 NAME A2F MLT A2 FEM
employed * log(income)	STFN2 NAME EMPINC MLT EMP LINC
regression parameters	/DEFINE $R LEXP 15 LOWINC INTLOW $
	EMPINC EMP NONW HEAD SIZE EXGD $
	EGINS A1 A2 A2F EDO EDNHS EDHS
end procedure	/PROCEND

This student will be called AA, the others BB, CC, DD, EE, and FF;
their model definition procedures are AAMODL through FFMODL,
respectively. We assume that all procedures have the following
features in common. They accept a matrix name as an argument, which
facilitates keeping track of the numerous data sets to be processed
(when the above procedure is executed, NAME will assume the value of
the argument supplied). They call the raw data variables by the same
names. And they define their regression model by stringing together
the arguments for the STPAK regression routine in ISX variable $R (Ch
4, Sec. 2.2, p. 60): dependent variable first, number of independent
variables second, then the list of independent variables.

2.2 Fitting and Evaluating Models

Relegating each student's coding to a separate procedure enables us to write evaluation procedures that are independent of the model being processed. The first fits a given student's model to an arbitrary number of data matrices.

Fitting a Student's Regression Models	
define procedure	/PROC FIT MODL NAME
dimension	<DIM> STDIM NAME 11 INC EDUC NONW $
	AGE FEM HLTH EMP HEAD INS EXPEND $
	SIZE
read [1]	STREAD NAME 10 (11F6.0) 250
execute model statements	MODL NAME
regress	STREG NAME $R
shift arguments left	/ARGLS MODL 3
repeat if "NAME" exists	/SKIP <DIM> NE NAME
end procedure	/PROCEND
fit model on data sets	FIT AAMODL AA BB CC DD EE FF

[1] The data matrices are stored consecutively on a single FORTRAN unit.

It defines and reads a data matrix, calls the model definition procedure supplied as its first argument, then runs the regression according to the parameters placed by the model definition procedure in $R. The /ARGLS statement (p. 77) performs a left-shift of arguments, leaving the first (known internally as MODL) unchanged, but moving the third to position two (known internally as NAME), the fourth to position three, etc. The /SKIP command (p. 78) returns to the statement labelled <DIM> if NAME exists after this shift, otherwise procedure execution terminates. In the above execute statement, AAMODL becomes the model definition procedure used, and data matrices AA through FF are processed in turn.

This program would generate two kinds of output: in-core regression blocks, perhaps for further processing, and standard regression printouts, to be analyzed and reported. Two DYNCOR regression blocks are produced per data matrix: one contains the names of accumulated variables, the other contains the information needed to compute additional regressions or to utilize the present coefficients in other analyses (e.g., of residuals). Both have the same last name as the data matrix, enabling us to have several regression blocks simultaneously in-core and permitting routines called later to link up the information, if necessary.

The analysis of printed output illustrates the effects of overfitting one's data, as shown in the table below. We see that the diagonal entries are generally the largest in each row (model), although some exceptions occur due to column (data set) effects. Controlling for rows and columns and fitting a diagonal indicator (i.e., an indicator of whether the model is being fit to the data set on which it was based), we estimated an R^2 boost for the diagonal of about 0.05 -- more than 20 percent above the average entry in the table.

R^2 FOR REFITTED COEFFICIENTS, BY
STUDENT MODELS AND STUDENT DATA SETS

DATA SET

		AA	BB	CC	DD	EE	FF
	AA	.36	.22	.15	.34	.14	.20
	BB	.24	.30	.20	.31	.17	.27
M	CC	.26	.22	.22	.31	.12	.20
O D	DD	.19	.20	.17	.32	.13	.23
E L	EE	.25	.31	.22	.35	.22	.29
	FF	.23	.29	.21	.30	.17	.31

The next step evaluates the predictive accuracy of the reported regression coefficients. Taking the coefficients obtained by each student on his own data, we compute his residuals on every other student's data, then produce an R^2-like quantity

$$1 - \text{SUM [residuals]}^2 / \text{SUM [dependent variable - its mean]}^2$$

Assuming that procedure FIT has been called to leave behind the DYNCOR regression and data blocks for the given student, the following procedure would print for each data matrix the sum of squared residuals and the variance of the dependent variable, which are sufficient for evaluating the above.

Evaluate Student's Model on Others' Data	
define procedure	/PROC EVAL NAME OTHR
row for residuals	<ENL> STENL OTHR 1 RSID
compute residuals	STREGP OTHR NAME TRUE
residual sum of squares	STFNOB OTHR SSQ RSID
dependent variable variance	STFNOB OTHR VAR $R
shift arguments left	/ARGLS NAME 3
repeat if "OTHR" exists	/SKIP <ENL> NE OTHR
end procedure	/PROCEND
evaluate model on data sets	EVAL AA AA BB CC DD EE FF

STREGP (p. 111) fills variable RSID in matrix OTHR (argument 2) with residuals from the regression associated with NAME (argument 1). STFNOB (p. 97) computes functions over all observations -- in this case, summing squared residuals, computing the variance of the dependent variable, and printing the results. As before, /ARGLS and /SKIP are used to cycle over different data sets, causing BB's data to be processed next, etc.

Iterating this procedure over different students' models, we obtain the table below. In many cases, the sum of squared residuals turns out larger than the raw sum of squared deviations of the dependent variable -- a startling fact. In all cases, the value of R^2

plummets. This usually succeeds in teaching the student to use some of his newly-learned statistical tools with caution.

R² FOR REPORTED COEFFICIENTS, BY
STUDENT MODELS AND STUDENT DATA SETS

DATA SET

		AA	BB	CC	DD	EE	FF
	AA	.36	-.04	.02	.20	-.09	.03
	BB	.08	.30	.09	.18	-.04	.15
M O D E L	CC	.13	.16	.22	.21	.02	.13
	DD	.12	.11	.12	.32	.02	.17
	EE	.06	.08	.03	.09	.22	.11
	FF	.15	.10	.09	.16	-.02	.31

While the fitting and evaluation procedures are shown being executed for just one student at a time, they might easily be run for all students in a procedure such as below. This procedure positions the read routine at the start of the file and fits and evaluates each model in succession by calling on the FIT and EVAL procedures defined earlier.

Fitting and Evaluating All Models on All Data	
define procedure	/PROC FITEVAL MODL NAME
rewind input file	/REWIND 10
fit models	<FIT> FIT MODL AA BB CC DD EE FF
evaluate on data sets	EVAL NAME AA BB CC DD EE FF
shift arguments left	/ARGLS 3
repeat if "MODL" exists	/SKIP <FIT> NE MODL
end procedure	/PROCEND
fit and evaluate models on data sets	FITEVAL AAMODL AA BBMODL BB CCMODL $ CC DDMODL DD EEMODL EE FFMODL FF

2.3 Large Data Set Evaluations

The final step in the exercise takes each student's model and fits it to the entire data base of 11,155 observations.

Student's Regression with All Observations	
define procedure	/PROC ACCREG MODL NAME
dimension	<DIM> STDIM NAME 11 INC EDUC NONW $
	AGE FEM HLTH EMP HEAD INS EXPEND $
	SIZE
read	STREAD NAME 10 (11F6.0) 250
execute model statements	MODL NAME
accumulate cross products	STREGA NAME 0
repeat if no end-of-file	/SKIP <DIM> NE $EOF EOF
regress	STREG NAME $R
end procedure	/PROCEND
fit model on all data	ACCREG AAMODL AA

This procedure reads a block of data, transforms it by passing it to
the model supplied, then calls the regression accumulation routine
STREGA (p. 110) to increment the cross-products sums. The variable
$EOF is set by ISX to the value EOF if an end-of-file is detected by
STREAD (see the ISX note, p. 92), and the /SKIP command sends the
program back to the top unless that occurs. When STREG gets control,
it finds a set of regression blocks in core that are sufficient for
the computations it wants to do, so it uses them. The following
output is produced for student AA.

REGPAK / REGANL   07/09/80   PAGE 13

```
SAMPLE SIZE  .  .  .  .  .  .  .  .11155
SUM OF WEIGHTS .  .  .  .  .  .  . 1.1155D+04
ESTIMATED STD DEV  .  .  .  .  . 1.8026D+00
R SQUARED  .  .  .  .  .  .  .  . 0.2069
```

VARIABLE	COEFFICIENT	ESTD STD DEV	T
0	6.0874D+00	7.4817D-02	81.3641
25 LOWINC	1.1114D-01	6.4705D-02	1.7176
24 INTLOW	-3.8678D-01	1.1619D-01	-3.3290
29 EMPINC	1.6940D-01	6.2774D-02	2.6987
7 EMP	-6.4721D-01	1.4178D-01	-4.5648
3 NONW	-3.6670D-01	3.9541D-02	-9.2740
8 HEAD	2.3035D-01	4.7689D-02	4.8303
11 SIZE	-1.4026D-01	8.4040D-03	-16.6899
12 EXGD	-1.5063D+00	5.2415D-02	-28.7386
27 EGINS	4.1245D-01	4.4548D-02	9.2586
20 A1	-4.8069D-02	4.8553D-03	-9.9002
21 A2	-4.3225D-01	5.6655D-02	-7.6297
28 A2F	8.1822D-01	6.7479D-02	12.1256
16 ED0	-4.4232D-01	1.5215D-01	-2.9071
17 EDNHS	-5.8602D-01	5.4689D-02	-10.7155
18 EDHS	-3.8858D-01	4.9002D-02	-7.9299

26 LEXP   DEPENDENT VARIABLE

ANALYSIS OF VARIANCE

SOURCE	DF	SS	MS	F
REGRESSION	15	9.4421D+03	6.2947D+02	193.726
ERROR	11139	3.6194D+04	3.2493D+00	
TOTAL	11154	4.5636D+04		

The final example runs these computations for all students, generates a random sample of 200 nonzero-expenditure observations for an examination of residuals, and saves all of the accumulations for future runs.

Student Analyses on All Observations	
define procedure	/PROC ACCANAL MODL NAME
rewind input file	<REW> /REWIND 10
dimension	<DIM> STDIM NAME 11 INC EDUC NONW $
	AGE FEM HLTH EMP HEAD INS EXPEND $
	SIZE
read	STREAD NAME 10 (11F6.0) 250
execute model statements	MODL NAME
accumulate cross products	STREGA NAME 0
eliminate zero expenditures	STCPY NAME EXPEND NAME
accumulate 200-obs rndm smpl	STSAMP NAME 0 200
repeat if no end-of-file	/SKIP <DIM> NE $EOF EOF
load xxx/ and "NAME" into "X" array	/LOADX A4 xxx/ NAME
define $NAM as chars 4-6	/DEFX $NAM 3 A 4
rename random sample matrix	DYNNAM DATA $NAM DATA NAME
save "NAME" blocks on unit 20	DYNOUT .... NAME 20 0
rows for resids, predictions	STENL NAME 2 RSID PRDN
regress	STREG NAME $R
plot resids vs predictions	STPLT NAME PRDN 1 RSID
delete "NAME" blocks	DYNDEL .... NAME
shift arguments left	/ARGLS 3
repeat if "MODL" exists	/SKIP <REW> NE MODL
end procedure	/PROCEND
fit models on all data	ACCANAL AAMODL AA BBMODL BB CCMODL $
	CC DDMODL DD EEMODL EE FFMODL FF

During the accumulation, the only changes from the previous example involve calling STCPY (p. 101) to eliminate zero expenditures and calling STSAMP (p. 119) to accumulate a random sample of 200 observations from among the 11,155 encountered. By convention, it stores this sample in a data matrix whose name is "/" followed by the first three identifiers of the source matrix; e.g., /AA for AA, /BB for BB, etc. /LOADX (p. 72) loads its arguments into X, a work array or register, internal to ISX; for AA, the first six characters in this "X" array will contain xxx/AA. Then, /DEFX (p. 69) defines $NAM to be the three characters in X starting with character four; i.e., /AA for AA, /BB for BB, etc. DYNNAM (p. 262) now renames the random sample matrix to the name of the source matrix, and the regression routine inserts residuals and predictions into it for plotting (AA's plot of 200 residuals and predictions appears below). DYNOUT (p. 272) stores all NAME blocks next in self-formatted fashion (that can be read in by DYNCOR input routines), and DYNDEL (p. 261) deletes them from core. Finally, the procedure is cycled over students using the /ARGLS and /SKIP statements.

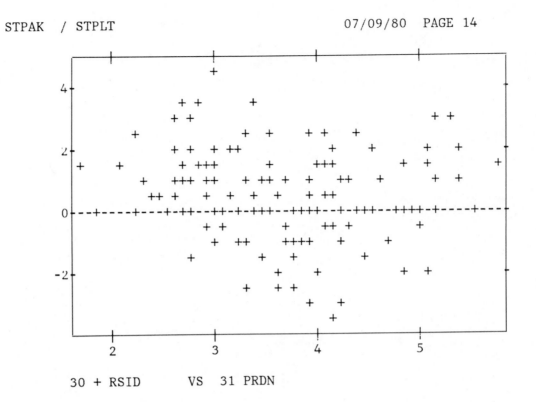

30 + RSID   VS   31 PRDN

CHAPTER 3

TIME SERIES ANALYSIS

This chapter introduces the analysis of time series data using TSPAK - STATLIB's Time Series Package (Ch. 6). First, we proceed step-by-step through a typical analysis of a specific time series. In the second part of the chapter we present a series of more advanced examples. In each case, we place more emphasis on the software "tools" than on building an "optimal" model.

1. INTRODUCTION TO TSPAK

The table below contains the international airline passenger data analyzed by Brown [2] and later by Box and Jenkins [3].

INTERNATIONAL AIRLINE PASSENGERS (THOUSANDS), BY MONTH AND YEAR

	Jan	Feb	Mar	Apr	May	Jun	Jul	Aug	Sep	Oct	Nov	Dec
1949	112	118	132	129	121	135	148	148	136	119	104	118
1950	115	126	141	135	125	149	170	170	158	133	114	140
1951	145	150	178	163	172	178	199	199	184	162	146	166
1952	171	180	193	181	183	218	230	242	209	191	172	194
1953	196	196	236	235	229	243	264	272	237	211	180	201
1954	204	188	235	227	234	264	302	293	259	229	203	229
1955	242	233	267	269	270	315	364	347	312	274	237	278
1956	284	277	317	313	318	374	413	405	355	306	271	306
1957	315	301	356	348	355	422	465	467	404	347	305	336
1958	340	318	362	348	363	435	491	505	404	359	310	337
1959	360	342	406	396	420	472	548	559	463	407	362	405
1960	417	391	419	461	472	535	622	606	508	461	390	432

We show how STATLIB might be used to model this data through 1957 and generate forecasts out through 1960. The first step consists of printing and plotting the data, transforming it as appropriate, and differencing it to remove non-stationarities (trend and seasonal structure). Then follows the iterative process of identifying time series model structure and estimating coefficients via regression (least squares). Finally, after a thorough analysis of the model residuals, forecasts are generated for 1958-1960 and compared with the actual data.

The analysis is presented in the form of ISX commands. ISX (Ch. 4) is STATLIB's command system. It is invoked by issuing operating system commands which will be described in a later section; it may be used in interactive or batch mode. TSPAK commands (and other STATLIB commands) which may be issued within ISX are described only briefly here; complete TSPAK documentation, including both ISX and FORTRAN calling sequences, is contained in Chapter 6.

1.1 Data Input

The first step is entering the data into the computer. Data for STATLIB's high-level packages, such as TSPAK, are stored in blocks managed by the STATLIB in-core data manager DYNCOR (Ch. 9). The space in which the blocks are stored is normally obtained by DYNCOR from the computer's operating system.

Entering the data into the blocks may be done in numerous ways; we show only the simplest one here, giving other examples later.

Reading Data	
read	DYNINP 10

Data are read from FORTRAN unit 10, which has been associated with a data set containing the two-word series name <DATA IALP>, length, format, "timing" information, and monthly data.

```
.DAT IALP 3 I(*)
 1949 1 12
DATA IALP 144 R(-3P12F4.0)
 112 118 132 129 121 135 148 148 136 119 104 118
 115 126 141 135 125 149 170 170 158 133 114 140
 145 150 178 163 172 178 199 199 184 162 146 166
 171 180 193 181 183 218 230 242 209 191 172 194
 196 196 236 235 229 243 264 272 237 211 180 201
 204 188 235 227 234 264 302 293 259 229 203 229
 242 233 267 269 470 315 364 347 312 274 237 278
 284 277 317 313 318 374 413 405 355 306 271 306
 315 301 356 348 355 422 465 267 404 347 305 336
 340 318 362 348 363 435 491 505 404 359 310 337
 360 342 406 396 420 472 548 559 463 407 362 405
 417 391 419 461 472 535 622 606 508 461 390 432
```

The basic data structure for TSPAK is the time series, stored as a singly dimensioned array in a DYNCOR block. To identify the element corresponding to a given time point, TSPAK uses a two-level time scale, which may represent years and months, weeks and days, etc. This information is stored in a separate DYNCOR block; here <.DAT IALP> identifies the first element of <DATA IALP> as (1949,1) and the number of secondary units (months) in a primary unit (year) as 12.

1.2 Preliminary Analysis

Analysis and inspection of the data prior to modeling are very important. Failure to detect outliers or structural patterns can lead to incorrect or useless models. We begin by printing the airline series.

Printing	
reduce page width [1]	OPTION * PAGSIZ 65
print	TSPRT DATA IALP 1949 1 1957 12

[1] Reduction of page width to 65 characters (and later of plot height to 20 lines) is done here to save space. Such reduction is often useful (or necessary) for terminal output, whereas full-page printout, with greater resolution, is usually desired on high-speed line printers. OPTION (p. 285) controls output for specific subroutines, groups of subroutines, or the entire library ("*").

TSPAK / TSPRT   DATA IALP   (000)   07/09/80   PAGE 1

	1949	1950	1951	1952	1953	1954
1	112.	115.	145.	171.	196.	204.
2	118.	126.	150.	180.	196.	188.
3	132.	141.	178.	193.	236.	235.
4	129.	135.	163.	181.	235.	227.
5	121.	125.	172.	183.	229.	234.
6	135.	149.	178.	218.	243.	264.
7	148.	170.	199.	230.	264.	302.
8	148.	170.	199.	242.	272.	293.
9	136.	158.	184.	209.	237.	259.
10	119.	133.	162.	191.	211.	229.
11	104.	114.	146.	172.	180.	203.
12	118.	140.	166.	194.	201.	229.
SUM	1520.	1676.	2042.	2364.	2700.	2867.

	1955	1956	1957
1	242.	284.	315.
2	233.	277.	301.
3	267.	317.	356.
4	269.	313.	348.
5	470.	318.	355.
6	315.	374.	422.
7	364.	413.	465.
8	347.	405.	467.
9	312.	355.	404.
10	274.	306.	347.
11	237.	271.	305.
12	278.	306.	336.
SUM	3608.	3939.	4421.

A quick inspection suggests that the data have been read in properly. We now proceed to plot the time series against time. Since the plot cannot fit on one page, it is split in two.

Plotting	
reduce plot height·	PPLOTP LINES 20
plot	TSPLT 1 DATA IALP 1949 1 1957 12

TSPAK   / TSPLT   07/09/80   PAGE 2

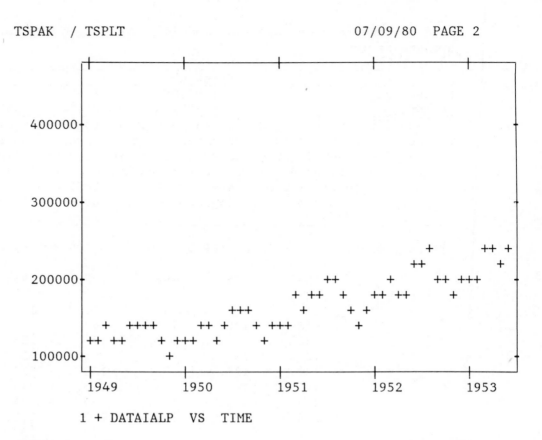

1 + DATAIALP VS TIME

TSPAK   / TSPLT   07/09/80   PAGE 3

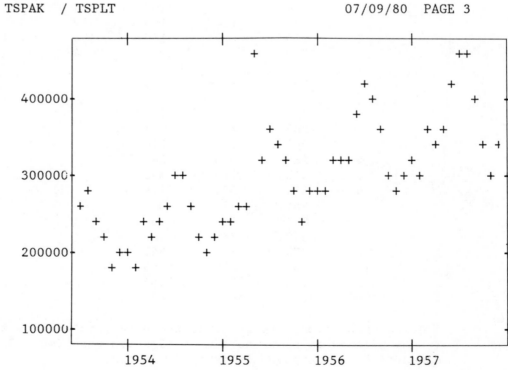

1 + DATAIALP VS TIME
JAN 1949-DEC 1957

We see immediately that the May 1955 value is out of line.
Comparison of the printed output with the data shows that 270000 was
erroneously entered as 470000. TSPUT (p. 167) is called to make the
correction.

Correcting	
replace May 1955 value	TSPUT DATA IALP 1955 5 1 270000

1.3 Data Transformation

The plot also shows variability increasing with level, indicating
perhaps a multiplicative, rather than additive, error structure. In
that case the logarithms of the data will have an additive structure,
which generally is required (or assumed) in modeling. The function
routine TSFN1 (p. 153) may be called to create a new series
<DATA LALP> containing the logarithms of <DATA IALP>.

Transforming	
logarithms	TSFN1 DATA LALP LOG DATA IALP
plot	TSPLT 1 DATA LALP 1949 1 1957 12

TSFN1: DATA LALP = LOG(DATA IALP), JAN 1949-DEC 1960

TSPAK / TSPLT   07/09/80   PAGE 4

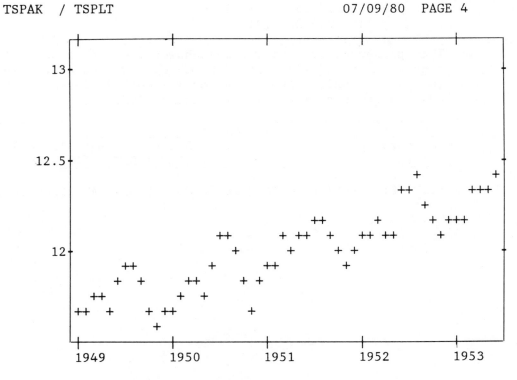

1 + DATALALP VS TIME

TSPAK / TSPLT   07/09/80 PAGE 5

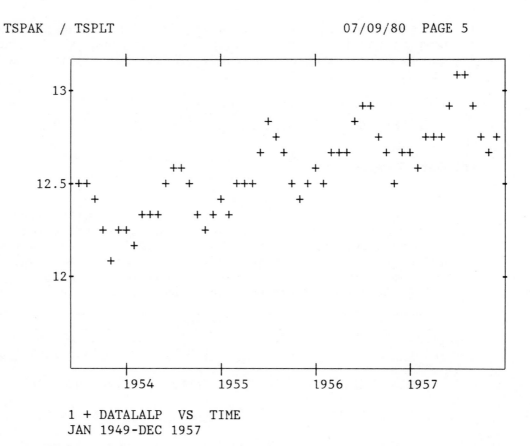

1 + DATALALP   VS   TIME
JAN 1949-DEC 1957

The presence of a strong seasonal component, with period 12 months,
suggests working with the 12-month differences of the series. TSDIFF
(p. 158) creates the series of 12-month differences <DATA 12LP> and
adjusts its starting point to January 1950.

Differencing	
difference	TSDIFF DATA LALP 12 DATA 12LP
plot	TSPLT 1 DATA 12LP 1949 1 1957 12

TSDIFF: DATA 12LP = 12 DIFF OF DATA LALP, JAN 1950-DEC 1960

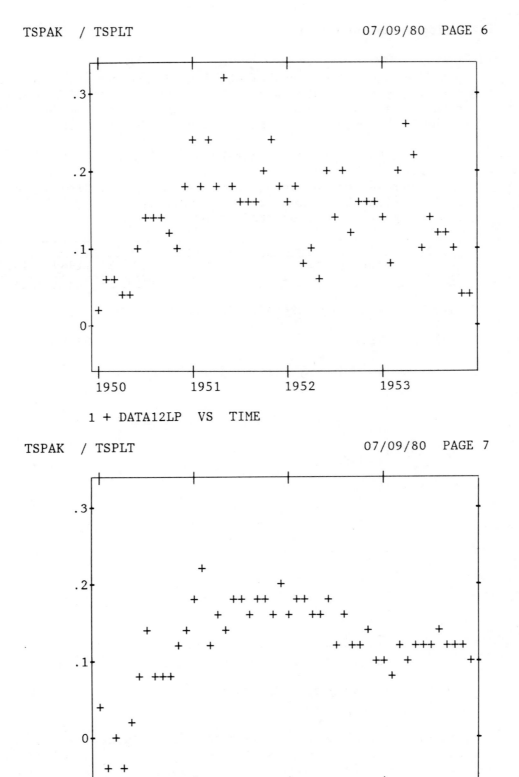

1 + DATA12LP VS TIME

1 + DATA12LP VS TIME
JAN 1950-DEC 1957

1.4 Autocorrelation Function

The 12-month differences of the logarithms appear to be more-or-less stationary (i.e., mean and variance independent of time). Under such conditions, identification of the appropriate model structure is aided by examination of the autocorrelation function

$$r(k) = corr\ (x(t),x(t-k)),\qquad k=0,1,...,$$

the correlation between the series and itself lagged (shifted) k months. TSACOR (p. 160) creates a new series <ACOR 12LP> containing the autocorrelations of <DATA 12LP>.

Autocorrelations	
autocorrelation series	TSACOR DATA 12LP 1949 1 1957 12
plot	TSPLT 1 ACOR 12LP 0 1 50 1

TSACOR: DATA 12LP, 32 LAGS, JAN 1950-DEC 1957

TSPAK / TSPLT   07/09/80   PAGE 8

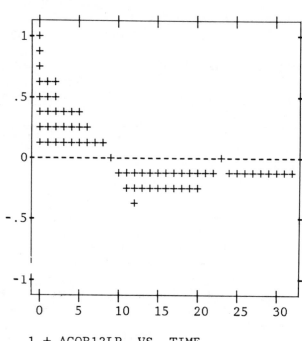

1 + ACOR12LP VS TIME
0-32

The autocorrelation series <ACOR 12LP> is defined at "times" (lags) 0,1,...,[N/3], where N is the length of the original series (in this case 96). The number of observations per "year" for an ACOR series is one, and in calling TSPAK routines, time points are referenced as (lag,1) rather than (year,month). Thus in the plot call above, the first point to be plotted is specified as (0,1) and the last as (50,1), a range large enough to plot the entire series, which actually exists from (0,1) through (32,1).

1.5 Autoregression

The autocorrelation plot suggests a first or, perhaps, second order autoregressive model for the series. To fit a first order model,

$$12LP(t)=A+B*12LP(t-1)+e(t),$$

we first describe the model structure to TSMODL (p. 161), then call the regression subroutine TSREG (p. 163) to estimate the coefficients.

First-order Autoregression	
independent vbl: 12LP lag 1	TSMODL AREG 12LP 1 1 INDV
dependent vbl: 12LP lag 0	TSMODL AREG 12LP 1 0 DEPV
regress	TSREG AREG 1949 1 1957 12

```
TSREG:   MODEL=AREG, TYPE=DATA, FEB 1950-DEC 1957
         DEPV=12LP

TSPRDN:  MODEL=AREG, TYPE=DATA/PRDN/RSID, FEB 1950-DEC 1957
         DEPV=12LP
```

The model description routine TSMODL simply stores the information it receives in a DYNCOR block for later use by the regression routine. TSREG calculates regression coefficients, leaving them and other intermediate results in DYNCOR blocks for use by other TSPAK subroutines. It also calls the prediction routine TSPRDN (p. 164) to compute predicted (fitted) values and residuals over the regression time period. These series are stored as <PRDN 12LP> and <RSID 12LP>, respectively.

TSPAK subroutines are divided generally into those that compute and those that print. We have seen examples of both. TSREG is a computing routine, and to print out the regression summary we must call TSREGA (p. 164). In addition, intermediate regression results such as means, variances and correlations would have been printed when TSREG was called had we requested them through OPTION (p. 285).

Regression Summary	
print regression summary	TSREGA AREG 12LP

REGPAK / REGANL   07/09/80   PAGE 9

        SAMPLE SIZE   95
        SUM OF WEIGHTS . . . .   9.5000D+01
        ESTIMATED STD DEV 4.3754D-02
        R SQUARED 0.4730

        VARIABLE   COEFFICIENT   ESTD STD DEV   T

        0   4.3603D-02   1.0854D-02   4.0171
        1 12LP...1   6.7792D-01   7.4201D-02   9.1364

        2 12LP....   DEPENDENT VARIABLE

        ANALYSIS OF VARIANCE

            SOURCE   DF   SS   MS   F

            REGRESSION   1   1.5980D-01   1.5980D-01   83.473
            ERROR   93   1.7804D-01   1.9144D-03

            TOTAL   94   3.3785D-01

    TSREGA: MODEL=AREG, TYPE=DATA, DEPV=12LP, FEB 1950-DEC 1957

Patterns in the autocorrelation function of the residuals may show
structure not yet removed and suggest additional terms to be
incorporated in the model.

Residual Autocorrelations	
residual autocorrelations	TSACOR RSID 12LP 1949 1 1957 12
plot	TSPLT 1 ACOR 12LP 0 1 50 1

    TSACOR: RSID 12LP, 31 LAGS, FEB 1950-DEC 1957

TSPAK / TSPLT   07/09/80   PAGE 10

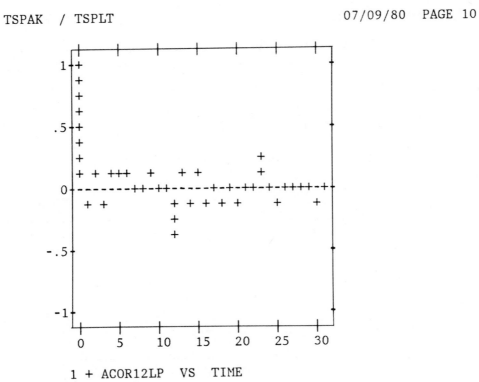

1 + ACOR12LP   VS   TIME
0-31

The residual series <RSID 12LP> may itself be plotted to check for
patterns in level and variance.

Residual Plot	
plot residuals	TSPLT 1 RSID 12LP 1949 1 1957 12

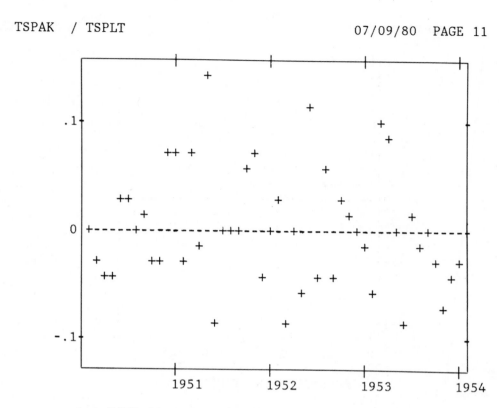

1 + RSID12LP VS TIME

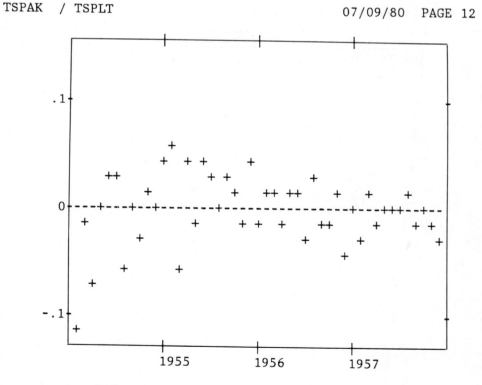

1 + RSID12LP VS TIME
FEB 1950-DEC 1957

1.6 Prediction

While the noticeable decrease in residual dispersion over time should lead us to further analysis, we will instead proceed to generate forecasts for the series, using data through the end of the regression period.

Forecasting	
forecast	TSPRDN AREG 1958 1 1960 12
plot data and forecasts	TSPLT 2 DATA 12LP PRDN 12LP $
	1958 1 1960 12

TSPRDN: MODEL=AREG, TYPE=DATA/PRDN/RSID, JAN 1958-DEC 1960
    DEPV=12LP

TSPAK / TSPLT   07/09/80 PAGE 13

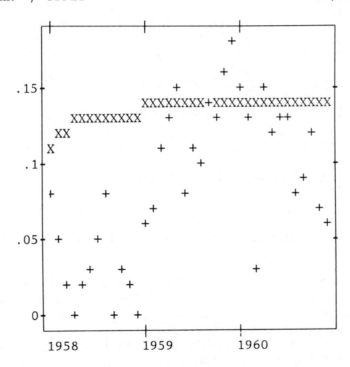

1 + DATA12LP 2 X PRDN12LP VS TIME
JAN 1958-DEC 1960

Recognizing that these forecasts are in terms of 12-month differences of logarithms, we apply the inverse transformations to obtain forecasts of IALP.

Inverse Transforming	
"undifference"	TSUNDF PRDN 12LP DATA LALP 12 $
	PRDN LALP
exponentiate	TSFN1 PRDN IALP EXP PRDN LALP
plot data and forecasts	TSPLT 2 DATA IALP PRDN IALP $
	1958 1 1960 12

TSUNDF: PRDN LALP = 12 UNDF OF PRDN 12LP, BASE = DATA LALP,
        FEB 1950-DEC 1960

TSFN1: PRDN IALP = EXP(PRDN LALP), FEB 1950-DEC 1960

TSPAK / TSPLT   07/09/80 PAGE 14

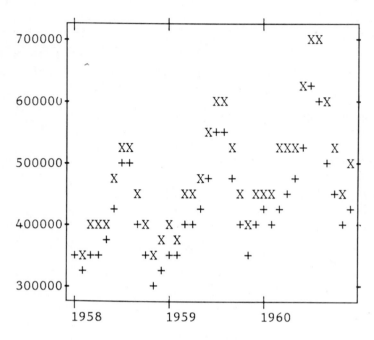

1 + DATAIALP   2 X PRDNIALP VS TIME
JAN 1958-DEC 1960

1.7 User-written Procedures for Autoregression

Adding additional terms to the model would require additional calls
to TSMODL and TSREG. In general, this process is iterative and can
be simplified by writing an ISX "procedure" to carry out the
repetitive operations. The following one, named AR, takes the
desired lag as an argument, adds it to the model by calling TSMODL,
then repeats the above commands for autoregression and residual
autocorrelation plotting.

Autoregression Procedure	
define procedure	/PROC AR LAG
new lag term	TSMODL AREG 12LP 1 LAG INDV
regress	TSREG AREG 1949 1 1957 12
autocorrelations	TSACOR RSID 12LP 1949 1 1957 12
plot	TSPLT 1 ACOR 12LP 0 1 50 1
end procedure	/PROCEND

The first-order autoregressive model may then be incremented to
second-order.

Execute Autoregression Procedure	
model, adding lag 2	AR 2

TSREG: MODEL=AREG, TYPE=DATA, MAR 1950-DEC 1957
         DEPV=12LP

TSPRDN: MODEL=AREG, TYPE=DATA/PRDN/RSID, MAR 1950-DEC 1957
         DEPV=12LP

TSACOR: RSID 12LP, 31 LAGS, MAR 1950-DEC 1957

TSPAK / TSPLT   07/09/80   PAGE 15

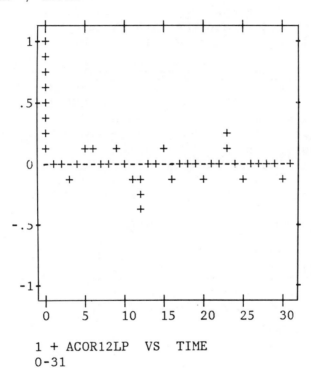

      1 + ACOR12LP VS TIME
      0-31

Each time it is called, the procedure adds one lag term to the model
and repeats the analysis. We next re-write the procedure to accept
as arguments all lag terms to be included in the model.   Subroutine
DYNDEL (p. 261) is called to delete the existing model <MODL AREG> if
any.

General Autoregression Procedure	
define procedure	/PROC AR LAG
delete old model	DYNDEL MODL AREG
dependent variable	TSMODL AREG 12LP 1 0 DEPV
independent variable	<IND> TSMODL AREG 12LP 1 LAG INDV
shift arguments left	/ARGLS 2
go to <IND> if LAG exists	/SKIP <IND> NE LAG
regress	TSREG AREG 1949 1 1957 12
autocorrelations	TSACOR RSID 12LP 1949 1 1957 12
plot	TSPLT 1 ACOR 12LP 0 1 50 1
end procedure	/PROCEND

The /ARGLS statement (p. 77) performs a left shift on the arguments, moving the second to position one (known internally as LAG), the third to position two, the fourth to position three, etc.

A model with lags 1 and 3, followed by one with lags 1, 2, 12, 13 and 14, would then be requested as follows.

Execute Autoregression Procedure	
model, lags 1 and 3	AR 1 3
model, lags 1,2,12,13,14	AR 1 2 12 13 14

Procedure AR is now quite general, except that it can only be used for variable 12LP and applies to a fixed time period. We now modify it to make the series name the first argument and to use the variable $T for the time period, and repeat the analyses.

More General Autoregression Procedure	
define procedure	/PROC AR VBL LAG
delete old model	DYNDEL MODL AREG
dependent variable	TSMODL AREG VBL 1 0 DEPV
independent variable	<IND> TSMODL AREG VBL 1 LAG INDV
shift arguments left	/ARGLS VBL 3
go to <IND> if LAG exists	/SKIP <IND> NE LAG
regress	TSREG AREG $T
autocorrelations	TSACOR RSID VBL $T
plot	TSPLT 1 ACOR VBL 0 1 50 1
end procedure	/PROCEND
define $T	/DEFINE $T 1949 1 1957 12
model, lags 1 and 3	AR 12LP 1 3
model, lags 1,2,12,13,14	AR 12LP 1 2 12 13 14

2. ADVANCED EXAMPLES

The remainder of this chapter continues the analysis of the airline passenger data by presenting a series of examples which demonstrate more advanced features of STATLIB. The reader is expected to have achieved a fair degree of proficiency and familiarity with TSPAK and ISX before tackling this section.

Each example is presented in the form of a procedure. In some cases this is not necessary; the statements could be coded directly if they are to be executed only once. If branching statements (/SKIP, p. 78) are to be used, however, the code must be incorporated into a procedure.

2.1 Probability Plotting

The first example is a procedure which generates normal quantile-quantile plots (i.e., plots of the sorted elements of the series vs. fitted normal distribution quantiles). The procedure is applied to the IALP residuals.

Normal Probability Plotting Procedure	
define procedure	/PROC NORMQQ TYPE NAME
copy	TSFN1 DATA NQQ EQL TYPE NAME
dimension	STDIM NQQ 1 NAME
fit normal quantiles	STFITD NQQ NAME NORMAL
normal probability plot	STPLT NQQ NORMAL 1 NAME
end procedure	/PROCEND
execute	NORMQQ RSID IALP

TSFN1: DATA NQQ = EQL(RSID 12LP), MAR 1950-DEC 1957

STDIM: NQQ, 1 VBLS:
        RSID

STENL: NQQ, 1 VBLS:
        NORMAL

STFITD: NQQ, VBL=RSID, NORMAL FIT, MEAN=0, STDEV=.0427

STPAK / STPLT   07/09/80   PAGE 16

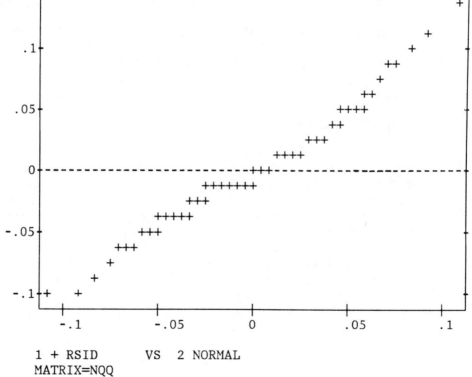

1 + RSID   VS   2 NORMAL
MATRIX=NQQ

STPAK subroutine STFITD (p. 115) is used to fit the quantiles. Since
it will be sorting the matrix and adding a second variable, we first
copy the series into a new one, <DATA NQQ>. The new variable, which
contains the normal quantiles, is named NORMAL.

This example is typical of situations in which one may wish to move from one high-level STATLIB package to another. The reverse transition is accomplished by calling STEXT (STPAK variable extract, p. 103) to extract one variable from a data matrix and TSTORG (TSPAK time origin definition, p. 169) to create its time control block.

2.2 Counting Outliers

The second example is a procedure which counts the number of residuals that are more than S standard deviations removed from zero.

Outlier Counting Procedure	
define procedure	/PROC CNTOUTL NAME S
standard deviation	TSFNTS STD RSID NAME 0 1 9999 1
divide	TSFN1 CNT OUTL DIV RSID NAME $XXX
absolute value	TSFN1 CNT OUTL ABS CNT OUTL
indicator	TSFN1 CNT OUTL GT CNT OUTL S
total	TSFNTS SUM CNT OUTL 0 1 9999 1
print	/ RSID NAME CONTAINS $XXX OUTLIERS
end procedure	/PROCEND
execute	CNTOUTL 12LP 3

TSFNTS: STD(RSID 12LP) = .0426809, MAR 1950-DEC 1957

TSFN1: CNT OUTL = DIV(RSID 12LP,.0426809), MAR 1950-DEC 1957

TSFN1: CNT OUTL = ABS(CNT OUTL), MAR 1950-DEC 1957

TSFN1: CNT OUTL = GT(CNT OUTL,3), MAR 1950-DEC 1957

TSFNTS: SUM(CNT OUTL) = 1, MAR 1950-DEC 1957

../ RSID 12LP CONTAINS 1 OUTLIERS

TSFNTS (p. 156) computes functions over all or part of a time series (TSFNM, p. 156, provides the same functions, but over multiple segments of a series). The single value it returns is stored as ISX variable $XXX, which is used in subsequent commands.

Recall that STATLIB subroutines may be called from FORTRAN programs as well as from ISX. The outlier-counting procedure may be written as a FORTRAN subroutine as follows:

```
           SUBROUTINE CNTOUT(NAME,S)
           IMPLICIT REAL*8(A-H,P-Z),LOGICAL(O)
           CALL TSFN1('CNT ','OUTL','DIV','RSID',NAME,
             TSFNTS('STD','RSID',NAME,0,1,9999,1))
           CALL TSFN1('CNT ','OUTL','ABS','CNT ','OUTL')
           CALL TSFN1('CNT ','OUTL','GT ','CNT ','OUTL',S)
           N=TSFNTS('SUM','CNT ','OUTL',0,1,9999,1)
           WRITE(6,90)NAME,N
           RETURN
        90 FORMAT(' RSID ',A4,' CONTAINS',I4,' OUTLIERS')
           END
```

2.3 Time Base Conversion

Next we consider a procedure which demonstrates aggregation over time and looping within procedures. The procedure ANNSMRY creates three time series containing the annual means, minima, and maxima respectively, of a monthly series.

Annual Summary Procedure	
define procedure	/PROC ANNSMRY NAME
means	TSFNM MEAN NAME AVG DATA NAME 12 S
minima	TSFNM MIN NAME MIN DATA NAME 12 S
maxima	TSFNM MAX NAME MAX DATA NAME 12 S
shift arguments left	/ARGLS 2
repeat if more	/SKIP -99 NE NAME
end procedure	/PROCEND
execute for IALP and ABCD	ANNSMRY IALP ABCD

```
TSFNM:   MEAN IALP = AVG(DATA IALP), JAN 1949-DEC 1960
         SEG LGTH = 12, NEW TIME = 1949-1960

TSFNM:   MIN  IALP = MIN(DATA IALP), JAN 1949-DEC 1960
         SEG LGTH = 12, NEW TIME = 1949-1960

TSFNM:   MAX  IALP = MAX(DATA IALP), JAN 1949-DEC 1960
         SEG LGTH = 12, NEW TIME = 1949-1960
```

/ARGLS performs a "left shift" on the procedure argument list, sliding each procedure argument to the left. The integer 2 as the last (in this case only) argument means that procedure argument 2 becomes procedure argument 1 (NAME), argument 3 becomes argument 2, and so on. The /SKIP statement returns to the first line in the procedure if NAME is not null (i.e., more series remain to be processed).

A plot of the three annual summary series may be helpful in understanding the structure of the data.

Plotting Annual Summary	
increase resolution	PPLOTP LINES 25
plot	TSPLT 3 MEAN IALP MIN IALP MAX IALP $
	1949 1 1957 1

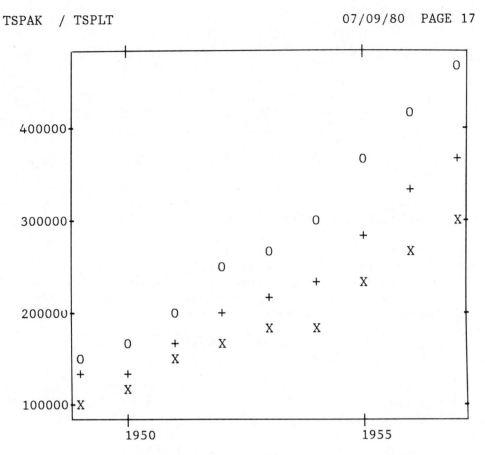

1 + MEANIALP 2 X MIN IALP 3 O MAX IALP
VS TIME
1949-1957

2.4 Box Plots

An even better tool for summarizing data is the box plot. The median
is used in place of the mean as a more robust measure of location.
Lower and upper quartiles are computed and plotted, with lines
connecting them to the extremes. The lower and upper quartiles are
normally connected with a vertical box, but on a printer plot this is
not practical.

Box-plot Procedure	
define procedure	/PROC BOXPLOT TYPE NAME K
suppress TSPAK messages	OPTION TSMSG PRINT OFF
medians	TSFNM BP.. MED MED TYPE NAME K S
lower quartiles	TSFNM BP.. LQ ORD TYPE NAME K S .25
upper quartiles	TSFNM BP.. UQ ORD TYPE NAME K S .75
minima	TSFNM BP.. MIN MIN TYPE NAME K S
maxima	TSFNM BP.. MAX MAX TYPE NAME K S
reset message printing	OPTION TSMSG PRINT *
save first 5 plot characters	PPLOTP CHAR -5
new plot characters	PPLOTP CHAR 5 X--||
bar from 4th to 2nd variable	PPLOTP BARV 4 2
bar from 5th to 3rd variable	PPLOTP BARV 5 3
plot	TSPLT 5 BP.. MED BP.. MIN BP.. $
	MAX BP.. LQ BP.. UQ 0 1 9999 1
reset plot characters	PPLOTP CHAR 5
skip line	/
print title under plot	/ BOX-PLOT FOR TYPE NAME , $
	SEGMENTS OF LENGTH K
delete temporary series	DYNDEL BP.. ....
end procedure	/PROCEND
execute for DATA IALP	BOXPLOT DATA IALP 12

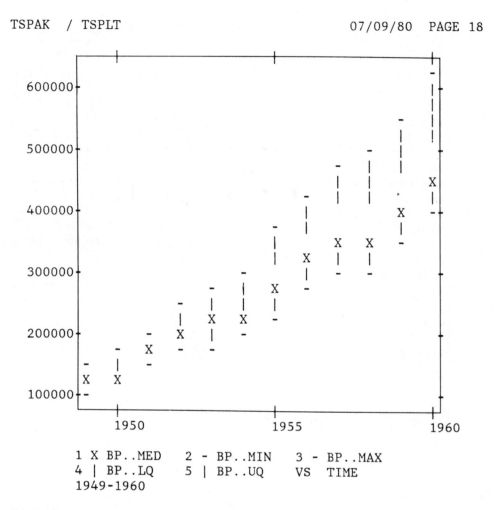

TSPAK / TSPLT   07/09/80   PAGE 18

1 X BP..MED   2 - BP..MIN   3 - BP..MAX
4 | BP..LQ   5 | BP..UQ   VS   TIME
1949-1960

BOX-PLOT FOR DATA IALP , SEGMENTS OF LENGTH 12

This procedure has been written for general use by including the
segment length K (typically 12 for monthly series) as an argument,
adding the OPTION statements to suppress messages from TSPAK, saving
and re-setting the plotting characters, printing the series name and
segment length under the plot, and deleting the temporary series when
finished.

2.5 Processing Sets of Time Series

The last example consists of a procedure which performs preliminary
data analysis (print, plot, box plot, scatter plot vs. <DATA IALP>,
and autocorrelation plot) and code which executes this procedure for
every DATA series on FORTRAN unit 15. <DATA IALP> is assumed to be
among those series stored on 15, and the procedure is made
intelligent enough to bypass the scatter plot of IALP against itself.
Because of the large amount of output, all printing is directed to
unit 8 (presumably a high-speed printer).

Preliminary Analysis Procedure	
define procedure	/PROC PRELIM TYPE NAME K
print	TSPRT TYPE NAME 0 1 9999 1
plot	TSPLT 1 TYPE NAME 0 1 9999 1
box-plot	BOXPLOT TYPE NAME K
skip plot if NAME is IALP	/SKIP <AC> EQ NAME IALP
horizontal variable	TSPLTH DATA IALP
scatter plot	TSPLT 1 TYPE NAME 0 1 9999 1
autocorrelations	<AC> TSACOR TYPE NAME 0 1 9999 1
plot	TSPLT 1 ACOR NAME 0 1 50 1
end procedure	/PROCEND
read data	DYNINP 15
output to unit 8	OPTION * UNIT 8
list of DATA series	/LIST DATA .... DATALST
execute PRELIM for each	DATALST PRELIM 12
reset output unit	OPTION * UNIT *

The command

        /LIST DATA .... DATALST

(see p.   80) creates an ISX procedure DATALST of the following form:

        /PROC DATALST
            $1 DATA ABCD $2 $3 $4 $5 $6 $7
            $1 DATA IALP $2 $3 $4 $5 $6 $7
            ...
            $1 DATA WXYZ $2 $3 $4 $5 $6 $7
        /PROCEND

One line is generated for each DYNCOR block whose first name is DATA. Variables $1, $2, ..., $7 are references to procedure arguments one through seven (an alternative to specifying symbolic arguments in the /PROC statement). Then the command

        DATALST PRELIM 12

results in substitution of PRELIM for $1 and 12 for $2, and is equivalent to

        PRELIM DATA ABCD 12
        PRELIM DATA IALP 12
        ...
        PRELIM DATA WXYZ 12

PART II

HIGH LEVEL ROUTINES

This part of the manual documents STATLIB's high level packages, including ISX (Interactive STATLIB Executive System), STPAK (Statistical Analyis of Two-Way Matrices), TSPAK (Time Series Analysis), SPPAK (Spectrum Analysis), TABLE (Table Manipulations and Analysis), DYNCOR (Dynamic Core Storage Management), and various service routines (e.g., print control, plot parameters). These routines are sufficient for many types of statistical analysis, and they offer the user a set of commands that are quite easy to use. In contrast, STATLIB's lower level routines, documented in Part III, provide more flexibility and power, but they require additional programming effort.

ISX (Ch. 4) is an interactive system for executing most STATLIB subroutines. It reads statements containing subroutine names and arguments in free form, interprets them, and issues the actual subroutine calls. The statements may be entered as a "program" or, on time-sharing systems, entered from a terminal, in which case they are executed immediately as encountered. In addition to its interactive capabilities and free-form punctuation-free input, ISX offers the advantage of not requiring compilation or link-editing (loading), as is required with FORTRAN programs. Furthermore, since calling sequences in ISX are virtually identical to those of the FORTRAN subroutines, the user need not "re-learn" the library in switching from one to the other.

STPAK (Ch. 5) is the principal package for handling two-way data matrices. One dimension consists of observations or cases (e.g., people); the other contains variables or measurements on these observations (e.g., age, race, sex). STPAK routines perform a variety of analysis operations, including printing, plotting, regression, cross-tabulations, and logit maximum likelihood. Auxiliary routines exist for creating new variables and modifying old ones, storing and retrieving results, and for performing a number of in-core data management functions.

TSPAK (Ch. 6) is used to manage and model time series data. The time series is a one-dimensional array containing a variable measured at a number of points in time (or space). Subroutines which perform many useful operations, from printing and plotting to autoregression, are included in this package.

SPPAK (Ch. 7) is a system of FORTRAN subroutines for spectrum analysis of time series. It can be combined with routines from TSPAK when one desires to perform analyses of time series in both time and frequency domains. Subroutines are included which perform such operations as univariate and multivariate spectrum analysis, Wiener filtering, Fourier transformation, convolution and many more.

Unusual features include the option of robust model fitting and outlier adjustment in the Wiener filtering routine. The robust option uses a redescending influence function constructed from a linear section and a descending part related to the extreme value distribution. Maximum likelihood estimation of Box-Cox transformation parameters is also available.

TABLE (Ch. 8) manages and analyzes multiway tables of data. Arbitrarily dimensioned tables are managed via calling sequences keyed to the names of dimensions and/or their rows and columns; so, for example, to obtain a race by sex count of employees from a five-way table in which the other dimensions are job level, salary range, and state, one simply tells the appropriate TABLE routine to project the table onto the race and sex dimensions. Routines are provided for many of the basic data handling operations associated with such tables.

DYNCOR (Ch. 9) provides storage management services for FORTRAN programs. In particular, it serves as the primary in-core data management system or all of STATLIB's other high level packages. Blocks of core are given names by the user. A "pointer" subscript may be returned to the calling program, which permits referencing a block's contents as a subscripted FORTRAN array. Most computer operating systems provide a facility for dynamic allocation of core storage, enabling DYNCOR to obtain storage space for blocks automatically as needed.

Service routines (Ch. 10) provide miscellaneous parameter settings for the low level routines used by the above packages. This includes suppressing or redirecting printing, labelling and/or numbering pages, overriding the default plot routine settings, suppressing the constant term in multiple linear regression, etc.

Each chapter contains an introduction, a statement of documentation conventions specific to it (general conventions are described below), the documentation itself, a series of examples, and finally a subject index and glossary of subroutines or commands. A composite subject index and glossary for all Part II routines appear as appendices to Part II.

DOCUMENTATION CONVENTIONS

Calling Sequence Notation

Calling sequences will be given in both FORTRAN (FTN) and ISX (ISX) formats. The following notation will be used in describing them.

   a. Arguments which are character strings (e.g., matrix or variable names, time series names, DYNCOR block identifiers) will be written in lower case. Unless otherwise stated, the length of the argument name equals the maximum permissable number of characters (e.g., "type" signifies up to four characters, "fun", up to three). In FORTRAN calls, character strings must be right-padded with blanks up to their maximum lengths; in ISX, the right-padding is done automatically.

b. Arguments which are usually arrays containing one-word character strings will be written in lower case and enclosed in single quotes (e.g., 'typ1typ2..'). In FORTRAN calls, the actual arguments must either be FORTRAN arrays or packed literal constants aligned on the appropriate word boundaries (e.g., 'DATARSID' for four-character words, 'AGE   SEX   ' for eight-character words). Unless otherwise noted, the length of the argument name signifies how many characters are permitted.

c. Arguments which are normally not character strings are written in upper case (e.g., N, X, N1Y, OCON). The first character of the name indicates the required type: A-H and P-Z denote real arguments, I-N denote integers, and O denotes logical variables. On IBM, all real variables are double precision (REAL*8), whereas integer and logical variables are of standard precision (length 4). In FORTRAN calls, all variables or constants must follow these conventions. Because ISX reads commands free-form, and thus makes the necessary conversions, it permits slightly greater flexibility: FORTRAN real or integer constants are acceptable for A-H and P-Z variables, integer or real (without exponent) constants for I-N variables, and .TRUE., TRUE, .FALSE., or FALSE for O variables.

d. Calling sequence arguments enclosed in square brackets (e.g., [C]) are optional. Where commands allow more than one optional argument, a given argument may be omitted only if succeeding ones are too. In ISX, where an array appears in square brackets (e.g., [X]), one or more array elements may be specified.

e. Where appropriate, alternative values for character string arguments are identified in calling sequences separated by "|". Default values for optional arguments are underlined.

f. FUNCTION subprograms are indicated by "..." before and after their FORTRAN calling sequences.

DYNCOR Blocks

Most routines of Part II use DYNCOR (Ch. 9) for core storage management, either to find their input data or to store their computational results. Block identifiers (two four-character words) may depend on the input data, the routine generating the results, or both. When a routine "creates" a given block, it usually sets up certain companion descriptor blocks as well; unless otherwise specified, all "created" blocks will overwrite identically named blocks that may exist.

DYNCOR block identifiers in the text (but not in the calling

sequences) are enclosed in angle brackets; e.g., <DATA ABCD>
identifies a block whose first identifier is DATA and whose last is
ABCD.

Errors and Messages

Common errors include misspelling a command or subroutine name,
leaving out the name of a data matrix, time series, or variable, or
having insuffient core storage available. All such errors result in
a message by the appropriate package's error handler; the command or
subroutine is not executed. Error handlers are named "pkgERR", where
"pkg" is the package prefix; as elsewhere, their printing may be
controlled through subroutine OPTION (p. 285). To facilitate finding
them with text editors, error messages contain the characters
" *** ". A counter is also incremented which eventually terminates
execution; the allowable number of errors, defaulted to 32, can be
modified through subroutine OPTION.

Most high-level routines generate a one- or two-line message
summarizing what they have done. This helps to make program printout
self-documenting in that the flow of execution can be determined from
the output alone. Messages are printed by the appropriate package's
message routine "pkgMSG", where "pkg" is the package prefix. Their
printing may also be controlled through subroutine OPTION.

CHAPTER 4

ISX - INTERACTIVE STATLIB EXECUTIVE SYSTEM

1. INTRODUCTION

ISX is an interactive (or batch) system for executing most STATLIB subroutines. It provides high-level language calling sequences for such packages as STPAK (Statistical Analysis of Two-Way Matrices, Ch. 5), TSPAK (Time Series Analysis, Ch. 6), SPPAK (Spectrum Analysis, Ch. 7), and TABLE (Table Manipulations and Analysis, Ch. 8), eliminating the rigid syntax requirements of FORTRAN, and enabling programs to be run interactively. ISX reads statements containing subroutine names and arguments in free-form, interprets them, and issues the actual subroutine calls. The following example illustrates its usage.

```
DYNINP 10
TSACOR DATA ABCD 1960 1 1972 10
TSPLT 1 ACOR ABCD 0 1 99 1
TSTAB DATA ABCD 1960 1972 TABL ABCD
TABPRT TABL ABCD 0 0
```

The first statement directs ISX to call DYNCOR (Dynamic Core Storage Management, Ch. 9) subroutine DYNINP, which reads self-formatted data from unit 10. TSPAK routines TSACOR and TSPLT compute and plot the autocorrelation function of a time series <DATA ABCD>. TSTAB creates a month-by-year table from this series for use by TABLE. One of its routines, TABPRT, generates a printout.

These statements may be entered as a "program" or, on time-sharing systems, entered from a terminal, in which case they are executed immediately as encountered. To minimize the amount of typing required, the user may define abbreviations for frequently used strings of characters (Sec. 4.6). For added flexibility, he may create ISX "procedures", or subroutines, consisting of one or more ISX statements (Sec. 5).

In addition to its interactive capabilities and free-form punctuation-free input, ISX offers the advantage of not requiring compilation or link-editing (loading), as is required with FORTRAN programs. Furthermore, since calling sequences in ISX are virtually identical to those of the FORTRAN subroutines, the user need not "re-learn" the library in switching from one to the other.

Section 2 explains general ISX documentation conventions. Section 3 lists STATLIB subroutines and special program-control commands that may be called through ISX. The latter are described in Sections 4 and 5, Section 5 containing ISX commands pertaining to user-defined procedures. Section 6 explains the structure of the ISX system and provides instructions for adding new subroutine calls to it. For ISX commands only, Section 7 is a subject index and Section 8 a one-page summary of calling sequences. Combined subject indices and a glossary of calling sequences for all ISX-callable routines are appendices to Part II.

2. CONVENTIONS AND NOTATION

2.1 ISX Statements

ISX statements consist of a command followed, optionally, by one or more arguments. The command may begin at any point on the line; arguments must be separated from it and from each other by one or more blanks. The command will either be the name of a subroutine (Sec. 3, p. 62), an ISX command (Secs. 4-5, p. 65), or a procedure (Sec. 5, p. 76).

Arguments may consist of any non-blank characters, except that "$" as the first character has special meaning (see Sec. 2.2, below). Also, because blanks are used as delimiters, a special argument consisting of exactly four periods ("....") has been set aside to denote a blank word.

Each input line may be from 1 to 80 characters long, although the input logical record length may be reduced through /ISXIO (p. 71). Statements may be continued on succeeding lines by coding the single character "$" as the last argument on the line. The total number of arguments (after substitution - see Sec. 6, p. 81), may not exceed 96 and the total length of the statement, after substitution and deletion of excess blanks, may not exceed 480 characters.

2.2 ISX Variables

Character strings may be stored as ISX "variables", which are identified by symbolic names and whose values may subsequently be used in ISX statements. Symbolic names have the form "$abc" (the single character "$" followed by up to three characters). Some variables are created by ISX to contain output which in FORTRAN would be placed in variables or arrays; others indicate when a nonstandard subroutine return (such as an end-of-file) has been taken. The user himself may define ISX variables as abbreviated strings of frequently used characters or as the results of arithmetic operations on other ISX variables. For additional details, see Section 4.6 (p. 66).

2.3 ISX Internal ("X") Array

An internal array "X" (containing 50 double-precision words) is used by ISX to receive values from library routines that return output into FORTRAN variables or arrays (e.g., DYNGET, DYNFNB, DYNOLD); use of this array enables results of various computations to be fetched and further processed. The command /DEFX (p. 69) defines ISX variables from it; these variables may be used in subsequent ISX statements (see Sec. 2.2). Routines which receive input from FORTRAN arrays (e.g., DYNPUT, DYNAPD, STPUT, TSPUT) will also use the array if their trailing arguments are omitted. See the text for examples.

2.4 Error Conditions

Errors detected by ISX result in the printing of the offending statement followed by an error message from subroutine ISXERR; the statement itself is not executed. The most common errors are calling non-existent routines, which result in the simple message "?", and having insufficient arguments for a given routine. The unit number for ISXERR printing is controlled by /ISXIO (p. 71) rather than OPTION; for a general description of STATLIB error handling conventions, see the Part II Introduction (p. 58).

2.5 Calling Sequences

Calling sequences are given here for ISX commands only; those of the high-level package subroutines appear in their respective chapters. Notation conventions for arguments are as described in the Part II Introduction (p. 56).

ISX commands (Secs. 4-5) may be abbreviated by specifying enough leading characters to uniquely identify them or, in some cases, by using the shorter "recommended" abbreviations. The necessary characters are underlined in the documentation.

3. ISX SUBROUTINES AND COMMANDS

ISX and FORTRAN calling sequences are generally identical, except that an argument requiring an array of k numbers or character strings (i.e., packed names within one set of quotes) is coded as k separate arguments. Some routines, if no argument is given for the array, will use the internal array "X" (see Sec. 2.3, p. 60) to store their results. /DEFX (p. 69) and /LOADX (p. 72) are useful in creating ISX variables from this array.

This section lists all routines callable from ISX, including the program-control commands described in Sections 4-5 and the high-level package subroutines described elsewhere in Part II. Details on the subroutines may be found in the appropriate chapter of Part II.

3.1 ISX

ISX commands (Secs. 4-5) perform numerous program-control functions. The following commands are available.

/	/DEFAR	/LIST	/SKIP
/ABEND	/DEFINE	/LOADX	/STOP
/ARGLS	/DEFX	/LOG	/SYS
/ARGS	/DO	/LOGDSK	/VERIFY
/BACKSP	/ENDFILE	/PROC	/WRITE
/CMDS	/ERRSET	/RESTORE	/XEQ
/COMMENT	/ISXIO	/REWIND	/XEQFILE
/DEFAI	/ISXLIST	/SAVE	

3.2 STPAK

STPAK (Ch. 5, p. 87) performs statistical analyses on two-way data matrices. The following entry points may be called through ISX.

STCODE	STFN0	STPUT	STTSFN
STCPY	STFN1	STRCDK	STUINS
STDIM	STFN2	STRCOD	STUSER
STDSP	STGET	STREAD	STWRIT
STENL	STLINK	STREG	STXRGN
STEXT	STLOGT	STREGA	STXTAB
STFITD	STNAM	STREGP	
STFNC	STPLT	STSAMP	
STFNOB	STPRT	STSORT	

3.3 TSPAK

TSPAK (Ch. 6, p. 145) is used to manage and model time series data. The following entry points may be called through ISX.

TSACOR	TSFN1	TSPLTH	TSRSDA
TSARFS	TSFN2	TSPOLO	TSTAB
TSCLIM	TSGET	TSPOLY	TSTABK
TSCSUM	TSHARM	TSPRDN	TSTIME
TSDIFF	TSLBLS	TSPRT	TSTORG
TSEXT	TSMODL	TSPUT	TSTYPE
TSFNM	TSMODR	TSREG	TSUNDF
TSFNTS	TSPACF	TSREGA	TSXCOR
TSFN0	TSPLT	TSRFSD	

3.4 SPPAK

SPPAK (Ch. 7, p. 185) performs spectrum analyses on times series data. The following entry points may be called through ISX.

SPACOR	SPDIF	SPGAIN	SPTFN
SPACOV	SPECT	SPMODL	SPWIND
SPBXCX	SPECTM	SPPARM	SPWINW
SPBXTR	SPECTN	SPPHAS	SPXAMP
SPCFT	SPECTX	SPREG	SPXCOR
SPCOHE	SPFTI	SPRFT	SPXCOV
SPCONC	SPFTIN	SPRFT2	SPXTRA
SPCONJ	SPFTMU	SPRVBD	
SPCONV	SPFTSQ	SPSFT	

3.5 TABLE

TABLE (Ch. 8, p. 225) manages and analyzes multi-way tables of data. The following entry points may be called through ISX.

TABAOV	TABENL	TABFT1	TABPRP
TABAVP	TABEXT	TABFT2	TABPRS
TABCON	TABFND	TABPLT	TABPRT
TABDIM	TABFN1	TABPRJ	TABREG
TABDSP	TABFN2	TABPRM	TABTRN

3.6 DYNCOR

DYNCOR (Ch. 9, p. 257) is the STATLIB dynamic core storage management package. The following entry points may be called through ISX.

DYNAPD	DYNEXT	DYNINB	DYNNAM
DYNCON	DYNFNB	DYNINL	DYNNEW
DYNCPY	DYNFN1	DYNINP	DYNOLD
DYNDEL	DYNFN2	DYNIN1	DYNOUE
DYNDMP	DYNGBG	DYNLST	DYNOUT
DYNENL	DYNGET	DYNMAP	DYNPUT
DYNERR			

3.7 SERVICE

Service routines (Ch. 10, p. 281) set and retrieve options and parameters for routines called indirectly through ISX. The following entry points may be called through ISX.

CORLEF	FMTCRD	OPTGET	REGPAR
CORREM	OPAGE	OPTION	RUNIF
DSPPAR	OPAGEP	PPLOTP	TIMER
ERRSET	OPTERR	REGGET	TIMZER

4. ISX COMMANDS

ISX commands, which all begin with the character "/", are used to control the operation of ISX, perform certain "housekeeping" functions, and provide some input/output operations. One important group of commands, relating to "procedures", is treated separately in Section 5 (p. 76). Certain commands, denoted "system-dependent", interface with the operating system in use. Their availability and argument lists may vary from one installation to another.

4.1 / - Print Message

/ [line]

prints the line on the ISX output unit.

4.2 /ABEND - Abnormal End

/ABEND

causes ISX to ABEND by calling a non-existent subroutine.

4.3 /BACKSP - Backspace

/BACKSP NUNIT [NREC]

backspaces NREC (1 if not specified) records on FORTRAN unit NUNIT.

4.4 /CMDS - List Available Commands

/CMDS [ALL|pkgnam|PROC]

ALL   lists all commands and the minimum number of
        arguments required by each
pkgnam lists commands in the given package and the
        minimum number of arguments required by each
PROC   lists all ISX procedures currently in core
        (see Sec. 5.1, p. 76)

If no argument is given, the names of packages available are listed. Procedures listed (PROC keyword) are preceded by and, if necessary, padded on the right by equal signs ("=").

4.5 /COMMENT - Comment

/COMMENT [line]

is ignored by ISX and may be used to document "programs".

4.6 /DEFINE - Define Variable

/DEFINE $abc [string]

$abc   = ISX variable to be assigned the value string
         (must be on the same input line as /DEFINE)
string = any group of characters

Any occurrence of the argument $abc in future statements will be
replaced by string. During substitution, non-existent or deleted ISX
variables are ignored, unless they are of the form $$abc, in which
case $abc is inserted into the line without substitution.

In executing the /DEFINE statement, substitution occurs first; thus,
"/DEFINE $ABC $XYZ" would assign to $ABC the current value of $XYZ.
If string is not given, $abc is deleted.

The first character following the dollar sign may not be an integer
(1-9).   If the first character following the dollar sign is a period
(e.g., "$.XY") and the variable is defined within an ISX procedure
(Sec. 5), the variable is considered to be local to the procedure and
is deleted when the procedure terminates; the only variables of this
form known within a procedure are those created within the procedure.
Otherwise, the global ISX variable $abc is stored in DYNCOR block
<DEFN $abc>.

Note that variables named $EOF, $ERR, $NAM, $TYP and $XXX are created
by ISX commands; their use for other purposes should be avoided.

Example:

/DEFINE $T 1960 1 1972 5

All subsequent appearances of $T are replaced by 1960 1 1972 5.

4.6.1 /DEFAI - Define From Integer Arithmetic Operation

/DEFAI $abc I1 opr I2

$abc = ISX variable to be assigned the result of the
        arithmetic operation (must be on the same input
        line as /DEFAI)
I1,I2 = integer operands
opr   = operation to be performed: + - * or /

A character string S is first constructed by evaluating I1 opr I2; the equivalent of a "/DEFINE $abc S" statement is then issued.

Examples:

        /DEFAI $2Y 2 * $Y
        /DEFAI $J $J + 1

sets $2Y equal to twice $Y and increments $J by one.

4.6.2 /DEFAR - Define From Real Arithmetic Function

        /DEFAR $abc fun [R1] [R2]

        $abc = ISX variable to be assigned the function value
                (must be on the same input line as /DEFAR)
        fun   = function (from the list below) to be performed
        R1,R2 = function arguments

A character string S is first constructed by evaluating fun(R1,R2); the equivalent of a "/DEFINE $abc S" statement is then issued. Trailing zeroes beyond the decimal point and, if S is an integer, the decimal point itself are stripped so that /SKIP statement (p. 78) character string comparisons may succeed. A central STATLIB function evaluator is used.

The following table gives the values which will be stored as $abc for available function codes (fun):

Function	$abc
ABS	|R1|
ADD	R1+R2
ASN	arcsin(R1)
DIV	R1/R2
EQ	ind(R1=R2)
EQL	R1
EXP	exp(R1)
FTN	FTNFUN(R1,R2)
GE	ind(R1≥R2)
GT	ind(R1>R2)
INT	[R1/R2]
INV	1/R1
LE	ind(R1≤R2)
LGS	1/(1+exp(-R1))
LGT	log(R1/(1-R1))
LOG	log(R1)
LT	ind(R1<R2)
MAX	max(R1,R2)
MIN	min(R1,R2)
MLT	R1*R2
MOD	mod(R1,R2)
NE	ind(R1≠R2)
NPR	PNORM(R1)
PWR	R1**R2
RNO	RNORM(0)
ROU	round(R1)
RUN	RUNIF(0)
SEQ	1
SIN	sin(R1)
SQR	R1**.5
SUB	R1-R2
TPR	PTDIST(R1,R2)
ZER	zero(R1,R2)

Logarithms are computed to the base e. The indicator function (ind) returns 1 if its argument is true, 0 if false. RNORM (p. 373) and RUNIF (p. 374) are random number generators for the normal and uniform distributions. PTDIST is a cumulative t-distribution function routine (p. 370). The zero function zeroes out the R2 low-order bytes of a real word.

Examples:

```
/DEFAR $YSQ MLT $Y $Y
/DEFAR $LZZ LOG $ZZ
```

defines ISX variables which are the square of $Y and the logarithm of $ZZ.

4.6.3 /DEFX - Define From Internal Array

/DEFX $abc N code [K1]

$abc = ISX variable to be developed from the internal
       "X" array (must be on the same input line as
       /DEFX)
N   = number of items to be extracted from that array
code = array-to-string conversion type:
       R - internal array elements are reals
       I - internal array elements are integers
       A8 - internal array elements are length-8
            character strings
       A4 - internal array elements are length-4
            character strings
       A - internal array elements are characters
K1   = initial element in the internal array (will be 1
       if not specified)

/DEFX provides a facility for using the internal array "X" (p. 60)
in subsequent ISX statements. First, an N-item character string S is
constructed from X according to the specified conversion type; the
elements are blank-separated except when code is A. The equivalent
of a "/DEFINE $abc S" statement is then issued. When code is R,
trailing zeroes beyond the decimal point and, if S is an integer, the
decimal point itself are stripped so that /SKIP statement (p. 78)
character string comparisons may succeed. The constucted string may
not be longer than 480 characters.

In some cases, ISX interface routines (see Sec. 6) that store their
results in X(1) issue the equivalent of a

        /DEFX $XXX 1 code

statement, where "code" is of the appropriate type. This provides
simplified retrieval and use of results in most cases. Details on
how $XXX is constructed are given in the subroutine documentation
sections.

Examples:

        DYNFNB DATA ABCD MAX
        /DEFX $MAX 1 R
        PPLOTP VMAX $MAX

DYNFNB (p. 263) is a function which returns in X(1) the maximum of
DYNCOR block <DATA ABCD>. /DEFX converts this real number to
character string, and issues the equivalent of a /DEFINE statement to
set its value. $MAX is then passed to PPLOTP (p. 287) to specify the
vertical maximum for a subsequent plot. Note that

        DYNFNB DATA ABCD MAX
        PPLOTP VMAX $XXX

is an alternative, using ISX variable $XXX.

```
DYNGET DATA ABCD 1 3 9
/DEFX $I 7 I
```

DYNGET (p. 260) returns words 3 through 9 of <DATA ABCD> into X. /DEFX converts these integers to character strings, and assigns them to $I.

4.7 /ENDFILE - Write End-of-File

/ENDFILE NWUNIT

writes an end-of-file on FORTRAN unit NWUNIT.

4.8 /ERRSET - Extended Error Handling (System-Dependent)

/ERRSET fun [NOAL] [MSG|NOMSG]

fun = function for which errors are to be controlled
NOAL = number of errors of the given type allowed
       (unlimitted if omitted or > 255)
MSG   causes standard system messages and tracebacks
       to be printed when the error occurs
NOMSG suppresses typeouts

Errors such as dividing by zero, exponentiating a large number, taking the logarithm of a negative number, and many others permit the user to take corrective actions and continue with execution. An extended error handling subroutine permits one to specify the number of allowable errors of each type and the disposition of messages during execution (in any case, a summary error table is printed at the end of the job). Subroutine ERRSET (p. 283) is FORTRAN- or ISX-callable, but its arguments are error numbers instead of mnemonics. /ERRSET accepts the function names supplied to /DEFAR (p. 67), STFN1 (p. 94), and other STATLIB function routines, translates them into the proper error numbers, and issues the appropriate call to ERRSET. For additional details and options, including the control of input/output errors, and especially the default corrective action, see the system FORTRAN Programmer's Guide.

The following table gives the error control codes allowed, the IBM code to which it is converted, and a description of the error type.

	IBM	
fun	code	Description
DIV	209	divide check: x/y
EXP	262	invalid argument range: exp(x)
INT	209	divide check: x/y
INV	209	divide check: x/y
LGS	262	invalid argument range: exp(x)
LGT	263	invalid argument range: log(x)
LOG	263	invalid argument range: log(x)
MLT	207	exponent overflow: x*y
MOD	209	divide check: x/y
PWR	245	invalid argument range: x**y
SQR	261	invalid argument range: sqrt(x)

Example:

```
/ERRSET DIV
/ERRSET LOG 1 MSG
STFN1 TAB EXPEND DIV EXPEND TOTAL
DYNFN2 DATA ABCD LOG DATA EFGH
```

permits unlimitted divisions by zero without messages, but limits out-of-range logarithmic errors to 1 with messages. Execution will terminate (abnormally) if <DATA EFGH> contains a data item less than or equal to zero.

4.9 /ISXIO - ISX Input/Output Unit

/ISXIO [NRUNIT|*] [NWUNIT|*] [LRECIN]

resets the input and output unit numbers, and optionally, the input logical record length (card size) for ISX routines. Reducing the card size enables one to insert comments into command lines and also eliminates problems introduced by text editors that insert line numbers in columns 73 through 80. An asterisk or omitted value indicates no change. Note that this affects ISX routines only; output for subroutine packages is controlled through OPTION (p. 285).

4.10 /ISXLIST - ISX Listing

/ISXLIST ddname [cc]

causes all ISX input lines to be written, without substitution, to the ddname specified. If ddname is specified as blank ("...." in ISX), output will be suppressed. ISX initializes ddname to SYSPRINT for batch processing on IBM OS/VS systems and to blank (i.e., suppresses output) on time-sharing. The second argument indicates the carriage control character to be used for each line; no carriage control character will be used if "N" is specified, while a blank will be used if the argument is omitted.

4.11 /LIST - List DYNCOR Block Identifiers

/LIST [type] [name]

type,name = identifiers of DYNCOR blocks to be listed.
At least one of the arguments must be blank
("....") or omitted, meaning "all".

prints identifiers of all blocks matching <type name> on the ISX
output unit. See Section 5.6 (p. 80) for ways to pass this
information into ISX procedures.

Examples:

/LIST DEFN

lists the identifiers of all blocks with first identifier DEFN.

/LIST .... ABCD

lists all blocks with name ABCD.

4.12 /LOADX - Load Internal Array

/LOADX code word1 [word2 ..]

loads word1, word2, ... into the "X" array (see Sec. 2.3, p. 60)
using the conversion specified by code:

    R   - convert to real
    I   - convert to integer
    A8 - store in double words (8-character)
    A4 - store in single words (4-character)
    A N J K - move up to N characters from the string
              "word1 word2 ..", beginning with the J-th
              character, into the "X" array, beginning with
              the K-th character. Before moving, the
              N-character target area in the "X" array is
              loaded with blanks.

Examples:

/LOADX R 123.4 567.8 999.99
/LOADX A4 ONE TWO
/LOADX A 1 1 1 .
/LOADX A 3 1 2 $TYP

loads X(1), X(2), X(3) with real numbers, loads X(1) with the
character string "ONE TWO ", and loads the first four characters of X
with "." followed by the first three characters (bytes) of the string
$TYP.

4.13 /LOG - Logoff (System-Dependent)

/LOG

causes the user to be logged off the system.

4.14 /LOGDSK - Update File Directory (System-Dependent)

/LOGDSK

updates the system file directory to include any data sets dynamically defined during the job. This protects against losing these data sets if the job terminates abnormally.

4.15 /RESTORE - Restore DYNCOR Blocks

/RESTORE [NRUNIT]

restores DYNCOR blocks written by /SAVE (below), presumably in an earlier job step. It rewinds the file first, then calls DYNINP (p. 270). If NRUNIT is omitted, unformatted reading occurs from FORTRAN unit 29. /RESTORE and /SAVE together enable the user to easily pick up in a future session where he left off in an earlier one.

4.16 /REWIND - Rewind

/REWIND NUNIT

rewinds FORTRAN unit NUNIT.

4.17 /SAVE - Save All DYNCOR Blocks

/SAVE [NWUNIT]

saves all DYNCOR blocks (except the DYNCOR and ISX command directories) on the given output unit, rewinding the file first, then calling DYNOUT (p. 272) in a loop. If NWUNIT is omitted, unformatted writing occurs on FORTRAN unit 29 (on IBM systems, RECFM should be VBS or VS). /SAVE and /RESTORE (above) together enable the user to easily pick up in a future session where he left off in an earlier one.

4.18 /STOP - Terminate Execution

/STOP

terminates execution and returns control to the routine that invoked ISX (see Sec. 6, p. 81). Execution is also terminated by an end-of-file in the input stream.

4.19 /SYS - Execute System Command (System-Dependent)

/SYS [(NOPRT)] command

executes any allowable system command. Each such command returns a system-dependent integer error code as the first word of the "X" array and as ISX variable $XXX. If non-zero, this code will be printed unless the optional argument "(NOPRT)" is included.

4.20 /VERIFY - Verification

/VERIFY [ON|OFF|*]

ON   turns on verification, causing a typeout of input
     commands as entered, after substitution
OFF turns off verification, suppressing typeouts
*   removes the last /VERIFY ON or OFF command

ISX initializes the verification mode to "OFF". Verification commands with arguments "ON" or "OFF" are stacked and removed by "/VERIFY *" on a last-in, first-out basis.

4.21 /WRITE - Write to Unit

/WRITE NWUNIT [line|*]

writes the specified line, after substitution for "$" variables, onto FORTRAN unit NWUNIT. If NWUNIT is "*", the current ISX output unit is used and printing may be suppressed or directed to a different unit via OPTION (p. 285), specifying "ISX". If its length exceeds 80 characters, the line is broken into records of length 80. If the second argument is "*", subsequent input lines are written, without substitution, until terminated by a line beginning with "/WRITEEND".

4.22 /XEQ - Execute Unit

/XEQ NRUNIT

FORTRAN unit NRUNIT is rewound, and commands are read and executed from it. Upon encountering an end-of-file, NRUNIT is rewound and control is returned to the normal input stream. /XEQ simply changes the input unit to NRUNIT; if it occurs within a procedure, commands will not be read from NRUNIT until all active procedures terminate.

4.23 /XEQFILE - Execute File (System-Dependent)

/XEQFILE fileid

reads and executes commands from the specified file. If not specified, filetype is taken as ISX and filemode as * on VP/CSS or VM/CMS systems. FORTRAN unit 30 is rewound and used; any existing definition for 30 will be cleared. Upon encountering an end-of-file, unit 30 is rewound and control is returned to the normal input stream. /XEQFILE simply changes the input unit to 30; if it occurs within a procedure, commands will not be read from 30 until all active procedures terminate.

/XEQFILE may return a system-dependent integer error code (non-zero if the file is not found) as the first word of the "X" array and as ISX variable $XXX.

Example:

/XEQF TSREGPRC

Commands from the file TSREGPRC are read and executed.

5. PROCEDURES

"Procedures" are user-written commands which contain sets of ISX
commands, subroutine calls, and/or calls to other procedures. A
procedure is created by /PROC (special procedures are generated by
/DO and /LIST) and executed by giving its name as a command.
Arguments may be given when a procedure is executed and/or re-defined
within the procedure through /ARGS or /ARGLS. Within a procedure,
arguments are referenced according to the names supplied in the /PROC
statement; alternatively, $1, $2, ... reference the first, second,
and succeeding arguments, but do not appear in the /PROC statement.
During substitution, non-existent arguments are ignored. Procedure
calls may be nested to any level, and procedures may be called
recursively.

5.1 /PROC - Procedure Definition

> /PROC procnam [arg1 arg2 ..|PRINT|DELETE]

```
procnam = procedure name
arg1 .. = symbolic procedure arguments (up to 8
          characters)
PRINT     prints an existing procedure
DELETE    deletes an existing procedure
```

Unless the argument is "PRINT" or "DELETE", this statement causes
succeeding input lines to be entered without substitution into a
procedure with name "procnam". The procedure name may be from 1 to 7
characters in length (the first character may not be "<"); the input
lines are packed and stored in DYNCOR block <=procnam=> (a single
"=", then the procedure name, then right padded to eight characters
with "="). Symbolic arguments within the procedure (arg1, arg2, ...)
will be replaced by the actual arguments supplied when the procedure
is called. The procedure definition is terminated by "/PROCEND".

The statements

```
/PROC procnam PRINT
/PROC procnam DELETE
```

may be used anywhere; otherwise, /PROC may not itself appear within a
procedure. When printed, symbolic arguments will have been replaced
by $1, $2, ..., and abolute skips by relative skips (see /SKIP,
p. 78).

Example:

```
/PROC PRT&CMD SERIES CMD
   TSPRT DATA SERIES 1965 1 1972 5
   CMD SERIES
/PROCEND
PRT&CMD INWD PLOT
```

    PRT&CMD GAIN DISPLAY

prints series INWD and executes procedure PLOT, then prints series
GAIN and executes procedure DISPLAY. SERIES and CMD are replaced by
the first and second arguments supplied when the procedure is called.
Indentation of lines within procedures is recommended for ease in
reading.

5.2 /ARGS - Redefine Arguments

    /ARGS [newarg1 newarg2 ..]

redefines, within a procedure, the values of its arguments arg1,
arg2, ... (or $1, $2, ...). /ARGS may only appear within procedures.

Examples:

    /ARGS 1926 INWD TSPRDN

causes the first three arguments to take on the values 1926, INWD,
and TSPRDN.

    /DEFINE $STR 1.6 ABCD
    /ARGS $1 $2 $STR

leaves arguments one and two unchanged, but defines arguments three
and four to 1.6 and ABCD.

5.3 /ARGLS - Redefine Arguments by Left Shift

    /ARGLS [newarg1 newarg2 .. newargn] K

redefines, within a procedure, the values of its arguments arg1,
arg2, ... (or $1, $2, ...) up through the nth (n may be zero), then
slides the Kth through last to positions (n+1) through (n+1+last-K).
The (n+1)th argument is set to the current value of the Kth, the
(n+2)th to the (K+1)th, etc., and the last (K-n-1) arguments are
deleted. Argument K may be equal to n+1, in which case no shift
occurs. /ARGLS may only appear within procedures.

Example:

    /ARGLS 2

slides all arguments one to the left: argument two replaces argument
one, three replaces two, etc., and the last argument is deleted.

    /ARGLS $1 $2 5

leaves the first two arguments unchanged, but slides the remaining
ones two to the left: argument five replaces argument three, six

replaces four, etc., and the last two are deleted.

5.4 /SKIP - Skip Lines in Procedure

/SKIP N|<lbl> rr [string1] [string2] [K]

skips N lines (relative addressing) or to the statement labelled
<lbl> (absolute addressing) in the procedure, conditional on the
relationship between string1 and string2. The label consists of one
to three alphanumeric characters enclosed in angle brackets. If rr
is EQ (equality) or NE (inequality), a character string comparison is
made between the first K characters of string1 and string2 (if K is
not specified, all characters will be compared). If rr is GE
(greater than or equal to), GT (greater than), LE (less than or equal
to), or LT (less than), string1 and string2 are converted to real
numbers and an arithmetic comparison made. If rr is U, an
unconditional skip occurs. In character comparisons, the strings
string1 and string2 will be considered unequal if string2 alone is
omitted and equal if both are omitted. In all cases, the skip will
take place if the rr condition occurs. If N is negative, the skip
will be to the |N|th previous line. A skip past the end of the
procedure may be used to terminate the procedure; a skip past the
beginning of the procedure will begin execution at the procedure's
first statement. With absolute addressing, the target statement may
be no more than 99 lines before or 1000 lines after the current line.
/SKIP may appear only within a procedure.

Examples:

        /DEFINE $TYP $1
        /SKIP 1 NE $1
        /DEFINE $TYP DATA

defines $TYP as $1 if given (i.e., nonblank), DATA otherwise.

        /ARGLS $1 3
        /SKIP -8 NE $2

"shifts" the arguments and repeats the eight preceding lines until
only one argument remains.

        /SKIP 4 EQ . $1 1

skips the four succeeding lines if the first character of argument 1
is a period.

        /PROC PRT&PLT SERIES
          TSPRT DATA SERIES 1965 1 1972 5
          PLOT SERIES
          /ARGLS 2
          /SKIP -3 NE SERIES
        /PROCEND
        PRT&PLT INWD GAIN

prints and plots <DATA INWD>, then redefines SERIES to GAIN, skips
back to the top, and prints and plots <DATA GAIN>. The second
argument shift leaves SERIES blank, so the skip is not taken and
execution of the procedure terminates.

```
/PROC EX2 ARG
  /SKIP <L1> EQ ARG XYZ
  REGRESS INPUT 3.5
  /SKIP <END> U
  <L1> REGRESS OUTPUT 4.3
<END> /PROCEND
```

skips to the statment labeled <L1> if the argument supplied is XYZ,
otherwise executes the first REGRESS statement and exits from the
procedure.

5.5 /DO - Do Loops


```
/DO procnam N1 N2 [N3]
```

```
procnam = the name of the procedure to be created
N1,N2   = the limits of the loop
N3      = the increment of the loop (1 if not
          specified)
```

creates a procedure procnam as follows:

```
/PROC procnam
  $1 $2 $3 $4 $5 $6 $7 N1
  $1 $2 $3 $4 $5 $6 $7 N1+N3
  $1 $2 $3 $4 $5 $6 $7 N1+2*N3
  ...
  $1 $2 $3 $4 $5 $6 $7 N2
/PROCEND
```

The procedure procnam may then be used to execute commands or other
procedures, with the index of the loop as the last argument of those
calls. Consistent with FORTRAN "do loop" requirements, N1 must be
less than or equal to N2, and N3 must be greater than zero.

Example:

```
/DO DOYR 1960 1970 5
DOYR ANLZ ABCD
```

is equivalent to:

```
ANLZ ABCD 1960
ANLZ ABCD 1965
ANLZ ABCD 1970
```

5.6 /LIST - List DYNCOR Block Identifiers (in Procedure)

```
/LIST type name procnam
```

type,name = identifiers of DYNCOR blocks to be
        listed. At least one of these must be
        blank ("...."), meaning "all".
procnam = the name of the procedure to be created

When the procnam argument is present, /LIST (see also Sec. 4.11, p. 72) enters the identifiers of matching blocks into a procedure as shown below, rather than printing them on the ISX output unit:

```
/PROC procnam
   $1 typ1 nam1 $2 $3 $4 $5 $6 $7
   $1 typ2 nam2 $2 $3 $4 $5 $6 $7
   ...
/PROCEND
```

The procedure procnam may then be used to execute commands or other procedures with the DYNCOR identifiers as the first two arguments.

DYNLST (p. 267) performs a similar function, but returns the block identifiers directly to the user (or calling procedure) rather than creating an intermediate procedure.

Example:

```
/LIST DATA .... DATALST
DATALST TSPRT 1960 1 1973 12
```

is equivalent to

```
TSPRT DATA nam1 1960 1 1973 12
TSPRT DATA nam2 1960 1 1973 12
   ...
```

6. ISX STRUCTURE

ISX consists of a control routine (ISXCTL), an interface routine for ISX commands (ISXCMD), and interface routines for each of STATLIB's high-level packages: STPAK (ISXST), TSPAK (ISXTS), SPPAK (ISXSP), TABLE (ISXTAB), DYNCOR (ISXDYN), and SERVICE (ISXSVC). Individual implementations of ISX can be created without some of the interface routines, resulting in more efficient use of core storage.

ISX is designed to allow new versions to be created without some of the Section 3 interface routines and/or with additional user-supplied interface routines. This is accomplished by passing as arguments to the control routine ISXCTL the names of the interface routines to be used.

ISXCTL reads a line of input, removes excess blanks, substitutes for "$" arguments, and stores the resulting line in common block ISX001 along with pointers to the beginning and end of each argument. Other arrays in ISX001 are loaded with the arguments stored as length-4 and length-8 character strings, and as integers. The "X" array (p. 60) is also contained in ISX001.

ISXCTL then procedes to interrogate the interface routines in turn, until the requested command is recognized and executed. The name of the command is entered in a hashed directory <ISX* *DY*>, along with the index of the interface routine and the index of the command within the interface routine, which saves searching on subsequent calls. If the command is not found, ISXCTL searches for a procedure with the given name (stored as DYNCOR block <=procnam>). If found, ISXCTL begins "reading" statements from the procedure rather than the input stream. If not, an error message is issued.

6.1 ISX Main Programs

The calling sequence for ISXCTL is as follows:

        CALL ISXCTL(S1,S2,S3,S4,S5,S6,S7,S8)

where S1, ..., S8 are names of ISX interface routines, declared EXTERNAL in the calling program. ISXCMD, the interface routine for ISX commands, is called automatically by ISXCTL and should not be included. The complete ISX main program is:

        EXTERNAL ISXDYN,ISXSVC,ISXST,ISXTAB,ISXTS,ISXSP,ISXDUM
        CALL ISXCTL(ISXDYN,ISXSVC,ISXST,ISXTAB,ISXTS,ISXSP,
            ISXDUM,ISXDUM)
        STOP
        END

Eight arguments must be included; ISXDUM is a dummy entry point.

6.2 ISX Interface Routines

Interface routines may be written by the user and used with ISX. The
following example shows the form of a routine for interfacing with
the subroutine package XYZPAK:

```
        SUBROUTINE ISXXYZ(LC,CNAME,K,*,*)
        REAL*8 CNAME,A8,X
        COMMON /ISX001/ A8(96),A(96),I(96),KMD(120),
            M,M1V(96),M2V(96),MD,X(50)
        INTEGER NC/4/,NARG(4)/2,3,0,1/
        REAL*8 C(4)/'XYZADD','XYZPRT','XYZMAP','XYZREG'/
        IF(LC.EQ.0) CALL ISXCLP(NC,C,NARG,'XYZPAK  ',&88)
        IF(K.EQ.0) CALL BSCANW(8,CNAME,1,C,1,8*NC,8,K,&88)
        IF(M.LT.NARG(K)) RETURN 2
        GO TO (10,20,30,40),K
     10 CALL XYZADD(A(1),A(2))
        GO TO 80
     20 CALL XYZPRT(A(1),I(2),I(3))
        GO TO 80
     30 CALL XYZMAP
        GO TO 80
     40 CALL XYZREG(A8(1))
     80 RETURN 1
     88 RETURN
        END
```

When ISXXYZ is called by ISXCTL, CNAME will contain the command (or
subroutine) name of length LC, padded on the right with blanks.   LC
will be zero if /CMDS has been called, in which case subroutine
ISXCLP prints arrays C (subroutine names) and NARG (minimum number of
arguments), then passes control to statement 88. If K is zero, CNAME
has not been called previously and BSCANW (p. 376) is called to
search C for its appearance, setting K to the appropriate value (1-4
here) if successful. If CNAME is not found, control passes to
statement 88 and a normal return is taken, telling ISXCTL to continue
its search. If the number of arguments M is less than the minimum
required for CNAME, a RETURN 2 is executed and ISXCTL prints an error
message. The computed GO TO statement transfers control to the
proper statement for execution of the desired subroutine.

In coding subroutine calls, arguments of the proper type are taken
from arrays in common block ISX001, which contains:

A8	- arguments as length-8 character strings
A	- arguments as length-4 character strings
I	- arguments as integers
KMD	- ISX statement (after substitution)
M	- number of arguments
M1V,M2V	- locations of first and last characters of arguments in KMD
MD	- number of arguments defined for current procedure (if any)
X	- "X" array

Character arguments are left-justified and padded with blanks. The last argument will spill over into succeeding array elements if it exceeds the word length.

An interface routine for any package can be modeled after ISXXYZ, with changes to the following lines:

      a. subroutine name in first line
      b. two lines defining NC, NARG and C
      c. computed GO TO statement through statement 40

ISX contains three entry points that may be of use in writing interface routines:

      CALL ISXERR(LMSG,ERRMSG,&xx)

prints the LMSG-character (LMSG < 28) error message ERRMSG after printing the command statement, then transfers to statement xx.

      CALL ISXCMX('$abc',I,VALUE,&xx)

creates ISX variable $abc from VALUE, with conversion types character (length 4), integer, or real according to I = 1, 2, or 3. If the first argument is the integer zero rather than '$abc', ISX variable $XXX is created from the first word of the "X" array and VALUE is ignored. Calling ISXCMX with I = -1 deletes the specified ISX variable. ISXCMX automatically transfers control to statement xx.

      CALL ISXPRC(procnam,LINE,N1,N2,&xx)

is used to build a procedure internally. Called once for each line, ISXPRC stores characters N1 through N2 of array LINE in successive lines of the procedure. The procedure is terminated by calling ISXPRC with N1 = 0. ISXPRC may also be used to delete (N1 = -1) and print(N1 = -2) procedures. The error return is taken if errors occur or when N1 ≤ 0.

7. SUBJECT INDEX

8. GLOSSARY OF ISX COMMANDS

CHAPTER 5

STPAK - STATISTICAL ANALYSIS OF TWO-WAY MATRICES

1. INTRODUCTION

STPAK is a system of FORTRAN subroutines for statistical analysis and modeling. Subroutines are included which perform such operations as printing, plotting, distribution fitting, cross-tabulation, regression, logit maximum likelihood, etc. Data management facilities are contained as well, enabling data to be organized and manipulated in various ways.

STPAK routines may be called directly in FORTRAN, or in ISX (Ch. 4), which accepts free-form input without FORTRAN punctuation. The following simple ISX program demonstrates the programming style of STPAK.

```
STDIM HLTH 6 AGE SEX WHITE INSURED INCOME EXP
STREAD HLTH 10 (6F5.0) 100
STPRT HLTH 0 0
STFN1 HLTH LEXP LOG EXP
STFN1 HLTH LINC LOG INCOME
STENL HLTH 2 PRDN RSID
STREG HLTH LEXP 5 AGE SEX WHITE INSURED LINC
STPLT HLTH PRDN 1 RSID
```

The call to STDIM (p. 91) stores dimensioning information for a matrix named HLTH, to consist of the 6 variables age, sex, racial status, insurance status, income, and medical expenditures. STREAD (p. 91) reads the matrix from FORTRAN unit 10 and stores it as a 600-word block (6 variables, 100 observations). STPRT (p. 105) prints the data, properly labeled. STFN1 (p. 94) creates new variables LEXP and LINC which are the logarithms of expenditures and income. STENL (p. 102) next enlarges the matrix to contain the variables PRDN and RSID. These names have special meaning to the regression routine STREG (p. 108), called next, which fills their locations in the data matrix with predictions and residuals from the regression of log expenditures on the 5 variables listed. Finally, STPLT (p. 106) generates a plot of residuals versus predictions.

Data matrices are managed by DYNCOR, the STATLIB dynamic in-core data management system (Ch. 9). They may be read in through DYNCOR or STPAK input routines, or created directly in the user program itself. Each data matrix is identified by a four-character name, usually supplied as the first argument to an STPAK routine. Variables are identified by their own eight-character names, and are strung out where required to identify an operation. Thus, to print the entire data matrix identified as HLTH:

        STPRT HLTH 0 0   ,

whereas to plot the 2 variables LEXP and PRDN versus INCOME:

        STPLT HLTH INCOME 2 LEXP PRDN   .

Section 2 describes STPAK conventions and procedures. Calling
sequence descriptions are given in Section 3. Subroutines performing
similar operations are grouped and organized alphabetically within
subsections. Section 4 contains sample programs, their accompanying
narratives, and the resulting output. Section 5 is a subject index.
Finally, Section 6 is a one-page summary of STPAK calling sequences.

2. CONVENTIONS AND NOTATION

2.1 Data Storage

STPAK routines create and maintain data matrices in core, storing the
data themselves as real numbers (REAL*8 on IBM) in DYNCOR blocks,
storing dimension control information in separate DYNCOR blocks (see
Sec. 2.2, below).

Each DYNCOR block is referenced by a first and last name (see p. 257
for an explanation of identification conventions). In STPAK, the
first indicates the type of block it is (e.g., DATA for data, *DAT
for dimension control blocks, REG for regression output, etc.), and
the last identifies the name of a particular set of data. References
to such blocks in the text have the two-word identifiers enclosed in
angle brackets (e.g., <DATA HLTH>, <*DAT HLTH>). For compactness,
STPAK subroutine calling sequences require only last names. But
through DYNCOR, using first and last names, the user can perform
further useful operations on these blocks, such as storing or
retrieving them externally, renaming, deleting, or copying them, etc.

The layout of an STPAK data matrix is analogous to that of a FORTRAN
data matrix. In FORTRAN, the coding

        DIMENSION X(6,100)

causes 600 contiguous words of core storage to be reserved and
treated logically as a 6 "row" by 100 "column" array; these locations
may be referenced as

        X(1,1), X(2,1), ..., X(6,1),
            X(1,2), ..., X(6,100)   .

A corresponding STPAK "dimension" statement is

        STDIM HLTH 6 AGE SEX WHITE INSURED INCOME EXP   .

This would cause other STPAK routines to regard, say, the 6*k contiguous words of storage occupied by <DATA HLTH> as a similarly stored 6 row by k column array. So, for example, a request to compute average expenditures (variable EXP) would result in averaging the row 6 contents within the block (i.e., words 6, 12, ..., 6*k).

2.2 Dimension Control Blocks

Dimension information is stored and maintained in a control block whose last name is the same as the data block but whose first name is *DAT (i.e., <*DAT mtrx>). Its contents are simply the variable names, each right-padded with enough blanks to fill out a real word (REAL*8 on IBM). The length of the block equals the number of variables.

DYNCOR may be used to obtain the lengths and locations of any blocks needed to perform a specific operation (see DYNOLD documentation, p. 260). The dimensions of the matrix are thus recovered by STPAK routines as the number of (real) words in <*DAT mtrx> and the ratio of the numbers of words in <DATA mtrx> and <*DAT mtrx>. In interpreting a request requiring specific variables, STPAK routines obtain these dimensions, then assume that the locations of variable names within the *DAT block match the rows of the matrix containing their data.

2.3 Block Expansion

Several routines create new variables in the data matrix and thus require space. A variable with a blank name signifies that a given row is available; in that case, the row will be used and the "blank" variable renamed. However, if a blank variable is not found, an attempt will be made to enlarge the matrix by calling DYNNEW (p. 260). Because enlarging typically requires that a new block of the desired length be created and the old one copied into it, care should be taken with large matrices to avoid inefficient management of core storage. The user should consider having enough blank variables initially to avoid enlarging, perhaps specifying more variables than needed when creating dimension contol blocks (STDIM, p. 91). Most STPAK routines that create matrices also include provisions for extra variables (c.f., STEXT, p. 103).

2.4 Observation Labels

Certain routines (e.g., STPRT, STDSP, STPLT) generate printed output with alphanumeric observation labels, if supplied. If a variable named OBL exists, its row in the data matrix is assumed to contain labels, each occupying one real word. Certain routines then give OBL data special treatment; e.g., "A" format codes are used for printing, sums and cross-products are not computed in regression, and other exceptions are made as noted.

2.5 Messages, Errors, and Printing Options

STATLIB-wide message and error conventions are described in the Part II Introduction (p. 58). Refer there (and to the Section 4 examples, p. 124) for further information on controlling the printing of messages and decisions on whether and when errors should terminate execution. The following conventions apply specifically to STPAK.

Error conditions result in a printed message by STERR. The most common errors arise in misspelling or leaving out the name of a matrix or variable. The messages "xxxx DATA BLOCK NOT FOUND" or "xxxx DIMENSION BLOCK NOT FOUND" mean that DYNCOR blocks <DATA xxxx> (the data matrix) or <*DAT xxxx> (the dimension control block) do not exist. The message "VBL=xxxxxxxx NOT FOUND" means that variable xxxxxxxx does not appear in the dimension control block; this is followed by the list of variables that do. Another frequent error results from insufficient core storage being available to create or enlarge a given block. A message from DYNCOR identifies the block and the number of words requested.

Each STPAK subroutine generates (through STMSG) a one- or two-line message summarizing what it has done. This helps to make program output self documenting in that the flow of execution can be determined from the output alone.

OPTION (p. 285) may be used to control STPAK printing, specifying ST* for all routines, STMSG for messages, STERR for error messages, or the subroutine name for routines that generate printed output.

2.6 Calling Sequence Notation

Calling sequences follow the STATLIB-wide conventions described in the Part II Introduction (p. 56). The following apply specifically to STPAK.

a. Matrix names may be up to four characters long, variable names up to eight. Since generic variable names have four characters, not eight, calling sequence notation convention (a) is violated; this is done here for compactness.

b. Because blank variables have the special significance of reserving space (Sec. 2.3, p. 89), instances often arise in creating matrices that one or more trailing variables are to be left blank. This is signified by including a variable with leading character ")". In FORTRAN calling sequence documentation, such cases are indicated by generic names which contain right parentheses: e.g., "var1..)". In ISX, an ")" variable is appended automatically to each subroutine call.

3. STPAK SUBROUTINES

3.1 Creating Data Matrices

3.1.1 STDIM - Dimension Control Block

STDIM specifies the number and names of variables for a data matrix by creating a dimension control block (see p. 89) and leaving it with the data manager DYNCOR. Such a block has *DAT as its first name, the matrix name as its second, and contains simply the variable names, each right-padded with enough blanks to fill out a real word (REAL*8 on IBM). The length of the *DAT block, obtained by other routines through DYNOLD (p. 260), is interpreted by STPAK as the number of variables in the matrix. The number of observations in the matrix is defined by the routine supplying the data when core storage is actually obtained (c.f., STREAD, below).

Calling Sequences:

    (FTN) CALL STDIM(mtrx,NVAR,'var1..)')

    (ISX) STDIM mtrx NVAR var1 var2 ..

        mtrx = data matrix name
        NVAR = number of variables
        var1.. = array of variable names

Example:

        STDIM HLTH 10 AGE SEX WHITE INSURED INCOME EXP

specifies 10 variables for HLTH, the last four of which are blank. Subsequently, STPAK routines can recover this information in block <*DAT HLTH>, will assume the data matrix (DYNCOR block <DATA HLTH>) to be 10 by k, and will assume that AGE occupies row 1, SEX row 2, etc. Rows 7-10 are blank, signifying their availability for use in storing other variables.

3.1.2 STREAD - Input

STREAD reads data sequentially into core and organizes them as a DYNCOR block whose first name is DATA. It requires a dimension control block (STDIM, above) to determine how many variables to read.

Calling Sequences:

    (FTN) CALL STREAD(mtrx,NUNIT,fmt,NOBS,&EOF)

    (ISX) STREAD mtrx NUNIT fmt NOBS

```
mtrx  = data matrix name
NUNIT = FORTRAN unit
fmt   = FORTRAN format statement, or "(*nn)" (see
        below)
NOBS  = number of observations to be read
&EOF  = end-of-file return
```

With an ordinary FORTRAN format statement, STREAD simply reads the data (the format codes should be compatible with REAL storage); for reasons of efficiency, it issues a single FORTRAN read statement for the entire data matrix. The user should be familiar with FORTRAN format input rules; e.g., if the format statement contains group repeat specifications, the last of these is used to read all records beyond the first. Before returning, STREAD adjusts the length of the matrix to the number of observations encountered, which will be NOBS unless an end-of-file is reached. A FORTRAN call reaching an end-of-file causes a branch to FORTRAN statement number EOF; in ISX, a special ISX variable is created (see below).

Data may be read free-form by specifying "*" as the format code. Numerical data, separated by one or more blanks, are then read from succeeding records. The width of the input record will be 80 unless the "*" format is followed by a shorter width (e.g., "*72"). Reading will stop and the length of the matrix adjusted if a data item is coded as "*".

Special variable names are OBL (observation labels, p. 89) and blank ("...." in ISX). OBL data are simply moved, not converted to real, during free-form input. Blank variables at the end of the *DAT block are initialized to zero and ignored during input. Blank variables not at the end of the list are processed as ordinary nonblank variables.

Example:

```
STDIM HLTH 20 AGE SEX WHITE INSURED INCOME EXP OBL
STREAD HLTH 10 (4F3.0,2F8.0,A8) 100
```

specifies 20 variables for HLTH and reads up to 100 records from unit 10. Since the last 13 variables are blank, STREAD infers that 7 items are to be read per record. Data are stored in DYNCOR block <DATA HLTH>.

ISX Notes:

Upon hitting an end-of-file, the ISX variable $EOF is set equal to the character string EOF. In conjunction with the ISX /SKIP command (p. 78), this would enable one to loop through a data base performing various matrix accumulations (e.g., cross-tab computations via STXTAB, p. 114; regression accumulations via STREGA, p. 110), then to proceed with the analysis once all the data have been processed.

If an asterisk is given as the FORTRAN unit, reading will occur from the current ISX input unit (the same unit from which commands are

being read). This enables programs to be read and executed from disk
(see the ISX /XEQ and /XEQFILE commands, p. 74) without dependence
on the input unit number.

Examples:

```
    /PROC INPUT
      <RD> STREAD HLTH 10 (4F3.0,2F8.0) 100
      ACCUM
      /SKIP <RD> NE $EOF EOF
    /PROCEND
    INPUT
    ANALYZE
```

executes user-written procedure INPUT, which reads matrix HLTH 100
observations at a time, calls procedure ACCUM, and skips back to the
the STREAD statement so long as $EOF has not been assigned the
end-of-file value (EOF). Skipping fails after the end-of-file is
reached, and procedure ANALYZE is then executed.

```
    STDIM HLTH 10 AGE SEX EXP
    STREAD HLTH * (*72) 5
    1 0 3  4 0 6  7 0 9  10 1 12  13 1 15
```

reads matrix HLTH free-form from columns 1-72 of the ISX input unit.

3.2 Elementary Operations

3.2.1 STCODE - Coding Dummy Variables

STCODE creates dummy variables indicating which of possibly several
equally spaced intervals contain a given variable's values. Each
dummy variable takes on the value 1 if the specified variable falls
within its interval, 0 otherwise.

Calling Sequences:

    (FTN) CALL STCODE(mtrx,cvar,XL,XU,XD,'var1..')

    (ISX) STCODE mtrx cvar XL XU XD var1 var2 ..

        mtrx   = data matrix name
        cvar   = coding variable
        XL   = mid-point of lowermost interval for cvar
        XU   = mid-point of uppermost interval for cvar
        XD   = distance between mid-points of adjacent
                  intervals (must divide XU - XL)
        var1.. = array of dummy variable names

The intervals are [XL-XD/2,XL+XD/2), [XL+XD/2,XL+3*XD/2), ..., and
[XU-XD/2,XU+XD/2]. Names for the dummy variables are taken
successively from the array of variable names provided.

Example:

      STCODE HLTH AGE 10 90 20 AGE10 AGE30 AGE50 AGE70 AGE90

creates dummy variables AGE10, AGE30, ..., AGE90 which contain zero-one indicators of whether AGE lies in [0,20), [20,40), ..., or [80,100] respectively.

3.2.2 STFN0, STFN1, STFN2 - Functions

Function routines may be used to perform a wide class of observation by observation operations on zero, one, or two variables. STFN0 creates a new variable which may depend on a constant:

$$z(i) = f(C) \quad .$$

STFN1 creates a new variable which is a function of an existing variable and, perhaps, a constant:

$$z(i) = f(x(i),C) \quad .$$

STFN2 creates a new variable which is a function of two existing variables:

$$z(i) = f(x(i),y(i)) \quad .$$

In all cases, computations may be performed in place; i.e., a new variable can have the same name as an old one. Space, if needed, is obtained by the function routines through STENL (p. 102). A central STATLIB function evaluator is used.

Calling Sequences:

    (FTN) CALL STFN0(mtrx,zvar,fun[,C])
    (FTN) CALL STFN1(mtrx,zvar,fun,xvar[,C])
    (FTN) CALL STFN2(mtrx,zvar,fun,xvar,yvar)

    (ISX) STFN0 mtrx zvar fun [C]
    (ISX) STFN1 mtrx zvar fun xvar [C]
    (ISX) STFN2 mtrx zvar fun xvar yvar

        mtrx = data matrix name
        zvar = z variable
        fun = function code
        xvar = x variable
        yvar = y variable
        C   = real constant

The following table gives the resulting values of z(i) for available function codes (fun):

Function	STFN0	STFN1	STFN2
ABS	$\|C\|$	$\|x(i)\|$	-
ADD	-	$x(i)+C$	$x(i)+y(i)$
ASN	arcsin(C)	arcsin(x(i))	-
DIV	-	$x(i)/C$	$x(i)/y(i)$
EQ	-	ind(x(i)=C)	ind(x(i)=y(i))
EQL	C	$x(i)$	-
EXP	exp(C)	exp(x(i))	-
FTN	FTNFUN(C)	FTNFUN(x(i),C)	FTNFUN(x(i),y(i))
GE	-	ind(x(i)≥C)	ind(x(i)≥y(i))
GT	-	ind(x(i)>C)	ind(x(i)>y(i))
INT	-	$[x(i)/C]$	$[x(i)/y(i)]$
INV	1/C	1/x(i)	-
LE	-	ind(x(i)≤C)	ind(x(i)≤y(i))
LGS	1/(1+exp(-C))	1/(1+exp(-x(i)))	-
LGT	log(C/(1-C))	log(x(i)/(1-x(i)))	-
LOG	log(C)	log(x(i))	-
LT	-	ind(x(i)<C)	ind(x(i)<y(i))
MAX	-	max(x(i),C)	max(x(i),y(i))
MIN	-	min(x(i),C)	min(x(i),y(i))
MLT	-	x(i)*C	x(i)*y(i)
MOD	-	mod(x(i),C)	mod(x(i),y(i))
NE	-	ind(x(i)≠C)	ind(x(i)≠y(i))
NPR	PNORM(C)	PNORM(x(i))	-
PWR	-	x(i)**C	x(i)**y(i)
RNO	RNORM(0)	-	-
ROU	round(C)	round(x(i))	-
RUN	RUNIF(0)	-	-
SEQ	i	-	-
SIN	sin(C)	sin(x(i))	-
SQR	C**.5	x(i)**.5	-
SUB	-	$x(i)-C$	$x(i)-y(i)$
TPR	-	PTDIST(x(i),C)	PTDIST(x(i),y(i))
ZER	-	zero(x(i),C)	-

Logarithms are computed to the base e. The indicator function (ind) returns 1 if its argument is true, 0 if false. FTNFUN is a dummy function, meant to be replaced by a user-supplied function in ISX (see below). RNORM (p. 373) and RUNIF (p. 374) are random number generators for the normal and uniform distributions. PTDIST is a cumulative t-distribution function routine (p. 370). The zero function zeroes out the C low-order bytes of a real word. A user-supplied FUNCTION subprogram may be passed in place of fun (see the FORTRAN note, below).

Subroutine ERRSET (p. 283), callable from ISX or FORTRAN, may be used to recover from such errors as division by zero, taking logarithms or square roots of negative numbers, etc. In ISX, the /ERRSET statement (p. 70) accomplishes this while providing a simpler calling sequence.

Examples:

```
STFN0 HLTH IDX SEQ
```

```
          STFN0 HLTH ONE EQL 1
```

sets variable IDX to (1,2,3,...) and variable ONE to (1,1,1,...).

```
          STFN1 HLTH WGTS LT AGE 60
```

defines an indicator variable WGTS to be 1.0 if AGE < 60, 0.0 otherwise.

```
          STFN2 HLTH W.S MLT WHITE SEX
```

sets variable W.S equal to the product of WHITE and SEX.

```
          STFN1 HLTH LEXP ADD EXP 1
          STFN1 HLTH LEXP LOG LEXP
```

creates a new variable LEXP containing the logarithms of (EXP+1).

FORTRAN Note:

A user-supplied FUNCTION subprogram may be used. It must return real values, be declared EXTERNAL in the calling program, and passed in place of the function name; if added to the calling sequence, up to three additional arguments (A1,A2,A3) will be passed along to the function. The function will be called by STFN0, STFN1, or STFN2 for each observation as follows:

$$z(i) = F(A1,A2,A3) \qquad \text{(by STFN0)}$$
$$z(i) = F(x(i),A1,A2,A3) \qquad \text{(by STFN1)}$$
$$z(i) = F(x(i),y(i),A1,A2) \qquad \text{(by STFN2)}$$

Example:

```
          EXTERNAL FN
          CALL STFN1('HLTH','AGEX    ',FN,'AGE     ')
```

ISX Note:

Dummy function FTNFUN is called if the function code is "FTN". It may be replaced by a user-written FORTRAN function; procedures for combining FORTRAN object modules with the ISX program are described in Part IV of this manual. The function FTNFUN should have the same calling sequence as the function F above, and should expect A1 to have been converted to real if called through STFN0 or STFN1. A2 and A3 are passed along as character strings, each occupying one real word; if, for internal purposes, it is necessary to obtain reals or integers, STATLIB routines DVALUE or IVALUE (p. 376) may be useful.

Examples:

```
          STFN1 HLTH UAGE FTN AGE 15
```

passes control to function FTNFUN, once for each observation. In each case, the first argument is age, the second argument is the real number 15.

STFN2 HLTH UEXP FTN INCOME EXP

calls FTNFUN once for each observation, passing along income and expenses.

3.2.3 STFNOB, STFNC - Functions Across Observations

STFNOB and STFNC compute aggregate statistics over all or within specific groups of observations; see also STXTAB (p. 114) for sums over groups.

STFNOB evaluates functions over the entire set of observations corresponding to a given variable and returns the value in an arithmetic assignment statement (or expression). Its one-line message also contains the function value. A centralized STATLIB function evaluator is called to perform the computations.

Calling Sequences (STFNOB):

    (FTN) ...STFNOB(mtrx,fun,xvar[,C])...

    (ISX) STFNOB mtrx fun xvar [C]

        mtrx = data matrix name
        fun = function code
        xvar = function argument variable
        C   = constant

The following function codes (fun) may be used:

Function	Result
AVG	Average
EXT	Extract Cth element (C integer)
MAX	Maximum
MED	Median
MIN	Minimum
ORD	Cth order statistic (C real)
SSQ	Sum of squares
STD	Standard deviation
SUM	Sum
VAR	Variance

C is required only for functions EXT and ORD. With EXT, C identifies the observation from which data are to be extracted, a value beyond the matrix meaning "last"; with ORD, C specifies a fractional order statistic between 0 and 1.

FORTRAN Note:

A user-written function may be declared EXTERNAL and passed as argument fun. It will be called as follows:

```
        STFNOB = F(NVAR,NOBS,X,A1,A2) ,
```

where X is dimensioned (NVAR,NOBS) and A1, A2 are optional arguments.
F should base its computation on X(1,1), X(1,2), ..., X(1,NOBS).

ISX Note:

The function value is stored both as the first real word of the ISX
"X" array and as ISX variable $XXX (see Ch. 4, Secs. 2.2-3, p. 60).
This variable might itself be used in a later statement, including
being saved under a different name through /DEFINE (p. 66).

Examples:

```
        STFNOB HLTH MED EXP
        STFN1 HLTH EXPM SUB EXP $XXX
        STFN1 HLTH EXPM ABS EXPM
        STFNOB HLTH AVG EXPM
        /DEFINE $MAD $XXX
```

computes and prints median expenditures, subtracts them from raw
expenditures, takes the absolute value of this difference, computes
and prints mean absolute deviation from the median, and finally saves
the last quantity as ISX variable $MAD.

STFNC evaluates functions over clusters of observations, storing the
aggregated results in a new matrix. The clusters are identified as
observations corresponding to constant contiguous values of a given
variable. STSORT (p. 120) may be used to sort the data if necessary,
although such data are usually naturally ordered. The function
evaluation methods and options are the same as for STFNOB.

Calling Sequences (STFNC):

```
    (FTN) CALL STFNC(xmtx,zmtx,cvar,fun,NVAR,'var1..'[,C])

    (ISX) STFNC xmtx zmtx cvar fun NVAR var1 var2 .. [C]

            xmtx   = data matrix containing function arguments
            zmtx   = data matrix to receive function values
            cvar   = variable defining clusters
            fun    = function code (character string, length 3)
            NVAR   = number of variables
            var1.. = array of variables names
            C      = constant (e.g., 2, .5)
```

Clusters of observations in matrix xmtx are determined, and fun is
applied to each of the NVAR variables named. Results are stored as
identically named variables in matrix zmtx. If a dimension control
block for zmtx is found, space is reserved in zmtx for all variables
listed there and in the array of variable names. If either list
includes variable cvar, values of that variable will be copied into
zmtx for identification. To facilitate creating output matrices in
successive calls to STFNC with different function codes, zmtx is not

reinitialized if it is found to exist and to have the required number of observations.

Examples:

        STFNC HLTH HFAM FAMILY AVG 2 AGE SEX
        STFNC HLTH HFAM FAMILY SUM 1 EXP
        STFNC HLTH HFAM FAMILY EXT 2 WHITE INSURED 1

creates matrix HFAM from matrix HLTH. Assuming that observations within HLTH are on individuals and that individuals within families (identified by FAMILY) are contiguous, HFAM would contain family-level data: average age and sex, total expenditures, and race and insurance status.

3.2.4 STRCOD, STRCDK - Recode

STRCOD recodes a given variable by mapping entire intervals into targeted single values. An interval is defined by its lower and upper end-points. These end-points and targets are supplied free-form in a character string and arranged in triplets. In FORTRAN calls, this string must be terminated by a right parenthesis.

Calling Sequences (STRCOD):

    (FTN) CALL STRCOD(mtrx,rvar,ovar,rstrng)

    (ISX) STRCOD mtrx rvar ovar rstrng

        mtrx   = data matrix name
        rvar   = recoded variable
        ovar   = old variable (may be the same as rvar)
        rstrng = L1 U1 Z1 L2 U2 Z2 ..)

Values of ovar in [L1,U1] are recoded to Z1, [L2,U2] to Z2, etc. The number of elements in rstrng may not exceed 200 (93 in ISX; see p. 60). If intervals have values in common, the one appearing first in the list takes precedence. A value not contained in any interval is copied without modification.

Examples:

        STRCOD HLTH EDUC EDUC   0 6 1   7 8 2

recodes EDUC in place so that [0,6] becomes 1, [7,8] becomes 2.

        STRCOD HLTH LEXPC LEXP   0 1.5 1   3 8 0

recodes LEXP into LEXPC so that [0,1.5] becomes 1, [3,8] becomes 0; values less than zero, in the open interval 1.5-3, or greater than eight are simply copied.

STRCDK recodes a given variable based on the values of K variables (possibly including itself). Intervals for the K variables and the target values for the recoded variable are supplied free-form in a character string and arranged in groups of size 2*K+1. In FORTRAN calls, this string must be terminated by a right parenthesis.

Calling Sequences (STRCDK):

   (FTN) CALL STRCDK(mtrx,rvar,cond,K,'var1..',rstrng)

   (ISX) STRCDK mtrx rvar cond K var1 var2 .. rstrng

   mtrx = data matrix name
   rvar = recoded variable
   cond = condition for recode: AND or OR
   K   = number of variables
   var1.. = array of variable names (may include rvar)
   rstrng = L11 U11 L12 U12 .. L1K U1K Z1
        L21 U21 L22 U22 .. L2K U2K Z2 ..)

Values of rvar are recoded to $Z1$, $Z2$, etc., according to which of the regions specified in rstrng contains the K variables listed. The number of elements in rstrng may not exceed 200 (92-K in ISX). With cond = "OR", the recoding occurs if any of the K variables lies in a given region; with cond = "AND", all K must lie in the region. If the recode conditions are satisfied in more than one region, the one appearing first in the list takes precedence. An observation for which none of the comparisons succeeds has its rvar value left alone.

Examples:

  STFN0 HLTH WGTS EQL 1
  STRCDK HLTH WGTS OR 2 EDUC EXP -99 -1 -99 -1 0

sets variable WGTS equal to the constant 1, then recodes it to zero if either EDUC or EXP is between -99 and -1 (e.g., missing data codes).

  STRCDK HLTH WGTS AND 2 SEX WHITE 0 0 1 1 0

further modifies WGTS to be zero if SEX is zero and WHITE is one.

3.2.5 STTSFN - Time Series Functions

Time series functions include generating cumulative sums, lagged differences, lagged values, or moving averages of a given variable. Time series operations are useful not only for observations indexed in time, but generally whenever observation indices correspond to the values of some equally spaced variable (e.g., cumulative sums of empirical density functions are empirical cdf's). For added flexibility in time series manipulations, see TSPAK (Ch. 6, p. 145).

Calling Sequences:

        (FTN) CALL STTSFN(mtrx,zvar,func,xvar[,ILAG])

        (ISX) STTSFN mtrx zvar func xvar [ILAG]

                mtrx = data matrix name
                zvar = z variable
                func = function code
                xvar = x variable
                ILAG = lag (positive or negative). If positive,
                       computations may be performed in place.

The following table lists available functions and gives the resulting
value of z(i):

Function	$z(i)$
CSUM	$x(1)+x(2)+\ldots+x(i)$
DIFF	$x(i)-x(i-ILAG)$
LAG	$x(i-ILAG)$
MAVG	$(x(i-ILAG+1)+\ldots+x(i))/(|ILAG|)$

For codes DIFF, LAG, and MAVG, the function result is zero if an
argument is undefined (e.g., $x(-1)$).

Example:

        STTSFN HLTH CRSI CSUM RSID

sets CRSI to be the cumulative sum of residuals.

        STTSFN HLTH RSID3 MAVG RSID 3

sets RSID3 to be a three-point moving average of residuals.
According to the definition above, the first two entries of RSID3
would not be defined, so they are set equal to zero.

3.3 Matrix Manipulations

3.3.1 STCPY - Copy Observations

STCPY creates a new data matrix by copying the dimension control
block and selected observations from an existing matrix. Regardless
of name, variables in the new matrix follow their ordering in the old
matrix; to permute or exclude variables, use STEXT (p. 103).

Calling Sequences:

        (FTN) CALL STCPY(omtx,ivar,nmtx)

        (ISX) STCPY omtx ivar nmtx

```
omtx = old data matrix name
ivar = indicator variable, or blank ("...." in ISX)
nmtx = new data matrix name (may be same as old)
```

If ivar is nonblank, it is assumed to be an indicator variable contained in omtx; observations will then be copied only if the corresponding entry of ivar is nonzero. If nmtx = omtx, the matrix will be copied in place.

Examples:

```
STCPY HLTH .... CPY1
STCPY HLTH WHITE CPY2
STFN1 HLTH NONW NE WHITE 1
STCPY HLTH NONW CPY3
```

generates a full copy of HLTH (CPY1), a copy of only whites (CPY2), and a copy of nonwhites (CPY3).

```
STCPY HLTH WHITE HLTH
```

copies HLTH into itself, retaining whites only.

3.3.2 STENL - Enlarge

STENL enlarges a matrix by adding variable names to the dimension control block and, if necessary, adjusting the data block itself. Variables which already exist result in no action being taken. Blank variables signify available space, so they are simply renamed and their correponding data initialized to zero. If too few blank variables exist, however, a block large enough to contain the new matrix is generated and the old matrix is copied into it.

Calling Sequences:

```
(FTN) CALL STENL(mtrx,NVAR,'var1..)')

(ISX) STENL mtrx NVAR var1 var2 ..

      mtrx   = data matrix name
      NVAR   = number of variables
      var1.. = array of variable names
```

Example:

```
STENL HLTH 2 PRDN RSID
```

adds variables PRDN and RSID to HLTH.

3.3.3 STEXT - Extract Variables

STEXT extracts selected variables from an existing data matrix and stores them as a new matrix.

Calling Sequences:

    (FTN) CALL STEXT(omtx,nmtx,NVAR,'var1..)')

    (ISX) STEXT omtx nmtx NVAR var1 var2 ..

        omtx   = old data matrix name
        nmtx   = new data matrix name (may be same as old)
        NVAR   = number of variables
        var1.. = array of variable names

Blank variables, or variables not found in the old matrix, have their corresponding data initialized to zero. Variables in the new matrix will be ordered as prescribed in the calling sequence. If nmtx = omtx and NVAR is less than or equal to the total number of variables, the matrix will be extracted in place. If NVAR is zero, the matrix is simply "cleaned up": the k nonblank variables are extracted into locations 1 through k, and the remaining locations are zeroed out. This feature can be useful in limiting the number of variables to be accumulated in regression (p. 107) or logit maximum likelihood (p. 117) computations and hence in reducing costs.

Examples:

        STEXT HLTH HLTH 5 AGE LINC LEXP

extracts HLTH into itself, carrying along the three variables AGE, LINC, and LEXP, and leaving space for two more.

        STEXT HLTH HEXT 2 AGE LEXP

extracts HLTH into HEXT, a matrix consisting of two variables.

        STEXT HLTH HLTH 0

cleans up matrix HLTH, moving all nonblank variables into the lowermost matrix locations, and zeroing out the remaining ones.

3.3.4 STLINK - Link Matrices

STLINK links matrices mtx1 and mtx2 with equal numbers of observations. Each nonblank variable in mtx2 is moved into mtx1. Space is obtained via subroutine STENL (p. 102); according to procedures previously described, this results in the replacement of data when an identically named variable is found, the usage of existing space corresponding to blank variables, and the generation of a larger block only if necessary.

Calling Sequences:

    (FTN) CALL STLINK(mtx1,mtx2)

    (ISX) STLINK mtx1 mtx2

        mtx1 = data matrix to be enlarged
        mtx2 = input data matrix

Another common linking joins observations from two matrices that are identically dimensioned (i.e., same variables, but possibly different numbers of observations); subroutine DYNCON (p. 263), which concatenates DYNCOR blocks, may be called to accomplish that.

Examples:

        STLINK HLTH HEXT

links the contents of HEXT to those of HLTH. If HEXT were generated from the above Section 3.3.3 example, variables AGE and LEXP will be found to exist, in which case the data will be copied but HLTH will not be enlarged.

        DYNCON DATA WHIT DATA NONW

links matrices WHIT (originally dimensioned k by n1) and NONW (dimensioned k by n2) along the "observations" dimension; WHIT's dimensions are subsequently k by (n1+n2).

3.3.5 STNAM - Rename

STNAM renames one or more variables.

Calling Sequences:

    (FTN) CALL STNAM(mtrx,NVAR,'ovr1..)','nvr1..)')

    (ISX) STNAM mtrx NVAR ovr1 nvr1 ovr2 nvr2 ..

        mtrx   = data matrix name
        NVAR   = number of variables to be renamed
        ovr1.. = array of old variable names
        nvr1.. = array of new variable names

STNAM goes through the list of variable names in order; the effect of renaming is cumulative. If a new variable name is found already to exist, the existing one is renamed to blank, thereby deleting it.

ISX Note:

In ISX the calling sequence requires old and new variables as successive pairs of arguments.

Example:

        STNAM HLTH 3 NONW WGTS PRDN .... RSID ....

renames NONW to WGTS and PRDN and RSID to blank, effectively deleting
the last two.

        STNAM HLTH 3 WGTS TEMP WGTS2 WGTS TEMP WGTS2

renames WGTS to WGTS2 and WGTS2 to WGTS, using TEMP as a temporary
name to avoid clashes.

3.4 Printing, Plotting, Display

3.4.1 STPRT, STWRIT - Printing

STPRT prints a data matrix, properly labelled. Variables are listed
in columns across the page, observations down. STWRIT writes the
data, minus labels and page-heading information. STWRIT generally
places an entire observation on one logical record, and is useful in
creating new machine-readable data files. In either case, some or
all of the variables may be printed, and the output format may be
explicitly given or determined from a format code supplied by the
user.

Calling Sequences:

    (FTN) CALL STPRT(mtrx,NVAR,'var1..',fmtcod)
    (FTN) CALL STWRIT(mtrx,NVAR,'var1..',NUNIT,fmtcod)

    (ISX) STPRT mtrx NVAR var1 var2 .. fmtcod
    (ISX) STWRIT mtrx NVAR var1 var2 .. NUNIT fmtcod

        mtrx   = data matrix name
        NVAR   = number of variables
        var1.. = array of variable names
        fmtcod = format or format code
        NUNIT = FORTRAN unit

If NVAR is zero, all nonblank variables are printed or written. The
output format is determined as follows: if the first character of
fmtcod is "(", fmtcod is assumed to be a FORTRAN format statement,
and the entire matrix of nonblank variables is dumped in a single
WRITE statement; if the first character is "A", "D", "E", "F", or
"G", fmtcod is assumed to be a FORTRAN format code (e.g., Aw, Fw.d),
and STPRT or STWRIT creates its own format statement using this code
exclusively. In the latter case, STPRT positions variable names over
their data, adds a carriage control character, adds observation
labels if variable OBL exists (see Sec. 2.4, p. 89), and prints up
to [120/w] variables at a time until the list is exhausted; STWRIT
writes all NVAR variables for each observation on one logical record.
If fmtcod does not begin with any of the above codes, F9.2 is

assumed.

The default FORTRAN output unit is 6 for STPRT. This may be changed
in the usual way through subroutine OPTION (p. 285). When calling
STWRIT, the user must supply the output unit himself.

Example:

```
        STPRT HLTH 0 0
        STWRIT HLTH 2 AGE INCOME 7 (2A8)
        STPRT HLTH 6 AGE WHITE SEX INCOME INSURED EXP F4.0
        STWRIT HLTH 3 AGE WHITE INSURED 20 F5.0
        STWRIT HLTH 0 7 A8
```

prints all nonblank variables in HLTH using format code F9.2, writes
age and income onto unit 7 using format (2A8), prints the 6 variables
age, white, sex, income, insurance status, and expense using format
(1X6F4.0), writes age, white, and insurance status onto unit 20 with
format (3F5.0), and writes, say, all 25 variables in the matrix onto
unit 7 with format (25A8).

3.4.2 STPLT - Plotting

STPLT plots one or more variables against a designated horizontal
axis variable. Subroutine PPLOT (p. 358) does the plotting; its
entry point PPLOTP (p. 287) enables minima or maxima to be set, plot
characters to be changed, axes or grids to be drawn, etc.

Calling Sequences:

    (FTN) CALL STPLT(mtrx,hvar,NVAR,'var1..')

    (ISX) STPLT mtrx hvar NVAR var1 var2 ..

        mtrx   = data matrix name
        hvar   = horizontal axis variable, or blank ("...." in
                  ISX)
        NVAR   = number of plotted variables
        var1.. = array of variables to be plotted

If hvar is blank, a "time" plot is produced; i.e., variables are
plotted one observation per column against observation indices. Time
plots too wide for one page will appear as separate plots on
consecutive pages, each with the same vertical scale. Alternatively,
"comic" mode plotting may be set through PPLOTP, which causes time
plots (not scatter plots) to be printed down the page. Page size,
normally assumed to be 132 print positions, may be changed via the
PAGSIZ code in subroutine OPTION (p. 285).

If the matrix contains observation labels (variable OBL, p. 89), and
if a single vertical axis variable is being plotted, the first
character of each label will be the plot character for its
observation. To suppress this feature, one may plot the same

variable twice: i.e., set NVAR = 2, var2 = var1.

Example:

       STPLT HLTH PRDN 2 LEXP PRDN

plots the 2 variables LEXP and PRDN versus PRDN.

3.4.3 STDSP - Display

STDSP generates a display consisting of several plots, individually scaled, on a page. The example in Section 4.1 (p. 129) illustrates the technique. Turned sideways, the display is simply 3 low-resolution plots of variables versus observation indices. For clarity, the plotted points are connected to their ordinate axes; the axes themselves are made up of two-digit integers which provide greater precision than can be obtained from the number of asterisks alone.

Calling Sequences:

    (FTN) CALL STDSP(mtrx,NVAR,'var1..')

    (ISX) STDSP mtrx NVAR var1 var2 ..

        mtrx   = data matrix name
        NVAR   = number of plotted variables
        var1.. = array of variables to be displayed

If NVAR = 0, the data corresponding to all nonblank variables except observation labels (variable OBL, p. 89) are displayed. Output is generated by subroutine DSPLAY (p. 356); further options are available using entry point DSPPAR (p. 282).

3.5 Regression Analysis

Regression is performed using REGPAK (Ch. 11, p. 297), the STATLIB regression package. STREGA may be used when the data are either in core or available one observation at a time to generate "accumulation" matrices (i.e., sums, cross-products). These can be stored using DYNCOR output routines or simply left behind for further accumulations by STREGA or for use by STREG, the regression routine. STREG will attempt to satisfy a given request from the accumulation matrix available; if unable to do so, however, it will create one from the data matrix in core, use it, then leave it behind as well. Residuals and predictions (i.e., fitted values) may be inserted by STREG or STREGP directly into a data matrix for further analysis. Other options and details are described below.

3.5.1 STREG - Regression

STREG carries out a linear regression by calling on REGPAK subroutines. The constant term is normally included, but may be suppressed through REGPAK parameter routine REGPAR (p. 290).

Calling Sequences:

    (FTN) CALL STREG(mtrx,depv,NINDV,'ind1..')

    (ISX) STREG mtrx depv NINDV ind1 ind2 ..

        mtrx   = data matrix name
        depv   = dependent variable, or blank ("...." in ISX)
        NINDV   = number of independent variables
        ind1.. = array of independent variables

Certain variable names, if present in the matrix, have special meaning to STREG. Variable WGTS causes weighted regression to be performed; weights are treated logically as the number of elements (possibly fractional) in an averaging process that would have yielded each observation (note: not as a count of exact replicates). Variables RSID or PRDN cause residuals or predictions to be computed and stored in the data matrix. Variable OBL signifies observation labels (p. 89) and will be temporarily zeroed out during accumulations to avoid machine overflows.

Example:

        STREG HLTH LEXP 5 AGE SEX WHITE INSURED LINC

regresses LEXP on the 5 variables AGE, SEX, WHITE, INSURED, and LINC.

Additional Details:

The entire regression consists of a number of steps. An accumulation phase is carried out first by REGACC (p. 323). Then, for numerical reasons, the cross-products matrix is normalized (if the constant is being suppressed) or reduced to a correlation matrix: means and standard deviations are computed by REGMSD (p. 323) and the matrix reduced by REGCOR (p. 324). Next, the appropriate subsection of the correlation matrix is extracted by REGSEL (p. 324) and inverted by REGINV (p. 325). During inversion, variables that would cause singularity or near-singularity are detected and automatically deleted; the collinearity threshold may be modified through REGPAR (p. 290). If depv is blank, the request is considered fulfilled and STREG returns. Otherwise, the regression coefficients are calculated by REGRES (p. 326) and various statistics reported by REGANL (p. 326). Finally, predictions and residuals are obtained and stored in the data matrix if variables PRDN or RSID are present.

Printed output is produced by the following subroutines, if needed by STREG for the current request: REGMSD, REGINV (if variables are deleted), and REGANL. The table below describes their output and identifies other subroutines called with printing turned off. As elsewhere, any of the printing may be controlled through subroutine OPTION (p. 285).

Subroutine	Page	Print	Output Description
REGACC	323	OFF	regression observations
REGMSD	323	ON	means, variances, standard deviations
REGCOR	324	OFF	correlation matrix
TRIDIS	349	OFF	correlation matrix display
REGINV	325	ON	deleted variables (collinearity threshold exceeded)
REGANL	326	ON	coefficients, ANOVA table

Intermediate results are stored under "standard" REGPAK format (see Ch. 11, Sec. 3.10, p. 312) in DYNCOR block <REG mtrx>. They may be retrieved through REGGET (p. 289), which accesses the regression block most recently referenced. Once the regression has passed beyond the accumulation phase, calling STREG with a blank dependent variable and NINDV = 0 updates the reference but does not perform additional computations.

STREG will try to avoid reaccumulating cross-products between calls and will first check to see if this block exists and can satisfy the current regression request. If not, accumulations are carried out from <DATA mtrx> and a new <REG mtrx> block is generated. To maximize the chances of being able to satisfy future regression requests, all but possibly the last few variables in the matrix are included: those last variables are eliminated if named WGTS, PRDN, RSID, OBL, blank, or if the leading character is "*". For large data matrices, substantial core and execution time savings may result from calling STEXT (p. 103) or STNAM (p. 104) to eliminate unnecessary variables from the accumulations.

Results of the accumulation phase can be managed in various ways through DYNCOR subroutines; e.g.,

        DYNOUT REG mtrx NUNIT 0

(p. 272) stores the <REG mtrx> block in a format understandable to DYNINP or DYNINL (p. 270).

        DYNDEL REG mtrx

(p. 261) deletes the <REG mtrx> block, which will force STREG to reaccumulate. For further ways to manage these blocks, see DYNCOR documentation.

Examples:

        STREG HLTH LEXP 4 AGE SEX WHITE INSURED
        STREG HLTH EXP 5 AGE SEX WHITE INSURED INCOME
        DYNOUT REG HLTH 20 0
        DYNOUT *DAT HLTH 20 0

performs two regressions (only one accumulation) and stores the
regression and dimension control blocks on unit 20.

```
DYNINP 20
STREG HLTH LEXP 5 AGE SEX WHITE INSURED LINC
STREG HLTH LEXP 3 WHITE INSURED LINC
```

in a subsequent job would retrieve that output and perform the
additional regressions without reaccumulating.

```
STENL HLTH 1 RSID
STREG HLTH LEXP 5 AGE SEX WHITE INSURED LINC
STFN1 HLTH RSID ABS RSID
STFN1 HLTH WGTS LT RSID 2.5
DYNDEL REG HLTH
STREG HLTH LEXP 5 AGE SEX WHITE INSURED LINC
```

results in a regression in which outlying observations are trimmed.
The first regression stores residuals in RSID. Next, a variable WGTS
is created which is 1 if |RSID| < 2.5, 0 otherwise. The contents of
this variable are to be used as weights in a subsequent regression;
first, however, it is necessary to force reaccumulations by calling
DYNDEL.

3.5.2 STREGA - Regression Accumulations

STREGA generates accumulation matrices for use by STREG. STREGA does
not require all observations to be in core at once, so the user may
process large data sets in segments. Observations may also be read
in one at a time through subroutine STUINP (p. 122).

Calling Sequences:

        (FTN) CALL STREGA(mtrx,NREC,&EOF)

        (ISX) STREGA mtrx NREC

                mtrx = data matrix name
                NREC = number of records to be processed, or zero
                &EOF = end-of-file return

As before, variables named WGTS, RSID, PRDN, OBL, blank, or beginning
with "*", receive special treatment; see STREG (above) for
conventions.

If NREC is zero, accumulations are carried out from the data matrix
in core; otherwise, the specified number of records will be processed
(by STUINP, p. 122) up to an end-of-file. STREGA stores results in
DYNCOR block <REG mtrx>, as required by STREG. Alternatively,
further accumulations may be carried out by STREGA itself: if, on a
subsequent call, the regression block is found to exist and to be
properly formatted (i.e., it has the correct number and names of
variables and was not modified in a call to STREG), it is added onto

without reinitialization.

As produced by STREGA, the <REG mtrx> block contains 20 words of parameter information and various sums: observations, weights, variables, and cross-products. This structure is particularly useful in that if two or more REG blocks are identically formatted but resulted from accumulations over disjoint sets of observations, the item-by-item sum of all but the first 20 words will correspond to accumulations over their union of observations. DYNCOR routines DYNGET, DYNPUT, and DYNFN2 (Ch. 9, Sec. 3, p. 260) may be used to perform these computations; see the example below.

STREGA does not generate printed output beyond its one-line message, although it calls REGACC (p. 323) to carry out the accumulations, which may. As elsewhere, subroutine OPTION (p. 285) may be called to force, suppress, or redirect printing.

Examples:

        STREGA HLTH 10000

generates regression blocks from a file of up to 10000 records; subroutine STUINP (p. 122) is called upon to supply one observation at a time.

        STREGA WHIT 0
        STREGA NONW 0

generates regression blocks WHIT and NONW from data matrices in core. Assuming these matrices to be identically formatted, the subsequent statements

        DYNGET REG WHIT 2 1 20
        DYNFN2 REG HLTH ADD REG WHIT REG NONW
        DYNPUT REG HLTH 2 1 20

result in an accumulation matrix for whites and nonwhites both. DYNGET obtains the first 20 words of the block in the ISX "X" array (p. 60), thereby protecting the regression block's nonadditive contents. After DYNFN2 adds the two blocks, DYNPUT restores the original 20 words.

ISX Note:

As with STREAD (p. 91), the ISX variable $EOF is set equal to the character string EOF upon reaching an end-of-file and may be used to control branching within a user-written procedure (c.f., Sec. 3.1.2 example, p. 93).

3.5.3 STREGP - Regression Prediction

STREGP calls REGPAK subroutines REGPRE (p. 327) and REGFOV (p. 329) to generate a number of quantities associated with the regression coefficient vector (from a previous call to STREG): residuals (y-b'x), predictions (b'x), residual standard errors (stdev[y-b'x]), prediction standard errors (stdev[b'x]), forecast standard errors (stdev[b'x+e]), and degrees of freedom. It requires as input a matrix of "observations", the name of the matrix from which the regression coefficient vector was generated, and an indicator of whether the computations are to involve the constant term. The constant term would be suppressed if, for example, one were interested in obtaining t statistics of linear combinations of the regression coefficients: e.g., predictions divided by their standard errors. In any case, this argument is ignored if the regression model itself does not contain a constant term.

Calling Sequences:

        (FTN) CALL STREGP(mtrx,rmtx,const)

        (ISX) STREGP mtrx rmtx CON|NOCON

                mtrx = data matrix name
                rmtx = regression data matrix name
                const = CON includes constant term, NOCON suppresses
                          constant term

Computational results are inserted back into the data matrix, according to the variable names it contains: RSID, PRDN, RSIDSTD, PRDNSTD, FCSTSTD, and DF signify residuals, predictions, residual standard errors, prediction standard errors, forecast standard errors, and degrees of freedom respectively. When weights are present (variable WGTS), residual and forecast standard errors correspond to observations with those weights (see Ch. 11, Sec. 4.2, p. 315).

Examples:

        STREG HLTH LEXP 3 AGE SEX INSURED
        STENL HLTH 2 RSID RSIDSTD
        STREGP HLTH HLTH CON

regresses log expenditures on age, sex, and insurance status, then inserts residuals and residual standard errors into matrix HLTH. Continuing this example:

        STDIM COMB 3 AGE SEX INSURED
        STREAD COMB * (*) 6
          10 1 1   10 0 -1   10 -1 0   -10 1 0
           5 0 1   5 -1 -1
        STENL COMB 3 PRDN PRDNSTD DF
        STREGP COMB HLTH NOCON
        STFN2 COMB T DIV PRDN PRDNSTD
        STFN2 COMB SIG TPR T DF
        STPRT COMB 7 AGE SEX INSURED PRDN PRDNSTD T SIG F7.2

Matrix COMB is input, and STREGP computes linear combinations of the coefficients, their standard errors, and the error degrees of

freedom.   Finally, t statistics   and their significance levels are
generated and the matrix printed.

3.6 Cross Tabulations

Routines   of this section generate cross-tab, or grouped   sum,
matrices.   Such matrices   contain sums of designated variables over
groups of observations, the groupings as determined by the values of
other variables.

Subroutine STXRGN specifies "regions" (rectangular intervals) that
identify observation groups. Subroutine STXTAB performs the actual
computations, storing "grouping" and "sum" variables together as a
standard STPAK matrix. Analysis and display may be performed via the
standard STPAK print, plot, and display routines (Sec. 3.4, p. 105).

3.6.1 STXRGN - Cross-tab Regions

STXRGN specifies rectangular regions into which observations will be
grouped by STXTAB (see below). Regions may be defined in up to 10
dimensions and are assumed to have equally spaced boundaries. For
each grouping variable to be used, one supplies the mid-points of its
lowermost and uppermost intervals and the distance between mid-points
of adjacent intervals. This information is simply stored in DYNCOR
block <RGN mtrx> for use by STXTAB.

Calling Sequences:

      (FTN) CALL STXRGN(mtrx,gvar,XL,XU,XD)

      (ISX) STXRGN mtrx gvar XL XU XD

            mtrx = data matrix name, or "DFLT" (meaning default)
            gvar = grouping variable
            XL   = mid-point of lowermost interval for gvar
            XU   = mid-point of uppermost interval for gvar
            XD   = distance between mid-points of adjacent
                   intervals (must divide XU - XL)

Subsequently, cross-tabs involving gvar will form groupings based on
which of the intervals [XL-XD/2,XL+XD/2), [XL+XD/2,XL+3*XD/2), ...,
or [XU-XD/2,XU+XD/2] contains its value.

Examples:

            STXRGN HLTH AGE 5 95 10
            STXRGN HLTH INCOME 5000 25000 10000
            STXRGN HLTH SEX 0 1 1

generates DYNCOR block <RGN HLTH>, which contains grouping rules for
AGE, INCOME, SEX. Subsequently, STXTAB will group them into the

following intervals:

```
AGE     - [0,10),[10,20),...,[90-100],
INCOME  - [0,10000),[10000,20000),[20000,30000],
SEX     - [-.5,.5),[.5,1.5].
```

3.6.2 STXTAB - Cross-tab Computations

STXTAB generates a cross-tabs matrix. It assumes that intervals for the grouping variables have been specified in calls to STXRGN (above) and that this information is stored in block <RGN mtrx> (in which it searches first) or <RGN DFLT>. Additionally, it receives a list of sum variables, each of which is to be totalled separately. A cross-tabs matrix is computed which has one "observation" per group: the value of each grouping variable at the grouping interval's centroid, and the running totals over that group for each sum variable. If the specified cross-tabs matrix xmtx is found to exist and to be formatted consistent with the current request (say, from a previous call to STXTAB), it is simply added onto. Thus, STXTAB does not require the entire data matrix to be in core at once, and the user may process large data sets in segments.

Calling Sequences:

    (FTN) CALL STXTAB(mtrx,xmtx,NG,NS,'var1..)')

    (ISX) STXTAB mtrx xmtx NG NS var1 var2 ..

```
        mtrx   = data matrix name
        xmtx   = cross-tabs matrix name
        NG     = number of grouping variables
        NS     = number of sum variables
        var1.. = array of variable names
```

The cross-tabs matrix will have NG + NS variables. Group variables are assumed to appear first in the list of names, and their values will be sorted according to the order named (i.e., var1 primary, var2 secondary, etc.).

As in regression, the existence of a variable named WGTS in the original matrix automatically causes weighted sums to be computed (i.e., the weight for each observation multiplies the value summed). Also, any sum variable not found in the original matrix is assumed to index a row of ones; thus, for unweighted sums, it would contain simply a count of points in each group, whereas for weighted sums, it would contain the sum of weights. Finally, a blank sum variable would cause space in xmtx to be reserved for future computations by STPAK routines.

Grouped sums are but one example of aggregation functions; see STFNC (p. 97) for others. STXTAB alone, however, allows weighted computations and has the special conventions for identifying rows containing ones.

Examples:

    STXTAB HLTH HTAB 2 2 AGE INCOME WHITE TOTL

generates   a   cross-tab   matrix   HTAB.   According   to   information
previously supplied to STXRGN (p. 113), HTAB would be 4 by 30,
structured as follows:

    AGE   = (5,5,5,15,15,15,...,95,95,95)
    INCOME = (5000,15000,25000,5000,15000,...,25000)
    WHITE = (total whites, given AGE and INCOME)
    TOTL   = (total people, given AGE and INCOME)

The statements

    STXTAB HLTH XTAB 2 2 SEX AGE EXP TOTL
    STFN2 XTAB EXP DIV EXP TOTL

generate cross-tabs matrix XTAB, then divide total expenditures by
total people to obtain average expenditures.   XTAB is 4 by 20,
structured as follows:

    SEX = (0,0,0,...,0,1,1,1,...,1)
    AGE = (5,15,25,...,95,5,15,...,95)
    EXP = (average expenditures, given AGE and SEX)
    TOTL = (total people, given AGE and SEX)   .

If necessary, STCPY (p. 101) may be called to compress observations
with TOTL = 0 from the matrix, thereby avoiding the division by zero
problem that would occur if a particular group were empty.   In ISX,
the /ERRSET statement (p. 70) provides another alternative.

3.7 Miscellaneous Subroutines

3.7.1 STFITD - Distribution Fitting

STFITD fits a gamma or normal distribution to a sequence of
observations by the method of moments. Parameters of the fitted
distribution are printed; fitted quantiles are then stored as a
variable in the data matrix.

Calling Sequences:

    (FTN) CALL STFITD(mtrx,fvar,dist)

    (ISX) STFITD mtrx fvar dist

        mtrx = data matrix name
        fvar = variable to be fitted
        dist = distribution - GAMMA or NORMAL

To compute the quantiles, STFITD uses secondary storage to sort fvar into ascending sequence. Quantile values are stored in variables GAMMA or NORMAL, according to the distribution involved.

Example:

>   STFITD HLTH RSID NORMAL
>   STPLT HLTH NORMAL 1 RSID

fits a normal distribution to the residuals and produces a residuals versus normal quantiles scatter-plot (i.e., a standard "probability plot").

3.7.2 STGET, STPUT - Editing

STGET retrieves values of a variable; STPUT enters data into a variable, replacing existing values.

Calling Sequences:

>   (FTN) CALL STGET(mtrx,kvar,K1,K2,X)
>   (FTN) CALL STPUT(mtrx,kvar,K1,K2,X)
>
>   (ISX) STGET mtrx kvar K1 K2
>   (ISX) STPUT mtrx kvar K1 K2 [X]
>
>   mtrx = data matrix name
>   kvar = variable name
>   K1   = beginning observation number
>   K2   = ending observation number
>   X   = array receiving (STGET) or containing (STPUT)
>   data

The one-line message generated by STGET includes up to 10 of the values retrieved. A request to retrieve beyond the bounds of the matrix results in successful retrieval up to the last observation but an error message.

STPUT may be used to expand the number of observations: in that case, observation K1 must be contiguous with other observations in the matrix (i.e., K1 ≤ NOBS+1), and the values of other variables beyond NOBS will be initialized to zero.

ISX Note:

STGET places retrieved values (up to 50) in the ISX "X" array. STPUT loads from this array unless an argument list is supplied; in the latter case, loading is done with real conversion unless the variable named is OBL (observation labels, p. 89).

Example:

>   STGET HLTH EXP 1 41
>   /DEFX $EXP 41 R

        STPUT HLTH EXP 3 6 73 67 17 93
        STPUT HLTH OBL 10 12 JESSICA STEFANI JENNIFER

retrieves in X(1), X(2), ..., X(41) and in ISX variable $EXP the
first 41 values of expenditures, replaces expenditures in
observations 3-6 with the values 73, 67, 17, and 93, and replaces
existing labels in observations 8-10.

3.7.3 STLOGT - Logit Maximum Likelihood

STLOGT maximizes the logit likelihood function and reports the
maximum likelihood estimates. The estimation problem arises in
binomial trials where the probability of success is assumed to vary
systematically with certain independent variables; e.g.,

$$p(i) = \text{Pr[success on observation i]}$$

$$= 1/(1+\exp{-}(b'x(i)))$$

where b is a vector of "logit regression coefficients". The log
likelihood function is

$$\sum_{i=1}^{\text{NOBS}} y(i)*\log(p(i)) + (n(i){-}y(i))*\log(1{-}p(i)) \quad .$$

where n(i) denotes the number of attempts and y(i) the number of
successes for observation i. This function is maximized by
Newton-Raphson iteration.

Calling Sequences:

    (FTN) CALL STLOGT(mtrx,pvar,NINDV,'ind1..')

    (ISX) STLOGT mtrx pvar NINDV ind1 ind2 ..

        mtrx   = data matrix name
        pvar   = proportions of success variable (=y(i)/n(i))
        NINDV = number of independent variables
        ind1.. = array of independent variables

Several variable names have special meaning to STLOGT. WGTS is
assumed to index the number of attempts (i.e., the n(i)'s); if
nonexistent, the n(i)'s are assumed to be 1. Variable PRDN will be
generated and filled with predictions of pvar: estimates of p(i)
obtaining by plugging in the maximum likelihood coefficients. If
present, variable RSID will be filled with standardized residuals:

$$(pvar(i){-}PRDN(i))/(PRDN(i)*(1{-}PRDN(i))/n(i))**.5$$

Example:

```
STFN1 HLTH EXP>20 GT EXP 20
STLOGT HLTH EXP>20 2 SEX AGE
```

estimates the probability that a person's expenditures exceed 20 dollars, given sex and age.

Additional Details:

STLOGT runs iterative weighted regressions to obtain the maximum likelihood estimates, storing intermediate results under "standard" REGPAK format (see p. 312) in DYNCOR block <LGT mtrx>. STLOGT calls to REGPAK subroutines have printing turned off, although previously issued OPTION calls (p. 285) for ordinary linear regression will still be in effect and should be cancelled.

Linear combinations or standard errors of linear combinations of the coefficients may be obtained through STREGP (p. 111). One first renames <LGT mtrx> to <REG mtrx> through DYNNAM (p. 262), then calls STREGP, utilizing the fact that logit and regression computations leave identically formatted blocks.

STLOGT provides two options for supplying starting values. If a <LGT mtrx> block is found to exist from a previous STLOGT call with identical variables, the coefficients in that block are used. This enables one to resume a set of computations that stopped short of convergence, or to iterate to convergence on a subset of the data before approaching the entire data set. Otherwise, STLOGT checks for whether a regression request (STREG, p. 108) with those variables has most recently been issued, in which case it converts the regression coefficients to logit "discriminant function estimates" using the method described in Efron [4]. Convergence from the discriminant function estimates usually comes in one or two iterations; also, because starting values for several different logit specifications can be obtained with only one regression accumulation, additional savings are possible.

OPTION may also be called with codes NOITER to control the number of iterations and CONV to control the convergence threshold for changes in the log likelihood function. Default settings are 10 and .01; to reset them, say, to 5 and .0001,

```
OPTION STLOGT NOITER 5
OPTION STLOGT CONV .0001
```

Examples:

```
STDIM COMB 2 SEX AGE
STREAD COMB * (*) 6
   1 10   1 20   1 30    0 10   0 20  0 30
STENL COMB 2 PRDN PRDNSTD
DYNNAM LGT HLTH REG HLTH
STREGP COMB HLTH CON
STFN2 COMB UCL ADD PRDN PRDNSTD
STFN2 COMB LCL SUB PRDN PRDNSTD
STFN1 COMB UCL LGS UCL
```

```
STFN1 COMB LCL LGS LCL
STPRT COMB 0 0
```

Continuing the above example, matrix PRD is input, DYNNAM renames the block containing the logit regression results, and STREGP computes linear combinations and standard errors of linear combinations of the coefficients. Upper (UCL) and lower (LCL) one standard error confidence limits are obtained, after which logistic transformations of them become the confidence intervals for the p(i)'s themselves. These results are printed.

```
STREG HLTH EXP>20 2 SEX AGE
STLOGT HLTH EXP>20 2 SEX AGE
STREG HLTH EXP>20 3 SEX AGE INCOME
STLOGT HLTH EXP>20 3 SEX AGE INCOME
```

provides discriminant function starting values for two logit models; only one regression accumulation is required for both.

3.7.4 STSAMP - Random Sampling

STSAMP causes a random sample of observations to be generated. Observations are read in through subroutine STUINP (p. 122) or taken from a data matrix already in core. "Sampling" does not necessarily imply a data reduction; i.e., the number of observations retained can equal the number encountered. This provides a convenient method for inputting data directly from a FORTRAN subroutine.

<u>Calling Sequences:</u>

    (FTN) CALL STSAMP(mtrx,NREC,NOBS,&EOF)

    (ISX) STSAMP mtrx NREC NOBS

        mtrx = data matrix name
        NREC = number of observations to be processed
        NOBS = number of observations to be sampled
        &EOF = end-of-file return

If NREC is zero, STSAMP assumes that source observations are contained in matrix <DATA mtrx>, and it generates a matrix <DATA /mtr> (i.e., "/" followed by the first three characters of "mtrx") consisting of a random sample of NOBS observations. The full collection of observations from which the sample is to be drawn does not have to be supplied in a single call: for each in-core matrix being sampled, STSAMP keeps track of the number of observations encountered and uses a selection algorithm which produces a random sample regardless of the total. If NREC is greater than zero, observations are read via STUINP (p. 122). In that case, if an end-of-file is reached before NOBS records have been encountered, the matrix will be shortened appropriately. Otherwise, the matrix will contain NOBS observations which are a random sample of the records encountered.

STATLIB uniform random number generator RUNIF (p. 291) is used for each observation to decide whether it should be kept and, if so, which observation it is to replace. A starting value may be supplied to RUNIF, enabling results to be replicated between computer jobs.

Example:

        STSAMP HLTH 10000 200

generates a random sample of 200 observations from a file of size 10000.

        STSAMP HLTH 0 150

generates a random sample of 150 observations from matrix HLTH; the output matrix is named /HLT.

ISX Note:

As with STREAD (p. 91), the ISX variable $EOF is set equal to the character string EOF upon reaching an end-of-file and may be used to control branching within a user-written procedure (c.f., Sec. 3.1.2 example, p. 93).

3.7.5 STSORT - Sorting

STSORT sorts a matrix according to the variables named.

Calling Sequences:

    (FTN) CALL STSORT(mtrx,NVAR,'var1..',code)

    (ISX) STSORT mtrx NVAR var1 var2 .. code

            mtrx   = data matrix name
            NVAR   = number of variables determining sort
            var1.. = array of variable names
            code   = direction of sort: A for ascending, D for
                     descending

The list of variables determines the sort sequence: var1 is primary, var2 secondary, etc.

Example:

        STSORT HLTH 2 WHITE RSID A

sorts the HLTH matrix so that nonwhites appear first, whites second. Within each of these groups, the residuals are arranged in ascending order.

3.7.6 STUSER - User Subroutines

STUSER provides a simple method for placing a data matrix directly under FORTRAN control. A user-written subroutine is passed to STUSER, which in turn calls the subroutine and passes to it the data matrix, its dimensions, and the list of variable names.

Calling Sequences:

    (FTN) CALL STUSER(mtrx,NOBS,SUB)

    (ISX) STUSER mtrx NOBS

        mtrx = data matrix name
        NOBS = number of observations
        SUB = user-supplied subroutine, declared EXTERNAL

If NOBS is zero, the existing matrix <DATA mtrx> is passed into SUB; otherwise, a new matrix (assumed previously dimensioned: STDIM, p. 91) is created and then passed into SUB. Subroutine SUB is permitted to reduce the value of NOBS, in which case the matrix itself will be shortened by STUSER. If added to the calling sequence, up to two additional arguments will be passed on to the subroutine. The subroutine will be called by STUSER as follows:

        CALL SUB(NVAR,NOBS,X,VAR,A1,A2)

where X is the data matrix (dimensioned NVAR by NOBS), and VAR is the vector of variable names (dimensioned NVAR).

Example:

        EXTERNAL XYZ
        CALL STUSER(HLTH,0,XYZ)

results in a call to subroutine XYZ by STUSER with the arguments shown above.

ISX Note:

In ISX, no subroutine name should appear in the call statement; dummy subroutine FTNSUB is called automatically. FTNSUB may be replaced by a user-written FORTRAN subroutine; procedures for combining FORTRAN object modules with the ISX program are described in Part IV of this manual. The subroutine should have the same calling sequence as the subroutine XYZ above. A1 and A2 are passed along as character strings, each occupying one real word; if, for internal purposes, it is necessary to obtain reals or integers, STATLIB routines DVALUE or IVALUE (p. 376) may be useful.

Example:

        STUSER HLTH 0
        STUSER MTRX 87

passes the existing matrix HLTH into subroutine FTNSUB, then creates a new matrix MTRX (previously dimensioned) consisting of 87 observations and passes it into FTNSUB.

3.8 User Input Control

As mentioned, certain STPAK routines may be made to operate on data which are available one observation at a time. To perform the input, subroutine STUINP may be supplied by the user. Alternatively, a FORTRAN unit and format may be supplied to STUINS for use by a default version of STUINP, described below.

3.8.1 STUINP - User Input

STUINP is called by STREGA (regression accumulations, p. 110) or STSAMP (matrix input, p. 119) when observations are to be processed one at a time. So that the processing routine knows what to do with the data, a dimension control block must exist prior to having STUINP supply data for for a given matrix.

Calling Sequences:

    (FTN) CALL STUINP(X,&EOF)

        X   = array in which data are to be stored
        &EOF = end-of-file return

Unless the end-of-file is taken (via a RETURN 1 statement), the calling subroutine expects that X(1), X(2), ..., X(NVAR) will have been filled with appropriate values; these must occupy real words and must correspond in position and number with variables in the dimension control block. If an end-of-file is reached, the calling subprogram considers data retrieval to be complete and continues with its normal processing.

In many applications, STUINP will be tailor-written for a particular matrix, so there would be no need to pass along input parameters. They may be obtained, however, from COMMON block ST002: the declaration

        COMMON /ST002/ NAME,NVAR,NVARR,NREC,NCT,KDUMY(83)

provides the data matrix name, the number of variables in the matrix, the number of the last nonblank variable, the number of records to be read, and the current record count.

Example:

        SUBROUTINE STUINP(X,*)
        IMPLICIT REAL*8 (A-H,P-Z)
        DIMENSION X(8)

```
      READ(10,1,END=90) (X(I),I=1,6)
      X(7)=DLOG(X(6))
      X(8)=DLOG(X(5))
      RETURN
   90 RETURN 1
   91 FORMAT(20F4.0)
      END
```

provides input logic for a data matrix such as described in Section 1 (p. 87).

3.8.2 STUINS - User Input Specifications

A default version of STUINP exists and may be used to obtain data, given FORTRAN unit and format specifications. Subroutine STUINS is called to supply that information.

<u>Calling Sequences</u>:

    (FTN) CALL STUINS(NUNIT,fmt)

    (ISX) STUINS NUNIT fmt

        NUNIT = FORTRAN unit
        fmt   = format statement, enclosed in parentheses

As with STREAD (p. 91), the number of data items read per record is determined as the position of the last nonblank variable name in the *DAT block; the remaining variables are initialized to zero.

<u>Example</u>:

        STUINS 10 (4F3.0,2F8.0,A8)

sets the default STUINP to issue read statements from FORTRAN unit 10 according to format (4F3.0,2F8.0,A8). The program calling STUINP will determine from the *DAT block that 7 variables are to be read, and will pass this information along in COMMON block ST002 (p. 122).

4. SAMPLE PROGRAMS

Examples of this section are drawn from the CHAS-NORC 1970 medical expenditures survey. The data apply to some 11,155 individuals, and consist of selected demographic measurements, a measure of their health status, and their total medical expenditures for the previous year. The objectives of the following programs are to investigate basic relationships between those variables. The complete input streams are shown for running the programs on an IBM VS/370 system; the resulting output appears afterward. See Chapter 15, Section 2 (p. 391) for information on running the ISX program under VS.

4.1 Example 1

Job Input Stream:

```
//jobname JOB (acctg info),parameters
// EXEC ISX
//GO.FT10F001 DD *
  4960  0 25  1  0     17
  4960  1 22  1  0      1
     0  1  1  1  0     37
  2900  1 46  1  0      0
     0  0 12  1  0      0
  2556  0 63  1  0      1

         . . .

        (40 CARDS)

//GO.SYSIN DD *
OPTION * PAGSIZ 65
PPLOTP LINES 20
STDIM HLTH 6 INCOME NONWHITE AGE FEMALE INSURED EXP
STREAD HLTH 10 (F5.0,4F3.0,F5.0) 40
STFN1 HLTH WHITE EQ NONWHITE 0
STFN1 HLTH LEXP ADD EXP 1
STFN1 HLTH LEXP LOG LEXP
STENL HLTH 2 PRDN RSID
STREG HLTH LEXP 4 AGE FEMALE WHITE INSURED
STPLT HLTH PRDN 1 RSID
STFITD HLTH RSID NORMAL
STPLT HLTH NORMAL 1 RSID
STDSP HLTH 3 LEXP PRDN RSID
STPRT HLTH 4 AGE WHITE EXP RSID 0
```

Description:

Optional preliminaries include setting the page width to 65 columns and the plotting depth to 20 lines. STDIM (p. 91) is called to describe the data matrix as having 6 variables: INCOME, NONWHITE, AGE, FEMALE, INSURED, and EXP respectively. STREAD (p. 91) reads the data into core: 40 records from unit 10, yielding a data matrix consisting of 240 words. Three calls to STFN1 (p. 94) result in the computation of variables WHITE (an indicator of whether NONWHITE is zero) and LEXP (the logarithms of expenditures plus 1.0), the latter to be used as a dependent variable in regression. First, however, STENL (p. 102) is called to create variables RSID and PRDN. These have special meaning to the regression routine, STREG (p. 108), which fills them with residuals and predictions when called. The regression is followed by a standard plot of residuals versus predictions via STPLT. Subroutine STFITD (p. 115) then fits normal quantiles to the residuals; the resulting (probability) plot of residuals against those quantiles by STPLT (p. 106) is a useful tool for deciding whether they are approximately normal. Subroutine STDSP (p. 107) generates side-by-side plots of the dependent variable, predictions, and residuals. Finally, a subset of variables is printed by STPRT (p. 105).

Output:

STATLIB ISX 12/01/78   07/09/80   PAGE 1

STDIM: HLTH, 6 VBLS:
         INCOME NONWHITE AGE FEMALE INSURED EXP

STREAD: HLTH (6 BY 40), UNIT=10, 6 VBLS READ

STENL: HLTH, 1 VBLS:
         WHITE

STFN1:   HLTH, WHITE=EQ(NONWHITE,0)

STENL: HLTH, 1 VBLS:
         LEXP

STFN1:   HLTH, LEXP=ADD(EXP,1)

STFN1:   HLTH, LEXP=LOG(LEXP)

STENL: HLTH, 2 VBLS:
         PRDN RSID

REGPAK / REGMSD   07/09/80   PAGE 2

SAMPLE SIZE   40
SUM OF WEIGHTS . . .   4.0000D+01
AVERAGE WEIGHT . . .   1.0000D+00

VARIABLE	MEAN	VARIANCE	STD DEV
1 INCOME	7.6488D+03	2.0747D+07	4.5549D+03
2 NONWHITE	3.2500D-01	2.2500D-01	4.7434D-01
3 AGE	3.0100D+01	6.3671D+02	2.5233D+01
4 FEMALE	6.2500D-01	2.4038D-01	4.9029D-01
5 INSURED	6.0000D-01	2.4615D-01	4.9614D-01
6 EXP	1.8003D+02	1.4255D+05	3.7756D+02
7 WHITE	6.7500D-01	2.2500D-01	4.7434D-01
8 LEXP	3.7582D+00	3.8010D+00	1.9496D+00

REGPAK / REGANL   07/09/80   PAGE 3

SAMPLE SIZE   40
SUM OF WEIGHTS . . . .   4.0000D+01
ESTIMATED STD DEV . . . . .   1.6259D+00
R SQUARED 0.3758

VARIABLE	COEFFICIENT	ESTD STD DEV	T
0	1.8097D+00	6.5304D-01	2.7712
3 AGE	2.8950D-02	1.0837D-02	2.6714
4 FEMALE	4.8294D-01	5.6273D-01	0.8582
7 WHITE	1.8262D+00	5.8922D-01	3.0994
5 INSURED	-7.6235D-01	5.6051D-01	-1.3601
8 LEXP	DEPENDENT VARIABLE		

ANALYSIS OF VARIANCE

SOURCE	DF	SS	MS	F
REGRESSION	4	5.5711D+01	1.3928D+01	5.268
ERROR	35	9.2530D+01	2.6437D+00	
TOTAL	39	1.4824D+02		

STREG: HLTH, DEPV=LEXP, 4 INDVS

STPAK / STPLT   07/09/80   PAGE 4

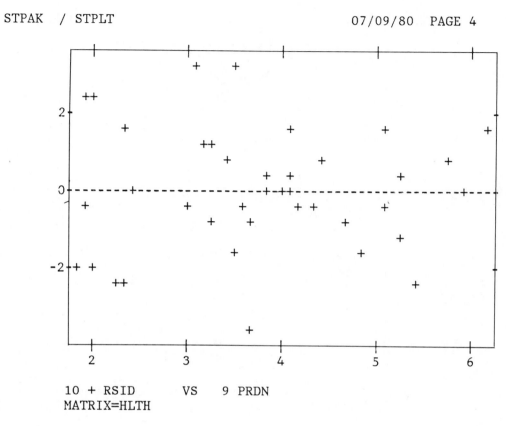

10 + RSID   VS   9 PRDN
MATRIX=HLTH

STENL: HLTH, 1 VBLS:
        NORMAL

STFITD: HLTH, VBL=RSID, NORMAL FIT, MEAN=0, STDEV=1.540312

STPAK / STPLT   07/09/80   PAGE 5

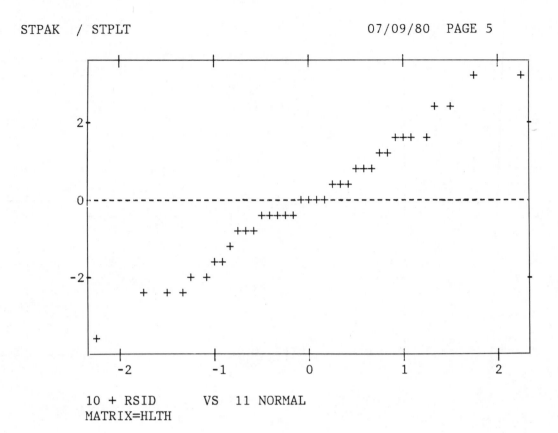

10 + RSID   VS   11 NORMAL
MATRIX=HLTH

STPAK / STDSP   07/09/80   PAGE 6

VBL: 8 LEXP   9 PRDN   10 RSID
MIN: 0.0   1.82   -3.67
MAX: 7.66   6.17   3.24

	LEXP		PRDN		RSID	
1.	0	*	42	****	0	*
2.	36	****	82	*********	15	**
3.	0	*	11	**	19	**
4.	0	*	9	*	20	**
5.	0	*	5	*	23	***
6.	0	*	0	*	26	***
7.	23	***	38	****	28	***
8.	43	****	68	********	32	***
9.	52	*****	77	*********	36	****
10.	51	*****	66	*******	42	****
11.	34	****	33	****	43	****
12.	39	****	42	****	44	****
13.	49	*****	58	*******	45	******
14.	47	*****	53	*****	46	******
15.	60	******	75	********	46	******
16.	42	****	40	****	47	******
17.	21	**	1	*	49	*****
18.	36	****	26	***	50	******
19.	31	***	14	**	52	******
20.	53	*****	52	*****	53	*****
21.	50	*****	45	*****	53	*****
22.	78	*********	94	***********	54	*****
23.	54	******	49	*****	55	*******
24.	56	******	51	*****	56	*******
25.	58	******	52	*****	58	*******
26.	55	*****	45	*****	58	*******
27.	74	********	78	*********	60	*******
28.	83	**********	90	***********	62	*******
29.	54	******	36	****	63	*******
30.	68	********	58	*******	65	*******
31.	55	******	32	***	68	********
32.	55	******	30	***	69	********
33.	72	********	51	*****	74	********
34.	99	**********	99	***********	74	********
35.	86	*********	75	********	75	********
36.	50	*****	12	**	75	********
37.	54	*****	1	*	86	*********
38.	58	******	3	*	89	**********
39.	80	*********	28	***	98	***********
40.	88	*********	38	****	99	**********

MATRIX=HLTH

STPAK / STPRT   07/09/80   PAGE 7

MATRIX=HLTH   OBS   1- 40

AGE	WHITE	EXP	RSID
11.00	1.00	0.0	-3.67
71.00	1.00	16.00	-2.58
18.00	0.0	0.0	-2.33
15.00	0.0	0.0	-2.24
8.00	0.0	0.0	-2.04
10.00	0.0	0.0	-1.82
59.00	0.0	5.00	-1.73
50.00	1.00	28.00	-1.44
64.00	1.00	55.00	-1.18
63.00	1.00	50.00	-0.77
14.00	1.00	13.00	-0.64
11.00	1.00	20.00	-0.63
51.00	1.00	45.00	-0.52
1.00	1.00	38.00	-0.48
34.00	1.00	101.00	-0.48
8.00	1.00	24.00	-0.37
12.00	0.0	4.00	-0.27
50.00	0.0	15.00	-0.21
5.00	0.0	10.00	-0.04
0.0	1.00	60.00	-0.01
16.00	1.00	47.00	0.05
79.00	1.00	406.00	0.09
22.00	1.00	65.00	0.20
41.00	1.00	74.00	0.26
0.0	1.00	90.00	0.39
16.00	1.00	67.00	0.40
65.00	1.00	309.00	0.50
73.00	1.00	589.00	0.63
18.00	1.00	62.00	0.75
9.00	1.00	186.00	0.85
13.00	1.00	71.00	1.03
46.00	0.0	70.00	1.12
25.00	1.00	254.00	1.46
71.00	1.00	2129.00	1.49
60.00	1.00	746.00	1.52
2.00	0.0	48.00	1.54
13.00	0.0	65.00	2.28
15.00	0.0	85.00	2.49
6.00	1.00	495.00	3.16
59.00	0.0	859.00	3.24

4.2 Example 2

<u>Job Input Stream:</u>

```
//jobname JOB (acctg info),parameters
// EXEC ISX
//GO.FT10F001 DD DSN=DATA,DISP=SHR
//GO.FT20F001 DD DSN=REG,DISP=SHR
//GO.SYSIN DD *
OPTION * PAGSIZ 65
PPLOTP LINES 20
OPTION STMSG PRINT OFF
STXRGN HLTH AGE 10 70 15
STXRGN HLTH INCOME 1 3 1
/PROC INPUT
   <DIM> STDIM HLTH 17 INCOME NONWHITE AGE FEMALE INSURED EXP
   STREAD HLTH 10 (6F6.0) 200
   STFN1 HLTH WHITE EQ NONWHITE 0
   STCODE HLTH AGE 10 70 15 AGE10 AGE25 AGE40 AGE55 AGE70
   STRCOD HLTH INCOME INCOME 0 4000 1 0 8000 2 0 1D20 3
   STCODE HLTH INCOME 1 3 1 INC0:4 INC4:8 INC:OTHR
   STFN1 HLTH LEXP ADD EXP 1
   STFN1 HLTH LEXP LOG LEXP
   STREGA HLTH 0
   STFN2 HLTH EXPW MLT EXP WHITE
   STFN1 HLTH EXP+ GT EXP 50
   STXTAB HLTH HTAB 2 5 AGE INCOME EXP EXPW EXP+ WHITE TOTL
   /SKIP <DIM> NE $EOF EOF
/PROCEND
INPUT
OPTION STMSG PRINT *
DYNOUT REG HLTH 20 0
DYNOUT *DAT HLTH 20 0
STREG HLTH LEXP 9 FEMALE WHITE INSURED AGE10 AGE25 AGE40 $
   AGE55 INC0:4 INC:OTHR
STPRT HTAB 0 0
STFN2 HTAB EXP DIV EXP TOTL
STFN2 HTAB EXPW DIV EXPW WHITE
STDSP HTAB 2 EXP EXPW
STCODE HTAB AGE 10 70 15 AGE10 AGE25 AGE40 AGE55 AGE70
STCODE HTAB INCOME 1 3 1 INC0:4 INC4:8 INC:OTHR
STFN2 HTAB EXP+ DIV EXP+ TOTL
STNAM HTAB 1 TOTL WGTS
STENL HTAB 1 RSID
STLOGT HTAB EXP+ 6 AGE10 AGE25 AGE40 AGE55 INC0:4 INC4:8
STPLT HTAB PRDN 1 EXP+
STPRT HTAB 4 WGTS EXP+ PRDN RSID
```

<u>Description:</u>

The data are now on a disk data set named DATA; it is assumed to contain 2100 observations. The data base will be passed to produce regression and cross-tabs output. Before the program reads data, however, OPTION (p. 285) sets the page size to 65 columns, PPLOTP

(p. 287) limits the plotting depth to 20 lines, OPTION suppresses
STPAK summary messages, and STXRGN (p. 113) defines regions for the
cross-tabs grouping variables. Within the INPUT procedure, STDIM
(p. 91) is called to supply dimensioning information: HLTH consists
of 17 variables, the 6 to be read in plus 11 which are blank for now.
Data are read next in blocks of size 200. STFN1 (p. 94) defines a
racial indicator variable named WHITE. STCODE (p. 93) creates dummy
variables AGE10, AGE25, AGE40, AGE55, AGE70, which indicate age
level. STRCOD (p. 99) recodes variable INCOME to take on the values
1, 2, or 3, and the recoded values are themselves coded to dummy
variables INC0:4, INC4:8, INC:OTHR. The logarithms of EXP+1 are
computed by STFN1, and STREGA (p. 110) performs a regression
accumulation on the 15 variables defined thus far. Preparation is
made next for cross-tabs computations. STFN2 (p. 94) computes a
variable EXPW which equals expenditures for whites, zero otherwise,
and STFN1 computes EXP+ as an indicator of whether expenditures
exceeds 50. The call to STXTAB (p. 114) accumulates EXPW, EXP+, EXP,
WHIT, TOTL versus AGE, INCOME in matrix HTAB. Since variable TOTL
does not exist in HLTH, its values are assumed to be 1. The last
statement in INPUT checks to see if the end-of-file has been reached,
and branches back to the top of the procedure otherwise. Following
the actual call to INPUT, calls to DYNOUT (p. 272) result in saving
the regression output on unit 20, after which a call to STREG
(p. 108) regresses LEXP on several dummy variables. Finally, an
analysis of the cross-tabs matrix is performed. STPRT (p. 105)
prints the matrix; STFN2 computes average expenditures for all
persons and for whites alone; and these are displayed by STDSP
(p. 107). To do logit maximum likelihood estimation on the
proportions of expenditures that exceed 50, AGE and INCOME are coded
to dummy variables, EXP+ is redefined to be the observed proportion
of successes, TOTL is renamed to WGTS, the matrix is enlarged to
contain a row for residuals, and STLOGT (p. 117) is called to perform
the computations. The final statements generate a plot of data
versus the predictions supplied by STLOGT and a printout of data,
predictions, and standardized residuals.

If the number of observations in the data base were evenly divisible
by 200, the last execution of STREAD in INPUT would have left a
matrix of length zero, and the subsequent recodes would have produced
error messages. DYNOLD (p. 260) might have been called to sense
this, and /SKIP (p. 78) could then have branched out of the
procedure, as follows:

                DYNOLD DATA HLTH 2
                /SKIP 100 EQ $XXX 0

Inserting these statements immediately after STREAD would prevent the
errors from occurring.

Output:

STATLIB ISX   12/01/78   07/09/80   PAGE 1

REGPAK / REGMSD   07/09/80   PAGE 2


```
        SAMPLE SIZE  . . . . 2100
        SUM OF WEIGHTS . . .   2.1000D+03
        AVERAGE WEIGHT . . .   1.0000D+00
```

	VARIABLE	MEAN	VARIANCE	STD DEV
1	INCOME	2.1448D+00	6.7556D-01	8.2192D-01
2	NONWHITE	3.2619D-01	2.1989D-01	4.6893D-01
3	AGE	3.1196D+01	5.4116D+02	2.3263D+01
4	FEMALE	5.3333D-01	2.4901D-01	4.9901D-01
5	INSURED	6.0762D-01	2.3853D-01	4.8840D-01
6	EXP	2.1365D+02	8.3047D+05	9.1130D+02
7	WHITE	6.7381D-01	2.1989D-01	4.6893D-01
8	AGE10	3.3143D-01	2.2169D-01	4.7084D-01
9	AGE25	1.9238D-01	1.5544D-01	3.9426D-01
10	AGE40	1.5000D-01	1.2756D-01	3.5716D-01
11	AGE55	1.3286D-01	1.1526D-01	3.3950D-01
12	AGE70	1.0619D-01	9.4959D-02	3.0815D-01
13	INC0:4	2.7571D-01	1.9979D-01	4.4698D-01
14	INC4:8	3.0381D-01	2.1161D-01	4.6001D-01
15	INC:OTHR	4.2048D-01	2.4379D-01	4.9375D-01
16	LEXP	3.6719D+00	4.0184D+00	2.0046D+00

REGPAK / REGANL   07/09/80   PAGE 3

SAMPLE SIZE   2100
SUM OF WEIGHTS . . . . 2.1000D+03
ESTIMATED STD DEV . . . . . 1.8737D+00
R SQUARED 0.1301

VARIABLE	COEFFICIENT	ESTD STD DEV	T
0	3.0397D+00	1.5097D-01	20.1349
4 FEMALE	4.3803D-01	8.2261D-02	5.3249
7 WHITE	5.4275D-01	9.2845D-02	5.8457
5 INSURED	4.4367D-01	9.5679D-02	4.6370
8 AGE10	-1.0521D+00	1.2210D-01	-8.6166
9 AGE25	-1.4990D-01	1.3601D-01	-1.1022
10 AGE40	3.8766D-02	1.4663D-01	0.2644
11 AGE55	1.6258D-01	1.4857D-01	1.0942
13 INC0:4	9.4809D-02	1.1367D-01	0.8341
15 INC:OTHR	2.0745D-01	1.0072D-01	2.0596

16 LEXP   DEPENDENT VARIABLE

ANALYSIS OF VARIANCE

SOURCE	DF	SS	MS	F
REGRESSION	9	1.0972D+03	1.2191D+02	34.726
ERROR	2090	7.3375D+03	3.5108D+00	
TOTAL	2099	8.4347D+03		

STREG: HLTH, DEPV=LEXP, 9 INDVS, OLD ACCUM

STPAK / STPRT   07/09/80   PAGE 4

MATRIX=HTAB   OBS   1- 15

AGE	INCOME	EXP	EXPW	EXP+	WHITE	TOTL
10.00	1.00	9310.00	2978.00	34.00	57.00	169.00
10.00	2.00	14103.00	7729.00	53.00	130.00	231.00
10.00	3.00	29522.00	22951.00	108.00	224.00	296.00
25.00	1.00	17586.00	6333.00	42.00	36.00	85.00
25.00	2.00	46946.00	17471.00	72.00	89.00	143.00
25.00	3.00	42963.00	38178.00	102.00	138.00	176.00
40.00	1.00	24353.00	16387.00	26.00	24.00	46.00
40.00	2.00	20916.00	12409.00	41.00	53.00	80.00
40.00	3.00	36621.00	27553.00	123.00	152.00	189.00
55.00	1.00	21032.00	17408.00	41.00	45.00	71.00
55.00	2.00	20213.00	16229.00	43.00	57.00	77.00
55.00	3.00	41967.00	23761.00	89.00	98.00	131.00
70.00	1.00	59947.00	55971.00	78.00	106.00	125.00
70.00	2.00	16181.00	14753.00	46.00	57.00	63.00
70.00	3.00	9506.00	8094.00	23.00	29.00	35.00

STFN2:   HTAB, EXP=DIV(EXP,TOTL)

STFN2:   HTAB, EXPW=DIV(EXPW,WHITE)

STPAK / STDSP   07/09/80   PAGE 5

VBL:	3 EXP	4 EXPW
MIN:	55.09	52.25
MAX:	529.41	682.79

```
    1.    0 *            0 *
    2.    1 *            1 *
    3.    9 *            7 *
    4.   32 ***         19 **
    5.   57 ******      22 ***
    6.   39 ****        35 ****
    7.   99 *********   99 **********
    8.   43 ****        28 ***
    9.   29 ***         20 **
   10.   50 *****       53 *****
   11.   43 ****        36 ****
   12.   55 ******      30 ***
   13.   89 *********   75 ********
   14.   42 ****        32 ***
   15.   45 *****       35 ****
       MATRIX=HTAB
```

STENL: HTAB, 5 VBLS:
         AGE10 AGE25 AGE40 AGE55 AGE70

STCODE: HTAB, VBL=AGE, 5 CELLS: 10 TO 70 BY 15, VBLS:
         AGE10 AGE25 AGE40 AGE55 AGE70

```
STENL:   HTAB, 3 VBLS:
         INC0:4  INC4:8  INC:OTHR

STCODE:  HTAB, VBL=INCOME, 3 CELLS: 1 TO 3 BY 1, VBLS:
         INC0:4  INC4:8  INC:OTHR

STFN2:   HTAB, EXP+=DIV(EXP+,TOTL)

STNAM:   HTAB, OLD/NEW VBLS:
         TOTL WGTS

STENL:   HTAB, 1 VBLS:
         RSID

STENL:   HTAB, 1 VBLS:
         PRDN
```

```
STPAK / STLOGT                                  07/09/80   PAGE 6


   SAMPLE SIZE  . . . . . . . .     15
   OBSERVATIONS . . . . . . . .   1917
   SUCCESSES  . . . . . . . . .    921
   LOG LIKELIHOOD RATIO . . . .   107.4938
```

VARIABLE	COEFFICIENT	ESTD STD DEV	T
0	1.0286D+00	1.5798D-01	6.5113
8 AGE10	-1.6510D+00	1.5800D-01	-10.4491
9 AGE25	-6.3974D-01	1.7134D-01	-3.7338
10 AGE40	-4.3877D-01	1.8216D-01	-2.4087
11 AGE55	-3.0895D-01	1.8333D-01	-1.6852
13 INC0:4	-4.8930D-01	1.1848D-01	-4.1297
14 INC4:8	-4.1627D-01	1.0860D-01	-3.8330

```
   5 EXP+       DEPENDENT VARIABLE
```

```
STLOGT: HTAB, DEPV=EXP+, ITERATION 1, LOGLIK=107.4938
```

STPAK / STLOGT   07/09/80   PAGE 7

          SAMPLE SIZE   15
          OBSERVATIONS 1917
          SUCCESSES 921
          LOG LIKELIHOOD RATIO 108.0554

          VARIABLE   COEFFICIENT   ESTD STD DEV   T

          0   1.1026D+00   1.6783D-01   6.5698
          8 AGE10   -1.7723D+00   1.6976D-01   -10.4403
          9 AGE25   -6.8316D-01   1.7843D-01   -3.8288
         10 AGE40   -4.8140D-01   1.9039D-01   -2.5285
         11 AGE55   -3.3875D-01   1.9171D-01   -1.7670
         13 INC0:4   -5.4650D-01   1.2546D-01   -4.3559
         14 INC4:8   -4.6141D-01   1.1415D-01   -4.0423

          5 EXP+   DEPENDENT VARIABLE

STLOGT: HTAB, DEPV=EXP+, ITERATION 2, LOGLIK=108.0554

STPAK / STLOGT   07/09/80   PAGE 8

          SAMPLE SIZE   15
          OBSERVATIONS 1917
          SUCCESSES 921
          LOG LIKELIHOOD RATIO 108.0556

          VARIABLE   COEFFICIENT   ESTD STD DEV   T

          0   1.1037D+00   1.6906D-01   6.5287
          8 AGE10   -1.7744D+00   1.7144D-01   -10.3502
          9 AGE25   -6.8370D-01   1.7924D-01   -3.8144
         10 AGE40   -4.8203D-01   1.9128D-01   -2.5200
         11 AGE55   -3.3917D-01   1.9257D-01   -1.7613
         13 INC0:4   -5.4758D-01   1.2658D-01   -4.3260
         14 INC4:8   -4.6222D-01   1.1500D-01   -4.0194

          5 EXP+   DEPENDENT VARIABLE

STLOGT: HTAB, DEPV=EXP+, ITERATION 3, LOGLIK=108.0556 (CONVGD)

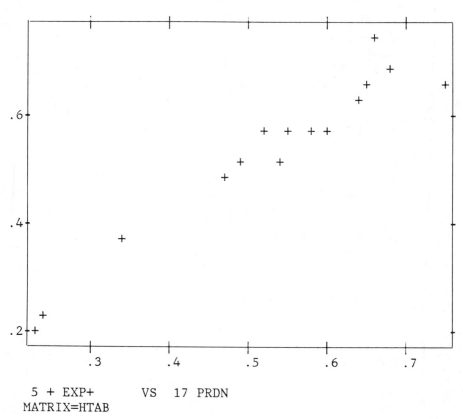

5 + EXP+   VS   17 PRDN
MATRIX=HTAB

MATRIX=HTAB   OBS   1- 15

WGTS	EXP+	PRDN	RSID
169.00	0.20	0.23	-0.84
231.00	0.23	0.24	-0.50
296.00	0.36	0.34	0.96
85.00	0.49	0.47	0.48
143.00	0.50	0.49	0.34
176.00	0.58	0.60	-0.65
46.00	0.57	0.52	0.63
80.00	0.51	0.54	-0.49
189.00	0.65	0.65	0.01
71.00	0.58	0.55	0.40
77.00	0.56	0.58	-0.29
131.00	0.68	0.68	-0.07
125.00	0.62	0.64	-0.27
63.00	0.73	0.66	1.25
35.00	0.66	0.75	-1.28

5. SUBJECT INDEX

Subroutine and Subject   Page

6. GLOSSARY OF SUBROUTINE CALLS (ISX)

CHAPTER 6

TSPAK - TIME SERIES PACKAGE

1. INTRODUCTION

TSPAK is a system of FORTRAN subroutines for time series management, analysis, and modeling. Its subroutines perform such operations as printing, plotting, and autoregression. TSPAK also provides a framework for managing time series easily and efficiently. SPPAK (Ch. 7, p. 185) performs frequency domain operations on time series.

TSPAK routines may be called directly in FORTRAN, or in ISX (Ch. 4), which accepts free-form input without FORTRAN punctuation. The following simple ISX program demonstrates the programming style of TSPAK.

```
DYNINP 8
TSPRT DATA ABCD 1960 1 1969 12
TSDIFF DATA ABCD 1 DATA ABC1
TSACOR DATA ABC1 1960 1 1969 12
TSPLT 1 ACOR ABC1 0 1 99 1
```

DYNINP (p. 270) reads one or more time series into core. One of these, <DATA ABCD>, is printed from January 1960 through December 1969 by TSPRT (p. 150). TSDIFF (p. 158) calculates the first differences of <DATA ABCD> and names them <DATA ABC1>. Finally, the autocorrelation function of these differences is computed by TSACOR (p. 160) and plotted by TSPLT (p. 150).

Time series are managed by DYNCOR, the STATLIB dynamic in-core data management system (Ch. 9, p. 257). They may be read directly by DYNCOR input routines or inserted into DYNCOR blocks by the user; some are also created by TSPAK. Each series is referenced by a first and last name, which is also the name of the DYNCOR block containing it. The first name will generally indicate what type of series it is (e.g., DATA for data, RSID for residuals, SPEC for spectrum) and will be called the "type". The last name further identifies the series and will be called simply "name". The use of DYNCOR blocks frees the user from explicitly providing storage for each series and enables him to identify and manage them easily and efficiently. Output series and arrays from TSPAK routines are also left in DYNCOR blocks, so that the user may access or ignore them as he chooses.

Each time series has associated with it a time control block which specifies three parameters. The first two describe the beginning time point in terms of primary and secondary units; e.g., years and months, years and quarters, days and hours, etc. For convenience they are referred to as years and months, respectively. The third quantity is the number of months per year (i.e., the number of increments in the secondary unit per increment in the primary unit). Thus, if <DATA ABCD> were a monthly series beginning in January 1956, its starting point would be 1956,1 and it would have 12 months per year.

In order to perform an operation on one or more time series, it is generally necessary to specify the operation, the series involved, and the time span to be included. In TSPAK, the subroutine called specifies the operation, the series are identified by their DYNCOR "types" and "names", and the time span is identified by its beginning and ending years and months. Thus, to print the series <DATA ABCD> through 1969, one issues the statement:

> TSPRT DATA ABCD 1956 1 1969 12

Section 2 of this chapter describes TSPAK conventions and procedures in greater detail. Section 3 contains descriptions of the commonly used subroutines. Section 4 describes low-level TSPAK routines which need not concern the casual user. Sample programs are shown in Section 5. Section 6 contains a subject index. Finally, Section 7 is a one-page summary of TSPAK calling sequences.

2. CONVENTIONS AND NOTATION

2.1 Data Storage

TSPAK routines create and maintain time series in core, storing the data themselves as real numbers (REAL*8 on IBM) in DYNCOR blocks and time control information in separate DYNCOR blocks (see Sec. 2.2, below). See Section 2.5 (p. 148) for information on entering data into blocks.

DYNCOR identifiers ("types" and "names") may be any four-character words except blank ("...." in ISX). Several additional considerations apply to types. First, to avoid confusion with time control blocks, types should not begin with the character "." and types differing only in their last (fourth) letter should be avoided. Some TSPAK routines require only names of series and assume specific types (e.g., DATA for regression). For this reason, DATA is recommended as the type for most series employed in model building.

2.2 Time Control Blocks

A specific time point may be identified by its "year" and "month". (Recall that years and months are generic for primary and secondary time units, respectively). If there are no secondary units (e.g., annual data), months/year is 1 and month should always be specified as 1.

To find the element corresponding to a specific time point, TSPAK must know the time point corresponding to the initial element in the series. As mentioned in Section 1, this information, along with the months/year value, is stored in a DYNCOR block keyed to the block containing the series itself. The control block has the same name as the series and a type consisting of "." followed by the first three characters of its type. Thus the time control block for <DATA ABCD> is <.DAT ABCD>. This block must contain three integer values corresponding to initial year, initial month and months/year, respectively; months/year must be positive. For example, <.DAT ABCD> might contain 1956,1,12. If the time control block does not exist, TSPAK assumes the values to be 1,1,1 (i.e., the series exists for t = 1,2,3,...).

Time labels printed by TSPAK will be in one of three forms: (a) "year" if months/year is 1 (e.g., 37), (b) "mmm yyyy" if months/year is 12 (e.g., JAN 1966), or (c) "year:month" otherwise, (e.g., 1957:3).

The time span used by a TSPAK routine generally depends on both the span requested in the call statement and the range over which all involved series exist. TSPAK subroutines intersect these spans, so that a precise specification of time usually is not required. Thus, for example, a print request from 0,1 through 9999,1 could (probably) be used to print an entire monthly series.

2.3 Messages, Errors, and Printing Options

STATLIB-wide message and error conventions are described in the Part II Introduction (p. 58). Refer there (and to the Section 5 examples, p. 173) for information on controlling the printing of messages and decisions on whether and when errors should terminate execution. The following conventions apply specifically to TSPAK.

TSPAK subroutines are divided broadly into two categories, those that compute and those that produce printed or plotted output. The computing routines produce (through TSMSG) a one- or two-line message summarizing what they have done. This helps to make the printed output "self-documenting" in that the flow of the program can be determined from the output alone.

An error condition detected by TSPAK results in a printed error message from TSERR. The name of the subroutine involved is printed along with the type of error, if known. The most common are "<type name> NOT FOUND", meaning that a required DYNCOR block did not exist, and "CORE NOT AVAILABLE FOR <type name>", meaning insufficient core storage was available to create a new block. In the latter case, the message will have been preceded by a DYNCOR error message giving the number of words requested. Incorrect calling sequence specification often results in very large amounts of core being requested.

OPTION (p. 285) may be used to control TSPAK printing, specifying TS* for all routines, TSMSG for messages, TSERR for error messages, or the subroutine name for routines that generate printed output.

2.4 Calling Sequence Notation

Calling sequences follow the STATLIB-wide conventions described in the Part II Introduction (p. 56). The following apply specifically to TSPAK.

   a. Character string arguments are assumed to be of length four, unless otherwise stated.

   b. The integer arguments N1Y, N1M, N2Y, N2M denote the beginning and ending years and months in a TSPAK call. The integer argument MPY denotes months per year.

2.5 DYNCOR Input Subroutines

Since DYNCOR blocks play a central role in TSPAK, DYNCOR routines may be useful to the TSPAK user. In particular, DYNCOR input routines DYNINP, DYNINL, DYNIN1, and DYNINB (p. 270) are often used with TSPAK to read data. Blocks are read into core sequentially from cards, disk, tape, etc. These routines (except DYNINB, see below) require that each block be preceded by a header record containing the following information:

        type name LENGTH t(fmt)

where t is "R" (real) for data and "I" (integer) for time control information, and fmt is a FORTRAN format, enclosed in parentheses, or "(*)", indicating free-form input. The header record is read free-form, and may be continued onto a successive record by coding a "$" as its last word.

To read all blocks from FORTRAN unit NRUNIT into core,

    (FTN) CALL DYNINP(NRUNIT)

    (ISX) DYNINP NRUNIT

are the FORTRAN and ISX calls respectively. A time control block, which may contain identification as well as time control information, will normally accompany the series. For example, an input stream might appear as follows:

```
.DAT ABCD 20 I(I5,2I3,1X17A4)
 1956  1 12 DISTRICT ABCD
DATA ABCD 168 R(12F6.0)
   1357  1426  1397  1410  1399 ...
   1459  1520  1502  1508  1470 ...
   ...
   ...                                      14 lines (cards),
                                            12 numbers/line
```

Data may also be input from a file lacking header cards or time control information:

```
    (FTN) CALL DYNINB(NRUNIT,type,name,LENGTH,t(fmt))
    (FTN) CALL TSTORG(type,name,N1Y,N1M,MPY)

    (ISX) DYNINB NRUNIT type name LENGTH t(fmt)
    (ISX) TSTORG type name N1Y N1M MPY
```

inputs series <type name> from FORTRAN unit NRUNIT and defines its time origin through TSTORG (p. 169). For example,

```
        DYNINB 10 DATA ABCD 168 R(*)
        TSTORG DATA ABCD 1956 1 12
```

could be used to read data from a file appearing as follows:

```
    1357 1426 1397 1410 ...
    ...
```

3. TSPAK SUBROUTINES

3.1 Printing and Plotting

3.1.1 TSPRT - Printing

TSPRT prints a time series and, if months/year is greater than 1, the "annual" sums of the series. A format generating routine is used to produce "clean" formatted output (c.f., p. 33); a common scaling factor, if any, is printed at the top of the page.

<u>Calling Sequences</u>:

    (FTN) CALL TSPRT(type,name,N1Y,N1M,N2Y,N2M)

    (ISX) TSPRT type name N1Y N1M N2Y N2M

<u>Example</u>:

        TSPRT DATA ABCD 1960 1 1969 12

prints <DATA ABCD> from 1960,1 through 1969,12.

3.1.2 TSPLT - Plotting

TSPLT plots one or more series against time (c.f., p. 175); for scatterplots, TSPLTH may be called to define a horizontal axis series. Plots are produced on the printer (or terminal) by PPLOT (p. 358); PPLOTP (p. 287) may be used to control plot parameter settings and options.

<u>Calling Sequences (TSPLT)</u>:

    (FTN) CALL TSPLT(N,'typ1typ2..','nam1nam2..',N1Y,N1M,N2Y,N2M)

    (ISX) TSPLT N typ1 nam1 typ2 nam2 .. N1Y N1M N2Y N2M

        N   = number of series to be plotted
        typ1.. = an array or character string of types
        nam1.. = an array or character string of names

<u>Examples</u>:

        TSPLT 1 DATA ABCD 1960 1 1969 12

plots <DATA ABCD> vs. time.

        TSPLT 2 DATA ABCD DATA WXYZ 1960 1 1969 12

plots <DATA ABCD> and <DATA WXYZ> vs. time (on a single plot).

A vertical axis will always be plotted at time point zero, if zero is within the range of the plot. In addition, several types have special meanings to TSPLT. RSID, ACOR, XCOR, and PACF as the first type listed cause a horizontal axis to be plotted at zero; the latter three also cause the vertical limits for the plot to be set to plus and minus one and vertical bars to be drawn to the zero axis. Frequency domain types (see SPPAK, Ch. 7, p. 186) also have special meaning.

TSPLTH may be used to specify the horizontal axis variable for the next call to TSPLT. If TSPLTH has not been called, time itself is used as the horizontal axis variable.

Calling Sequences (TSPLTH):

        (FTN) CALL TSPLTH(type,name)

        (ISX) TSPLTH type name

Example:

            TSPLTH DATA WXYZ
            TSPLT 1 DATA ABCD 1960 1 1969 12

plots <DATA ABCD> vs. <DATA WXYZ>.

Page size, normally assumed to be 132 print positions, may be changed through OPTION (p. 285) via the PAGSIZ code. Time plots too wide for one page will appear on two or more successive plots, each with the same vertical scale. Alternatively, time plots may be printed "down-the-page" by a "MODE COMIC" request to PPLOTP.

3.2 Time Series Generation

Routines of this section are used to generate special time series.

3.2.1 TSPOLY - Polynomials

TSPOLY generates time series containing powers of t, where t = 0,1,2,... . Powers of degree 1 through ND are computed, the k-th degree series containing $0,1**k,2**k,...$. The type for the new series is specified by the user; names are assigned by TSPOLY as P:01, P:02, ..., P:ND.

The origin for the series, i.e., the time point for which the value is zero, will normally be the first point in the series. TSPOLO may be called to set the origin to a different time point for the next TSPOLY call.

Calling Sequences (TSPOLY):

    (FTN) CALL TSPOLY(ND,N1Y,N1M,N2Y,N2M,MPY,type)

    (ISX) TSPOLY ND N1Y N1M N2Y N2M MPY type

          ND = maximum degree to be computed

Example:

        TSPOLY 2 1960 1 1969 12 12 DATA

creates <DATA P:01> containing 0,1,2,3,...,119 and <DATA P:02>
containing 0,1,4,9,...,119^2.

Calling Sequences (TSPOLO):

    (FTN) CALL TSPOLO(N1Y,N1M)

    (ISX) TSPOLO N1Y N1M

Example:

        TSPOLO 1959 10
        TSPOLY 2 1960 1 1969 12 12 DATA

creates   <DATA P:01> containing 3,4,5,...,122 and <DATA P:02>
containing 9,16,25,...,122^2.

3.2.2 TSHARM - Harmonic Series

TSHARM generates series containing sines and cosines of a desired
period.

Calling Sequences:

    (FTN) CALL TSHARM(PD,N1Y,N1M,N2Y,N2M,MPY,type,namc,nams)

    (ISX) TSHARM PD N1Y N1M N2Y N2M MPY type namc nams

          PD   = period (in "months")
          namc = name for cosine series
          nams = name for sine series

Example:

        TSHARM 6 1960 1 1969 12 12 DATA COS2 SIN2

generates <DATA COS2> and <DATA SIN2> containing cosines and sines of
period 6.

3.3 Elementary Operations

3.3.1 TSFN0, TSFN1, TSFN2 - Functions (Transformations)

Function routines may be used to perform a wide class of observation-by-observation operations on zero, one, or two time series. TSFN0 creates a new series which may depend on a constant:

$$z(t) = f(C) \quad .$$

TSFN1 creates a new series which is a function of an existing series and, perhaps, a constant:

$$z(t) = f(x(t),C) \quad .$$

TSFN2 creates a new series which is a function of two existing series:

$$z(t) = f(x(t),y(t-LAG)) \quad .$$

A central STATLIB function evaluator is used.

Calling Sequences:

```
(FTN) CALL TSFN0(ntyp,nnam,fun,N1Y,N1M,N2Y,N2M,MPY[,C])
(FTN) CALL TSFN1(ntyp,nnam,fun,typ1,nam1[,C])
(FTN) CALL TSFN2(ntyp,nnam,fun,typ1,nam1,typ2,nam2,LAG)

(ISX) TSFN0 ntyp nnam fun N1Y N1M N2Y N2M MPY [C]
(ISX) TSFN1 ntyp nnam fun typ1 nam1 [C]
(ISX) TSFN2 ntyp nnam fun typ1 nam1 typ2 nam2 LAG

      ntyp,nnam = type and name for z
      fun       = function code
      typ1,nam1 = type and name of x
      typ2,nam2 = type and name of y
      LAG       = time lag for y
      C         = real constant
```

The following table gives the resulting values of z(t) for available function codes (fun):

fun	TSFN0	TSFN1	TSFN2
ABS	|C|	|x(t)|	-
ADD	-	x(t)+C	x(t)+y(t-LAG)
ASN	arcsin(C)	arcsin(x(t))	-
DIV	-	x(t)/C	x(t)/y(t-LAG)
EQ	-	ind(x(t)=C)	ind(x(t)=y(t-LAG))
EQL	C	x(t)	-
EXP	exp(C)	exp(x(t))	-
FTN	FTNFUN(C)	FTNFUN(x(t),C)	FTNFUN(x(t),y(t-LAG))
GE	-	ind(x(t)≥C)	ind(x(t)≥y(t-LAG))
GT	-	ind(x(t)>C)	ind(x(t)>y(t-LAG))
INT	-	[x(t)/C]	[x(t)/y(t-LAG)]
INV	1/C	1/x(t)	-
LE	-	ind(x(t)≤C)	ind(x(t)≤y(t-LAG))
LGS	1/(1+exp(-C))	1/(1+exp(-x(t)))	-
LGT	log(C/(1-C))	log(x(t)/(1-x(t)))	-
LOG	log(C)	log(x(t))	-
LT	-	ind(x(t)<C)	ind(x(t)<y(t-LAG))
MAX	-	max(x(t),C)	max(x(t),y(t-LAG))
MIN	-	min(x(t),C)	min(x(t),y(t-LAG))
MLT	-	x(t)*C	x(t)*y(t-LAG)
MOD	-	mod(x(t),C)	mod(x(t),y(t-LAG))
NE	-	ind(x(t)≠C)	ind(x(t)≠y(t-LAG))
NPR	PNORM(C)	PNORM(x(t))	-
PWR	-	x(t)**C	x(t)**y(t-LAG)
RNO	RNORM(0)	RNORM(0)	-
ROU	round(C)	round(x(t))	-
RUN	RUNIF(0)	RUNIF(0)	-
SEQ	t	t	-
SIN	sin(C)	sin(x(t))	-
SQR	C**.5	x(t)**.5	-
SUB	-	x(t)-C	x(t)-y(t-LAG)
TPR	-	PTDIST(x(t),C)	PTDIST(x(t),y(t-LAG))
ZER	-	zero(x(t),C)	-

Logarithms are computed to the base e. The indicator function (ind) returns 1 if its argument is true, 0 if false. FTNFUN is a dummy function, meant to be replaced by a user-supplied function in ISX (see below). RNORM (p. 373) and RUNIF (p. 374) are random number generators for the normal and uniform distributions. PTDIST is a cumulative t-distribution function routine (p. 370). The zero function zeroes out the C low-order bytes of a real word. A user-supplied FUNCTION subprogram may be passed in place of fun (see the FORTRAN note, below).

Subroutine ERRSET (p. 283), callable from ISX or FORTRAN, may be used to recover from such errors as division by zero, taking logarithms or square roots of negative numbers, etc. In ISX, the /ERRSET statement (p. 70) accomplishes this while providing a simpler calling sequence.

Examples:

        TSFN1 DATA LABC LOG DATA ABCD

creates a new series <DATA LABC> containing logarithms of <DATA ABCD>.

> TSFN1 DATA AB50 SUB DATA ABCD 50

subtracts 50 from each element of <DATA ABCD>.

> TSFN2 DATA ABYZ SUB DATA ABCD DATA WXYZ 0

creates a new series <DATA ABYZ> containing <DATA ABCD> minus <DATA WXYZ>.

> TSFN0 DATA NOIS RNO 1960 1 1969 12 12

creates a new series <DATA NOIS> containing normal random numbers.

The operation may be done "in place" using TSFN1. With TSFN2, however, the time span of the new series is dependent on the time spans of both input series, which may not coincide. Thus caution must be exercised in using the same type and name for new and old series.

FORTRAN Note:

A user-supplied FUNCTION subprogram may be used. It must return real values, be declared EXTERNAL in the calling program, and be passed in place of the function name; if added to the calling sequence, up to three additional arguments (A1,A2,A3) will be passed along to the function. The function will be called by TSFN0, TSFN1 or TSFN2 for each observation as follows:

$$z(t) = F(A1,A2,A3) \qquad \text{(by TSFN0)}$$
$$z(t) = F(x(t),A1,A2,A3) \qquad \text{(by TSFN1)}$$
$$z(t) = F(x(t),y(t\text{-}LAG),A1,A2) \qquad \text{(by TSFN2)}$$

Example:

```
EXTERNAL FN
CALL TSFN1('DATA','FABC',FN,'DATA','ABCD',36.D0)
```

ISX Note:

Dummy function FTNFUN is called if the function code is "FTN". It may be replaced by a user-written FORTRAN function; procedures for combining FORTRAN object modules with the ISX program are described in Part IV of this manual. The function FTNFUN should have the same calling sequence as the function F above, and should expect A1 to have been converted to real if called through TSFN0 or TSFN1. A2 and A3 are passed along as character strings; if, for internal purposes, it is necessary to obtain reals or integers, STATLIB routines DVALUE and IVALUE (p. 376) may be useful.

3.3.2 TSFNTS, TSFNM - Functions of Series and Moving Functions

TSFNTS evaluates a function over part or all of a time series. Its one-line message contains the function value.

TSFNM creates a new series, each element of which is a function of N points of an existing series. The function may be evaluated point-by-point or once for each N-point segment. An example of the latter is creating an annual series from a monthly series where the value for each year is the sum of the monthly values, or simply the first month's value.

Calling Sequences:

        (FTN) ...TSFNTS(fun,type,name,N1Y,N1M,N2Y,N2M[,C])...
        (FTN) CALL TSFNM(ntyp,nnam,fun,type,name,N,code[,C])

        (ISX) TSFNTS fun type name N1Y N1M N2Y N2M [C]
        (ISX) TSFNM ntyp nnam fun type name N code [C]

                ntyp,nnam = type and name for new series
                fun   = function code
                type,name = type and name of existing series
                N   = length of segment
                code   = "R","C","L", or "S" (see below)
                C   = constant

The following function codes (fun) may be used:

Function	Result
AVG	Average
EXT	Extract Cth element (C integer)
MAX	Maximum
MED	Median
MIN	Minimum
ORD	Cth order statistic (C real)
SSQ	Sum of squares
STD	Standard deviation
SUM	Sum
VAR	Variance

C is required only for functions EXT and ORD. With EXT, C specifies the integer location to be extracted; with ORD, C specifies a fractional order statistic between 0 and 1. A user-supplied function may be passed in place of fun (see the FORTRAN note, below).

If code is L(left), C(centered) or R(right), the new series y(t) will be a function of the old series x(t) as follows:

        R: y(t) = fun[x(t-N+1), ..., x(t)]
        C: y(t) = fun[x(t-[(N-1)/2]), ..., x(t+[N/2])]
        L: y(t) = fun[x(t), ..., x(t+N-1)]

If code is S(segments), the function will be evaluated once per segment and the new series will have a different time scale than the original one. The precise action taken depends on the relationship between N and the "months/year" value of the existing series. If N is a divisor of months/year, the new series will have a months/year value equal to that ratio, and the first point in the resultant series will correspond to the first complete segment in the old series. If N does not divide months/year, the new series will have a time origin of 1,1 with 1 month/year, and the segments will consist of the first N points, the second N points, etc., in the old series.

Examples:

        TSFNTS MED DATA ABCD 0 1 9999 1

computes the median value of series <DATA ABCD>.

        TSFNM DATA MABC AVG DATA ABCD 12 R

computes 12-month "right" moving averages of <DATA ABCD>.

        TSFNM DATA QABC SUM DATA ABCD 3 S

converts monthly series <DATA ABCD> to quarterly series <DATA QABC> by summing over months within quarters.

        TSFNM DATA YABC EXT DATA ABCD 12 S 1

converts <DATA ABCD> to an annual series <DATA YABC> by extracting the 1st month within each year.

        TSFNM DATA 2YMX MAX DATA ABCD 24 S

creates <DATA 2YMX> containing the maxima of successive 24-month segments of <DATA ABCD>. Since 24 does not divide 12, <DATA 2YMX> begins at 1,1 with months/year=1. Also, the first value will be the maximum of the first 24 points in <DATA ABCD>, regardless of its starting month.

FORTRAN Note:

A user-supplied function may be declared EXTERNAL and passed as argument fun. It should have calling sequence

        ... FN(KDIM,N,X,A1,A2) ...

where X is dimensioned (KDIM,N), and A1,A2 are optional arguments which may be passed to TSFNTS or TSFNM; FN should base its computation on X(1,1),...,X(1,N). (Note: FN will always be called with KDIM=1.)

        EXTERNAL USERFN
        CALL TSFNM('DATA','FNAB',USERFN,'DATA','ABCD',6,'S',35)

applies the user-supplied function USERFN to semi-annual segments of

<DATA ABCD>.

ISX Note:

The function value returned by TSFNTS is stored both as the first
real word of the ISX "X" array and as ISX variable $XXX (see Ch. 4,
Secs. 2.2-3, p. 60). This variable might itself be used in a later
statement, such as one using /DEFINE (p. 66) to save the value under
a different name.

3.3.3 TSDIFF, TSUNDF - Differencing

TSDIFF computes KDIF-point differences of a time series:

$$y(t) = x(t) - x(t-KDIF).$$

TSUNDF performs the inverse operation to differencing, referred to
here as "undifferencing".

Calling Sequences (TSDIFF):

    (FTN) CALL TSDIFF(type,name,KDIF,ntyp,nnam)

    (ISX) TSDIFF type name KDIF ntyp nnam

        type,name = type and name of x
        ntyp,nnam = type and name for y

Example:

      TSDIFF DATA ABCD 1 DATA ABC1

computes <DATA ABC1> as first differences of <DATA ABCD>.

Undifferencing typically will be done after regression and prediction
have been performed on a differenced series

$$y(t) = x(t) - x(t-KDIF)$$

to obtain predictions for x:

$$\hat{x}(t) = x(t-KDIF) + \hat{y}(t),$$

where t-KDIF ranges over the period of the regression. However, if
multi-step predictions for more than KDIF units past the regression
period have been computed,

$$\hat{x}(t) = \hat{x}(t-KDIF) + \hat{y}(t).$$

TSUNDF uses predictions for x rather than x itself after the
regression period (as does the prediction routine TSPRDN, p. 164) in
order to allow multi-step predictions. TSTIME (p. 168) may be used

to override this feature.

Calling Sequences (TSUNDF):

    (FTN) CALL TSUNDF(type,name,btyp,bnam,KDIF,ntyp,nnam)

    (ISX) TSUNDF type name btyp bnam KDIF ntyp nnam

        type,name = type and name of $\hat{y}$
        btyp,bnam = type and name of x
        ntyp,nnam = type and name for $\hat{x}$

Example:

    TSUNDF PRDN ABC1 DATA ABCD 1 PRDN ABCD

computes <PRDN ABCD> by adding <PRDN ABC1> to <DATA ABCD> lagged one in the "past" and to <PRDN ABCD> lagged one in the "future".

3.3.4 TSCSUM - Cumulative Sums

TSCSUM computes the cumulative sums of a time series,

$$y(t) = x(t1) + x(t1+1) + \ldots + x(t)$$

Calling Sequences:

    (FTN) CALL TSCSUM(type,name,ntyp,nnam,N1Y,N1M,N2Y,N2M)

    (ISX) TSCSUM type name ntyp nnam N1Y N1M N2Y N2M

        type,name = type and name of x
        ntyp,nnam = type and name for y

Example:

    TSCSUM DATA ABCD DATA CSAB 1960 1 1969 12

computes cumulative sums of DATA ABCD over the years 1960 to 1969.

3.4 Correlation

The auto- and cross-correlation routines in TSPAK compute correlations directly. For very long series, faster routines are available in SPPAK, the STATLIB spectrum analysis package (Ch. 7, p. 185).

3.4.1 TSACOR - Autocorrelation

TSACOR computes the autocorrelation function, or correlogram, of a series,

$$r(k) = cor(y(t),y(t-k)).$$

Calling Sequences:

(FTN) CALL TSACOR(type,name,N1Y,N1M,N2Y,N2M)

(ISX) TSACOR type name N1Y N1M N2Y N2M

The autocorrelation function will be called <ACOR name>, and will be defined for $0,1,2,...,[N/3]$, where N is the series length. The number of observations per "year" for an ACOR series is one, and in calling TSPAK routines, time points are referenced as (lag,1) rather than (year,month). Thus, the first and last series points are (0,1) and ([N/3],1).

Example:

```
TSACOR DATA ABCD 1960 1 1969 12
TSPLT 1 ACOR ABCD 0 1 99 1
```

computes and plots the autocorrelation function of <DATA ABCD>.

3.4.2 TSPACF - Partial Autocorrelation

TSPACF computes the partial autocorrelation function of a time series.

Calling Sequences:

(FTN) CALL TSPACF(type,name,N1Y,N1M,N2Y,N2M)

(ISX) TSPACF type name N1Y N1M N2Y N2M

The partial autocorrelation function will be called <PACF name>, and will be defined for $0,1,2,...,[N/3]$; the number of observations per "year" is one.

Example:

```
TSPACF DATA ABCD 1960 1 1969 12
TSPLT 1 PACF ABCD 0 1 99 1
```

computes and plots the partial autocorrelation function of <DATA ABCD>.

3.4.3 TSXCOR - Cross-correlation

TSXCOR computes the cross-correlation function between two series,

$$r(k) = cor(y(t),x(t-k)),$$

i.e., for x leading y by k points.

Calling Sequences:

    (FTN) CALL TSXCOR(typ1,nam1,typ2,nam2,nnam,N1Y,N1M,N2Y,N2M)

    (ISX) TSXCOR typ1 nam1 typ2 nam2 nnam N1Y N1M N2Y N2M

        typ1,nam1 = type and name of x
        typ2,nam2 = type and name of y
        nnam   = name to be assigned to cross-correlation
                    function (type=XCOR).

The cross-correlation function <XCOR nnam> will be defined for time points -[N/3] through [N/3]; the number of observations per "year" is one.

Example:

        TSXCOR DATA ABCD DATA WXYZ ABYZ 1960 1 1969 12
        TSPLT 1 XCOR ABYZ -37 1 37 1

computes and plots the cross-correlation function of <DATA ABCD> and <DATA WXYZ>.

3.5 Regression

TSPAK uses REGPAK (Ch. 11, p. 297) to perform regression analysis. The routines in this section define the model (TSMODL, below), perform the regression (TSREG, p. 163), and print an analysis of the regression (TSREGA, p. 164). Intermediate results are stored in a DYNCOR block for use by other routines or by the user.

3.5.1 TSMODL - Model Definition

TSMODL is called to build a model for use during a subsequent regression. The model, which is simply a list of variable names, lags (for autoregression), and codes, is stored in a DYNCOR block with type MODL and name as given. Each call to TSMODL adds one or more entries to the list. TSMODR may be used to replace variable names in a model, or the entire model may be deleted by calling DYNDEL (p. 261).

Calling Sequences (TSMODL):

(FTN) CALL TSMODL(modl,name,NLAGS,LAGS,code)

(ISX) TSMODL modl name NLAGS LAGS code

    modl = model name
    name = variable name (a type of DATA will
            normally be assumed during regression -
            see TSTYPE, p. 169).
    NLAGS = number of lags being defined on this call
    LAGS = array of length NLAGS of integers
            containing non-negative lags (or a
            scalar, if NLAGS=1)
    code = type-of-variable code. Recognized values
            (others will be ignored by TSREG):
            INDV - independent variable
            DEPV - dependent variable
            WGTS - weights for weighted least squares

Example:

        TSMODL MDL6 ABCD 1 0 DEPV
        TSMODL MDL6 ABCD 3 1 2 3 INDV

The model block <MODL modl> may be thought of as a 3 by k matrix of
integer constants containing variable name, lag, and code for each
entry. Thus, the above example gives

                ABCD   0   DEPV
                ABCD   1   INDV
                ABCD   2   INDV
                ABCD   3   INDV

Model blocks may, of course, be read in with DYNINP (p. 270) as an
alternative to creating them with TSMODL, variable names and codes
being read with A format and lags with I format.

TSMODR finds the first appearance of a given code and changes all
occurrences of the associated variable name to the specified new name
(nnam).

Calling Sequences (TSMODR):

    (FTN) CALL TSMODR(modl,code,nnam)

    (ISX) TSMODR modl code nnam

Example:

        TSMODR MDL6 DEPV WXYZ

3.5.2 TSREG - Regression

TSREG performs regression (least squares) using the model and time span specified. Models must first be created through TSMODL (above). The series to be used must all have the same type; this will normally be DATA unless changed through TSTYPE (p. 169).

Calling Sequences:

    (FTN) CALL TSREG(modl,N1Y,N1M,N2Y,N2M)

    (ISX) TSREG modl N1Y N1M N2Y N2M

After computing the regression, TSREG calls TSPRDN (p. 164) to compute predictions (fitted values) and residuals over the same time interval. Coefficients are not printed by TSREG; TSREGA (below) may be called to print an analysis of the regression.

Weighted least squares will be performed if one or more variables with code WGTS are included in the model. Zero weights may be used to ignore data points. The series containing the weights do not have to exist over the entire time span being used; a weight of one is assumed for non-existent values. The weight used for each observation will be the product of those specified.

REGPAK subroutines REGACC (p. 323), REGMSD (p. 323), and REGCOR (p. 324), which accumulate cross-products, compute means and standard deviations, and compute correlation coefficients, respectively, are called by TSREG but normally will not print. Subroutine OPTION (p. 285) may be called to request printing. A constant (intercept) term will be included unless suppressed by:

    REGPAR CON OFF

(p. 290).

All intermediate results are stored under "standard" REGPAK format (see Ch. 11, Sec. 3.10, p. 312) in DYNCOR block <REG modl>. Through REGGET (p. 289), these may be accessed directly by the user. If more than one dependent variable is included in the model, then BU, BZERO, B and S2 are not accessible via REGGET; BZERO, B and S2 are stored, in that order, in DYNCOR block(s) <modl depv>. If TSREG is called with the last four arguments equal to zero, no regression is performed, but the appropriate REG block is activated for use by REGGET.

Example:

    TSREG MDL6 1960 1 1969 12

3.5.3 TSREGA - Analysis of Regression

TSREGA prints an analysis of regression by calling REGPAK subroutine
REGANL (p. 326). The output includes a standard ANOVA table as well
as the regression coefficients, their standard errors, and their t
values. Sample output appears in Section 5.1 (p. 174).

Calling Sequences:

        (FTN) CALL TSREGA(modl,name)

        (ISX) TSREGA modl name

                name = name of dependent variable, or blank
                        indicating all dependent variables.

Example:

        TSREGA MDL6 ABCD

3.6 Prediction, Forecasting, Forecast Variances

Subroutines of this section compute and print forecasts, residuals,
forecast variances and confidence limits based on regression.

3.6.1 TSPRDN - Prediction (Forecasting)

TSPRDN calculates predictions and residuals (if DATA exist) for all
dependent variables in the specified model, based on the last
regression using that model. Types of PRDN for predictions and RSID
for residuals are assigned unless otherwise specified through TSTYPE
(p. 169).

Calling Sequences:

        (FTN) CALL TSPRDN(modl,N1Y,N1M,N2Y,N2M)

        (ISX) TSPRDN modl N1Y N1M N2Y N2M

TSREG sets an internal "calendar" to the last time point used for
regression (it may be reset through TSTIME, p. 168). TSPRDN uses
only DATA for "past" values of independent variables and only PRDNs
for "future" values. An error will result if PRDNs are required and
are not available (in an autoregressive model beginning immediately
after the regression period, PRDNs will always be available since
TSPRDN is generating them). TSPRDN computes residuals
(RSID=DATA-PRDN) for that portion of the time interval for which DATA
exist.

TSREG calls TSPRDN for the regression time interval, so PRDNs and

RSIDs will normally be in existence when the user calls TSPRDN. If he specifies as the beginning time point (N1Y,N1M) the month immediately following the last existing one, the PRDN and RSID series will be extended. Otherwise any existing series will be deleted.

Example:

TSPRDN MDL6 1970 1 1974 12

3.6.2 TSRSDA - Residual Analysis

TSRSDA prints data (DATA), predictions (PRDN), residuals (DATA minus PRDN), percent errors, and running square roots of the average squared residual (c.f., p. 176). Annual and overall summaries are also printed.

Calling Sequences:

(FTN) CALL TSRSDA(name,N1Y,N1M,N2Y,N2M)

(ISX) TSRSDA name N1Y N1M N2Y N2M

Example:

TSRSDA ABCD 1970 1 1972 12

3.6.3 TSRFSD - Regression Forecast Standard Deviations

TSRFSD computes forecast standard deviations (errors), under the assumption that the values of the independent variables are known (zero variance), by calling REGPAK subroutine REGFOV (p. 329). Data for the independent variables must be available and the time interval must be specified properly. The standard deviations are stored as the series RFSD name.

Calling Sequences:

(FTN) CALL TSRFSD(modl,N1Y,N1M,N2Y,N2M)

(ISX) TSRFSD modl N1Y N1M N2Y N2M

The RFSD series may be used with TSCLIM (p. 166) to compute confidence limits for observed values or for forecast errors.

Example:

TSRFSD MDL5 1965 1 1967 12

3.6.4 TSARFS - Autoregressive Forecast Standard Deviations

TSARFS computes standard deviations (errors) of multi-step forecasts and of cumulative sums of multi-step forecasts from a univariate autoregressive model. The types assigned to the resulting series are ARFS and ACFS, respectively, with the name being the same as that of the dependent variable. The standard deviations are computed ignoring variation in the regression coefficients, i.e., assuming that the error of estimation is negligible compared with the compounding successive one-step prediction errors. TSARFS is intended primarily for univariate models; additional variables in a model will be ignored in variance calculations and will cause a warning message to be printed.

Calling Sequences:

   (FTN) CALL TSARFS(modl,N1Y,N1M,N2Y,N2M)

   (ISX) TSARFS modl N1Y N1M N2Y N2M

The ARFS and ACFS series may be used with TSCLIM (p. 166) to compute confidence limits for observed values or forecast errors.

Example:

   TSARFS MDL6 1970 1 1972 12

3.6.5 TSCLIM - Confidence Limits

TSCLIM computes upper and lower confidence limits. The limits will normally be centered about predictions or zero, using standard deviations computed by TSRFSD (p. 165) or TSARFS (p. 166).

Calling Sequences:

   (FTN) CALL TSCLIM(type,name,stdv,T)

   (ISX) TSCLIM type name stdv T

      type = PRDN if confidence limits are to be about
             predictions, or blank if about zero.
      name = name of series
      stdv = type of series containing standard deviations.
      T   = t value

Then

      <UCL name> = <type name> + T <stdv name>

      <LCL name> = <type name> - T <stdv name>

Examples:

        TSCLIM PRDN ABCD RFSD 2

provides confidence limits about predictions or forecasts.

        TSCLIM .... ABCD RFSD 2

provides confidence limits for forecast errors.

3.7 Miscellaneous Subroutines

3.7.1 TSEXT - Extraction

TSEXT extracts from an existing time series into a new series.

Calling Sequences:

        (FTN) CALL TSEXT(type,name,N1Y,N1M,N2Y,N2M,ntyp,nnam)

        (ISX) TSEXT type name N1Y N1M N2Y N2M ntyp nnam

                type,name = type and name of existing series
                ntyp,nnam = type and name for new series

Example:

        TSEXT DATA ABCD 1966 1 1966 12 DATA AB66

3.7.2 TSGET, TSPUT - Editing

TSGET retrieves and prints elements of a time series. TSPUT enters data into a series, extending it or replacing existing values.

Calling Sequences:

        (FTN) CALL TSGET(type,name,N1Y,N1M,N,A,&ERR)
        (FTN) CALL TSPUT(type,name,N1Y,N1M,N,A,&ERR)

        (ISX) TSGET type name N1Y N1M N
        (ISX) TSPUT type name N1Y N1M N [X]

                N   = number of data values
                X   = array containing (TSPUT) or receiving
                             (TSGET) data
                &ERR   = error return

TSGET attempts to retrieve the N points beginning at the specified date. If they do not exist, the closest (i.e., first or last) N (or fewer) points of the series are extracted and an error return taken. TSGET prints the series name, time label, and up to twelve of the values retrieved; printing may be suppressed through OPTION (p. 285).

If N is zero, the series name and beginning and ending time points are printed, along with any identification information contained in words four through twenty of the time control block, and the beginning and ending times and months/year value are returned in X as integers (the beginning and ending time points are returned as months relative to year 1).

TSPUT requires that new points be contiguous with the existing series. If the series does not exist, it is created, using the months/year value in its time control block (Sec. 2.2, p. 146). If the latter is not found, months/year is assumed to be 1.

ISX Note:

The ISX "X" array (p. 60) is used for array X by TSGET and, if only five arguments are supplied, by TSPUT. The number of data values transmitted is limited to 50.

Examples:

        TSGET DATA ABCD 1967 6 3
        TSPUT DATA ABCD 1968 6 3

replaces <DATA ABCD>, 6/68-8/68 with <DATA ABCD>, 6/67-8/67.

        TSTORG DATA EFGH 1970 1 12
        TSPUT DATA EFGH 1970 1 2 123 456

creates a new monthly series <DATA EFGH> with two elements, a value of 123 for January and 456 for February, 1970.

        TSGET DATA WXYZ 0 0 0

prints the time span for <DATA WXYZ>.

3.7.3 TSTIME - Reset Calendar

TSTIME is used to reset the value of the internal "calendar", which is normally set by TSREG to the last time point used in regression. This is necessary if one wishes to use DATA rather than PRDNs in forecasting from a regression model using TSPRDN; otherwise, TSPAK "pretends" that the DATA are not yet available and requires a PRDN series for each independent variable. Alternatively, the "EQL" function of TSFN1 may be used to create PRDNs, setting them equal to DATA.

Calling Sequences:

    (FTN) CALL TSTIME(N2Y,N2M,MPY)

    (ISX) TSTIME N2Y N2M MPY

Example:

TSTIME 1972 12 12

3.7.4 TSTORG - Define Time Origin

TSTORG may be used to specify the time origin and months/year for a
series by creating a time control block (Sec. 2.2, p. 146).

Calling Sequences:

   (FTN) CALL TSTORG(type,name,N1Y,N1M,MPY)

   (ISX) TSTORG type name N1Y N1M MPY

      type,name = type and name of series

Example:

   TSTORG DATA ABCD 1958 7 12

3.7.5 TSTYPE - Change Default Types

TSTYPE redefines the types to be used by TSPAK for data, prediction,
and residual series from their default values of DATA, PRDN and RSID,
respectively.

Calling Sequences:

   (FTN) CALL TSTYPE(data,prdn,rsid)

   (ISX) TSTYPE data prdn rsid

Example:

   TSTYPE RSID RPRD RSD2

3.8 Interface Routines

Time series data may be used with STPAK (Ch. 5, p. 87) directly, by
calling STDIM (p. 91) to dimension the block as a data matrix
containing one variable, possibly after calling TSEXT (p. 167) to
extract a subset of the series.   STLINK (p. 103) can be used to
combine several matrices into one. Observation labels for the matrix
may be generated as time series by TSLBLS (3.8.1) and linked into the
matrix as variable OBL.

Subroutines TSTAB (3.8.2) and TSTABK (3.8.3) generate tables from one
or more time series for use with TABLE (Ch. 8, p. 225), a package of
subroutines for managing and analyzing multiway tables of data.

STPAK variables may be extracted with STEXT (p. 103) for use with TSPAK. TABLE data may be extracted using TABEXT (p. 233), possibly after transposing (e.g., MON by YEAR, not YEAR by MON) using TABTRN (p. 234). TSTORG (p. 169) should be called to create the time control block.

3.8.1 TSLBLS - Time Labels

TSLBLS generates a time series containing time labels, as described in Section 2.2 (p. 146), by calling TSLBL (p. 172).

Calling Sequences:

    (FTN) CALL TSLBLS(N1Y,N1M,N2Y,N2M,MPY,type,name)

    (ISX) TSLBLS N1Y N1M N2Y N2M MPY type name

Example:

       TSLBLS 1960 1 1969 12 12 DATA OBLS

3.8.2 TSTAB - Table Interface

TSTAB generates a month by year table from a time series. If the series is monthly (months/year=12), the names JANUARY, ..., DECEMBER are assigned to the categories of the dimension MON; otherwise, those names are MON....1, MON....2, etc. The YEAR dimension will contain categories whose names are the years (e.g. 1960, 1961, ...). DIM blocks (p. 231) are created.

Calling Sequences:

    (FTN) CALL TSTAB(type,name,N1Y,N2Y,ntyp,nnam)

    (ISX) TSTAB type name N1Y N2Y ntyp nnam

Example:

       TSTAB DATA ABCD 1960 1969 TABL ABCD

3.8.3 TSTABK - Multiple Series Tables

TSTABK generates a TIME by SER (for series) table from one or more time series, all of which have the same number of months per year. Categories of TIME are the rows, and there is one column for each specified time point that intersects with at least one series (missing values for other series are filled with zeroes). Time labels are obtained through TSLBL (p. 172), and appear as described in Section 2.2 (p. 146). The number of columns (e.g., categories of

SER) equals the number of series specified, and this identification consists of types and names joined together. DIM blocks (p. 231) are created.

Calling Sequences:

    (FTN) CALL TSTABK(NS,'typ1type2..','nam1nam2..',
                      N1Y,N1M,N2Y,N2M,ntyp,nnam)

    (ISX) TSTABK NS typ1 nam1 typ2 nam2 ..
                     N1Y N1M N2Y N2M ntyp nnam

Example:

        TSTABK 3 DATA ABCD PRDN ABCD RSID ABCD
                1960 1 1969 12 TABL ABCD

Stores DATA, PRDNs, and RSIDs in two-way table <TABL ABCD>. Columns have the identifiers DATAABCD, PRDNABCD, RSIDABCD, respectively. The times spanned by the rows will be January 1960 through December 1969, possibly shortened at each end by months for which none of the series exists.

4. TSPAK SERVICE ROUTINES

These subroutines perform low-level functions and are called by other
TSPAK routines.

4.1 TSNEW, TSOLD - Create New, Find Old Series

TSNEW creates and TSOLD finds time series; both return a DYNCOR
pointer to the calling routine for access to the series. These
routines are basically TSPAK versions of DYNNEW and DYNOLD (p. 260);
beginning and ending dates and months/year are included in the
calling sequences.

Calling Sequences:

        (FTN) CALL TSNEW(type,name,N1,N2,MPY,X,JX,&ERR)
        (FTN) CALL TSOLD(type,name,N1,N2,MPY,X,JX,&ERR)

            N1,N2 = originating and terminating times for
                    series, in months (internal time scale)
                    These must be specified for TSNEW,
                    are returned by TSOLD.
            X   = reference array
            JX   = pointer subscript
            &ERR = error return for insufficient core (TSNEW)
                    or series not found (TSOLD).

Example:

        CALL TSOLD('DATA','ABCD',N1,N2,MPY,X,JX,&88)

TSNEWZ and TSOLDZ are identical routines, except that they compute
pointer subscripts relative to a common time point. Thus the
elements of the series are referenced as $X(JX,N1)$, ..., $X(JX,N2)$ with
TSNEWZ/TSOLDZ, $X(JX,1)$, ..., $X(JX,N2-N1+1)$ with TSNEW/TSOLD.

4.2 TSLBL - Generate Time Label

TSLBL generates an 8-character time label as described in Section 2.2
(p. 146) and as printed in Section 5.1 (p. 176).

Calling Sequence:

        (FTN) CALL TSLBL(J,MPY,Z)

            J = time point in months
            Z = resulting label.

5. SAMPLE PROGRAMS

A simple program to print a series and plot the autocorrelation function of its first differences was shown in Section 1. This section includes programs for regression and autoregression. The series used, <DATA BSMI>, is the number of telephones connected monthly in the Bell System. The complete input stream for running the programs on an IBM VS/370 system is shown, along with the resulting output (on time-sharing systems, of course, the output would directly follow each command). See Chapter 15, Section 2 (p. 391), for information on running the ISX program under VS.

5.1 Example 1

Job Input Stream:

```
//jobname JOB (acctg info),parameters
// EXEC ISX
//GO.FT10F001 DD *
.DAT BSMI 3 I(*)
1958 1 12
DATA BSMI 144 R(6F10.0)
      649272    585962    613382    659719    663652    753861    58A
      761317    771585    893150    831657    682389    709289    58B
      673992    647747    720583    740174    730661    872632    59A
      849480    831191    981109    860698    753983    733483    59B
      . . .
     1044607    961709   1036480   1066902   1083818   1326445    69A
     1288264   1294247   1516104   1291272   1006215   1022506    69B
.DAT BSMO 3 I(3I4)
1958    1   12
DATA BSMO 144 R(6F10.0)
      574655    538706    575524    607960    609011    741620    58A
      678571    696770    747775    690003    583113    596674    58B
      561179    552045    619124    621598    633552    831782    59A
      733895    740848    810971    715875    647590    609748    59B
      . . .
      852865    800555    877302    927355   1019776   1306526    69A
     1141544   1202415   1184662   1053750    869494    888568    69B
//GO.SYSIN DD *
OPTION * PAGSIZ 75
PPLOTP LINES 20
DYNINP 10
TSMODL REG1 BSMO 1 0 INDV
TSMODL REG1 BSMI 1 0 DEPV
TSREG REG1 1958 1 1967 12
TSREGA REG1 BSMI
TSPLT 1 RSID BSMI 1961 1 1964 12
TSTIME 1969 12 12
TSPRDN REG1 1968 1 1969 12
TSRSDA BSMI 1968 1 1969 12
```

Description:

OPTION (p. 285) is called to set the page size for output to 75 columns. DYNINP (p. 270) reads the series into core. TSMODL (p. 161) is called twice to define the independent (BSMO) and dependent (BSMI) variables for a model called REG1. TSREG (p. 163) then performs regression on this model from 1/58 through 12/67; it also calls TSPRDN (p. 164) to compute predicted values <PRDN BSMI> and residuals <RSID BSMI> over this time period (computer page 1). TSREGA (p. 164) produces a statistical analysis of the regression (computer page 2) and TSPLT (p. 150) plots a portion of the residuals (computer page 3). TSTIME (p. 168) is called to allow TSPRDN to make use of <DATA BSMO> in computing prediction from 1/68 through 12/69 (rather then requiring <PRDN BSMO>). Finally TSRSDA (p. 165) produces a summary of the predictions and errors (computer page 4).

Output:

STATLIB ISX 12/01/78   07/09/80 PAGE 1

TSREG: MODEL=REG1, TYPE=DATA, JAN 1958-DEC 1967
        DEPV=BSMI

TSPRDN: MODEL=REG1, TYPE=DATA/PRDN/RSID, JAN 1958-DEC 1967
        DEPV=BSMI

REGPAK / REGANL   07/09/80 PAGE 2

    SAMPLE SIZE 120
    SUM OF WEIGHTS . . . . 1.2000D+02
    ESTIMATED STD DEV . . . . . 5.0546D+04
    R SQUARED 0.9034

    VARIABLE   COEFFICIENT   ESTD STD DEV   T

    0   5.2476D+04   2.5140D+04   2.0874
     1 BSMO....   1.0672D+00   3.2118D-02   33.2274

     2 BSMI....   DEPENDENT VARIABLE

    ANALYSIS OF VARIANCE

        SOURCE   DF   SS   MS   F

        REGRESSION   1   2.8207D+12   2.8207D+12   1104.061
        ERROR   118   3.0147D+11   2.5549D+09

        TOTAL   119   3.1222D+12

TSREGA: MODEL=REG1, DEPV=BSMI, JAN 1958-DEC 1967

TSPAK   / TSPLT   07/09/80   PAGE 3

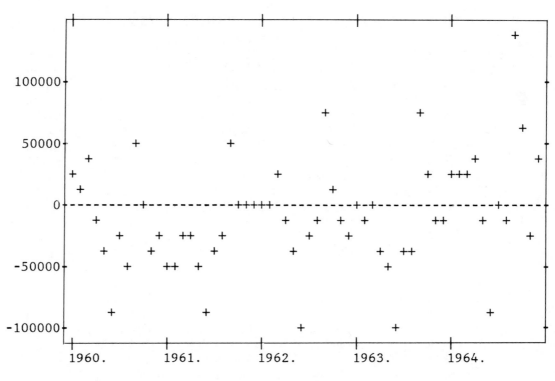

1 + RSIDBSMI   VS   TIME
JAN 1960-DEC 1964

TSPRDN: MODEL=REG1, TYPE=DATA/PRDN/RSID, JAN 1968-DEC 1969
        DEPV=BSMI

TSPAK / TSRSDA   07/09/80   PAGE 4

BSMI		DATA	PRDN	RESIDUAL	%	SQRT(ASR)
JAN	1968	969257.	926665.2	42591.8	4.39	42591.8
FEB	1968	929314.	883379.1	45934.9	4.94	44294.9
MAR	1968	979370.	928371.7	50998.3	5.21	46636.5
APR	1968	834954.	937851.8	-102897.8	-12.32	65408.1
MAY	1968	1022257.	1112684.9	-90427.9	-8.85	71119.7
JUN	1968	1233478.	1333145.6	-99667.6	-8.08	76619.9
JUL	1968	1219987.	1227555.5	-7568.5	-0.62	70993.9
AUG	1968	1255857.	1297638.3	-41781.3	-3.33	68031.8
SEP	1968	1436696.	1210956.0	225740.0	15.71	98874.3
OCT	1968	1299135.	1134270.3	164864.7	12.69	107315.2
NOV	1968	1051811.	1028809.3	23001.7	2.19	102555.8
DEC	1968	952873.	906421.3	46451.7	4.87	99101.1
		13184989.	12927749.0	257240.0	1.95	99101.1
JAN	1969	1044607.	962665.6	81941.4	7.84	97888.0
FEB	1969	961709.	906839.6	54869.4	5.71	95460.3
MAR	1969	1036480.	988745.1	47734.9	4.61	93043.4
APR	1969	1066902.	1042162.3	24739.7	2.32	90300.9
MAY	1969	1083818.	1140795.3	-56977.3	-5.26	88688.0
JUN	1969	1326445.	1446818.8	-120373.8	-9.07	90739.1
JUL	1969	1288264.	1270747.7	17516.3	1.36	88410.3
AUG	1969	1294247.	1335710.1	-41463.1	-3.20	86669.0
SEP	1969	1516104.	1316763.9	199340.1	13.15	95110.7
OCT	1969	1291272.	1177052.8	114219.2	8.85	96061.7
NOV	1969	1006215.	980412.3	25802.7	2.56	94104.2
DEC	1969	1022506.	1000768.3	21737.7	2.13	92229.6
		13938569.	13569481.7	369087.3	2.65	84803.1
					2.31	92229.6

5.2 Example 2

Job Input Stream:

```
//jobname JOB (acctg info),parameters
// EXEC ISX
//GO.FT29F001 DD DSN=FCST.DATA,DISP=SHR
//GO.SYSIN DD *
OPTION * PAGSIZ 75
PPLOTP LINES 20
DYNINL 29 .... BSMI
TSMODL AREG BSMI 3 1 12 13 INDV
TSMODL AREG BSMI 1 0 DEPV
TSREG AREG 1958 1 1967 12
TSREGA AREG BSMI
TSACOR RSID BSMI 1958 1 1967 12
TSPLT 1 ACOR BSMI 0 1 29 1
TSPRDN AREG 1968 1 1969 12
TSRSDA BSMI 1968 1 1969 12
```

Description:

This example is similar to the previous one, except that an autoregressive model is applied to BSMI. In this case, DYNINL (p. 270) is used to read in the series from disk, bypassing any blocks with names other than BSMI. TSMODL (p. 161) creates the model (AREG) using lags 1, 12 and 13. As before, the regression is computed and the analysis printed. At this point, the autocorrelation function of the residuals is computed by TSACOR (p. 160) and plotted by TSPLT (p. 150). TSPRDN (p. 164) calculates a multi-step forecast for BSMI, using the forecast values, as required, after 12/67. TSRSDA (p. 165) again summarizes the forecasts and forecast errors.

Output:

```
STATLIB ISX  12/01/78                    07/09/80  PAGE 1

TSREG:  MODEL=AREG, TYPE=DATA, FEB 1959-DEC 1967
        DEPV=BSMI

TSPRDN: MODEL=AREG, TYPE=DATA/PRDN/RSID, FEB 1959-DEC 1967
        DEPV=BSMI
```

REGPAK / REGANL   07/09/80   PAGE 2

    SAMPLE SIZE 107
    SUM OF WEIGHTS . . . . 1.0700D+02
    ESTIMATED STD DEV . . . . . 3.9371D+04
    R SQUARED 0.9397

    VARIABLE   COEFFICIENT   ESTD STD DEV   T

    0   1.9639D+04   2.3388D+04   0.8397
    1 BSMI...1   2.5925D-01   9.6889D-02   2.6757
    2 BSMI..12   1.0112D+00   4.1622D-02   24.2955
    3 BSMI..13   -2.6155D-01   1.0174D-01   -2.5708

    4 BSMI....   DEPENDENT VARIABLE

    ANALYSIS OF VARIANCE

        SOURCE   DF   SS   MS   F

        REGRESSION   3   2.4875D+12   8.2916D+11   534.927
        ERROR   103   1.5966D+11   1.5500D+09

        TOTAL   106   2.6471D+12

TSREGA: MODEL=AREG, DEPV=BSMI, FEB 1959-DEC 1967

TSACOR: RSID BSMI, 35 LAGS, FEB 1959-DEC 1967

TSPAK   / TSPLT   07/09/80   PAGE 3

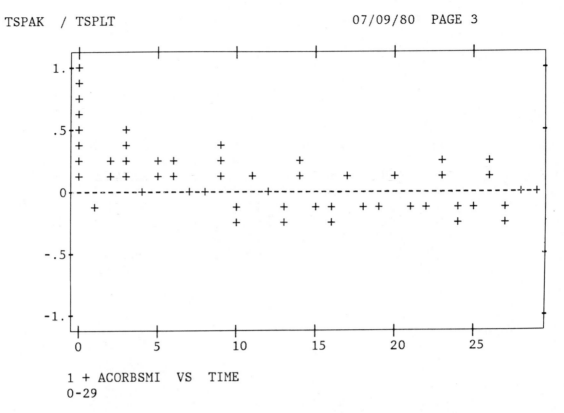

1 + ACORBSMI VS TIME
0-29

TSPRDN: MODEL=AREG, TYPE=DATA/PRDN/RSID, JAN 1968-DEC 1969
        DEPV=BSMI

TSPAK / TSRSDA   07/09/80   PAGE 4

BSMI	DATA	PRDN	RESIDUAL	%	SQRT(ASR)
JAN 1968	969257.	925390.4	43866.6	4.53	43866.6
FEB 1968	929314.	882886.3	46427.7	5.00	45165.3
MAR 1968	979370.	993755.3	-14385.3	-1.47	37801.0
APR 1968	834954.	936577.2	-101623.2	-12.17	60444.2
MAY 1968	1022257.	1029002.9	-6745.9	-0.66	54147.1
JUN 1968	1233478.	1268274.2	-34796.2	-2.82	51430.1
JUL 1968	1219987.	1130746.5	89240.5	7.31	58351.4
AUG 1968	1255857.	1263235.6	-7378.6	-0.59	54645.0
SEP 1968	1436696.	1425527.1	11168.9	0.78	51654.1
OCT 1968	1299135.	1185346.6	113788.4	8.76	60795.7
NOV 1968	1051811.	1054121.1	-2310.1	-0.22	57970.6
DEC 1968	952873.	912637.5	40235.5	4.22	56704.9
	13184989.	13007500.7	177488.3	1.35	56704.9
JAN 1969	1044607.	963059.7	81547.3	7.81	58988.5
FEB 1969	961709.	920079.1	41629.9	4.33	57921.4
MAR 1969	1036480.	1032167.9	4312.1	0.42	55968.4
APR 1969	1066902.	974408.6	92493.4	8.67	58918.4
MAY 1969	1083818.	1067853.4	15964.6	1.47	57290.2
JUN 1969	1326445.	1309864.1	16580.9	1.25	55813.1
JUL 1969	1288264.	1170951.0	117313.0	9.11	60625.8
AUG 1969	1294247.	1304885.8	-10638.8	-0.82	59138.5
SEP 1969	1516104.	1469070.2	47033.8	3.10	58618.8
OCT 1969	1291272.	1226309.0	64963.0	5.03	58922.0
NOV 1969	1006215.	1093492.9	-87277.9	-8.67	60432.2
DEC 1969	1022506.	950309.7	72196.3	7.06	60967.7
	13938569.	13482451.4	456117.6	3.27	64951.3
				2.34	60967.7

6. SUBJECT INDEX

Subroutine and Subject   Page

7. GLOSSARY OF SUBROUTINE CALLS (ISX)

CHAPTER 7

SPPAK - SPECTRUM ANALYSIS PACKAGE

1. INTRODUCTION

SPPAK is a system of FORTRAN subroutines for spectrum analysis of time series. Subroutines are included which perform such operations as univariate and multivariate spectrum analysis, Wiener filtering, Fourier transformation, and many more.

SPPAK subroutines may be called directly in FORTRAN, or in ISX (Ch. 4) which accepts free-form input without FORTRAN punctuation. The following simple ISX program demonstrates the programming style of SPPAK.

```
DYNINP 8
SPECT DATA ABCD 1960 1 1975 12
SPREG 1 DATA ABCD AR 1960 1 1975 12
SPECTM AR ABCD EFGH
TSPLT 2 SPEC ABCD SPEC EFGH 1 1 99999 1
```

DYNINP (p. 270) reads one or more time series into core. SPECT (p. 195) estimates the spectrum of univariate time series <DATA ABCD> by smoothing the periodogram, using data from January 1960 to December 1975. SPREG (p. 189) uses the same data to estimate Wiener filter coefficients, leaving the results labeled AR. SPECTM (p. 197) computes the spectrum corresponding to AR, and calls it <SPEC EFGH>. Finally, TSPLT (p. 150) plots the two estimates of the spectrum of <DATA ABCD>.

SPPAK is closely related to TSPAK, STATLIB's time series analysis package (Ch. 6), and as with TSPAK, data are managed by DYNCOR, the dynamic in-core data management system (Ch. 9). The conventions outlined in TSPAK Sections 1 and 2 are directly applicable here.

Section 2 describes SPPAK conventions and procedures. Section 3 contains descriptions of SPPAK subroutines for time series modeling. Section 4 describes subroutines for spectrum analysis and frequency domain manipulations. Two sample programs are given in Section 5. Sections 6 and 7 contain summary information: a subject index and a one-page glossary of calling sequences.

2. CONVENTIONS AND NOTATION

2.1 Relation to TSPAK

All SPPAK routines could have been included in TSPAK since they deal with time series. However, the classification of subroutines by time and frequency domains is natural, and keeps both TSPAK and SPPAK documentation down to reasonable size. SPPAK routines use TSPAK routines internally, and operate on the same kinds of data. The separation of TS and SP routines is for documentation clarity and convenience only. The reader is expected to be familiar with TSPAK's data storage conventions and its various routines, many of which are useful in spectrum analysis.

2.2 SPPAK Data Storage

SPPAK routines create and maintain data blocks in core, storing the data themselves as real numbers (REAL*8 on IBM) in DYNCOR blocks, storing time control information in separate DYNCOR blocks. Data and time control block storage conventions are identical to those of TSPAK (Ch. 6, Secs. 2.1-2, p. 146).

Each DYNCOR block is referenced by a first and last name (see p. 257 for an explanation of identification conventions). In SPPAK, the first indicates the type of block it is (e.g., DATA for data, SPEC for spectrum, PDGM for periodogram, etc.), and the last identifies the name of a particular series. References to such blocks in the text have the two-word identifers enclosed in angle brackets (e.g., <DATA BSMO>, <.DAT BSMO>).

Blocks with first names of DATA, PRDN, RSID, ACOR, PACF and XCOR have special meaning in TSPAK and are handled differently by some of its routines. Similarly, certain DYNCOR first names, or "types", have special meaning to SPPAK:

PDGM	- Periodogram
SPEC	- Spectrum
FTFM	- Fourier Transform
GAIN	- Gain
PHAS	- Phase
COHE	- Coherence
XAMP	- Cross-amplitude Spectrum
XPGR	- Real Part of Cross-periodogram
XPGI	- Imaginary Part of Cross-periodogram
XSPR	- Real Part of Cross-spectrum
XSPI	- Imaginary Part of Cross-spectrum
ACOV	- Autocovariance Function
XCOV	- Cross-covariance Function

In addition, "L" followed by the first three characters of one of the first seven of the above is recognized as the logarithm of the quantity.

Frequency domain data do not require an analogue of TSPAK's time control blocks (p. 146), using the default (1,1,1); i.e. frequency domain quantities are stored as time series starting at 1,1 and having 1 "month/year". However, the TSPAK plotting routine TSPLT (p. 150) recognizes these idenfifiers and plots the data on a frequency scale (0.0 to 0.5).

Fourier transforms of real data (FTFM) are stored with real and imaginary parts packed into a single DYNCOR block (see Sec. 4.5, p. 203). Periodograms, spectra, gain, phase, coherence, and cross-amplitude spectra (PDGM, SPEC, GAIN, PHAS, and XAMP) have only their values at frequencies 0.0 to 0.5 stored. The real (imaginary) parts of cross-spectra (XSPR and XSPI) and cross-periodograms (XPGR and XPGI) are symmetric (antisymmetric), so again only frequencies 0.0 to 0.5 are saved (see Secs. 4.5.7-8, p. 207).

High level SPPAK routines (e.g., SPREG, SPECT, SPECTX) and some low level routines create DYNCOR blocks with standard first names. Some lower level routines do computations in place, either leaving the identifiers unchanged (e.g., SPRFT), or renaming the output with standard ones (e.g., SPACOR).

2.3 Messages, Errors, and Printing Options

STATLIB-wide message and error conventions are described in the Part II Introduction (p. 58). Refer there (and to the Section 5 examples, p. 213) for further information on controlling the printing of messages and decisions on whether and when errors should terminate execution. Since TSPAK and SPPAK are so closely related, SPPAK uses TSPAK error and message handling routines. The following conventions apply specifically to SPPAK.

Error conditions result in a printed message by TSERR. The most common errors arise in misspelling or leaving out the name of a series or variable. Another frequent error results from insufficient core storage being available to create or enlarge a given block. A message from DYNCOR identifies the block and the number of words requested.

Each high level SPPAK subroutine generates (through TSMSG) a one- or two-line message summarizing what it has done. This helps to make program output self documenting in that the flow of execution can be determined from the output alone.

OPTION (p. 285) may be used to control SPPAK printing, specifying SP* for all routines, TSMSG for messages, TSERR for error messages, or the subroutine name for routines that generate printed output.

2.4 Calling Sequence Notation

Calling sequences follow the STATLIB-wide conventions described in the Part II Introduction (p. 56). The following apply specifically to SPPAK.

a. Character string arguments are assumed to be of length four or less, unless otherwise noted.

b. N1Y, N1M, N2Y, and N2M will be used to denote the beginning and ending years and months in an SPPAK call.

3. SPPAK SUBROUTINES FOR MODELING TIME SERIES

3.1 Model Building Routines

3.1.1 SPREG - Wiener Filter Parameter Estimation

SPREG builds a Wiener (minimum mean square error) filter on a specified series. SPREG estimates the spectrum of the time series and factors it to obtain a (large) autoregressive model. The form of the model will be determined by the routine, although some control may be exercised through SPDIF (p. 191) and SPMODL (p. 191). Univariate and bivariate models can be constructed. SPREG has the ability to build robust/resistant models, controlled through OPTION (p. 285). TSPRDN (p. 164) can be used to generate predictions using models from SPREG.

Calling Sequences:

        (FTN) CALL SPREG(NS,'typ1typ2..','nam1nam2..',mdln,
                    N1Y,N1M,N2Y,N2M)

        (ISX) SPREG NS typ1 nam1 typ2 nam2 .. mdln N1Y N1M N2Y N2M

        NS   = number of series (1 or 2)
        typ1typ2..   = types
        nam1nam2..   = names
        mdln   = name of model to be built
        N1Y-N2M   = starting and ending years and months

Example:

        SPREG 2 DATA BSMO DATA FRBI MOVE 1960 1 1969 12

builds a bivariate model, named MOVE, for <DATA BSMO> and <DATA FRBI>, using data from the sixties.

SPREG builds only stationary models. If the input is non-stationary, differencing must be supplied through SPDIF (p. 191). If any differencing is done, it must be sufficient to yield a stationary time series with mean essentially zero. If no differencing is done, SPREG will correct for a possibly nonzero mean.

SPREG generates a minimal amount of output, mostly diagnostic. Extra output may be obtained through SPXTRA (p. 190). The length of the autoregressive model and the smoothing in the spectrum estimation can be controlled through SPMODL (p. 191).

SPREG has the ability to build robust/resistant models, adjusting outliers in the process. The specialized code is activated through OPTION (p. 285): in ISX,

        OPTION SPREG ROBUST ON

The robust option causes the original data to be copied into blocks
<ORIG nam1>, <ORIG nam2>, etc., for safe keeping. After fitting a
preliminary model, a nonlinear filtering algorithm is applied which
fits a re-descending influence function PSI to the residuals and
adjusts the data as

$$DATA = PRDN + PSI(RSID) \quad .$$

The function PSI is constructed of a linear function near the origin
and a descending part related to the extreme value distribution.
DATA corresponding to small to medium sized values of RSID will
remain unchanged, while DATA corresponding to large values of RSID
will be adjusted toward the fitted value, PRDN. Two iterations of
model fitting and outlier adjustment are performed.

Example:

```
        OPTION SPREG ROBUST ON
        SPREG 1 DATA BSMO MOVE 1960 1 1969 12
```

builds a univariate model on an outlier adjusted version of
<DATA BSMO>. The original version of BSMO is now stored as
<ORIG BSMO>.

3.1.2 SPXTRA - Extra Output from SPREG

SPXTRA causes SPREG to print model coefficients, forecasts and
standard deviations of forecasts. SPREG will also stop at the end of
each year, and "forecast" the future, printing yearly totals for the
actual and fitted values.

Calling Sequences:

```
    (FTN) CALL SPXTRA(M)

    (ISX) SPXTRA M

        M = number of months ahead to be forecast
```

Since SPREG computes yearly totals, M should be a small multiple of
the months per year of the data. SPXTRA refers only to the next call
to SPREG, and may be cancelled if calls to another STATLIB package
occur between SPXTRA and SPREG.

Example:

```
        SPXTRA 24
```

will cause SPREG to print model coefficients, monthly forecasts two
years into the future (with standard deviations), yearly totals of
the forecasts (with standard deviations) one and two years ahead, and
yearly sums of the fitted and actual values, using each year of the
fitting period as a base year.

3.1.3 SPMODL - Specifying Model Parameters

SPMODL overrides default values of the model length and spectrum smoothing parameters in SPREG (p. 189).

Calling Sequences:

    (FTN) CALL SPMODL(MDLEN,MSMTH)

    (ISX) SPMODL MDLEN MSMTH

        MDLEN = length of model desired
        MSMTH = spectrum smoothing parameter (non-negative)

Example:

        SPMODL 21 10

requests a model of length 21 (excluding any differencing polynomial factor), with smoothing over 10 adjacent frequencies when estimating the spectrum.

If either of the arguments of SPMODL is negative or zero, a default value is taken in its place. The default values for MDLEN and MSMTH are $SQRT(2*N)$ and $SQRT(N)$, respectively, where N is the number of data points.

SPMODL refers only to the next call to SPREG, and may be cancelled if calls to another STATLIB package occur between SPMODL and SPREG.

3.1.4 SPDIF - Specifying Differencing

SPDIF creates a DYNCOR block containing the coefficients of a differencing polynomial. SPREG (p. 189) and SPBXCX (p. 192) search for this block and perform the indicated differencing to reduce their input to stationary series.

Calling Sequences:

    (FTN) CALL SPDIF(name,NLAG,LAG)

    (ISX) SPDIF name NLAG LAG1 LAG2 ..

        name = name of series
        NLAG = number of entries in LAG
        LAG   = array of lags at which differences are to be
               taken (i.e. LAG1, LAG2, ..., LAGN)

Example:

        SPDIF BSMO 2 1 12

will cause any series with name BSMO to be differenced at lags 1 and 12 before being used by SPREG. The differencing polynomial will be contained as a factor in any model built by SPREG.

SPDIF stores the differencing polynomial in block <DIFF name>. It remains in core until deleted through DYNDEL (p. 261) or removed by a call to SPDIF with NLAG = 0.

3.2 Box-Cox Transformation

3.2.1 SPBXCX - Estimation of Box-Cox Parameters

SPBXCX determines a maximum likelihood estimate of the power, a, in a Box-Cox transformation:

$$x' = \begin{cases} ((x+b)^a - 1)/a + ct + d & a \neq 0 \\ \log(x+b) + ct + d & a = 0 \end{cases}$$

Calling Sequences:

    (FTN) CALL SPBXCX(type,name,N1Y,N1M,N2Y,N2M)

    (ISX) SPBXCX type name N1Y N1M N2Y N2M

        type,name = type and name of input series
        N1Y-N2M   = starting and ending years and months

The parameters a, b, c, and d are stored in DYNCOR block <BXCX name> for future use by SPBXTR (p. 193). The detrending parameters c and d may be suppressed through OPTION (p. 285); in ISX,

        OPTION SPBXCX TREND OFF

The parameter b is chosen to make (x+b) nonnegative, and also to position the data in such a way that the members of the Box-Cox family are rich in different shapes. If the input series is non-stationary, differencing must be specified before estimating Box-Cox parameters. This must be done by calling SPDIF (p. 191) before calling SPBXCX. Parameters a and b can be reset directly if, for example, rounding is desired.

Example 1:

        SPBXCX DATA BSMO 1960 1 1969 12

will estimate the parameters of a Box-Cox transformation for <DATA BSMO>.

Example 2:

The user can manually reset the parameters to any desired value.   If the parameters a, b, c, and d in Example 1 were estimated as .47, -1.04E+06, 1.44E-01, and 2.43E+03, the nearby square root transformation can be obtained by

    TSPUT BXCX BSMO 1 1 4 .5 -1000000. 0. 0.

Note that parameters a and b have been rounded, and parameters c and d have been set to 0.0, since the old values are no longer valid.

3.2.2 SPBXTR - Box-Cox Transformation

SPBXTR performs the Box-Cox transformation (or inverse transformation) using parameters determined by SPBXCX (p. 192).

Calling Sequences:

    (FTN) CALL SPBXTR(type,name,I,nnam)

    (ISX) SPBXTR type name I nnam

        type = type for input (and output) series
        name = name for input series
        I   = 1 for Box-Cox transformation
             = -1 for inverse Box-Cox transformation
        nnam = name for output series

Example:

    SPBXTR PRDN TRMO -1 BSMO

computes the inverse transformation of <PRDN TRMO> to obtain <PRDN BSMO>.

4. SPPAK SUBROUTINES FOR SPECTRUM ANALYSIS

4.1 High Level Routines

4.1.1 SPPARM - Parameter Setting

SPPARM sets parameters and controls the flow of the high level routines for spectrum (SPECT) and cross-spectrum (SPECTX) estimation.

<u>Calling Sequences:</u>

    (FTN) CALL SPPARM(code,val)

    (ISX) SPPARM code val

        code = character string (see below)
        val = character string or number (see below)

code	val	Description
%EXT	<u>.20</u>	(val*LEN) zeroes to be appended before FFT
%TAP	<u>.10</u>	(val*LEN) data to be tapered on each end
WINP	<u>3</u>	Number of frequencies in Daniell window
MEAN	(<u>ON</u>|OFF)	Mean correction
TRND	(ON|<u>OFF</u>)	Detrending
TAPR	(<u>ON</u>|OFF)	Tapering with cosine window
NORM	(<u>ON</u>|OFF)	Standardize to variance 1.
FTFM	(ON|<u>OFF</u>)	Save Fourier transform
PDGM	(ON|<u>OFF</u>)	Save periodogram
SPEC	(<u>ON</u>|OFF)	Compute and save spectrum
ACOR	(ON|<u>OFF</u>)	Compute and save autocorrelation
GAIN	(ON|<u>OFF</u>)	Compute and save gain
XPGM	(ON|<u>OFF</u>)	Save cross-periodogram
XSPE	(ON|<u>OFF</u>)	Compute and save cross-spectrum
PHAS	(<u>ON</u>|OFF)	Compute and save phase
XAMP	(ON|<u>OFF</u>)	Compute and save cross-amplitude spectrum
COHE	(<u>ON</u>|OFF)	Compute and save coherence
XCOR	(ON|<u>OFF</u>)	Compute and save cross-correlation
RSET		Reset temporary values
LIST		List parameter settings

Underlined values are defaults. A code consisting of an asterisk (*) followed by the first three characters of one of the above codes is taken to be a temporary assignment, and can be reset by RSET. Other changes are permanent for the execution, unless specifically reset. Codes GAIN through XCOR apply only to SPECTX.

<u>Examples:</u>

        SPPARM LIST

lists the parameter settings currently in effect.

        SPPARM WINP 11

changes to a Daniell window of width 11.

        CALL SPPARM('*PDGM','ON')

in a FORTRAN program, saves the periodogram. To revert to deleting
the periodogram,

        CALL SPPARM('*PDGM','OFF')   , or

        CALL SPPARM('RSET')

4.1.2 SPECT - Univariate Spectrum Estimation

SPECT is a high level subroutine designed to estimate the spectrum
and/or Fourier transform, periodogram, and autocorrelation function
of a time series. The flow of the subroutine is controlled by SPPARM
(p. 194).

Calling Sequences:

    (FTN) CALL SPECT(type,name,N1Y,N1M,N2Y,N2M,&ERR)

    (ISX) SPECT type name N1Y N1M N2Y N2M

            type,name = type and name of series to be analyzed
            N1Y-N2M   = starting and ending years and months
            &ERR   = error return

SPECT will extract the needed data using TSEXT (p. 167) and remove
the mean (if MEAN is ON) and linear trend (if TRND is ON). If TAPR
is ON, %TAP of the data will be tapered with a cosine bell. SPECT
calls SPFTI (p. 206) to append zeroes, the number being determined by
%EXT. If NORM is ON, the series is normalized to unit variance. If
FTFM is ON, SPRFT (p. 203) leaves the Fourier transform in
<FTFM name>. If PDGM is ON, SPFTSQ (p. 207) leaves the periodogram
in <PDGM name>. If SPEC is ON, SPWIND (p. 200) smooths the
periodogram and leaves the spectrum in <SPEC name>. If ACOR is ON,
SPACOV (p. 198) and SPACOR (p. 199) leave the autocorrelation
function in <ACOR name>.

Examples:

        SPECT DATA BSMO 1960 1 1969 12

leaves an estimate of the spectrum in <SPEC BSMO>. Assuming SPPARM
defaults were used, the data would be mean corrected, but not
detrended. A Daniell window of width 3 would be used to smooth the
periodogram.

        SPPARM TRND ON
        SPPARM ACOR ON

```
SPPARM WINP 7
SPECT DATA BSMO 1960 1 1969 12
```

leaves another estimate of the spectrum in <SPEC BSMO>, and an estimate of the autocorrelation function in <ACOR BSMO>. This time the data would be detrended (and mean corrected) and a Daniell window of width 7 used.

4.1.3 SPECTX - Multivariate Spectra

SPECTX is a multivariate version of SPECT (p. 195). In addition to Fourier transforms, periodograms, spectra, and autocorrelation functions, SPECTX will compute cross-periodograms, cross-spectra, cross-amplitude spectra, cross-correlation functions, gain, phase and coherence. The flow of the subroutine is controlled by SPPARM (p. 194).

Calling Sequences:

```
(FTN) CALL SPECTX(NS,NX,'typ1typ2..','nam1nam2..',
                  N1Y,N1M,N2Y,N2M,&ERR)

(ISX) SPECTX NS NX typ1 nam1 typ2 nam2 N1Y N1M N2Y N2M
```

NS	= number of series
NX	= number of series for which cross-spectra with all other series are to be computed
typ1typ2..	= types
nam1nam2..	= names for series to be analyzed
N1Y-N2M	= starting and ending years and months
&ERR	= error return

SPECTX first does the computations in SPECT, obtaining Fourier transforms, periodograms, autospectra, etc. for each of the NS series. Then SPECTX computes cross-spectra, cross-correlation functions etc. Since these quantities are associated with pairs of names, new names must be supplied for cross-spectrum quantities. SPECTX assigns the names 0001, 0002, ..., taking first nam1 with all succeeding names, then nam2 with all succeeding names, until the first NX names have been used with all succeeding names. Names other than 0001, 0002, etc. may be supplied through SPECTN (p. 198).

SPECTX retrieves FTFM blocks two at a time, and multiplies them using SPFTMU (p. 207) to obtain the (complex) cross-periodogram. If XPGM is ON, the real and imaginary parts of the cross-periodogram are stored in <XPGR namx> and <XPGI namx>, where namx is the name assigned by SPECTX to this pair. If XCOR is ON, SPXCOV (p. 199) and SPXCOR (p. 200) are called to compute the cross-correlation function, which is stored in <XCOR namx>. If XSPE is ON, SPWIND (p. 200) smooths the cross-periodogram and leaves the real and imaginary parts of the estimated cross-spectrum in <XSPR namx> and <XSPI namx>. If PHAS is ON, SPPHAS (p. 210) leaves the estimated phase in <PHAS namx>. If XAMP is ON, SPXAMP (p. 209) leaves the estimated

cross-amplitude spectrum in <XAMP namx>. If GAIN is ON, SPGAIN
(p. 209) leaves the estimated gain in <GAIN namx>. If COHE is ON,
SPCOHE (p. 210) leaves the estimated coherence in <COHE namx>.

Example:

             SPECTX 3 2 DATA BSMO DATA BSMI DATA FRBI 1960 1 1969 12

will compute spectra for all three series, and phase and coherence
for all pairs. The names for the pairs will be:

                       (BSMO BSMI) - 0001
                       (BSMO FRBI) - 0002
                       (BSMI FRBI) - 0003

so that <COHE 0002> is the coherence of BSMO and FRBI.

4.1.4 SPECTM - Autoregressive Spectrum

SPECTM computes the spectrum corresponding to an autoregressive time
series model.

Calling Sequences:

     (FTN) CALL SPECTM(mdln,name,snam)

     (ISX) SPECTM mdln name snam

          mdln = name of model (from either TSPAK or SPPAK)
          name = name of dependent variable
          snam = name of output spectrum

If model mdln is non-stationary (i.e. the characteristic equation has
a zero on the unit circle), the spectrum has a pole (i.e. an infinite
value). In this case, SPECTM avoids division by zero by doing a 3
point moving average of the squared Fourier transform of the
coefficients whenever the maximum is greater than the minimum times
$10**10$. A warning message is printed when this is done.

SPECTM determines the number of frequencies (i.e. the length) for
<SPEC snam> by matching the length of <SPEC name> or <PDGM name> if
either exists. Otherwise the number of frequencies will be the
largest lag in the model.

Example:

If MOVE is an autoregressive model for BSMO, then

             SPECTM MOVE BSMO ARMO

computes <SPEC ARMO>, the spectrum corresponding to model MOVE, an
autoregressive spectrum estimate for BSMO.

4.1.5 SPECTN - Names for Cross-spectra

SPECTN overrides the assignment of names by SPECTX (p. 196).

Calling Sequences:

    (FTN) CALL SPECTN(N,'nam1nam2..')

    (ISX) SPECTN N nam1 nam2 ..

        N   = number of names
        nam1nam2.. = names for cross-spectrum quantities

Example:

        SPECTN 2 MOMI MOFR

assigns name MOMI to the first pair of names, MOFR to the second pair.

4.2 Transforming Spectra to/from Covariance Functions

4.2.1 SPACOV - Autospectrum to/from Autocovariance

SPACOV uses a Fast Fourier Transform (F.F.T.) to transform autospectra to autocovariance, or autocovariance to autospectra.

Calling Sequences:

    (FTN) CALL SPACOV (I,type,name)

    (ISX) SPACOV I type name

        I   = 1 for autospectrum to autocovariance
                     = -1 for autocovariance to autospectrum
    type,name = type and name of series to be transformed

When I=+1, the output is <ACOV name>. When I=-1, the output is <SPEC name>.

Examples:

        SPACOV 1 PDGM BSMO

computes <ACOV BSMO>, the autocovariance of BSMO.

        SPACOV -1 ACOV BSMO

computes <SPEC BSMO>. If <ACOV BSMO> has been windowed, this is an estimate of the spectrum of BSMO. If <ACOV BSMO> was unchanged from the first call, however, <SPEC BSMO> will be just the periodogram again, not a good estimate of the spectrum.

4.2.2 SPXCOV - Cross-spectrum to/from Cross-covariance

SPXCOV uses the Fast Fourier Transform (F.F.T.) to transform cross-spectra to cross-covariance, or cross-covariance to cross-spectra.

Calling Sequences:

>   (FTN) CALL SPXCOV(I,typr,namr,typi,nami,type,name,&ERR)

>   (ISX) SPXCOV I typr namr typi nami type name

>   I   = 1 for cross-spectrum to cross-covariance
>   = -1 for cross-covariance to cross-spectrum
>   typr,namr = type and name for real part of cross-
>   spectrum
>   typi,nami = type and name for imaginary part of cross-
>   spectrum
>   type,name = type and name for cross-covariance
>   &ERR   = error return

Examples:

>   SPXCOV 1 XPGR BSMO XPGI BSMO XCOV BSMO

computes the cross-covariance of BSMO from the cross-periodogram.

>   SPXCOV -1 XPGR BSMO XPGI BSMO XCOV BSMO

is the inverse of the first example, computing the cross-periodogram from the cross-covariance.

4.2.3 SPACOR - Autocovariance to Autocorrelation

SPACOR normalizes autocovariances to autocorrelations.

Calling Sequences:

>   (FTN) CALL SPACOR(type,name)

>   (ISX) SPACOR type name

>   type,name = type and name of series to be normalized
>   (usually ACOV)

SPACOR divides by the lag 0 term of <type name>, and renames the series <ACOR name>.

Example:

```
     SPACOR ACOV BSMO
```

standardizes <ACOV BSMO> to <ACOR BSMO>.

4.2.4 SPXCOR - Cross-covariance to Cross-correlation

SPXCOR normalizes cross-covariances to cross-correlations.

Calling Sequences:

        (FTN) CALL SPXCOR(type,name,typ1,nam1,typ2,nam2,&ERR)

        (ISX) SPXCOR type name typ1 nam1 typ2 nam2

                type   = type of series to be normalized (usually
                              XCOV)
                name   = name of series to be normalized
                typ1,typ2   = types of series containing normalizing
                              factors at lag 0. (usually ACOV)
                nam1,nam2   = names of series containing normalizing
                              factors, at lag 0.

SPXCOR divides <type name> by the square root of the product of the
lag 0 terms of <typ1 nam1> and <typ2 nam2>. Series <type name> is
renamed <XCOR name>.

Example:

        SPXCOR XCOV 0001 ACOV BSMO ACOV BSMI
        SPACOR ACOV BSMO
        SPACOR ACOV BSMI

normalizes <XCOV 0001> to be <XCOR 0001> by dividing by the square
root of the variances (i.e. the autocovariance lag 0 term) of BSMO
and BSMI. Note that <ACOV BSMO> and <ACOV BSMI> are normalized to
ACOR's after the cross-covariances are normalized.

4.3 Smoothing for Spectra

4.3.1 SPWIND - Computation of Windowed Spectra

SPWIND smooths spectra using either uniform weights (Daniell window)
or user-supplied weights.

Calling Sequences:

        (FTN) CALL SPWIND(type,name,ntyp,nnam)

        (ISX) SPWIND type name ntyp nnam

type,name = type and name of series to be smoothed
ntyp,nnam = type and name of smoothed series

SPWIND normally performs a uniformly weighted smoothing of length WINP determined by SPPARM (p. 194). If SPWINW (p. 201) has been called, SPWIND uses SPCONC (p. 202) to circularly convolve user-supplied weights with <type name>. SPWIND assumes that <type name> is a symmetric series (such as a periodogram), unless the first value is exactly zero (as in the imaginary part of a cross-periodogram), in which case <type name> is assumed antisymmetric.

Example:

        SPPARM WINP 11
        SPWIND PDGM BSMO SPEC BSMO

sets <SPEC BSMO> equal to an 11 point moving average of <PDGM BSMO>.

4.3.2 SPWINW - Specification of Window Weights

SPWINW directs SPWIND (p. 200) to employ user-supplied weights (in the frequency domain) instead of the Daniell window.

Calling Sequences:

    (FTN) CALL SPWINW(name,LEN)

    (ISX) SPWINW name LEN

        name = name of user-supplied WGTS block
              = OFF to return to Daniell window
        LEN   = length (used only when name = PRZN)

SPWINW directs SPWIND to look for a DYNCOR block <WGTS name> of frequency domain weights. This block must be supplied by the user unless Parzen weights are desired. When name is PRZN, modified Parzen weights with a frequency domain cutoff at (LEN-1) will be generated.

Examples:

        SPWINW XYZ

directs SPWIND to convolve its input with <WGTS XYZ>.

        SPWINW PRZN 20

directs SPWIND to convolve its input with <WGTS PRZN>, which SPWINW creates.

4.4 Convolution Using Fast Fourier Transform

The convolution of series X(t) and Y(t) is defined to be

$$Z(t) \quad = \quad \sum_{j} \quad X(t-j)*Y(j)$$

4.4.1 SPCONV - Non-circular Convolution

SPCONV convolves two time series assuming a non-periodic definition for both.

Calling Sequences:

     (FTN) CALL SPCONV(typ1,nam1,typ2,nam2,ntyp,nnam,&ERR)

     (ISX) SPCONV typ1 nam1 typ2 nam2 ntyp nnam

          typ1,typ2 = types of series to be convolved
          nam1,nam2 = names of series to be convolved
          ntyp,nnam = type and name of the convolution
          &ERR   = error return

SPCONV assumes that <typ1 nam1> and <typ2 nam2> are zero where not defined. The length of series <ntyp nnam> is the sum of the lengths of <typ1 nam1> and <typ2 nam2>, possibly plus a few zero observations to make the length acceptable to FFT.

Example:

          SPCONV DATA BSMO WGTS XYZ DATA ABC

sets   <DATA ABC>   equal   to the   convolution   of <DATA BSMO> and
<WGTS XYZ>.

4.4.2 SPCONC - Circular Convolution

SPCONC convolves two series assuming a period determined by the longer.

Calling Sequences:

     (FTN) CALL SPCONC(typ1,nam1,typ2,nam2,ntyp,nnam,&ERR)

     (ISX) SPCONC typ1 nam1 typ2 nam2 ntyp nnam

          typ1,typ2 = types of series to be convolved
          nam1,nam2 = names of series to be convolved
          ntyp,nnam = type and name of the convolution
          &ERR   = error return

SPCONC assumes that both <typ1 nam1> and <typ2 nam2> are periodic, with period determined by the longer. The length of series <ntyp nnam> will be the maximum of the lengths of <typ1 nam1> and <typ2 nam2>, possibly plus a few zero observations to make the length acceptable to FFT.

Example:

        SPCONC DATA ABC DATA XYZ DATA FGH

sets <DATA FGH> equal to the convolution of <DATA ABC> and <DATA XYZ>, assuming that both are periodic.

4.5 Fourier Transformation via Fast Fourier Transform

Fourier transformation for SPPAK is done by R. C. Singleton's algorithm FFT [5]. All transformations are done in place, destroying the input. Fourier transforms of real data are stored in packed form. When transforming N data points, the returned block contains the real part of the coefficient of $\exp(2\pi i \cdot k \cdot t/N)$ in position k+1 ($0 \leq k \leq N/2$), and the imaginary part in position N-k+1 ($0 < k < N/2$). When transforming complex data, the real and imaginary parts are returned in separate blocks. FFT requires that the number of data points be highly composite (i.e. have many factors) with no factors larger than 23. Failure to use SPFTI (p. 206) or SPFTIN (p. 206) to extend series to a suitable length may result in an error message from FFT.

The F.F.T. of X(t), $0 \leq t < N$, is

$$a(k) = \sum_{t=0}^{N-1} X(t) \cdot \exp(2\pi i \cdot k \cdot t/N) \qquad 0 \leq k \leq N$$

The inverse F.F.T. of a(k) is

$$X(t) = (1/N) \sum_{k=0}^{N} a(k) \cdot \exp(-2\pi i \cdot t \cdot k/N) \qquad 0 \leq t < N$$

4.5.1 SPRFT - F.F.T. of a Real Series

SPRFT computes the Fourier transform (or inverse Fourier transform) of a single real time series.

Calling Sequences:

        (FTN) CALL SPRFT(I,type,name,&ERR)

        (ISX) SPRFT I type name

            I   = 1 for Fourier transformation

                              = -1 for inverse Fourier transformation
              type   = type of series to be transformed
              name   = name of series to be transformed
              &ERR   = error return

SPRFT assumes that <type name> has a length acceptable to FFT. SPRFT
uses Singleton's REALTR to speed the calculation.

Examples:

              SPRFT 1 DATA BSMO

replaces <DATA BSMO> by its Fourier transform.

              SPRFT -1 DATA XYZ

replaces <DATA XYZ> by its inverse Fourier transform.

              SPRFT 1 DATA ABCD
              SPRFT -1 DATA ABCD

leaves <DATA ABCD> unchanged except for roundoff error.

4.5.2 SPRFT2 - F.F.T. of Two Real Series

SPRFT2 computes the Fourier transform (or inverse Fourier transform)
of two real time series simultaneously.

Calling Sequences:

    (FTN) CALL SPRFT2(I,typ1,nam1,typ2,nam2,&ERR)

    (ISX) SPRFT2 I typ1 nam1 typ2 nam2

              I   = 1 for Fourier transformation
                         = -1 for inverse Fourier transformation
              typ1,typ2 = types of series to be transformed
              nam1,nam2 = names of series to be transformed
              &ERR   = error return

SPRFT2 assumes that both <typ1 nam1> and <typ2 nam2> have the same
length, and that length is acceptable to FFT.   SPRFT2 speeds the
calculation   by   doing   a   single   complex   transformation, then
unscrambling the two real results.

Example:

              SPRFT2 1 DATA ABCD DATA WXYZ

replaces <DATA ABCD> and <DATA WXYZ> by their respective Fourier
transforms.

4.5.3 SPSFT - F.F.T. of a Real Symmetric Series

SPSFT computes the Fourier transform (or inverse Fourier transform) of a single real symmetric time series.

<u>Calling Sequences:</u>

        (FTN) CALL SPSFT(I,type,name,&ERR)

        (ISX) SPSFT I type name

                I   = 1 for Fourier transform
                             = -1 for inverse Fourier transform
                type,name = type and name of series to be transformed
                &ERR   = error return

SPSFT assumes that <type name> is half of a symmetric series (such as ACOR or SPEC, for example), and that after extension by reflection, the length is acceptable to FFT.

<u>Example:</u>

            SPSFT -1 ACOR BSMO

computes the inverse Fourier transform of <ACOR BSMO>. Note that this computation is done by SPACOV (p. 198), which also sets the time control block for ACOV.

4.5.4 SPCFT - F.F.T. of a Complex Series

SPCFT computes the Fourier transform (or inverse Fourier transform) of a complex time series.

<u>Calling Sequences:</u>

        (FTN) CALL SPCFT(I,typr,namr,typi,nami,&ERR)

        (ISX) SPCFT I typr namr typi nami

                I   = 1 for Fourier transformation
                             = -1 for inverse Fourier transformation
                typr,namr = type and name for real part of input/output
                typi,nami = type and name for imaginary part of in
                             input/output
                &ERR   = error return

SPCFT assumes that <typr namr> and <typi nami> have the same length, and that length is acceptable to FFT.

<u>Example:</u>

            SPCFT 1 XPGR 0001 XPGI 0001

replaces <XPGR 0001> and <XPGI 0001> by the real and imaginary parts of the Fourier transform of

<XPGR 0001>   +   i*<XPGI 0001>

4.5.5 SPFTI - Initialization for FFT, by Fraction

SPFTI extends a series with zeroes to a length acceptable to FFT, adding at least a specified fraction of the original length.

Calling Sequences:

    (FTN) CALL SPFTI(type,name,PEXT,&ERR)

    (ISX) SPFTI type name PEXT

        type,name = type and name of series to be extended
        PEXT   = minimal fraction to be extended
        &ERR   = error return

SPFTI extends <type name> to at least (1+PEXT) times the original length if PEXT ≤ 1. If PEXT > 1, it is assumed to be in percent, and divided by 100 before use.

Example:

        SPFTI DATA BSMO .3

extends <DATA BSMO> by at least 30% with zeroes, as does

        SPFTI DATA BSMO 30.

4.5.6 SPFTIN - Initialization for FFT, by Number

SPFTIN is the same as SPFTI (p. 206), except that the minimal extension is specified by number, not a fraction of the total length.

Calling Sequences:

    (FTN) CALL SPFTIN(type,name,N,&ERR)

    (ISX) SPFTIN type name N

        type,name = type and name of series to be extended
        N   = minimal length of extension
        &ERR   = error return

Example:

        SPFTIN DATA BSMO 100

extends <DATA BSMO> by at least 100 zeroes, to a length acceptable to FFT.

4.5.7 SPFTSQ - Square of Fourier Transform

SPFTSQ computes the absolute value squared of a Fourier transform of real data, scaled by the reciprocal of the length of the transform. That is, SPFTSQ computes the periodogram from the Fourier transform.

Calling Sequences:

    (FTN) CALL SPFTSQ(type,name,&ERR)

    (ISX) SPFTSQ type name

        type,name = type and name of input/output
        &ERR   = error return

SPFTSQ assumes that the input is the Fourier transform of real data, in packed form (see Sec. 4.5, p. 203). The computation is done in place, destroying the transform. Since for real data the periodogram is symmetric, only the first N/2+1 terms are saved; that is,

$$\sum_{t=0}^{N-1} X(t)*\exp(2\pi i*t*k/N) \qquad 0 \le k \le N-1$$

becomes

$$(1/N) \left| \sum_{t=0}^{N-1} X(t)*\exp(2\pi i*t*k/N) \right|^2 \qquad 0 \le k \le N/2$$

Example:

        SPFTSQ FTFM BSMO

squares the Fourier transform of BSMO, which should be renamed <PDGM BSMO>.

4.5.8 SPFTMU - Multiplication of Fourier Transforms

SPFTMU multiplies the Fourier transform of one real time series by the complex conjugate of a second, and scales the result by the reciprocal of the length of the transforms. That is, SPFTMU computes the cross-periodogram from Fourier transforms.

Calling Sequences:

    (FTN) CALL SPFTMU(typ1,nam1,typ2,nam2,&ERR)

        (ISX) SPFTMU typ1 nam1 typ2 nam2

            typ1,nam1 = type and name of first Fourier transform
            typ2,nam2 = type and name of second Fourier transform
                         (to be conjugated)
            &ERR   = error return

SPFTMU assumes that the inputs are Fourier transforms of real data, in packed form (see Sec. 4.5, p. 203). The computation is done in place, destroying the Fourier transforms. The real part of the product is returned in <typ1 nam1>, and the imaginary part in <typ2 nam2>. Since the real and imaginary parts are symmetric and antisymmetric respectively, the first N/2+1 terms are saved, as was done with SPFTSQ (p. 207).

Example:

        SPFTMU FTFM BSMI FTFM BSMO

leaves the real part of the cross-periodogram of BSMI and BSMO in <FTFM BSMI>, and the imaginary part in <FTFM BSMO>.

4.5.9 SPCONJ - Complex Conjugate of a Fourier Transform

SPCONJ replaces the Fourier transform of a real series by its complex conjugate.

Calling Sequences:

    (FTN) CALL SPCONJ(type,name)

    (ISX) SPCONJ type name

        type,name = type and name of series to be conjugated

SPCONJ assumes that the input is the Fourier transform of real data in packed form (see Sec. 4.5, p. 203). The signs of the last N/2-1 terms are changed in place.

Example:

        SPCONJ FTFM BSMO

replaces <FTFM BSMO> by its complex conjugate.

4.6 Miscellaneous Computations on Spectra

The subroutines for computing cross-amplitude spectra, gain, phase, and coherence are used most efficiently through SPECTX (p. 196). However, they may be called directly.

4.6.1 SPXAMP - Cross-amplitude Spectrum

SPXAMP computes the cross-amplitude spectrum as the absolute value of the cross-spectrum.

<u>Calling Sequences:</u>

    (FTN) CALL SPXAMP(typ1,nam1,typ2,nam2,ntyp,nnam,&ERR)

    (ISX) SPXAMP typ1 nam1 typ2 nam2 ntyp nnam

typ1,nam1	= type and name of real part of cross-spectrum
typ2,nam2	= type and name of imaginary part of cross-spectrum
ntyp	= type for cross-amplitude spectrum (usually XAMP)
nnam	= name for the cross-amplitude spectrum
&ERR	= error return

<u>Example:</u>

    SPXAMP XSPR 0001 XSPI 0001 XAMP 0001

computes the cross-amplitude spectrum <XAMP 0001> from the real and imaginary parts of the cross-spectrum of BSMO and BSMI in Ex. 4.1.3 (p. 197).

4.6.2 SPGAIN - Gain

SPGAIN computes gain as the ratio of the cross-amplitude spectrum (see Sec. 4.6.1, p. 209) and the auto-spectrum.

<u>Calling Sequences:</u>

    (FTN) CALL SPGAIN(typ1,nam1,typ2,nam2,ntyp,nnam,&ERR)

    (ISX) SPGAIN typ1 nam1 typ2 nam2 ntyp nnam

typ1,nam1	= type and name of cross-amplitude spectrum
typ2,nam2	= type and name of auto-spectrum
ntyp	= type for output (usually GAIN)
nnam	= name for output
&ERR	= error return

<u>Example:</u>

    SPGAIN XAMP 0001 SPEC BSMO GAIN 0001

computes <GAIN 0001> as the ratio of <XAMP 0001> and <SPEC BSMO>. In Ex. 4.1.3 (p. 197), this is the gain of the linear filter relating BSMO and BSMI.

4.6.3 SPPHAS - Phase

SPPHAS computes the phase from the cross-spectrum. The phase is returned in units of radians/2π.

Calling Sequences:

    (FTN) CALL SPPHAS(typ1,nam1,typ2,nam2,ntyp,nnam,&ERR)

    (ISX) SPPHAS typ1 nam1 typ2 nam2 ntyp nnam

        typ1,nam1 = type and name of real part of cross-
                     spectrum
        typ2,nam2 = type and name of imaginary part of cross-
                     spectrum
        ntyp   = type of output (usually PHAS)
        nnam   = name of output
        &ERR   = error return

Since phase, in the units returned, is only determined up to an additive integer, integers are added at each frequency to make the phase as smooth as possible.

Example:

        SPPHAS XSPR 0001 XSPI 0001 PHAS 0001

computes the phase <PHAS 0001> from the real and imaginary parts of the cross-spectrum of BSMI and BSMO in Ex. 4.1.3.

4.6.4 SPCOHE - Coherence

SPCOHE computes the coherence as the ratio of the cross-amplitude spectrum to the square root of the product of auto-spectra.

Calling Sequences:

    (FTN) CALL SPCOHE(typ1,nam1,typ2,nam2,typ3,nam3,&ERR)

    (ISX) SPCOHE typ1 nam1 typ2 nam2 typ3 nam3

        typ1,nam1 = type and name for first auto-spectrum
        typ2,nam2 = type and name for second auto-spectrum
        typ3,nam3 = type and name for cross-amplitude spectrum
        &ERR   = error return

SPCOHE returns the coherence in <typ3 nam3>, destroying the cross-amplitude spectrum. It is appropriate to change typ3 to COHE.

Example:

        SPCOHE SPEC BSMO SPEC BSMI XAMP 0001

DYNNAM XAMP 0001 COHE 0001

replaces <XAMP 0001> (the cross-amplitude spectrum in Ex. 4.1.3) with
the coherence of BSMO and BSMI, <COHE 0001>.

4.6.5 SPTFN - Transfer Function

SPTFN computes the transfer function of a linear model relating two
time series. It also computes the frequency response function as the
square root of the ratio of the cross-amplitude spectrum and the
auto-spectrum for comparison.

Calling Sequences:

    (FTN) CALL SPTFN(mdln,depv,name)

    (ISX) SPTFN mdln depv name

        mdln = model name
        depv = dependent variable in model mdln
        name = name of cross-amplitude spectrum, auto-spectrum
              and returned transfer function

If a linear model for Y(t) in terms of X(t) is

$$Y(t) = \sum_{j=1}^{M} a(j)*Y(t-j) \quad + \quad \sum_{j=0}^{N} b(j)*X(t-j) \quad + e(t)$$

SPTFN computes the parametric transfer function in <TFNP name> as

$$Z(k) = \left| \frac{\sum_{j=0}^{N} b(j)*exp(2\pi i*k*j/NF)}{1 - \sum_{j=1}^{M} a(j)*exp(2\pi i*k*j/NF)} \right| \quad 0 \le k \le NF$$

where NF is the number of frequencies in <XAMP name>.

The non-parametric estimate of the transfer function is stored in
<TFNN name>. SPTFN assumes that <XAMP name> and <SPEC name> are in
core and that model mdln involves only variables depv and name.

Example:

    SPTFN AR BSMO BSMI

computes the non-parametric transfer function of BSMO and BSMI, and
stores it in <TFNN BSMI>. The parametric transfer function
determined by model AR is computed and stored in <TFNP BSMI>.

4.6.6 SPRVBD - Residual Variance Bound

SPRVBD computes a nonparametric estimate of a lower bound on the residual variance that can be obtained by regressing one series on another.

Calling Sequences:

     (FTN) CALL SPRVBD(nams,namc,BD)

     (ISX) SPRVBD nams namc

          nams = name of SPEC block (independent variable)
          namc = name of COHE block (coherence between
                  independent and dependent variable)
          BD   = variance bound (real variable, returned in
                  FORTRAN)

In ISX, the value of the variance bound is returned as variable $XXX and as the first real word of the ISX "X" array (see Ch. 4, Sec. 2.3, p. 60). SPRVBD computes

$$(1/N) \sum_{j=1}^{N} (1 - COHE^2(j)) * SPEC(j)$$

This quantity estimates the variance of the residuals of the best linear model for the dependent variable in terms of <DATA nams>.

Example:

          SPRVBD BSMO 0001
          / RESIDUAL VARIANCE BOUND = $XXX

prints an estimate of the residual variance of <DATA BSMI> regressed on <DATA BSMO>, in Ex. 4.1.3.

5. SAMPLE PROGRAMS

A simple program for two types of univariate spectrum analysis was shown in Section 1. This section includes programs for bivariate spectrum estimation and Wiener filtering for forecasting. The complete input stream for running the programs on an IBM VS/370 system is shown, along with the resulting output. See Chapter 15, Section 2 (p. 391) for information on running the ISX program under VS.

5.1 Example 1

Job Input Stream:

```
//jobname JOB (acctg info),parameters
// EXEC ISX
//GO.FT10F001 DD *
.DAT BSMI 3 I(3I5)
 1955    1    12
DATA BSMI 211 R(6F10.0)
   609659.    584307.    637432.    610417.    642036.    773145.
   693415.    766089.    837552.    742869.    739833.    706529.

   ...
  1348858.
.DAT BSMO 3 I(3I5)
 1955    1    12
DATA BSMO 238 R(6F10.0)
   483691.    470184.    521791.    530970.    562872.    698156.
   586854.    658930.    671317.    599174.    578424.    514115.

   ...
  1100036.    999462.   1106675.   1231703.   1387781.   1450519.
  1465293.   1503307.   1389156.   1298208.
//GO.SYSIN DD *
DYNINP 10
OPTION * PAGSIZ 65
PPLOTP LINES 24
SPPARM LIST
SPECTN 1 IO
SPECTX 2 1 DATA BSMI DATA BSMO 1960 1 1965 12
TSFN1 LSPE BSMI LOG SPEC BSMI
TSFN1 LSPE BSMO LOG SPEC BSMO
TSPLT 1 LSPE BSMI 1 1 999 1
TSPLT 1 LSPE BSMO 1 1 999 1
TSPLT 1 COHE IO 1 1 999 1
TSPLT 1 PHAS IO 1 1 999 1
```

Description:

DYNINP (p. 270) reads the series into core. OPTION (p. 285) is called to set the page size for output to 65 columns. PPLOTP (p. 287) limits plots to 24 lines. SPPARM (p. 194) is called to print the default parameter settings. SPECTN (p. 198) initializes the name of the cross-quantities to IO. SPECTX (p. 196) computes spectra, phase and coherence for <DATA BSMI> and <DATA BSMO>. Logarithms of spectra (LSPE) are computed by TSFN1 (p. 153). TSPLT (p. 150) plots the various results.

Output:

STATLIB ISX   12/01/78   07/09/80   PAGE 1

SPPARM: %EXT=.2, %TAP=.1, WINP=3, OPTIONS:
          MEAN ON
          TRND
          TAPR ON
          NORM ON
          FTFM
          PDGM
          SPEC ON
          ACOR
          GAIN
          XPGM
          XSPE
          PHAS ON
          XAMP
          COHE ON
          XCOR

SPECTX: JAN 1960-DEC 1965
          TSDETR: DATA BSMI, MEAN=860970.2
          TSDETR: DATA BSMO, MEAN=762380
          IO = DATA BSMO, DATA BSMI
          SPDANL: DANIELL WINDOW,3-PT MA

TSFN1: LSPE BSMI = LOG(SPEC BSMI), 1-45

TSFN1: LSPE BSMO = LOG(SPEC BSMO), 1-45

TSPAK / TSPLT   07/09/80   PAGE 2

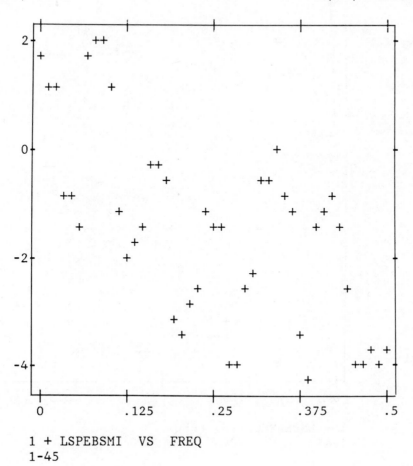

1 + LSPEBSMI   VS   FREQ
1-45

TSPAK / TSPLT   07/09/80 PAGE 3

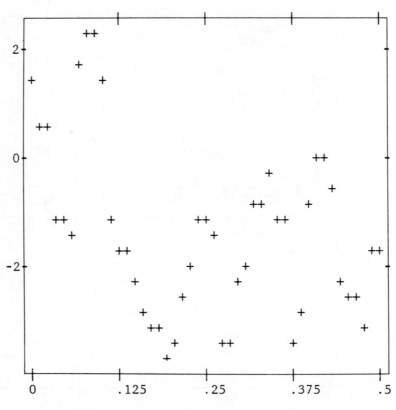

1 + LSPEBSMO   VS   FREQ
1-45

TSPAK / TSPLT   07/09/80   PAGE 4

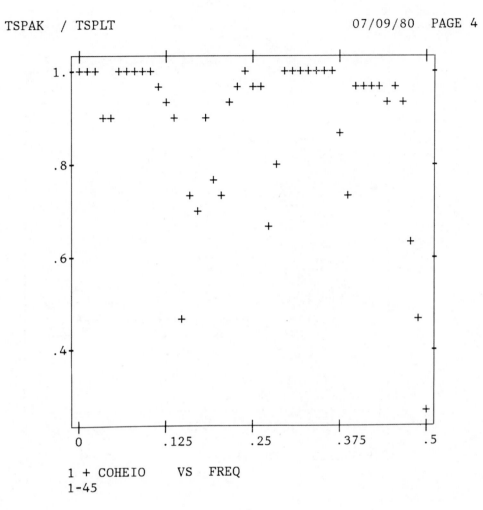

1 + COHEIO   VS   FREQ
1-45

TSPAK   / TSPLT   07/09/80   PAGE 5

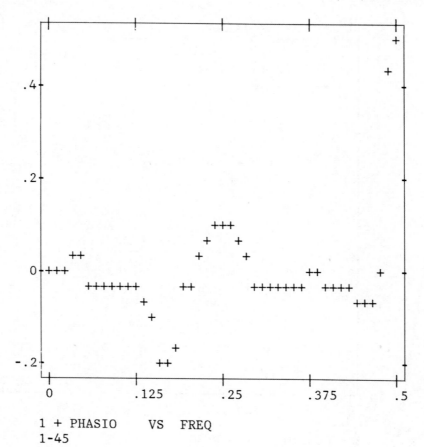

1 + PHASIO   VS   FREQ
1-45

5.2 Example 2

Job Input Stream:

```
//jobname JOB (acctg info),parameters
//   EXEC ISX
//GO.FT10F001 DD *
.DAT BSMI 3 I(3I5)
 1955     1   12
DATA BSMI 211 R(6F10.0)
    609659.    584307.    637432.    610417.    642036.    773145.
    693415.    766089.    837552.    742869.    739833.    706529.
    . . .
   1348858.
.DAT BSMO 3 I(3I5)
 1955     1   12
DATA BSMO 238 R(6F10.0)
    483691.    470184.    521791.    530970.    562872.    698156.
    586854.    658930.    671317.    599174.    578424.    514115.
    . . .
   1100036.    999462.   1106675.   1231703.   1387781.   1450519.
   1465293.   1503307.   1389156.   1298208.
//GO.SYSIN DD *
DYNINP 10
OPTION * PAGSIZ 65
PPLOTP LINES 24
SPDIF BSMO 2 1 12
SPREG 1 DATA BSMO AR 1960 1 1969 12
TSPRDN AR 1970 1 1971 12
TSARFS AR 1970 1 1971 12
TSCLIM PRDN BSMO ARFS 1.0
TSEXT DATA BSMO 1960 1 1969 12 DATA BSMO
PPLOTP CHAR 4 +*--
TSPLT 4 DATA BSMO PRDN BSMO UCL BSMO LCL BSMO 1968 1 1971 12
```

Description:

DYNINP (p. 270) reads the series into core, and OPTION (p. 285) sets
the page size and plotting format. SPDIF (p. 191) specifies that the
model for BSMO will contain two differencing operations, at lags 1
and 12.   SPREG (p. 189) constructs model AR, and prints diagnostic
statistics. TSPRDN (p. 164), TSARFS (p. 166), and TSCLIM (p. 166)
are called from TSPAK to generate forecasts and confidence limits.
TSEXT extracts <DATA BSMO> into itself, shortening the series to make
the following plot neater. TSPLT (p. 150) plots the results.

Output:

```
STATLIB ISX  12/01/78                          07/09/80  PAGE 1

SPDIF:  DIFFERENCING FOR BSMO AT 2 LAGS
```

```
SPREG:   MODEL=AR, JAN 1960-DEC 1969
         DEPV = DATA BSMO
         NO MEAN ADJUSTMENT
         VARIANCE AFTER DIFFERENCING = 2.4649D9
         WIENER'S ESTIMATE OF RESIDUAL VARIANCE = 9.3351D8
         RESIDUAL MEAN SQUARE = 1.0158D9
         VARIANCE TEST: COMPARE .4052313 WITH STANDARD NORMAL
         KOLMOGOROV-SMIRNOV TEST ON RESIDUALS
         MAXIMUM DEVIATION OF -.799463 AT FREQUENCY .2013889

TSPRDN:  MODEL=AR, TYPE=DATA/PRDN/RSID, JAN 1970-DEC 1971
         DEPV=BSMO

TSARFS:  MODEL=AR, VBL=BSMO, JAN 1970-DEC 1971

TSCLIM:  BSMO, UCL/LCL = PRDN +/- 1 * ARFS


TSPAK  / TSPLT                                    07/09/80  PAGE 2
```

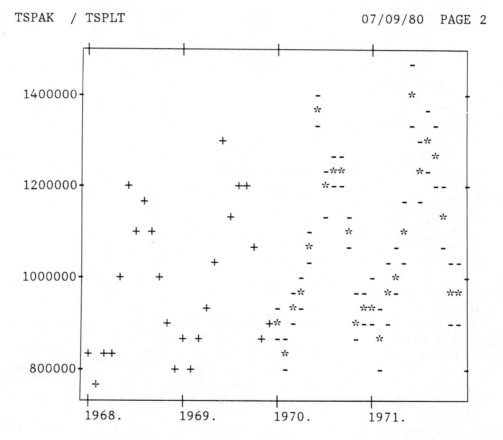

```
1 + DATABSMO  2 * PRDNBSMO  3 - UCL BSMO  4 - LCL BSMO
VS   TIME
JAN 1968-DEC 1971
```

6. SUBJECT INDEX

7. GLOSSARY OF SUBROUTINE CALLS (ISX)

TABLE   225

CHAPTER 8

TABLE - TABLE MANIPULATIONS AND ANALYSIS

1. INTRODUCTION

TABLE is a system of FORTRAN subroutines for the management and analysis of multiway tables of data. Routines are provided for many basic data handling operations, including transposition, extraction, concatenation, projection, and simple arithmetic. Analysis of variance software and various interfaces with STATLIB analysis and display routines are important additional features.

TABLE routines may be called directly in FORTRAN, or in ISX (Ch. 4), which accepts free format input without FORTRAN punctuation. The following simple ISX program demonstrates the programming style of TABLE.

```
DYNINP 5
TABDIM DATA ABCD 3 MON YEAR SER 12 5 2
TABPRT DATA ABCD 2 YEAR MON
TABAOV DATA ABCD 2 MON YEAR M/YR EFCT
TABAVP ABCD
TABPRT RSID ABCD 2 YEAR MON
TABPRT M/YR EFCT 2 YEAR MON
```

The call to DYNINP (p. 270) reads data blocks from FORTRAN unit 5 into core. TABDIM (p. 231) dimensions block <DATA ABCD> as MON (month) by YEAR (year) by SER (series); these dimensions have lengths 12, 5, and 2 respectively. TABPRT (p. 241) generates a properly labeled month by year printout for every series. Next, an analysis of variance of <DATA ABCD> is performed: month-year interactions are computed and stored in a table identified as <M/YR EFCT>. TABAVP (p. 239) prints out the standard sum of squares breakdown. TABPRT then produces month by year printouts, successively, of the residuals <RSID ABCD> and the effects <M/YR EFCT>.

Tables are managed by DYNCOR, the STATLIB dynamic in-core data management system (Ch. 9). They may be read in through DYNCOR input routines, or created directly in the user program itself. Each table is identified by DYNCOR through two four-character names, usually supplied as the first arguments to TABLE routines. Dimensions are identified by their own four-character names, and values along these dimensions (called "categories") have names of eight characters. Operations are specified by stringing out these identifiers (table, dimension, and category) down to the appropriate level; e.g.,

```
TABREG DATA ABCD SER SER....2 1 SER....1
```

regresses the category of dimension SER identified as SER....2

against SER....1;

     TABPRT DATA ABCD 2 YEAR MON

prints a table along the month and year dimensions.

Section 2 is a brief description of TABLE's conventions and procedures. Section 3 describes table storage methods. Calling sequences are given in Section 4, followed by two sample programs in Section 5. Finally, Section 6 contains a glossary and Section 7 a subject index.

2. CONVENTIONS AND NOTATION

2.1 Generic Names

The terms "type" and "name" are used freely throughout the text; consistent with other high-level package chapters, they are generic for the first and second identifiers of DYNCOR blocks. Also used here are "dimi" for the name of the ith dimension and "catk" for the name of the kth category within given dimension. Category names may be up to eight characters long; the others, up to four.

2.2 Messages, Errors, and Printing Options

STATLIB-wide message and error conventions are described in the Part II Introduction (p. 58). Refer there (and to the Section 5 examples, p. 244) for further information on controlling the printing of messages and decisions on whether and when errors should terminate execution. The following conventions apply specifically to TABLE.

Error conditions result in a printed message by TABERR. The most common errors arise in misspelling or leaving out the name of a qualifier. Another frequent error results from insufficient core storage being available to create or enlarge a given block. A message from DYNCOR identifies the block and the number of words requested.

Each TABLE subroutine generates (through TABMSG) a one- or two-line message summarizing what it has done. This helps to make program output self documenting in that the flow of execution can be determined from the output alone.

OPTION (p. 285) may be used to control TABLE printing, specifying TAB* for all routines, TABMSG for messages, TABERR for error messages, or the subroutine name for routines that generate printed output.

TABLE   227

2.3 Calling Sequence Notation

Calling sequences follow the STATLIB-wide conventions described in the Part II Introduction (p. 56). The following apply specifically to TABLE.

a. Table and dimension names may be up to four characters long, category names up to eight. Since generic category names have four characters, not eight, calling sequence notation convention (a) is violated; this is done here for compactness.

b. The constraint on dimension and category names is that they be identifiable; i.e., dimension names within a table and category names within a dimension should be unique.

3. TABLE STORAGE

Each table is stored as a DYNCOR block. It has two 4-character
identifiers, type and name, through which the user is able to
reference the block directly. For example,

```
DIMENSION X(1,1)
CALL DYNOLD('DATA','ABCD',2,LEN,X,JX)
```

permits direct reference to an existing block with type DATA, name
ABCD, as

$$X(JX,1), X(JX,2), ..., X(JX,LEN).$$

See DYNOLD documentation (p. 260) for details.

Associated with a table are two control blocks of dimension
information (Secs. 3.2-3, below). These are kept up-to-date as
tables are changed, so that output from any one TABLE routine may be
input, without modification, to another. Table control blocks are
created by calling TABDIM (p. 231) with information on the ordering
of dimensions, dimension sizes, dimension names, and the names of
categories within each dimension.

3.1 Data Layout

The layout of a table is best understood by analogy with the FORTRAN
DIMENSION statement. The coding

```
DIMENSION X(12,5,2)
```

causes 120 contiguous words of core storage to be reserved; in
ascending order, these may be referred to as

$$X(1,1,1), X(2,1,1), ..., X(12,1,1), X(1,2,1), ...,$$
$$X(12,5,1), X(1,1,2), ..., X(12,5,2) .$$

A corresponding TABLE dimension statement is

```
TABDIM DATA ABCD 3 MON YEAR SER 12 5 2
```

This would cause other TABLE routines to regard the 120 contiguous
words of storage occupied by <DATA ABCD> as a similarly stored 12 by
5 by 2 table. In addition, it assigns the names MON, YEAR, SER to
those respective dimensions. So, the statement

```
TABPRT DATA ABCD 2 YEAR MON
```

would generate a table consisting of two 12 by 5 sections, the first
(or second) of which would contain the first (or second) sixty words
of table <DATA ABCD>.

TABLE   229

3.2 Dimension Information Control Block

TABDIM (p. 231) creates a DYNCOR control block containing dimension information for a given table. Included are the ordering of dimensions, dimension names, dimension sizes, and certain results of computation for use by other TABLE routines. The naming convention is that this block has the same second identifier (name) as the table, but a first identifier (type) consisting of ":" followed by the first 3 characters of the table's type.

Information is stored in an 8 by NDIM layout; the ith column holds the following:

Row#	Contents
1	ith dimension name
2-4	work space used by TABLE routines
5	product of 1, ..., (i-1)th dimension lengths
6	ith dimension length
7	product of i+1, ..., NDIMth dimension lengths
8	location of category names in category control block (Sec. 3.3, below)

Thus,

        TABDIM DATA ABCD 3 MON YEAR SER 12 5 2

results in a block <:DAT ABCD> with contents

MON	*	*	*	1	12	10	1
YEAR	*	*	*	12	5	2	13
SER	*	*	*	60	2	1	18

3.3 Category Names Within Dimensions

Category names may be up to eight characters long, contained in a control block with the same second identifier (name) as the table, but with a first identifier (type) consisting of ";" followed by the first 3 characters of the table's type. Category names are ordered sequentially by dimension. Unless otherwise specified (Sec. 4.1, p. 231), those of the ith dimension are defaulted to

        dimi...1, dimi...2, ..., dimi...n .

The above call to TABDIM would have generated the block <;DAT ABCD> with contents

MON....1	MON....2	MON....3	MON....4	MON....5	MON....6
MON....7	MON....8	MON....9	MON...10	MON...11	MON...12
YEAR...1	YEAR...2	YEAR...3	YEAR...4	YEAR...5	SER....1
SER....2	.				

Note that through these naming conventions it is easy to manipulate control blocks along with the table itself. The statement

        DYNOUT .... ABCD 7 0

uses DYNCOR output routine DYNOUT (p. 272) to dump all blocks with
name ABCD onto unit 7; a subsequent program that retrieves them all
would not have to redimension <DATA ABCD>.

TABLE   231

4. TABLE SUBROUTINES

4.1 Dimension Information

4.1.1 TABDIM - Dimensioning

Calling Sequences:

        (FTN) CALL TABDIM(type,name,NDIM,'dim1dim2..',NCAT)

        (ISX) TABDIM type name NDIM dim1 dim2 .. NCAT

                type,name = table identifiers
                NDIM   = number of dimensions
                dim1dim2.. = dimension names
                NCAT   = number of categories array, or zero

DYNCOR block <type name> is described as a table having NDIM dimensions dim1, dim2, etc., with NCAT(1) categories in dim1, NCAT(2) in dim2, etc. If NCAT(1) is 0, the numbers of categories within each dimension are taken as the lengths of DYNCOR blocks <DIM dim1>, <DIM dim2>, etc., with category names as their contents; otherwise, NCAT(1) through NCAT(NDIM) are taken as the numbers of categories within their respective dimensions, and default category names

        dimi...1, dimi...2, .. ,

are assigned to dimension dimi. In that case, DYNCOR blocks <DIM dim1>, <DIM dim2>, etc., are created containing these names.

Examples:

                DYNPUT DIM MON 2 0 12 JAN FEB MAR ... DEC
                DYNPUT DIM YEAR 2 0 5 1965 1966 ... 1969
                DYNPUT DIM SER 2 0 2 BSMI BSMO
                TABDIM DATA ABCD 3 MON YEAR SER 0

creates three blocks <DIM MON>, <DIM YEAR>, <DIM SER> using DYNPUT (p. 260), then dimensions <DATA ABCD> as a 3-dimensional MON by YEAR by SER table; dimension lengths and category names for the table are taken from these newly-created DYNCOR blocks.

                TABDIM DATA ABCD 3 MON YEAR SER 12 5 2

dimensions <DATA ABCD> also MON by YEAR by SER with the same dimension lengths, but category names are

        MON....1, MON....2, ..., MON....5, ..., MON...12,
        YEAR...1, YEAR...2, ..., YEAR...5,
        SER....1, SER....2 .

New DYNCOR blocks <DIM MON>, <DIM YEAR>, <DIM SER> containing these names are also generated.

4.2 Table Manipulation

4.2.1 TABCON - Concatenation

Calling Sequences:

>   (FTN) CALL TABCON(typ1,nam1,dimn,typ2,nam2)
>
>   (ISX) TABCON typ1 nam1 dimn typ2 nam2
>
>   typ1,nam1 = first table identifiers
>   dimn   = dimension name
>   typ2,nam2 = second table identifiers

Table <typ2 nam2> is concatenated (joined) to table <typ1 nam1> on dimension dimn. The operation is permitted only if the two tables have all dimensions (except possibly dimn) identical, as would be the case after extraction (p. 233) or applying functions over a dimension (p. 238).

Example:

>   TABCON DATA ABCD MON DATA EFGH

concatenates <DATA EFGH> to <DATA ABCD> on the MON dimension. If, for example, <DATA EFGH> were MON by YEAR by SER, with dimension lengths 1, 5, and 2, <DATA ABCD> would now be 13 by 5 by 2.

4.2.2 TABENL - Enlarging

Calling Sequences:

>   (FTN) CALL TABENL(type,name,dimn,NCAT,'cat1cat2..')
>
>   (ISX) TABENL type name dimn NCAT cat1 cat2 ..
>
>   type,name = table identifiers
>   dimn   = dimension name
>   NCAT   = number of categories
>   cat1cat2.. = category names

Table <type name> is enlarged on an existing dimension dimn by the NCAT listed categories cat1, cat2, etc.

Example:

>   TABENL DATA ABCD SER 2 RESIDUAL ESTIMATE

TABLE   233

enlarges the SER dimension by two categories - RESIDUAL and ESTIMATE.

4.2.3 TABEXT - Extraction

Calling Sequences:

(FTN) CALL TABEXT(type,name,dimn,NCAT,'cat1cat2..',ntyp,nnam)

(ISX) TABEXT type name dimn NCAT cat1 cat2 .. ntyp nnam

```
type,name   = old table identifiers
dimn        = dimension name
|NCAT|      = number of categories
cat1cat2..  = category names
ntyp,nnam   = new table identifiers
```

The NCAT listed categories cat1, cat2, etc., of dimension dimn are extracted from table <type name>. Results are stored in new table <ntyp nnam>. If NCAT>0, the categories will be extracted in the order specified; if catk is listed, but does not appear in <type name>, space for that category is reserved and zeroed out. If NCAT<0, all categories except those listed are extracted.

Example:

TABEXT DATA ABCD YEAR 1 YEAR...5 DATA EFGH

extracts from <DATA ABCD> a table consisting of category YEAR...5 of YEAR. The resulting table, <DATA EFGH>, is also MON by YEAR by SER, but YEAR has dimension length 1.

4.2.4 TABPRJ - Projection

Calling Sequences:

(FTN) CALL TABPRJ(type,name,fun,NDIM,'dim1dim2..',ntyp,nnam)

(ISX) TABPRJ type name fun NDIM dim1 dim2 .. ntyp nnam

```
type,name   = old table identifiers
fun         = projection function - AVG,SUM,MIN,or MAX
|NDIM|      = number of dimensions
dim1dim2..  = dimension names
ntyp,nnam   = new table identifiers
```

Table <type name> is projected into a lower dimensional table <ntyp nnam> according to function fun. If NDIM>0, projection is onto the dimensions listed; i.e., <ntyp nnam> will have NDIM dimensions dim1, dim2, etc. If NDIM<0, projection is over those dimensions; i.e., <ntyp nnam> will have all the dimensions of <type name> except dim1, dim2, etc.

Example:

TABPRJ DATA ABCD SUM 1 SER DATA EFGH
TABPRJ DATA ABCD SUM -2 MON YEAR DATA EFGH

both project <DATA ABCD> by summation onto the SER dimension
(equivalently, over the MON and YEAR dimensions). Results are stored
in <DATA EFGH>, a one-dimensional table.

4.2.5 TABPRP - Propagation

Calling Sequences:

(FTN) CALL TABPRP(type,name,NDIM,'dim1dim2..',NCAT)

(ISX) TABPRP type name NDIM dim1 dim2 .. NCAT

```
type,name  = table identifiers
NDIM       = number of dimensions
dim1dim2.. = dimension names
NCAT       = number of categories array, or zero
```

Table <type name> is propagated (reproduced) over NDIM additional
dimensions dim1, dim2, etc. Information on the numbers of categories
per dimension is contained in vector NCAT; conventions are identical
to those established for TABDIM (p. 231). The new table has dim1,
dim2, etc., appearing at the end of the ordered list of dimensions.

Example:

TABPRP DATA ABCD 1 DIMN 8

adds onto <DATA ABCD> one new dimension DIMN. It is of length 8,
with category names

DIMN...1, DIMN...2, .., DIMN...8.

<DATA ABCD> is thus MON by YEAR by SER by DIMN. In addition, DYNCOR
block <DIM DIMN> containing these names is created.

4.2.6 TABTRN - Transposition

Calling Sequences:

(FTN) CALL TABTRN(type,name,NDIM,'dim1dim2..')

(ISX) TABTRN type name NDIM dim1 dim2 ..

```
type,name  = table identifiers
NDIM       = number of dimensions
dim1dim2.. = dimension names
```

TABLE   235

Table <type name> is transposed so that the |NDIM| dimensions dim1, dim2, etc., appear in the order listed. If NDIM>0, they appear first; otherwise, they are last. The ordering of dimensions not listed remains unchanged.

Example:

        TABTRN DATA ABCD 3 SER MON YEAR

reorders elements of <DATA ABCD> to be stored SER by MON by YEAR.

4.3 Arithmetic Functions

4.3.1 TABFN1, TABFN2, TABFT1, TABFT2 - Functions of Elements

Function routines may be used to perform a wide class of operations on one or two categories of a dimension within a single table or on every element of one or two tables. TABFN1 and TABFT1 create a new variable which is a function of an existing variable and, perhaps, a constant:

$$z(i) = f(x(i),C)$$

For TABFN1, the variables involved are the categories of one dimension, but for TABFT1, the variables are all of the elements of a table. Similarly, TABFN2 and TABFT2 create a new variable which is a function of two existing variables:

$$z(i) = f(x(i),y(i))$$

In all cases, computations may be performed in place; i.e. a new category (table) can have the same name as an old category (table). If space is needed for TABFN1 or TABFN2, it is obtained automatically through TABENL (p. 232). A central STATLIB function evaluator is used.

Calling Sequences:

        (FTN) CALL TABFN1(type,name,dimn,catz,fun,catx[,C])
        (FTN) CALL TABFN2(type,name,dimn,catz,fun,catx,caty)

        (ISX) TABFN1 type name dimn catz fun catx [C]
        (ISX) TABFN2 type name dimn catz fun catx caty

                type,name = table identifiers
                dimn   = dimension name
                catz   = category receiving function values
                fun   = function
                catx,caty = categories containing function arguments
                C   = real constant

```
(FTN) CALL TABFT1(typz,namz,fun,typx,namx[,C])
(FTN) CALL TABFT2(typz,namz,fun,typx,namx,typy,namy)

(ISX) TABFT1 typz namz fun typx namx [C]
(ISX) TABFT2 typz namz fun typx namx typy namy
```

```
    typz,namz   = table receiving function values
    fun         = function
    typx,namx,  = tables containing function arguments
      typy,namy
    C           = constant
```

For TABFT2, <typy namy> is transposed if necessary to the same dimension ordering as <typx namx>.

The following table gives the resulting values of z(i) for available functions:

Function	TABFN1	TABFN2
ABS	|x(i)|	-
ADD	x(i)+C	x(i)+y(i)
ASN	arcsin(x(i))	-
DIV	x(i)/C	x(i)/y(i)
EQ	ind(x(i)=C)	ind(x(i)=y(i))
EQL	x(i)	-
EXP	exp(x(i))	-
FTN	FTNFUN(x(i),C)	FTNFUN(x(i),y(i))
GE	ind(x(i)≥C)	ind(x(i)≥y(i))
GT	ind(x(i)>C)	ind(x(i)>y(i))
INT	[x(i)/C]	[x(i)/y(i)]
INV	1/x(i)	-
LE	ind(x(i)≤C)	ind(x(i)≤y(i))
LGS	1/(1+exp(-x(i)))	-
LGT	log(x(i)/(1-x(i)))	-
LOG	log(x(i))	-
LT	ind(x(i)<C)	ind(x(i)<y(i))
MAX	max(x(i),C)	max(x(i),y(i))
MIN	min(x(i),C)	min(x(i),y(i))
MLT	x(i)*C	x(i)*y(i)
MOD	mod(x(i),C)	mod(x(i),y(i))
NE	ind(x(i)≠C)	ind(x(i)≠y(i))
NPR	PNORM(x(i))	-
PWR	x(i)**C	x(i)**y(i)
RNO	RNORM(0)	-
ROU	round(x(i))	-
RUN	RUNIF(0)	-
SEQ	i	-
SIN	sin(x(i))	-
SQR	x(i)**.5	-
SUB	x(i)-C	x(i)-y(i)
TPR	PTDIST(x(i),C)	PTDIST(x(i),y(i))
ZER	zero(x(i),C)	-

Logarithms are computed to the base e. The indicator function (ind)

TABLE   237

returns 1 if its argument is true, 0 if false. FTNFUN is a dummy function, meant to be replaced by a user-supplied function in ISX (see below). RNORM (p. 373) and RUNIF (p. 374) are random number generators for the normal and uniform distributions. PTDIST is a cumulative t-distribution function routine (p. 370). The zero function zeroes out the C low-order bytes of a real word. A user-supplied FUNCTION subprogram may be passed in place of fun (see the FORTRAN note, below).

Subroutine ERRSET (p. 283), callable from ISX or FORTRAN, may be used to recover from such errors as division by zero, taking logarithms or square roots of negative numbers, etc. In ISX, the /ERRSET statement (p. 70) accomplishes this while providing a simpler calling sequence.

Examples:

        TABFN1 DATA ABCD SER ABCD0001 LOG SER1
        TABFN2 DATA ABCD SER DIFFLOG SUB ABCD0001 SER1

stores in category ABCD0001 the logarithms of SER1 elements, then in category DIFFLOG the difference of ABCD0001 and SER1.

        TABFT1 DATA WXYZ RNO DATA ABCD
        TABFT2 DATA ABCD ADD DATA ABCD DATA WXYZ

creates <DATA WXYZ> which is dimensioned like <DATA ABCD> and contains random normal deviates. <DATA WXYZ> and <DATA ABCD> are then added element-wise and the results placed in <DATA ABCD>.

FORTRAN Note:

A user-supplied function subprogram may be used. It must return real values, be declared EXTERNAL in the calling program, and passed in place of the funtion name; if added to the calling sequence, up to three additional arguments (A1,A2,A3) will be passed along to the funtion. The function will be called (by TABFN1, TABFN2, TABFT1, or TABFT2 for each element) as follows:

        $z(i) = F(x(i),A1,A2,A3)$ (by TABFN1 or TABFT1)
        $z(i) = F(x(i),y(i),A1,A2)$ (by TABFN2 or TABFT2)

ISX Note:

Dummy function FTNFUN is called if the function code is "FTN". It may be replaced by a user-written FORTRAN function; procedures for combining FORTRAN object modules with the ISX program are described in Part IV of this manual. The function FTNFUN should have the same calling sequence as the function F above, and should expect A1 to have been converted to real if called through TABFN1. A2 and A3 are passed along as character strings, each occupying one real word; if, for internal purposes, it is necessary to obtain reals or integers, STATLIB routines DVALUE or IVALUE (p. 376) may be useful.

Example:

```
EXTERNAL FN
CALL TABFN1('DATA','ABCD','SER ','DIFFLOG',FN,'SER1    ')
```

4.3.2 TABFND - Functions Over a Dimension

Calling Sequences:

(FTN) CALL TABFND(type,name,fun,dimn,ntyp,nnam[,C])

(ISX) TABFND type name fun dimn ntyp nnam [C]

type,name	= old table identifiers
fun	= function
dimn	= dimension operated upon
ntyp,nnam	= new table identifiers
C	= constant

Function fun is applied to dimension dimn of table <type name>, the results stored in new table <ntyp nnam>. The function may be any of the listed character strings below or user-supplied (see the FORTRAN note). Dimension dimn of <ntyp nnam> will have a single category, named the same as the function:

Function	Result
AVG	Average
EXT	Extract Cth element (C integer)
MAX	Maximum
MED	Median
MIN	Minimum
ORD	Cth order statistic (C real)
SSQ	Sum of squares about mean
STD	Standard deviation
SUM	Sum
VAR	Variance

C is required only for functions EXT and ORD. With EXT, C specifies the integer location to be extracted; with ORD, C specifies a fractional order statistic between 0 and 1.

Example:

        TABFND DATA ABCD AVG MON DATA EFGH

computes averages over the MON dimension for every category of YEAR, SER; results are stored in table <DATA EFGH> as category AVG of dimension MON.

FORTRAN Note:

A user-written function may be passed in place of fun. The result will be stored as category "EXTERNAL". Up to two additional arguments may be added and will be passed on to the function. The

TABLE   239

function should be written to treat dimension dimn as the first row

$$X(1,1),\ X(1,2),\ \ldots\ ,\ X(1,\mathrm{NOBS})$$

of a KDIM by NOBS matrix: calling sequence

$$\ldots\ \mathrm{fun(KDIM,NOBS,X)}\ \ldots$$

Example:

```
EXTERNAL EX2
CALL TABFND('DATA','ABCD',EX2,'YEAR','DATA','EFGH')
```

applies user function EX2 to the YEAR dimension for every category of MON, SER; results are stored in table <DATA EFGH> as category EXTERNAL of YEAR.

4.4 Analysis and Display

Routines of this section print, display, plot, and perform linear regressions on data. Interfaces are provided for STATLIB soubroutines DSPLAY (many plots per page display, p. 356), PPLOT (plotting, p. 358), and the regression package REGPAK (Ch. 11, p. 297). In addition, a special routine for balanced analysis of variance models is included. All of these routines are written to operate on rows of two way arrays (e.g., REGPAK routines regress one row against others); they therefore require a specific physical ordering of data. Corresponding routines of this section first call TABTRN (p. 234), if necessary, to set up this ordering.

4.4.1 TABAOV,TABAVP - Analysis of Variance

Calling Sequences:

    (FTN) CALL TABAOV(type,name,NDIM,'dim1dim2..',etyp,enam)

    (ISX) TABAOV type name NDIM dim1 dim2 .. etyp enam

        type,name   = table identifiers
        NDIM   = number of dimensions identifying effects
        dim1dim2.. = dimensions identifying effects
        etyp enam   = table of effects

One step in the analysis of variance of <type name> is performed. The NDIMth order effects due to dim1, dim2, etc., are computed and stored in table <etyp enam>. A residual table <RSID name> is generated if necessary, then automatically updated, as is the DYNCOR block <AOV name> containing the sum of squares breakdown (analysis of variance table). TABAOV adds onto the <AOV name> table if it exists, so that prior to issuing analysis of variance calls for a second table of the same name, <AOV name> should be deleted (see DYNDEL,

p. 261).

To print out the sum of squares breakdown,

    (FTN) CALL TABAVP(name)

    (ISX) TABAVP name

Example:

        TABAOV DATA ABCD 1 MON MON EFCT
        TABAOV DATA ABCD 1 YEAR YEAR EFCT
        TABAOV DATA ABCD 2 MON YEAR M/YR EFCT
        TABAVP ABCD

stores MON effects in <MON EFCT>, YEAR effects in <YEAR EFCT>, MON by YEAR effects in <M/YR EFCT>, then prints out the entire sum of squares breakdown.

4.4.2 TABDSP - Display

Calling Sequences:

    (FTN) CALL TABDSP(type,name,dimv,dimh)

    (ISX) TABDSP type name dimv dimh

        type,name = table identifiers
        dimv   = vertical dimension name
        dimh   = horizontal dimension name

Table <type name> is passed into subroutine DSPLAY (p. 356), which plots horizontal dimension categories side-by-side against vertical dimension labels. If <type name> has exactly one dimension, it is used as the vertical dimension; dimv, dimh are ignored. The plots are of low resolution in order to have many appear on each page. If necessary, TABTRN is called to order the data as required: dimh becomes the first dimension, dimv the second. A separate display is generated for each combination of categories of the remaining dimensions.

Example:

        TABDSP DATA ABCD MON YEAR

generates a MON by YEAR display for every category of SER. The ordering of dimensions becomes YEAR by MON by SER.

4.4.3 TABPLT - Plotting

Calling Sequences:

TABLE   241

(FTN) CALL TABPLT(type,name,dimn,cath,NCAT,'cat1cat2..')

(ISX) TABPLT type name dimn cath NCAT cat1 cat2 ..

```
type,name  = table identifiers
dimn       = dimension name
cath       = horizontal axis category
NCAT       = number of vertical axis categories
cat1cat2.. = vertical axis categories
```

Table <type name> is passed into subroutine PPLOT (p. 358), which plots elements of the NCAT categories cat1, cat2, etc., against those of cath. If cath is blank, a time plot is produced; i.e., the elements are plotted in the order in which they occur. If necessary, TABTRN (p. 234) is called to make dimn the first dimension. PPLOTP(p. 287) may be called to control plot parameter settings and options.

Examples:

TABPLT DATA ABCD SER SER....2 1 SER....1

plots elements of SER....1 against those of SER....2.

TABPLT DATA ABCD SER .... 1 SER....1

plots the category SER....1 versus time.

4.4.4 TABPRT, TABPRM - Printing

TABPRT prints all dimensions of a table in an easily readable rectangular matrix with proper dimension and category labels. The categories of one dimension appear in the columns of the matrix; the combinations of the categories of the remaining dimensions are nested in the rows. The corresponding labels appear above and to the left of the matrix of values. TABPRM, similarly, prints several conformable tables together in one matrix so that the rows of the tables corresponding to each combination of row categories are printed adjacent to one another. This routine facilitates the comparison of tables of like dimensions. Several parameter settings may be modified through TABPRS (below). The printing format for table values may be supplied and the table can be printed as several matrices of lesser dimension than the full table.

Calling Sequences:

(FTN) CALL TABPRT(type,name,NDIM,'dim1dim2..')

(ISX) TABPRT type name NDIM dim1 dim2 ..

```
type,name  = table identifiers
NDIM       = number of dimensions
dim1dim2.. = dimension names
```

TABTRN (p. 234) is called to transpose <type name> so that the
|NDIM| dimensions dim1, dim2, etc. appear in the order listed. The
categories of the first dimension of the table appear in the columns
of the matrix. In the nesting of all combinations of the categories
of the remaining dimensions in the rows, the categories for the
second dimension vary the fastest; the third dimension, the second
fastest; etc. If <type name> has exactly one dimension, it is used
as the column dimension. An appropriate format is determined unless
specified through TABPRS. A common exponent (if any) will be written
above the table. If the matrix will not fit on one page, it will be
split horizontally and vertically as necessary. Each sub-table will
be completely labeled.

    (FTN) CALL TABPRM(KTAB,'type1typ2..','nam1nam2..',NDIM,
                    'dim1dim2..')

    (ISX) TABPRM KTAB typ1 nam1 typ2 nam2 .. NDIM dim1 dim2 ..

        KTAB   = number of tables
        typ1typ2..,   = table identifiers
         nam1nam2..
        NDIM   = number of dimensions
        dim1dim2..   = dimension names

The KTAB tables are transposed by TABTRN (p. 234) in the order
specified by dim1dim2.. . If NDIM=0, the tables are transposed if
necessary like <typ1 nam1>. As in TABPRT, the tables are printed
together in a matrix, but the fastest changing label in the rows is
the one identifying the type and name of the table.

TABPRS may be called to modify the default printing logic of TABPRT
and TABPRM, which normally print tables as one matrix containing all
dimensions and which generate a format statement thought to be
appropriate for the given data.

Calling Sequences (TABPRS):

    (FTN) CALL TABPRS(code,VALUE)

    (ISX) TABPRS code VALUE

        code = character string code identifying parameter
        VALUE = parameter value (see below)

code VALUE	Description
TDIM N	sets maximum number of dimensions in printed table to N; reset by 0
FORM fmtcod	constructs format statement using format codes supplied: fmtcod = A9, D9.w, E9.w, or F9.w, where $0 \le w \le 9$; default reset by blank

Both codes modify printing in TABPRT and TABPRM and are permanent
until reset. Setting TDIM causes the tables(s) to be printed as

TABLE   243

several matrices each containing the first TDIM dimensions of the table for every combination of categories of the remaining dimensions.

4.4.5 TABREG - Regression

Calling Sequences:

    (FTN) CALL TABREG(type,name,dimn,catd,NCAT,'cat1cat2..')

    (ISX) TABREG type name dimn catd NCAT cat1 cat2 ..

type,name	= table identifiers
dimn	= dimension name
catd	= dependent variable category
NCAT	= number of independent variable
cat1cat2..	= independent variable categories

Table <type name> is passed into REGPAK subroutines (Ch. 11, p. 297), which regresses elements of catd against those of the NCAT categories cat1, cat2, etc. If necessary, TABTRN (p. 234) is called to make dimn the first dimension.

All intermediate results are stored under "standard" REGPAK format (see Ch. 11, Sec. 3.10, p. 312) in DYNCOR block <REG mod1>. Through REGGET (p. 289), these may be accessed directly by the user. If TABREG is called with dimension name blank ("...." in ISX),

        TABREG type name .... 0 0 0   ,

no regression is performed, but the appropriate REG block is activated for use by REGGET.

Example:

        TABREG DATA ABCD SER SER....2 1 SER....1

performs a linear regression of SER....2 on SER....1.

5. SAMPLE PROGRAMS

In section 1, movement of the time series <DATA BSMI>, the number of telephones connected monthly in the Bell System, is examined monthly over a six-year period. In section 2, the table <EMP TABL> is hypothetical human resources count data for employees of a company classified according to loss and three other dimensions. The objective of the program is to examine the differences in loss for three areas of the company from the average loss for the entire company. The complete input streams are shown for running the programs on the IBM VS/370 system, along with resulting output. See Chapter 15, Section 2 (p. 391), for information on running the ISX program under VS.

5.1 Example 1

Job Input Stream:

```
//jobname JOB (acctg info),parameters
//   EXEC ISX
//GO.FT10F001 DD *
DATA BSMI 72 R(6F10.0)
    684418.    643274.    759817.    689162.    773371.    893521.
    794136.    919291.    975007.    879541.    791770.    678332.
    738429.    678523.    774154.    756131.    797407.    924279.
    888043.    987544.    993634.    941983.    818995.    686061.
    752250.    694044.    754978.    800224.    823449.    914445.
    950725.    995552.   1062799.    968416.    800832.    751783.
    790400.    766346.    834918.    853731.    844265.   1054548.
   1005658.   1021164.   1194403.   1016114.    848100.    839063.
    786334.    784995.    917827.    874370.    862804.   1127593.
   1052950.   1100072.   1275551.   1044364.    962091.    883662.
    865972.    841846.    979926.    926128.    938801.   1207102.
   1078439.   1222488.   1334681.   1090884.    984492.    857221.
DIM MON 12 R(6(A8,2X))
JANUARY     FEBRUARY   MARCH      APRIL      MAY         JUNE
JULY        AUGUST     SEPTEMBR   OCTOBER    NOVEMBER    DECEMBER
DIM YEAR 6 R(6A5)
 1961 1962 1963 1964 1965 1966
//GO.SYSIN DD *
OPTION * PAGSIZ 75
DYNINP 10
TABDIM DATA BSMI 2 MON YEAR 0
TABPRT DATA BSMI 2 YEAR MON
TABDSP DATA BSMI YEAR MON
TABDSP DATA BSMI MON YEAR
TABAOV DATA BSMI 1 MON MON EFCT
TABAOV DATA BSMI 1 YEAR YEAR EFCT
TABAVP BSMI
TABPRT MON EFCT 0 0
TABPRT RSID BSMI 2 YEAR MON
TABFND DATA BSMI SUM MON DATA SUM
```

TABLE   245

```
TABFND DATA BSMI STD MON DATA STD
TABCON DATA BSMI MON DATA SUM
TABCON DATA BSMI MON DATA STD
TABPRT DATA BSMI 2 YEAR MON
```

Description:

The call to OPTION (p. 285) sets page size to 75 columns for most
STATLIB output routines. DYNINP (p. 270) reads in the data series
<DATA BSMI> and accompanying dimension information blocks <DIM MON>,
<DIM YEAR> from FORTRAN unit 10. TABDIM (p. 231) dimensions
<DATA BSMI> month by year, after which it is printed by TABPRT
(p. 241). Successive calls to TABDSP (p. 240) generate first, for
each month, a time plot across years, then, for each year, a time
plot across months. Next, analysis of variance is performed: month
and year main effects are computed and stored by TABAOV (p. 239), the
sum of squares breakdown is printed by TABAVP (p. 239), and finally
TABPRT prints the tables containing monthly effects and residuals.
The final sequence of coding computes (TABFND, p. 238) and
concatenates (TABCON, p. 232) sums and standard deviations over
months; TABPRT prints the resulting table.

Output:

STATLIB ISX 12/01/78   07/09/80 PAGE 1

TABDIM: DATA BSMI, 2 DIMNS:
        MON YEAR

TABLE / TABPRT   07/09/80 PAGE 2

DATA BSMI

MON	YEAR 1961	1962	1963	1964	1965	1966
JANUARY	684418.	738429.	752250.	790400.	786334.	865972.
FEBRUARY	643274.	678523.	694044.	766346.	784995.	841846.
MARCH	759817.	774154.	754978.	834918.	917827.	979926.
APRIL	689162.	756131.	800224.	853731.	874370.	926128.
MAY	773371.	797407.	823449.	844265.	862804.	938801.
JUNE	893521.	924279.	914445.	1054548.	1127593.	1207102.
JULY	794136.	888043.	950725.	1005658.	1052950.	1078439.
AUGUST	919291.	987544.	995552.	1021164.	1100072.	1222488.
SEPTEMBR	975007.	993634.	1062799.	1194403.	1275551.	1334681.
OCTOBER	879541.	941983.	968416.	1016114.	1044364.	1090884.
NOVEMBER	791770.	818995.	800832.	848100.	962091.	984492.
DECEMBER	678332.	686061.	751783.	839063.	883662.	857221.

TABLE / TABDSP   07/09/80   PAGE 3

DATA BSMI ... YEAR X MON

VBL:	1 JANUARY	2 FEBRUARY	3 MARCH	4 APRIL
MIN:	684418.00	643274.00	754978.00	689162.00
MAX:	865972.00	841846.00	979926.00	926128.00

Year								
1961	0	*	0	*	2	*	0	*
1962	29	***	17	**	8	*	28	***
1963	37	****	25	***	0	*	46	******
1964	58	*******	61	********	35	****	69	********
1965	56	*******	71	**********	72	*********	78	*********
1966	99	************	99	************	99	************	99	************

VBL:	5 MAY	6 JUNE	7 JULY	8 AUGUST
MIN:	773371.00	893521.00	794136.00	919291.00
MAX:	938801.00	1207102.00	1078439.00	1222488.00

Year								
1961	0	*	0	*	0	*	0	*
1962	14	**	9	*	33	****	22	***
1963	30	****	6	*	55	*******	25	***
1964	42	*****	51	*******	74	*********	33	****
1965	54	*******	74	*********	91	***********	59	*******
1966	99	************	99	************	99	************	99	************

VBL:	9 SEPTEMBR	10 OCTOBER	11 NOVEMBER	12 DECEMBER
MIN:	975007.00	879541.00	791770.00	678332.00
MAX:	1334681.00	1090884.00	984492.00	883662.00

Year								
1961	0	*	0	*	0	*	0	*
1962	5	*	29	***	14	**	3	*
1963	24	***	42	******	4	*	35	****
1964	60	*******	64	********	29	***	78	********
1965	83	**********	77	*********	88	**********	99	************
1966	99	************	99	************	99	************	87	**********

TABLE   247

TABLE / TABDSP   07/09/80   PAGE 4

DATA   BSMI ... MON   X YEAR

VBL: 1 1961   2 1962   3 1963   4 1964
MIN: 643274.00   678523.00   694044.00   766346.00
MAX: 975007.00   993634.00   1062799.00   1194403.00

JANUARY   12 **   19 **   15 **   5 *
FEBRUARY   0 *   0 *   0 *   0 *
MARCH   35 ****   30 ****   16 **   16 **
APRIL   13 **   24 ***   28 ***   20 ***
MAY   39 ****   37 ****   35 ****   18 **
JUNE   75 *********   77 *********   59 *******   67 *******
JULY   45 ******   66 ********   69 ********   55 *******
AUGUST   83 **********   98 *********** 81 ********** 59 *******
SEPTEMBR   99 *********** 99 *********** 99 *********** 99 ***********
OCTOBER   71 *********   83 **********   74 *********   58 *******
NOVEMBER   44 ******   44 ******   28 ***   19 **
DECEMBER   10 **   2 *   15 **   16 **

VBL: 5 1965   6 1966
MIN: 784995.00   841846.00
MAX: 1275551.00   1334681.00

JANUARY   0 *   4 *
FEBRUARY   0 *   0 *
MARCH   27 ***   28 ***
APRIL   18 **   17 **
MAY   15 **   19 **
JUNE   69 *******   74 ********
JULY   54 *******   48 ******
AUGUST   64 ********   77 *********
SEPTEMBR   99 *********** 99 ***********
OCTOBER   52 ******   50 ******
NOVEMBER   36 ****   28 ***
DECEMBER   20 ***   3 *

TABLE / TABAVP   07/09/80   PAGE 5

ANALYSIS OF VARIANCE - BSMI

SOURCE	DF	SS	MS	%SS	#CAT	#EFF
MON EFCT	11	1.0631E+12	9.6643E+10	65.5	12	1
YEAR EFCT	5	4.8765E+11	9.7530E+10	30.0	6	1
RSID	55	7.2786E+10	1.3234E+09	4.5	72	0
TOTL	71	1.6235E+12	2.2866E+10	100.0	72	0

TABLE / TABPRT   07/09/80   PAGE 6

MON   EFCT

XXXX	MON JANUARY	FEBRUARY	MARCH	APRIL	MAY	JUNE
	-130444.	-165240.	-63141.	-83454.	-60062.	120170.

MON   EFCT

XXXX	MON JULY	AUGUST	SEPTEMBR	OCTOBER	NOVEMBER	DECEMBER
	61580.	140940.	239268.	90139.	-32365.	-117391.

TABLE / TABPRT   07/09/80   PAGE 7

RSID BSMI

MON	YEAR 1961	1962	1963	1964	1965	1966
JANUARY	24725.6	36774.7	26902.8	-1548.2	-55939.5	-30915.4
FEBRUARY	18377.4	11664.5	3492.7	9193.6	-22482.7	-20245.6
MARCH	32821.8	5196.8	-37672.0	-24333.1	8250.7	15735.8
APRIL	-17520.9	7486.2	27886.3	14792.3	-14894.0	-17749.9
MAY	43296.3	25370.3	27719.5	-18065.6	-49851.8	-28468.7
JUNE	-16785.6	-27989.5	-61516.3	11985.6	34705.3	59600.4
JULY	-57581.1	-5636.0	33353.2	21685.1	18651.8	-10473.1
AUGUST	-11786.1	14505.0	-1179.8	-42168.9	-13586.2	54215.9
SEPTEMBR	-54397.4	-77732.3	-32260.2	32742.8	63565.5	68081.6
OCTOBER	-734.6	19745.5	22485.7	3582.6	-18492.7	-26586.6
NOVEMBER	33998.1	19261.2	-22594.7	-41927.7	21738.0	-10474.9
DECEMBER	5586.4	-28646.5	13382.7	34061.6	28335.3	-52719.6

TABFND: DATA BSMI TO DATA SUM, DIMN=MON, FUN,CATG=SUM

TABFND: DATA BSMI TO DATA STD, DIMN=MON, FUN,CATG=STD

TABCON: DATA SUM TO DATA BSMI, CON DIMN=MON

TABCON: DATA STD TO DATA BSMI, CON DIMN=MON

TABLE   249

TABLE / TABPRT   07/09/80   PAGE 8

DATA BSMI   (0)

| MON | YEAR | | | | | |
	1961	1962	1963	1964	1965	1966
JANUARY	68442.	73843.	75225.	79040.	78633.	86597.
FEBRUARY	64327.	67852.	69404.	76635.	78500.	84185.
MARCH	75982.	77415.	75498.	83492.	91783.	97993.
APRIL	68916.	75613.	80022.	85373.	87437.	92613.
MAY	77337.	79741.	82345.	84427.	86280.	93880.
JUNE	89352.	92428.	91445.	105455.	112759.	120710.
JULY	79414.	88804.	95073.	100566.	105295.	107844.
AUGUST	91929.	98754.	99555.	102116.	110007.	122249.
SEPTEMBR	97501.	99363.	106280.	119440.	127555.	133468.
OCTOBER	87954.	94198.	96842.	101611.	104436.	109088.
NOVEMBER	79177.	81900.	80083.	84810.	96209.	98449.
DECEMBER	67833.	68606.	75178.	83906.	88366.	85722.
SUM	948164.	998518.	1026950.	1106871.	1167261.	1232798.
STD	10711.	11207.	11776.	13130.	14963.	16041.

5.2 Example 2

Job Input Stream:

```
//jobname JOB (acctg info),parameters
//  EXEC ISX
//GO.FT10F001 DD *
EMP TABL 24 R(8F5.0)
   58.  25. 421. 108. 161.  85. 938. 476.
  227.  72.2322. 387. 368. 209.1764. 869.
  146.  42.2155. 242. 368.  96.1962. 444.
EMP RATE 12 R(4F10.3)
        0.121      0.188      0.146      0.152
        0.089      0.157      0.173      0.194
        0.063      0.148      0.158      0.178
DIM SEX 2 R(9A8)
MALE     FEMALE
DIM RACE 2 R(9A8)
WHITE    MINORITY
DIM AREA 3 R(9A8)
HDQTRS EAST     WEST
DIM LOSS 2 R(9A8)
QUIT    STAY
//GO.SYSIN DD *
OPTION * PAGSIZ 75
DYNINP 10
TABDIM EMP TABL 4 RACE LOSS SEX AREA 0
TABDIM EMP RATE 3 RACE SEX AREA 0
TABPRT EMP TABL 4 SEX LOSS RACE AREA
TABPRT EMP RATE 3 SEX RACE AREA
TABPRJ EMP TABL SUM 3 SEX LOSS RACE SXRC TABL
TABFN2 SXRC TABL LOSS LOSSRATE ADD QUIT STAY
TABFN2 SXRC TABL LOSS LOSSRATE DIV QUIT LOSSRATE
TABEXT SXRC TABL LOSS 1 LOSSRATE AVE RATE
TABTRN AVE RATE 3 LOSS SEX RACE
TABDIM AVE RATE 2 SEX RACE 0
TABPRP AVE RATE 1 AREA 0
TABFT2 DIF RATE SUB EMP RATE AVE RATE
TABPRS FORM F9.3
TABPRM 3 EMP RATE AVE RATE DIF RATE 0
```

Description:

OPTION (p. 285) is called to set the page size for output to 75 columns. DYNINP (p. 270) reads into core the two tables <EMP TABL> and <EMP RATE> and accompanying dimension information blocks <DIM SEX>, <DIM RACE>, and <DIM AREA>. TABDIM dimensions both tables (p. 231). <EMP TABL> contains the counts for the employees classified according to loss and three other descriptive dimensions. <EMP RATE> contains the loss rates calculated by dividing the number of losses by the total number of employees. Both tables are printed by TABPRT (p. 241). Table <EMP TABL> is projected into the sex-race-loss table <SXRC TABL> by summing over the AREA categories (TABPRJ, p. 233). Successive calls to TABFN2 (p. 235) create an additional LOSS

TABLE   251

category containing the loss rates. TABEXT (p. 233) extracts this LOSSRATE category and stores the result in <AVE RATE> which is then redimensioned by calling TABTRN (p. 234) and TABDIM. Next, the loss rates in <AVE RATE> are reproduced over the AREA dimension by TABPRP (p. 234), and the differences in loss rates between <EMP rate> and <AVE rate> are stored in the table <DIF RATE> by TABFT2 (p. 235). Finally, TABPRS (p. 241) specifies a common format for printing the three rate tables together by TABPRM (p. 241).

Output:

STATLIB ISX   12/01/78   07/09/80   PAGE 1

TABLE / TABPRT   07/09/80   PAGE 2

EMP   TABL

AREA	RACE	LOSS	SEX MALE	FEMALE
HDQTRS	WHITE	QUIT	58.	161.
		STAY	421.	938.
	MINORITY	QUIT	25.	85.
		STAY	108.	476.
EAST	WHITE	QUIT	227.	368.
		STAY	2322.	1764.
	MINORITY	QUIT	72.	209.
		STAY	387.	869.
WEST	WHITE	QUIT	146.	368.
		STAY	2155.	1962.
	MINORITY	QUIT	42.	96.
		STAY	242.	444.

TABLE / TABPRT   07/09/80   PAGE 3

EMP   RATE

		SEX	
AREA	RACE	MALE	FEMALE
HDQTRS	WHITE	0.121	0.146
	MINORITY	0.188	0.152
EAST	WHITE	0.089	0.173
	MINORITY	0.157	0.194
WEST	WHITE	0.063	0.158
	MINORITY	0.148	0.178

TABPRJ: EMP TABL TO SXRC TABL, FUN=SUM, 3 DIMNS:
        SEX LOSS RACE

TABFN2: SXRC TABL, DIMN=LOSS, NEW CATG: LOSSRATE = ADD(QUIT,STAY)

TABFN2: SXRC TABL, DIMN=LOSS, NEW CATG: LOSSRATE = DIV(QUIT,LOSSRATE)

TABEXT: SXRC TABL TO AVE RATE, DIMN=LOSS, 1 CATGS:
        LOSSRATE

TABTRN: AVE RATE, 3 DIMNS:
        LOSS SEX RACE

TABDIM: AVE RATE, 2 DIMNS:
        SEX RACE

TABPRP: AVE RATE, 1 DIMNS:
        AREA

TABFT2: DIF RATE = SUB(EMP RATE,AVE RATE)

TABLE

253

AREA	RACE	TABL	SEX MALE	FEMALE
HDQTRS	WHITE	EMP RATE	0.121	0.146
		AVE RATE	0.081	0.161
		DIF RATE	0.040	-0.015
	MINORITY	EMP RATE	0.188	0.152
		AVE RATE	0.159	0.179
		DIF RATE	0.029	-0.027
EAST	WHITE	EMP RATE	0.089	0.173
		AVE RATE	0.081	0.161
		DIF RATE	0.008	0.012
	MINORITY	EMP RATE	0.157	0.194
		AVE RATE	0.159	0.179
		DIF RATE	-0.002	0.015
WEST	WHITE	EMP RATE	0.063	0.158
		AVE RATE	0.081	0.161
		DIF RATE	-0.018	-0.003
	MINORITY	EMP RATE	0.148	0.178
		AVE RATE	0.159	0.179
		DIF RATE	-0.011	-0.001

6. SUBJECT INDEX

TABLE   255

7. GLOSSARY OF SUBROUTINE CALLS (ISX)

CHAPTER 9

DYNCOR - DYNAMIC CORE STORAGE MANAGEMENT

1. INTRODUCTION

DYNCOR is a system of subroutines which provides storage management services for FORTRAN programs. It is used extensively by ISX and by the high-level packages in Part I. Calls to DYNCOR subroutines allocate and free blocks of core during execution of the program. Dynamic allocation of storage means that the amount of space required does not need to be known at compilation time. Furthermore, the ability to release space for re-use leads to more efficient use of storage. Temporary work space can be obtained through DYNCOR or directly through system dynamic allocation routines if they exist (such as on IBM). If the system routines do not exist, the user may provide a large segment of core (DYNDEF, p. 275) and use DYNCOR for storage management.

A second function provided by DYNCOR is access by name. The user supplies two alphanumeric names ("type" and "name") for each block, according to which the block may then be referenced. This facility is particularly useful when the blocks are arrays being manipulated by a package of subroutines (e.g. matrices, time series, multi-way tables), for it allows referencing these items by alphanumeric names rather than location.

DYNCOR also provides certain operations on blocks, such as input/output, copying, and renaming. Most of these operations can be performed on a particular block or on all blocks with a particular type or name.

A directory of blocks is itself stored in a DYNCOR block. The user may request direct pointers to blocks; DYNCOR keeps these pointers current as blocks are moved.

Section 2 describes DYNCOR conventions and procedures. DYNCOR routines are described in Section 3, input/output routines in Section 4, and storage management in Section 5. Section 6 contains a subject index and 7 a glossary of subroutine calls.

2. CONVENTIONS AND NOTATION

2.1 Pointer Subscripts

A special type of subscript, called a pointer subscript, permits

access to elements in storage blocks. The pointer subscript (J) and
a reference array (L) are passed to DYNCOR routines when a block is
created or accessed.   DYNCOR sets the value of J so that L(J) is the
first element in the block. For example,

        CALL DYNOLD('TABL','ABC ',1,LEN,L,J,&32)

permits   reference   to   the   block   <TABL ABC>   as L(J),L(J+1),...,
L(J+LEN-1). An alternative is to dimension L(1,1); the Kth element
of the block is then L(J,K).   This may be generalized to
multi-dimensioned arrays: e.g., for a 3x4x5 array L is dimensioned
(1,3,4,1) and the K1,K2,K3-th element referenced as L(J,K1,K2,K3).
The number 1 in the calling sequence indicates that the reference
array L is single precision. Blocks always begin on odd words (i.e.,
"double word boundaries" on IBM) to assure double precision access.

To consolidate storage, garbage collection is performed during the
process of allocating a new block, if necessary. When a block is
moved due to garbage collection (or because the user is increasing
its size), all pointer subscripts associated with it are incremented
by the amount the block was moved. A pointer subscript should not be
used as an ordinary variable, since its value may be changed at
unpredictable times. A pointer remains associated with a block until
reused or released through DYNPTD (p. 268). In the latter case, the
value of the pointer is set to one.   If the block is deleted or
renamed, the pointer is set to point to the string "DYN*DLTD"; it
will be reset if a new block with the same type and name is
subsequently created.

Caution must also be exercised in passing DYNCOR blocks as arguments
to subroutines that may cause new blocks to be allocated.   If
subroutine SUB in

        CALL SUB(...,L(J),...)

generates a new block, and if L(J) refers to an address in a dynamic
storage block, the address represented by "L(J)" may become incorrect
while SUB has control. Subroutine DYNLOC (p. 269) may be used by SUB
to obtain DYNCOR pointers to its arguments.   Generally it is
efficient to do this only for arrays. If the subroutine is expecting
a scalar, a variable should be used in place of L(J), with assignment
statements preceding and/or following the call; i.e.

        LJ = L(J)
        CALL SUB(...,LJ,...)
        L(J) = LJ

Certain compilers (e.g., H-level on IBM) perform optimization which
can result in values of pointer subscripts being used "too early" in
computing addresses. This occurs because the compiler "thinks" that
a call to a subroutine cannot change the value of J when J is not an
argument.   This optimization problem may be avoided by putting all
pointer subscripts in COMMON.

If overlays are used, COMMON blocks containing DYNCOR pointers should

be placed in the root segment, or each pointer released through
DYNPTD (p. 268).

Pointer subscripts may themselves be located in DYNCOR blocks. The
first word of each block containing one or more pointer subscripts
must contain the character string "PTRS". Use of this feature is not
recommended, except in cases where a variable number of pointer
subscripts must be maintained. Pointers in a block will be deleted
if the block is deleted (or shortened sufficiently).

2.2 Error Conditions

An error return is included as the last argument for most routines
(optional on IBM). It will be taken if insufficient space is
available for a new block or if an old block does not exist.

DYNNEW prints an error message if core is not available to satisfy a
request. The block identifier and number of (single precision) words
requested are printed. Errors from some DYNCOR routines are printed
by DYNERR (p. 276). OPTION (p. 285) may be called to control DYNNEW
and DYNERR printing.

DYNCOR checks for validity of its internal pointers. If one has been
destroyed (over-written), DYNERR prints a dump and execution is
terminated.

DYNCOR occasionally enlarges its control blocks, <DYN* *DY*> and
<DYN* *BP*>. Insufficient core to enlarge one of these blocks will
result in the error message from DYNNEW, but execution may continue
with the old, smaller control block. Eventually, however, the
control block may be completely exhausted and DYNERR will terminate
execution, as above.

2.3 Notation

Calling sequences follow the STATLIB-wide conventions described in
the Part II Introduction (p. 56).

Each DYNCOR block has two single-word (4-character on IBM) labels, a
"type" and a "name". These may be any valid words (usually
alphanumeric), except that the type "DYN*" is reserved for DYNCOR
control blocks and a type or name may not consist entirely of blanks.
Specifying a blank type or name ("...." in ISX, since blanks are used
as delimiters) has a special meaning, such as "all" or "the same",
for some routines. In calling sequence descriptions, four-letter
lower-case words (e.g., type, name) will be used for arguments
requiring these labels. In the text, block identifiers will be
enclosed in angle brackets, i.e., <type name>.

3. BASIC ROUTINES

3.1 DYNNEW, DYNOLD, DYNENL - Generate, Find, Enlarge Blocks

DYNNEW generates a new block of length |LEN|. If a block with the same type and name already exists, its length will be adjusted. If the new length is greater than the old, the block will be enlarged or moved. If LEN < 0, the block will be made non-relocatable. If LEN = 0, the block is deleted.

DYNOLD locates an existing block and returns its length in LEN. LEN is set to zero and an error return taken if the block does not exist.

DYNENL enlarges an existing block by LEN words and returns a pointer to the first word added to the block. If the block does not exist, a new one is created.

Calling Sequences:

```
        (FTN) CALL DYNNEW(type,name,LPR,LEN,L,J,&ERR)
        (FTN) CALL DYNOLD(type,name,LPR,LEN,L,J,&ERR)
        (FTN) CALL DYNENL(type,name,LPR,LEN,L,J,&ERR)

        (ISX) DYNNEW type name LPR LEN
        (ISX) DYNOLD type name LPR
        (ISX) DYNENL type name LPR LEN
```

```
            type,name = type and name of block (nonblank)
            LPR       = precision of L (1-single, 2-double)
            LEN       = length of block in words of precision LPR
            L,J       = reference array and pointer
            &ERR      = error return
```

ISX Note:

DYNOLD stores the length of the block (zero if not found) in the first word of the ISX "X" array and as ISX variable $XXX (see Ch. 4., Secs. 2.2-3, p. 60).

Example:

```
        DYNOLD DATA AAAA 2
```

defines $XXX to be the length, in double-precision words, of <DATA AAAA>.

3.2 DYNPUT, DYNGET, DYNAPD - Array-to-Block Movements

DYNPUT moves data from array X into a block, generating or expanding the block if necessary. If the initial position (N1) specified is zero, a new block of the requested length (N2) is generated.

DYNGET moves data from an existing block into array X. If the initial position (N1) specified is zero, the entire block is moved and, in FORTRAN, its length returned in N2. An attempt to get data past the end of a block will result in an error return (data up to the end of the block will be moved).

DYNAPD appends array X to an existing block. If the block does not exist a new one is generated. DYNAPD is equivalent to DYNPUT except that the initial position (N1) is assumed to be one greater than the current length of the block.

Calling Sequences:

```
(FTN) CALL DYNPUT(type,name,LPR,N1,N2,X,&ERR)
(FTN) CALL DYNGET(type,name,LPR,N1,N2,X,&ERR)
(FTN) CALL DYNAPD(type,name,LPR,NW,X,&ERR)

(ISX) DYNPUT type name LPR N1 N2 [X]
(ISX) DYNGET type name LPR N1 N2
(ISX) DYNAPD type name LPR NW [X]
```

type,name	= type and name of block (non-blank)
LPR	= precision of X (1-single, 2-double)
N1	= initial position (first word in block to be moved)
	= 0 generate new block (DYNPUT)
	= 0 move entire block and (FTN only) set N2=LEN (DYNGET)
N2	= final position (in DYNCOR block)
NW	= number of words to be appended
X	= array to be moved
&ERR	= error return

ISX Note:

The elements of the DYNCOR block retrieved by DYNGET are stored in the ISX "X" array (p. 60), up to a maximum of 100 single-precision words. DYNAPD and DYNPUT will load directly in character form if array elements are supplied; otherwise loading is from the X array.

```
DYNPUT DATA ANUM 1 1 3 146 463 286
/LOADX I 146 463 286
DYNPUT DATA NUM 1 1 3
```

loads 146, 463 and 286 into <DATA ANUM> in character form and into <DATA NUM> in integer form. (/LOADX, p. 72, is called to load the numbers into the "X" array with conversion to integers.)

3.3 DYNDEL - Delete Blocks

DYNDEL deletes blocks, with a blank name or type meaning "all" (see example below). Pointer subscripts to a deleted block are set to point to the string "DYN*DLTD"; their values will be properly reset if a new block with the same type and name is subsequently generated. To delete pointers from DYNCOR's directory, and thereby free them for use as ordinary variables, use DYNPTD (p. 268).

Calling Sequences:

    (FTN) CALL DYNDEL(type,name,&ERR)

    (ISX) DYNDEL type name

        type,name = type and name of block(s)
        &ERR   = error return

Examples:

        DYNDEL TABL ABC

deletes <TABL ABC>.

        DYNDEL TABL ....

deletes every block whose type is TABL.

3.4 DYNCPY, DYNNAM - Copy, Rename Blocks

DYNCPY generates a copy of and DYNNAM renames the requested block(s). A blank old type or name indicates "all" and a blank new type or name indicates "the same" (see example below). If a block with the new name already exists, it is deleted.

Calling Sequences:

    (FTN) CALL DYNCPY(type,name,ntyp,nnam,&ERR,&ERR2)
    (FTN) CALL DYNNAM(type,name,ntyp,nnam,&ERR)

    (ISX) DYNCPY type name ntyp nnam
    (ISX) DYNNAM type name ntyp nnam

        type,name = type and name of old blocks(s)
        ntyp,nnam = type and name of new block(s) (DYNCPY)
                  = new type and name for old block(s) (DYNNAM)
        &ERR   = error return (block not found)
        &ERR2   = error return (insufficient core)

Examples:

        DYNCPY TABL ABC SPEC DEFG

generates a copy of <TABL ABC> called <SPEC DEFG>.

        DYNCPY TABL .... SPEC ....

generates copies of all TABL blocks, each retaining the block name and having a type of SPEC.

3.5 DYNCON - Concatenate Blocks

DYNCON concatenates block <typ2 nam2> to block <type name>, creating <type name> if it does not already exist. Block <typ2 nam2> is not deleted.

<u>Calling Sequences:</u>

> (FTN) CALL DYNCON(type,name,typ2,nam2,&ERR,&ERR2)

> (ISX) DYNCON type name typ2 nam2

>> type,name = block to be enlarged
>> typ2,nam2 = block to be concatenated to <type name>
>> &ERR   = error return (<typ2 nam2> not found)
>> &ERR2   = error return (insufficient core)

3.6 DYNEXT - Extraction

DYNEXT extracts from an existing block into a new block.

<u>Calling Sequences:</u>

> (FTN) CALL DYNEXT(type,name,LPR,N1,N2,ntyp,nnam,&ERR,&ERR2)

> (ISX) DYNEXT type name LPR N1 N2 ntyp nnam

>> type,name = block to be extracted from
>> LPR   = precision (1-single, 2-double)
>> N1,N2   = first and last words to be extracted
>> ntyp,nnam = block to contain extracted data
>> &ERR   = error return (<type name> not found or
>>   (N1,N2) out-of-range)
>> &ERR2   = error return (insufficient core)

N2 may be greater than the length of the existing block, in which case the N1th through last elements of the block are extracted.

3.7 DYNFN1, DYNFN2, DYNFNB - Functions

DYNFN1 creates a new block which is an element-by-element function of an existing block and, perhaps, a constant:

$$z(i) = f(x(i),C) \quad .$$

DYNFN2 creates a new block which is an element-by-element function of two existing blocks:

$$z(i) = f(x(i),y(i)) \quad ;$$

if the x and y arrays are of unequal length, z's length will be the shorter of the two.

DYNFNB is a function subprogram which returns a function of an entire block.

All blocks are assumed to contain real numbers.   Built-in functions are available through central STATLIB function routines; alternatively, the user may supply his own (see below).

Calling Sequences:

    (FTN) CALL DYNFN1(ztyp,znam,fun,xtyp,xnam[,C])
    (FTN) CALL DYNFN2(ztyp,znam,fun,xtyp,xnam,ytyp,ynam)
    (FTN) ...DYNFNB(type,name,fun[,C])...

    (ISX) DYNFN1 ztyp znam fun xtyp xnam [C]
    (ISX) DYNFN2 ztyp znam fun xtyp xnam ytyp ynam
    (ISX) DYNFNB type name fun [C]

        ztyp,znam = type and name for z
        xtyp,xnam = type and name for x
        ytyp,ynam = type and name for y
        type,name = type and name for existing block
        fun   = function code
        C   = constant

The following table gives the resulting values of z(i) for function codes (fun) available with DYNFN1 and DYNFN2:

Function	DYNFN1	DYNFN2
ABS	$\|x(i)\|$	-
ADD	$x(i)+C$	$x(i)+y(i)$
ASN	$\arcsin(x(i))$	-
DIV	$x(i)/C$	$x(i)/y(i)$
EQ	$ind(x(i)=C)$	$ind(x(i)=y(i))$
EQL	$x(i)$	-
EXP	$exp(x(i))$	-
FTN	$FTNFUN(x(i),C)$	$FTNFUN(x(i),y(i))$
GE	$ind(x(i)\geq C)$	$ind(x(i)\geq y(i))$
GT	$ind(x(i)>C)$	$ind(x(i)>y(i))$
INT	$[x(i)/C]$	$[x(i)/y(i)]$
INV	$1/x(i)$	-
LE	$ind(x(i)\leq C)$	$ind(x(i)\leq y(i))$
LGS	$1/(1+exp(-x(i)))$	-
LGT	$log(x(i)/(1-x(i)))$	-
LOG	$log(x(i))$	-
LT	$ind(x(i)<C)$	$ind(x(i)<y(i))$
MAX	$max(x(i),C)$	$max(x(i),y(i))$
MIN	$min(x(i),C)$	$min(x(i),y(i))$
MLT	$x(i)*C$	$x(i)*y(i)$
MOD	$mod(x(i),C)$	$mod(x(i),y(i))$
NE	$ind(x(i)\neq C)$	$ind(x(i)\neq y(i))$
NPR	$PNORM(x(i))$	-
PWR	$x(i)**C$	$x(i)**y(i)$
RNO	$RNORM(0)$	-
ROU	$round(x(i))$	-
RUN	$RUNIF(0)$	-
SEQ	i	-
SIN	$sin(x(i))$	-
SQR	$x(i)**.5$	-
SUB	$x(i)-C$	$x(i)-y(i)$
TPR	$PTDIST(x(i),C)$	$PTDIST(x(i),y(i))$
ZER	$zero(x(i),C)$	-

Logarithms are computed to the base e. The indicator function (ind) returns 1 if its argument is true, 0 if false. FTNFUN is a dummy function, meant to be replaced by a user-supplied function in ISX (see below). RNORM (p. 373) and RUNIF(p. 374) are random number generators for the normal and uniform distributions. PTDIST is a cumulative t-distribution function routine (p. 370). The zero function zeroes out the C low-order bytes of a real word. A user-supplied function subprogram may be passed in place of fun (see the FORTRAN note, below).

Subroutine ERRSET (p. 283), callable from ISX or FORTRAN, may be used to recover from such errors as division by zero, taking logarithms or square roots of negative numbers, etc. In ISX, the /ERRSET statement (p. 70) accomplishes this while providing a simpler calling sequence.

The following function codes (fun) may be used with DYNFNB:

Function	Result
AVG	Average
EXT	Extract Cth element (C integer)
MAX	Maximum
MED	Median
MIN	Minimum
ORD	Cth order statistic (C real)
SSQ	Sum of squares
STD	Standard deviation
SUM	Sum
VAR	Variance

C is required only for functions EXT and ORD. With EXT, C identifies the observation from which data are to be extracted, a value beyond the last block element meaning "last"; with ORD, C specifies a fractional order statistic between 0 and 1.

FORTRAN Note:

A user-supplied function subprogram may be used. It must return real values, be declared EXTERNAL in the calling program, and passed in place of the function name; if added to the calling sequence, up to three additional arguments (A1,A2,A3) will be passed along to the function. The function will be called (by DYNFN1 or DYNFN2, for each element) as follows:

```
DYNFN1:  z(i) = F(x(i),A1,A2,A3)
DYNFN2:  z(i) = F(x(i),y(i),A1,A2)
DYNFNB:  DYNFNB = F(KDIM,N,X,A1,A2)
```

With DYNFNB, function F should dimension X as (KDIM,N) and perform its operation over X(1,1),..., X(1,N). (KDIM will always be passed as 1 by DYNFNB.)

Examples:

```
EXTERNAL USERFN
CALL DYNFN1('DATA','AB50','ADD','DATA','ABCD',50D0)
Z = DYNFNB('DATA','AB50',USERFN)
```

creates <DATA AB50> as <DATA ABCD> plus 50, then sets FORTRAN variable Z equal to the result of applying user-supplied function USERFN to it.

ISX Note (DYNFN1 and DYNFN2):

Dummy function FTNFUN is called if the function code is "FTN". It may be replaced by a user-written FORTRAN function; procedures for combining FORTRAN object modules with the ISX program are described in Part IV of this manual. The function FTNFUN should have the same calling sequence as the function F above, and should expect A1 to have been converted to real if called through DYNFN1. A2 and A3 are passed along as character strings; if, for internal purposes, it is necessary to obtain reals or integers, STATLIB routines DVALUE and

IVALUE (p. 376) may be useful.

Examples:

>   DYNFN1 DATA AGE FTN DATA AGE 15

passes control to function FTNFUN, once for each word in <DATA AGE>. In each case, the first argument is age, the second argument is the real number 15.

>   DYNFN2 DATA EXP FTN DATA INC DATA EXP

calls FTNFUN, passing along paired contents of <DATA INC> and <DATA EXP>.

ISX Note (DYNFNB):

The function value is stored in the first real word of the ISX "X" array and as ISX variable $XXX (see Ch. 4, Secs. 2.2-3, p. 60).

Example:

>   DYNFNB DATA AAAA MAX

defines $XXX as the maximum entry in <DATA AAAA>.

3.8 DYNLST - Generate and Use Lists of Blocks

DYNLST generates a list of types and names of all blocks with a particular type or name, then supplies these one set at a time to the user.

In calling DYNLST, the user supplies a blank type and/or name to indicate "all". A block with the same type and name, except that "*DL*" replaces the blank type and/or name, is created and filled with the list of requested block identifiers. The first type and name are returned to the user as LT and LN. On subsequent calls the remaining types and names are returned. On the first call after the list has been exhausted, the block containing the list is deleted, a blank type and name are returned, and an error return taken.

Calling Sequence:

>   (FTN) CALL DYNLST(type,name,LT,LN,&ERR)

>   (ISX) DYNLST type name

>   type,name = requested type and name (at least one
>   must be blank)
>   LT,LN   = type and name of a block in the list
>   &ERR   = error return (taken after block exhausted)

Example:

```
10   CALL DYNLST('DATA','      ',LT,LN,&20)
     CALL TSPLT(LT,LN,0,1,9999,1)
     ...
     GO TO 10
20   ...
```

Each block whose type is DATA is processed, first being plotted by TSPLT.   Control passes to statement 20 after the last block has been processed.

ISX Note:

The type and name of each block are stored as ISX variables $TYP and $NAM. $TYP and $NAM will be blank on the first call after the last block has been processed. In conjunction with the ISX /SKIP command (p. 78), this would enable one to loop through all or a selected group of DYNCOR blocks, processing them in turn.

The ISX command /LIST (p. 80) provides a function similar to DYNLST, storing the types and names in an ISX procedure such that they can easily be passed as arguments to other commands or procedures.

Example:

```
/PROC PLOT
  <TOP> DYNLST DATA ....
  /SKIP <BOT> EQ $TYP
  TSPLT $TYP $NAM 0 1 9999 1
  ...
  /SKIP <TOP> U
  <BOT> / PROCEDURE "PLOT" RETURNING
/PROCEND
PLOT
```

This example accomplishes the same task as the FORTRAN example above. The first skip command branches to the bottom of the procedure if $TYP is blank; the last skip command branches unconditionally to the top.

3.9 DYNPTR, DYNPTD - Define, Delete Pointers

Pointer subscripts are automatically defined when a block is referenced through DYNNEW or DYNOLD (p. 260) and are updated whenever the block is moved (Sec 2.1). Additional pointers to a block may be defined through DYNPTR. The value of the new pointer subscript itself must be set by the user.

DYNPTD sets the value of pointer subscripts to 1 and deletes DYNCOR references to them, so that they will no longer be updated.   This must be done if the variable is to be used for other purposes, or if the routine containing the subscript is to be overlaid.

Calling Sequences:

```
(FTN) CALL DYNPTR(type,name,LPR,J,&ERR)
(FTN) CALL DYNPTD(J)
```

```
type,name = type and name of block
LPR       = precision of reference array using J
            (1-single, 2-double)
J         = pointer subscript.  "ALL " causes all
            pointers to be deleted (DYNPTD).
&ERR      = error return
```

Example:

```
CALL DYNOLD('DATA','ABCD',2,LEN,X,J,&88)
CALL DYNPTR('DATA','ABCD',2,J13,&88)
J13 = J + 12
CALL DYNPTD(JJ)
```

sets J13 to point to the 13th element of <DATA ABCD>, and deletes JJ
as a pointer subscript.

3.10 DYNLOC - Location in Block

Given an array LX, DYNLOC locates the block containing it, if any,
and returns a pointer to LX in the standard DYNCOR framework. The
type and name are returned to the calling program. If LX is not
contained in a DYNCOR block, the type and name are set to blanks and
an error return is taken. The pointer subscript is set to point to
LX whether it belongs to a block or not.

DYNLOC should be used by subroutines which accept arrays (possibly
contained in DYNCOR blocks) as arguments and generate new blocks
prior to using them, since the addresses passed for the arrays will
be incorrect if the arrays are stored in DYNCOR blocks which are
moved when new blocks are created.

Calling Sequence:

```
(FTN) CALL DYNLOC(LX,LT,LN,LPR,L,J,&ERR)
```

```
LX    = array to be located
LT,LN = type, name of block
LPR   = precision of L (1-single, 2-double)
L,J   = reference array and pointer subscript
&ERR  = error return
```

4. INPUT/OUTPUT

DYNCOR input/output routines provide facilities for dumping and reading blocks on cards, tape, disk, etc., for general data input, and for printing the contents of blocks.

4.1 DYNINP, DYNINL, DYNIN1, DYNINB - Input

DYNCOR input routines read formatted or unformatted blocks written by DYNOUT (p. 272) or prepared by the user. Formatted input is assumed if the FORTRAN unit is in [1,999]. A unit NRUNIT greater than 1000 implies unformatted reading from unit NRUNIT-1000. A new block is generated for each block read; an existing block with duplicate type and name will be deleted.

Formatted input consists of a header record (card) followed by records containing the contents of the block. The header record is read free-form from columns 1-80, with the following contents:

            type name LEN [t(fmt)]

where LEN is the length of the block to be read, t = "R" or "I" indicates real or integer words are being read, and fmt is a FORTRAN format statement, enclosed in parentheses. The last argument, t(fmt), must not begin in a column greater than 20. A "$" as the last word on the line indicates continuation to a second record. Format statements may contain up to 152 characters.

Formatted input may be read free-form by specifying "*" as the format code. Numerical data, separated by one or more blanks, are then read from succeeding records. Input of the current block will be stopped and the block length adjusted if a data item is coded as "*". Thus, by specifying LEN as a maximum value, blocks of unknown length may be read in conveniently. The width of the input record will be 80 unless the "*" format is followed by a shorter width (e.g., "*72").

Unformatted blocks consist of two logical records. The first contains four words (type, name, LEN, where LEN is number of single words, and the character string "DYN*"), and the second contains the contents of the block.

A negative unit number will cause the name of each block read in to be listed. Printing is further controlled through OPTION (p. 285), specifying DYNMSG. If an end-of-file is encountered while the contents of a block are being read, the size of the block is reduced accordingly, "*EOF*" is indicated on the printed message if printing is on and the end-of-file return is taken.

Four entry points are available: DYNINP reads in groups of blocks, DYNINL searches for specified blocks, and DYNIN1 reads blocks one at a time. DYNINB reads data (only) into a single block; header information is included in the calling sequence.

In ISX, the variable $EOF will be created and assigned the string
"EOF" if an end-of-file is encountered; otherwise, an existing $EOF
will be deleted. The input unit number may be specified as "*",
indicating that the current ISX input unit is to be used. This
permits programs and data to be read and executed from disk (see the
ISX /XEQ and /XEQFILE commands, p. 74) without dependence on the
input unit number.

Calling Sequences (DYNINP):

    (FTN) CALL DYNINP(NRUNIT,&EOF)

    (ISX) DYNINP NRUNIT

        |NRUNIT| = FORTRAN unit number
        &EOF   = end-of-file return.

DYNINP reads blocks from unit NRUNIT up through a "pseudo
end-of-file" (blanks in columns 1-72 if formatted, blank type and
name if not), resulting in a normal return, or an end-of-file,
resulting in &EOF return. Blocks for which insufficient space is
available are bypassed.

Calling Sequences (DYNINL):

    (FTN) CALL DYNINL(NRUNIT,'typ1typ2..)','nam1nam2..)',&EOF)

    (ISX) DYNINL NRUNIT typ1 nam1 typ2 nam2 ..

DYNINL is identical to DYNINP, except that the only blocks read are
those satisfying

        a. type = typi or typi = blank   and
        b. name = nami or nami = blank

for some i. In FORTRAN calls, if one list is shorter than the other,
it is considered to be padded with blanks.

Note that in ISX, the types and names of blocks to be read are passed
as pairs of arguments, with blank ("....") meaning all.

Calling Sequences (DYNIN1):

    (FTN) CALL DYNIN1(NRUNIT,OBLK,LT,LN,&EOF,&PEOF)

    (ISX) DYNIN1 NRUNIT

reads the header record for the next block and returns type (LT) and
name (LN). If OBLK = .TRUE., the block is also read in. If not, the
block may be bypassed by repeating the above call or read in by

        CALL DYNIN1(0,0,type,name,&EOF),

where type and name may be different than those above. The &PEOF
return is taken if a "pseudo end-of-file" (blank record) is read.

In ISX, a block is always read in (OBLK=.TRUE.) and its type and name
are stored as ISX variables $TYP and $NAM. $TYP and $NAM will be
blank if an end-of-file or pseudo end-of-file is encountered. In
conjunction with the ISX /SKIP command (p. 78), this would enable
one to read through a selected group of DYNCOR blocks, processing
them in turn.

Calling Sequences (DYNINB):

        (FTN) CALL DYNINB(NRUNIT,type,name,LEN,fmt,&EOF)

        (ISX) DYNINB NRUNIT type name LEN fmt

                fmt = "t(format)"   (same as on header record)
                     where t = R   real numbers
                            = I   integers

DYNINB reads data into a single block according to the specified
format. If |NRUNIT| is greater than 1000, fmt is ignored and an
unformatted read occurs on unit |NRUNIT-1000|.

Examples:

            DYNIN1 8
            /DEF $TN $TYP $NAM
            DYNINL -8 .... AAAA .... BBBB
            DYNINB 12 DATA GAIN 16 R(*72)

reads one block from unit 8, defines $TN to be its type and name,
then reads in all blocks with names AAAA or BBBB from the remainder
of the file. Finally, up to 16 data items are read free-form from
columns 1 through 72 of unit 12 into block <DATA GAIN>.

4.2 DYNOUT, DYNOUE - Output

DYNOUT writes a specified block or a group of blocks onto a given
FORTRAN unit. Blocks are written with header records for use by
DYNINP (p. 270). A "pseudo end-of-file", which terminates reading,
may be written using DYNOUE.

The form of output from DYNOUT depends on the requested unit and
optional format supplied.

   a. Printer: A printer heading (type, name, length) is generated for
      each block if the requested unit is 6. Printing may be
      suppressed or the actual output unit changed through OPTION
      (p. 285); page control is provided by OPAGE (p. 284). The
      contents of the block(s) will be printed in hexadecimal (on IBM)
      or, if supplied, following a format passed by the calling

program.

b. Formatted output: A header record compatible with DYNINP (p. 270) will be generated if the requested unit is not 6 and is in the range [1,999]. (The unit number must be within the range allowed by the computer operating system as well.) The contents of the block(s) will be output one byte per column ("A" format), or according to a format passed by the calling program.

c. Unformatted output: A unit NWUNIT greater than 1000 will result in unformatted output on unit NWUNIT-1000 compatible with DYNINP. Two logical records are generated for each block: a header record and the contents of the block. (For unformatted output on IBM systems, RECFM should be VBS or VS.)

A negative unit number (NWUNIT) will suppress the header record (or page heading). DYNOUT will list the type, name and unit number for each block written if the requested unit is not the printer (6) and if header records are not being suppressed; the printing may be controlled through OPTION (p. 285), specifying DYNMSG.

Calling Sequences (DYNOUT):

    (FTN) CALL DYNOUT(type,name,NWUNIT,fmt,&ERR)

    (ISX) DYNOUT type name NWUNIT [fmt]

                type,name = type, name of blocks (blank, or "...." in
                            ISX, indicates all)
                |NWUNIT| = FORTRAN unit
                fmt   = "t(format)" (see below)
                            where t = R real numbers
                                    = I integers
                          = 0 use default format
                &ERR   = error return

The argument fmt may contain a format beginning in the second character position: e.g. "R(8F10.3)". Here the R in position 1 indicates that the block contains real (floating point) quantities. The length of the fmt argument may not exceed 64 characters. If the second position does not contain a left parenthesis, the default format for the specified unit will be used.

ISX Notes:

If the fourth argument is supplied, it is used as the output format by DYNOUT. Otherwise, the format to be used is assumed to be contained in the ISX "X" array (p. 60), possibly placed there by FMTCRD (p. 283). If NWUNIT is '*', output is directed to the current ISX output unit.

Examples:

        DYNOUT .DAT .... 13 I(3I4)
        DYNOUT DATA .... 13 R(12F6.0)

        DYNOUT DIM YEAR 13 0

outputs all .DAT blocks on unit 13 using 3I4 format, all DATA blocks using a 12F6.0 format, and the block <DIM YEAR> using the default format.

DYNOUE generates a "pseudo end-of-file" to terminate reading by DYNINP (p. 270).

Calling Sequences (DYNOUE):

        (FTN) CALL DYNOUE(NWUNIT)

        (ISX) DYNOUE NWUNIT

                NWUNIT = FORTRAN unit (unit+1000 for unformatted
                          output)

5. STORAGE MANAGEMENT

Segments of core may be made available for storing blocks through DYNDEF (Sec. 5.1) and, if a system allocation routine is available, through DYNMSA (Sec. 5.2). Any number of segments may be used; i.e., calls to DYNDEF and DYNMSA may cause noncontiguous segments to be linked together. Usually, successive calls to DYNMSA (by DYNNEW) result in contiguous core, which simply enlarges the existing segment.

A hashed directory is maintained in block <DYN* *DY*>. A list of back pointers (i.e., pointers to the pointer subscripts) is maintained as block <DYN* *BP*> and used to update pointers when blocks are moved. During garbage collection by DYNGBG (Sec. 5.3), each relocatable block is moved as far "up" as possible (possibly into preceding segments).

5.1 DYNDEF - Define Segment

A calling program may declare a segment of core to be available for use by DYNCOR through DYNDEF. This routine will normally need to be called only if a system core allocation capability does not exist. The array may be located in the calling program or in COMMON.

Calling Sequence:

    (FTN) CALL DYNDEF(NW,C)

        NW = number of single words in C
        C = array

5.2 DYNMSA - Main Storage Allocation of Segment

DYNMSA calls a main storage allocation routine, if available, to allocate a segment for DYNCOR. If the core obtained is adjacent to an existing segment, the two are merged. DYNMSA is called by DYNNEW (p. 260) when necessary, and will not normally be called by the user.

Calling Sequence:

    (FTN) CALL DYNMSA(NW,&ERR)

        NW   = number of single words
        &ERR = error return (if core not available)

5.3 DYNGBG - Compression (Garbage Collection)

DYNGBG is called by DYNNEW (p. 260) when garbage collection is required.

Calling Sequences:

    (FTN) CALL DYNGBG

    (ISX) DYNGBG

5.4 DYNMAP - Storage Map

DYNMAP prints out a map of storage, showing the type, name, length and location of each block. Printing may be controlled through OPTION (p. 285).

Calling Sequences:

    (FTN) CALL DYNMAP

    (ISX) DYNMAP

5.5 DYNDMP - Control Block Dump

DYNDMP dumps the COMMON block DYN001 and active entries in DYNCOR blocks <DYN* *DY*> (directory) and <DYN* *BP*> (back-pointers). Printing may be controlled through OPTION (p. 285).

Calling Sequences:

    (FTN) CALL DYNDMP

    (ISX) DYNDMP

5.6 DYNERR - Error Dump, Tracing

DYNERR is called when DYNCOR routines detect internal errors, usually resulting from the COMMON block DYN001 or the directory blocks being destroyed. A dump of the COMMON block and the directory and back-pointer DYNCOR blocks is printed and execution terminated.

DYNERR may also be called to initiate tracing for debugging purposes. When tracing is on, DYNNEW and, optionally, DYNOLD print a one-line message containing type, name, precision, length and a relative pointer. DYNNAM indicates block renaming, and DYNGBG prints the number of times it has been called. Calls to DYNDEL result in a message from DYNNEW with precision equal to -1. Note that some messages may be misleading since several DYNCOR routines use DYNNEW and DYNOLD for internal purposes and others access blocks directly.

Printing may be controlled through OPTION (p. 285).

Calling Sequences:

      (FTN) CALL DYNERR(trace)

      (ISX) DYNERR [TRACE|NOTRACE]

           trace = TRACE initiates tracing, NOTRACE terminates
                  tracing

6. SUBJECT INDEX

7. GLOSSARY OF SUBROUTINE CALLS (ISX)

CHAPTER 10

SERVICE ROUTINES

1. INTRODUCTION

Routines in this chapter provide auxiliary services for STATLIB's high-level packages. They include entry points for altering certain parameter settings of the low-level routines in Part III, routines that control the decisions of many STATLIB routines concerning printing and other options, and routines that provide job status descriptions. The routines described here are all callable from ISX (through ISXSVC: see p. 64). Additional information on some of them, and on lower-level utility routines, is contained in Chapter 13 (p. 355).

Section 2 contains subroutine documentation. Interrelated subroutines are grouped into common subsections; otherwise, the listings are alphabetical. Calling sequences follow the STATLIB-wide conventions described in the Part II Introduction (p. 56). Section 3 is a subject index. Section 4 is a one-page summary of SERVICE routine calling sequences.

2. COMMANDS

2.1 CORLEF, CORREM - Core Available

(FTN) CALL CORLEF

(ISX) CORLEF

prints the size of the largest block of core available from the operating system. This message is helpful in determining the proper region size to reserve, since STATLIB's dynamic core allocation routines may cause the standard operating system message to say that the entire region allotted to the program has been used.

(FTN) CALL CORREM(NWORDS)

(ISX) CORREM

returns the size, in single-precision words, of the largest block of core available from the operating system. In ISX, the argument is returned in the first word of the "X" array and as ISX variable $XXX (see Ch. 4, Secs. 2.2-3, p. 60).

2.2 DSPPAR - Parameter Settings for Plotting Display

(FTN) CALL DSPPAR(code,VALUE)

(ISX) DSPPAR code VALUE

sets parameters for STATLIB subroutine DSPLAY (p. 356).

DSPLAY produces many plots on a page, individually scaled. The STPAK example (p. 129) illustrates the technique. Turned sideways, that display shows three low-resolution "time" plots; i.e., variables plotted one observation per column against observation indices. For clarity, the plotted points are connected to their variable's axis; a set of axis "labels" also provides values of points to greater precision than can be obtained from the number of asterisks alone.

OPTION (p. 285) may be used to set certain DSPLAY parameters, as follows: PAGSIZ (default = 132), PRINT (ON), and UNIT (6). Variable names and observation labels are provided automatcally to DSPLAY by the high-level calling program. Other DSPLAY parameters are set through DSPPAR, according to the table below.

code VALUE	Description
AXIS X	draws an axis at X for each variable
BAR OFF	turns off the BAR option for each variable. Normally, each point will connected to the axis or its variable's minimum by a line.
LABEL K	sets number of digits comprising axis label to K (default = 2)
LIN K	sets number of columns per display to K (default = 10)
VMIN X VMAX X	sets the corresponding limits to X. Values outside the limits will not be displayed.

2.3 ERRSET - System Error Settings (IBM-dependent)

(FTN) CALL ERRSET(IERNO,INOAL,INOMES,ITRACE)

(ISX) ERRSET IERNO INOAL INOMES ITRACE

   IERNO = IBM FORTRAN library routine error number
   INOAL = number of errors before program terminates
       (>255 allows an unlimitted number)
   INOMES = number of error messages to be printed
       (<0 suppresses all messages)
   ITRACE = 1 specifies no traceback in the error messages
       2 specifies a traceback

Errors made in calling routines in the IBM FORTRAN library (e.g., READ, WRITE, DLOG) search an option table to determine their recovery instructions. Usually, they print a message containing their error number (characters 4-6 in the code "IHCxxxI"), their name, and a traceback of the subroutines called leading to them. ERRSET, part of the IBM library itself, allows the user to alter the contents of this table. For additional details, see an IBM FORTRAN IV Programmer's Guide.

In ISX, the /ERRSET statement (p. 70) accepts the function names supplied to the central STATLIB function evaluator (used by /DEFAR, STFN1, TSFN1, etc.), translates them into the proper error numbers, and issues the ERRSET call. This provides a considerably simpler calling sequence.

2.4 FMTCRD - Card Format Generator

(FTN) CALL FMTCRD(type,name,FMT)

(ISX) FMTCRD type name

   type,name = DYNCOR block identifiers
   FMT   = 16-character array to receive format

generates a "clean" 80-column card format for outputting a DYNCOR block containing real numbers. In ISX, the format is stored in the "X" array (p. 60) for use by DYNCOR output routine DYNOUT (p. 272).

Example:

```
        FMTCRD DATA AAAA
        DYNOUT DATA AAAA 7
```

constructs a format statement for <DATA AAAA> and writes the data block onto unit 7.

2.5 OPAGE, OPAGEP - Automatic Page Control

```
        (FTN) ...OPAGE(M,K)...

        (ISX) OPAGE M K
```

M = FORTRAN unit on which output will occur.
K > 0 adds K to line count (i.e., K lines will be written on unit M by subsequent WRITE statements in calling program). If fewer than K lines remain on the current page, a new page will be started.
K = 0 sets to start a new page on next call to OPAGE regardless of line count.
K < 0 starts a new page immediately and sets the line count for unit M to $|K|$.

OPAGE, used extensively by STATLIB subroutines, provides automatic page control, printing the date, page number, and an optional title at the top of each page. With each call, the user tells OPAGE how many lines he intends to write with a subsequent WRITE statement. If insufficient lines remain on the current page (OPAGE maintains an internal line count), a new page will be started. OPAGE is a logical function that returns a value of .TRUE. if a new page has been started; the user may use this information to print page headings, etc. Page control is provided for up to 10 unit numbers.

Calling Sequences (OPAGEP):

```
        (FTN) CALL OPAGEP(M,code,VALUE)

        (ISX) OPAGEP M code VALUE
```

sets parameter options for unit M (M=0 means all), according to the table below. If the pause feature is ON, OPAGE pauses before starting each page by reading a line from unit 5.

code VALUE	Description
C x	sets new-page carriage control character to x (default="1")
L K	sets lines per page to K
N K	sets number for next page to K
P ON|OFF	turns pause on or off
T tstrng	prints tstrng, an eight-character title, at the top of each page

Example:

        OPAGEP 6 T UPSTATE

sets page titles for unit 6 to UPSTATE.

2.6 OPTION, OPTGET, OPTERR - Execution, Print Options

OPTION allows the user to control printing and subroutine execution for all of STATLIB. Selected options (e.g., print/no print, output unit number, page size, device type) are stored in a table; the subroutines themselves retrieve this information during execution through entry point OPTGET. A separate entry point OPTERR increments and returns an error counter which may be used to force execution to terminate.

        (FTN) CALL OPTION(idname,code,VALUE)

        (ISX) OPTION idname code VALUE

        idname = 6-character identifier, padded on the right
                 with blanks. Generally, it is a subroutine
                 name or a package prefix followed by the
                 universal character "*".
        code   = character string code for the option type;
                 only two characters are required. Standard
                 values are shown in table below.
        VALUE = value to be entered in option table (see
                 below), or "*" indicating remove last matching
                 (idname,code) entry from the table.

code VALUE	Description
PRINT ON	forces printing
OFF	suppresses printing
UNIT K	sets output unit number (e.g., 8)
PAGSIZ K	sets page size to K (e.g., 72)
DEVICE TERM	format for terminal
PRTR	format for high-speed printer
ERRLIM K	terminate execution after K errors (default = 32)
VLINEC v	sets vertical line character to v (default = "|")

In retrieving option values, the most recent entry with matching idname will be used. A match occurs if the user entered (a) the actual subroutine name, (b) the first k characters of the subroutine name followed by the universal character ("*"), (c) the universal character followed by the last k characters of the subroutine name, or (d) the universal character by itself. Since packages generally have all subroutines beginning with the same characters, calling OPTION with the package prefix and the universal character matches every subroutine in the package. Message and error routines, which all end with the characters MSG and ERR, can easily be controlled as well.

OPTION should be called with VALUE=* to remove old entries rather than specifying the previous value, since the table can hold only 20 entries and will ignore further calls once full. For example, a procedure should specify "PRINT *" rather than "PRINT ON" to remove the effect of an earlier "PRINT OFF" call.

Examples:

```
OPTION REG* PRINT OFF
OPTION REGANL PRINT ON
OPTION *MSG UNIT 8
OPTION * PAGSIZ 80
OPTION TS* PRINT *
```

turns off printing by all REGxxx (i.e., REGPAK) routines except REGANL, directs all message routines to print on FORTRAN unit 8, sets the page size for the entire library to 80 columns, and removes a previous print entry for TSxxxx (i.e., TSPAK) routines.

Calling Sequences (OPTGET):

    (FTN) CALL OPTGET(idname,code,IVALX,IVAL)

    (ISX) OPTGET idname code IVALX

        idname = 6-character identifier, padded on the right
                 with blanks; generally a subroutine name
        code   = character string code for the option type,
                 as above
        IVALX = single-word value to be returned if no
                 (idname,code) match occurs
        IVAL   = single-word value returned

In ISX, the argument IVAL is returned in the first word of the "X" array and as ISX variable $XXX (see Ch. 4, Secs. 2.2-3, p. 60).

Example:

```
OPTGET TSREGA UNIT 6
/WRITE $XXX BSMI AUTOREGRESSIVE MODEL
```

obtains the TSREGA output unit as $XXX and adds a comment to the output.

Calling Sequences (OPTERR):

        (FTN) CALL OPTERR(idname,NERR)

        (ISX) OPTERR idname

            idname = 6-character identifier, padded on the right
                     with blanks. If nonblank, the error counter
                     is incremented by 1.
            NERR   = current value of the error counter

In ISX, the argument NERR is returned in the first word of the "X"
array and as ISX variable $XXX (see Ch. 4, Secs. 2.2-3, p. 60).

OPTERR is called by STATLIB's high level packages ISX (Ch. 4), STPAK
(Ch. 5), TSPAK (Ch. 6), SPPAK (Ch. 7), and TABLE (Ch. 8) whenever
error messages are printed.   OPTERR increments an internal error
counter and terminates execution if this counter exceeds an allowable
threshold.   The number of errors permitted, defaulted to 32, can be
modified throught OPTION's ERRLIM code (see above).

Example:

            OPTGET * ERRLIM 32
            /DEFINE $OLD $XXX
            OPTERR ....
            /DEFAI $NEW $XXX + 2
            OPTION * ERRLIM $NEW
            EXECUTE
            OPTION * ERRLIM $OLD

causes execution to terminate if ISX procedure EXECUTE produces two
errors.   It saves the current error limit as variable $OLD, obtains
the current error count and increments it by two, modifies the error
limit, calls the procedure, then resets the error limit to its
original value.

2.7 PPLOTP - Parameter Settings for Plotting

        (FTN) CALL PPLOTP(code[,A1][,A2])

        (ISX) PPLOTP code [A1] [A2]

is used to set PPLOT (p. 358) parameters. PPLOT is called by all
STATLIB plot routines and provides automatic scaling, labeling,
titling, etc. Numerous examples are given in Chapter 3;   in
particular, the "box" plot (p. 52) illustrates the effects of
various PPLOTP parameter setting calls.

OPTION (p. 285) may be used to set certain PPLOT parameters, as
follows: PAGSIZ (default = 132), PRINT (ON), UNIT (6), VLINEC ("|"),
and DEVICE (PRTR). When DEVICE is PRTR, the plot is enclosed in a
box.   Variable   names   and   observation   labels   are provided

automatically by the high-level calling program. Other PPLOT
parameters are set through PPLOTP, according to the table below.

code A1 A2	Description
MODE COMIC	causes subsequent time plots (not scatter plots) to be printed in "comic mode", i.e., down the page
CINE	resets PPLOT to "cine mode" (across the page)
LINES K	limits the number of plot lines for scatter plots and "cine" time plots to K (default=45, maximum=45).
CHAR K [cstrng]	changes the first K plot characters to those in cstrng (default = +XO*#12...) or, if K<0, returns the first K plot characters in the cstrng argument. In ISX, the "X" array is used for the last argument if cstrng is omitted.
CHAR M	indicates that the characters to be plotted are stored in the data matrix. The last vertical variable will not be plotted, but will contain the plotting characters (one character per variable). Reset by CHAR 0.
VMIN X VMAX X HMIN X HMAX X	sets the corresponding limits to X. Values falling outside the limits will not be plotted.
VAXIS X cc HAXIS X cc	draws axes at X. The second argument contains the characters to be used: the first character for scatter and "cine" time plots, second for "comic" time plots.
TITLE NC tstrng	prints the NC-character (NC<25) title in tstrng at the top of the plot
BAR K X	turns on the BAR option for the K-th variable plotted. Each point will then be connected to the point X by a vertical line.
BARV K1 K2	turns on the BAR option for the K1-th variable plotted. Each point will then be connected by a vertical line to the K2-th variable.
VGRID HGRID	turns on the vertical and horizontal grid options
VTIC X HTIC X	sets the tick-mark spacing to X
TIME XO XI	defines the time origin and time increment for time plots
TNAM timevbl	specifies the name for the time variable in time plots (default = TIME)
OBL	uses observation labels on time axis for cine time plots
RESET *	resets all parameters (except MODE, LINES, CHAR) if resetting is off
OFF	causes all parameters to not be reset after succeeding plots. Normally all parameters except MODE, LINES, and CHAR are reset
ON	resets all parameters (except MODE, LINES, CHAR) and turns re-setting back on

Note: Twice the number of bars (BAR,BARV) plus the number of axes (HAXIS,VAXIS) may not exceed 16.

When more than one plotting character falls in the same print position, priority is as follows: (1) variables in the order given, (2) axes in reverse order, (3) horizontal grid lines, (4) vertical grid lines, (5) bars in reverse order.

Examples:

```
PPLOTP LINES 15
PPLOTP HMAX 1977
PPLOTP VAXIS 1975.75 I-
PPLOTP VMIN 0
PPLOTP TITLE 23 INWD DATA & PREDICTIONS
TSPLT 2 DATA INWD PRDN INWD 1965 1 1975 10
```

sets the plot depth to 15 lines, calls for a horizontal maximum of 1977, a vertical axis at 1975.75 (October), a vertical minimum of 0, a 23-character title, and plots two time series via TSPLT.

2.8 REGGET - Retrieving Regression Results

(FTN) CALL REGGET(code,N1,N2,X)

(ISX) REGGET code N1 N2

        code = results identifier
        N1,N2 = beginning and ending element numbers (for
                 arrays)
        X   = real or integer array receiving data

In ISX, up to 100 single-precision, 50 double-precision, words are stored in the "X" array (p. 60). If a single item is being retrieved (N1=N2), that item is also defined as variable $XXX.

All high-level STATLIB regression routines use REGPAK elementary routines to perform their calculations. Many REGPAK variables can be retrieved through REGGET; the table below indicates the retrieval codes (coresponding to their names in the REGPAK chapter) and the results. REGPAK work space contents, array lengths, and variable definitions are discussed in greater detail in Chapter 11 (p. 297).

code N1 N2 X	Description
AVG 1 NVT X	averages
B 1 NV-1 X	regression coefficients
BU 1 NVT X	regression coefficients (unscrambled)
BZERO 1 1 X	regression constant
C 1 f(NVT) X	correlation matrix
DF 1 1 K	degrees of freedom
KVAR 1 NV K	vector of variable indices
NOBS 1 1 K	number of observations
NV 1 1 K	number of variables in regression
NVT 1 1 K	number of variables accumulated
R2 1 1 X	R-squared
SSE 1 1 X	sum of squared errors
SST 1 1 X	sum of squares - dependent vbl
STD 1 NVT X	standard deviations
SUM 1 NVT X	sums
SWGT 1 1 X	sum of weights
S2 1 1 X	estimate of sigma-squared
V 1 f(NV-1) X	correlation matrix inverse
XNAM 1 NVT X	vector of variable names
XPX 1 f(NVT) X	cross products matrix

$$f(I) = I(I+1)/2$$

2.9 REGPAR - Regression Parameter Settings

(FTN) CALL REGPAR(code,VALUE)

(ISX) REGPAR code VALUE

    code = parameter identifier
    VALUE = new parameter setting

All high-level STATLIB regression routines use REGPAK elementary routines to perform their calculations. REGPAK parameters can be set through REGPAR; the table below indicates the codes available through ISX. For additional details, see Chapter 11, Section 3.8 (p. 310).

code VALUE	Description
CON ON	constant term included
OFF	constant term suppressed
CTHR X	collinearity threshold = X
CVAR X	coef of var'n threshold = X
EXW X	exponential weight factor = X
STOR STD	standard storage mode
COM	compressed storage mode
EXP	expanded storage mode

Default values are CON ON, CTHR .9999, CVAR .000001, EXW 1.0 and STOR STD.

2.10 RUNIF - Random Number Starting Values

(FTN) ...RUNIF(K)...

(ISX) RUNIF K

RUNIF generates uniform random numbers on (0,1) using a combination congruential and Tausworthe generator. RUNIF provides uniform random numbers for all STATLIB routines requiring them; a positive value of K sets its starting value, enabling results to be replicated between jobs. A negative value obtains a new starting value from the system clock. In ISX, the starting value is returned in $XXX. From ISX, RUNIF is called directly only for the purpose of specifying a starting value; the random number generated is not accessible. For additional details, see Chapter 13, Section 4.16 (p. 374).

2.11 TIMER, TIMZER - Print Execution Time

(FTN) CALL TIMER

(ISX) TIMER

prints the time of day and elapsed time since the first and most recent calls to TIMER. A first call to TIMER is made automatically when ISX is initiated; subsequent calls will give total CPU time since entering ISX.

Calling Sequences (TIMZER):

(FTN) CALL TIMZER

(ISX) TIMZER

resets the timer to zero and prints a message if TIMER has already been called.

3. SUBJECT INDEX

4. GLOSSARY OF SUBROUTINE CALLS (ISX)

PART III

LOW LEVEL ROUTINES

This part of the manual documents STATLIB's low level routines, including REGPAK (regression package), TRIPAK (triangular matrix package), and miscellaneous utility routines. These routines carry out the basic calculations for STATLIB's high level packages (Part II). They are documented here to service applications requiring FORTRAN programming.

REGPAK (Ch. 11) is a package of subroutines, each of which performs an operation associated with regression analysis. Executive subroutines are included to provide simplified calling for most situations. REGPAK's modular structure, with several levels of subroutines, results in substantial flexibility in its use. Other features include compressed storage of symmetric arrays, no fixed limit for the number of variables, and automatic deletion of linearly dependent variables.

TRIPAK (Ch. 12) performs operations on compressed triangular (and symmetric) matrices. These operations include addition, multiplication, inversion, dot product, and evaluation of quadratic forms. Utility routines are also included which provide printing, character display, and compatibility with two-dimensional arrays.

Utility routines (Ch. 13) provide miscellaneous services for the user and for other STATLIB routines. They include subroutines for plotting and display, subroutines for controlling print decisions, paging, and labelling, subroutines for performing calculations associated with standard probability distributions, and subroutines for character string manipulation and conversion. The latter routines are building blocks of the ISX system itself.

Each chapter contains an introduction, the documentation itself, and finally a subject index and glossary of subroutines calls. Where subroutines are callable from ISX, a reference is made to the appropriate page in Chapter 10, but ISX calling sequences are not provided. A composite subject index and glossary for all Part III routines appear as appendices to Part III.

DOCUMENTATION CONVENTIONS

Calling Sequence Notation

Calling sequences will be given in FORTRAN formats only. The following notation will be used in describing them.

a. Arguments which are character strings (e.g., parameter codes) will be written in lower case. Unless otherwise stated, the length of the generic name equals the required number of characters (e.g., "code" signifies four characters). Character strings must be right-padded with blanks up to this length.

b. Arguments which are normally FORTRAN scalars are written in upper case (e.g., N, X, N1Y, OCON). The first character of the name indicates the required type: A-H and P-Z denote real arguments, I-N denote integers, and O denotes logical variables. On IBM, all real variables are double precision (REAL*8), whereas integer and logical variables are of standard precision (length 4). Unless otherwise noted, all variables or constants must follow these conventions.

c. Calling sequence arguments enclosed in square brackets (e.g., [A1]) are optional.

d. FUNCTION subprograms are indicated by "..." before and after their calling sequences.

CHAPTER 11

REGPAK - REGRESSION ANALYSIS PACKAGE

1. INTRODUCTION

REGPAK is a package of subroutines designed to perform regression analysis. The package is constructed in modular form, with several "levels" of subroutines. This allows it to easily be modified or expanded to perform additional functions or to use different numerical algorithms. REGPAK will perform weighted as well as unweighted least squares. Subroutines are also included for recursive estimation (updating).

All data input and transformations are provided by the user; printed output by REGPAK is optional. Other features include compressed storage of symmetric arrays, no fixed limit for the number of independent variables, and automatic deletion of linearly dependent variables.

The remainder of Section 1 describes REGPAK's features, conventions, and procedures. Section 2 documents its "executive" routines, which should be sufficient for most application. Service routines are described in Section 3 and extended functions in Section 4. Section 5 discusses the "elementary" routines, called on by the executive routines to perform the basic operations, and useful themselves in carrying out nonstandard sequences of operations. Section 6 presents some sample programs. Section 7 contains a subject index. Finally, Section 8 summarizes REGPAK subroutine variables and calling sequences.

1.1 Subroutine Structure

REGPAK contains several types of subroutines: executive, service, elementary, and triangular matrix operators.

a. Executive (Secs. 2, 4). REGPAK executive subroutines perform "basic regression" (Sec. 2, p. 304) and "extended functions" (Sec. 4, p. 315) by calling REGPAK elementary routines. Most user requirements should be satisfied by use of executive and service routines. There is no fixed limit to the number of variables or observations allowed with either executive or elementary routines. Executive routines have the prefix REGX, usually followed by a single letter. Special entry points (e.g., REGXA1 in REGXA, p. 304) and "combination" routines (e.g., REGXAR , p. 307, for accumulation and regression) have two suffix letters.

b. Service (Sec. 3, p. 308). Service routines perform special functions in conjunction with the elementary and executive routines. Included are entry points for features such as weighted least squares and labels. REGPAK service routines have names consisting of the prefix REG and three suffix letters.

c. Elementary (Sec. 5, p. 323). REGPAK elementary subroutines each perform an operation needed for or associated with regression. They may be called directly when the executive routines are not sufficient. The number of variables allowed with elementary routines is restricted only by machine size. Elementary routines have names consisting of the prefix REG and three suffix letters.

d. TRIPAK (Triangular Matrix Package). TRIPAK performs operations on the linearly stored triangular matrices used by REGPAK. TRIPAK subroutine names have prefixes TRI, SYM and ISYM. These routines are documented in Chapter 12, p. 343.

1.2 Features of the Package

All (symmetric) 2-dimensional arrays are stored linearly as triangular matrices in the calling program (Chapter 12, p. 343). This compressed form of storage results in a core reduction of almost one-half. Programs operating on these arrays may over-write them, so one such array may be all that is required.

Independent variables which are "almost" linear combinations of other variables (i.e., whose multiple correlation with preceding variables exceeds a critical value) will automatically be deleted. The collinearity threshold can easily be modified.

1.3 The Data Matrix

REGPAK accepts data in the form of a two-way array. The accumulator routine, REGACC (p. 323), and corresponding executive routine REGXA1 (p. 304) accept a vector X, where X(1), X(2), ..., X(NVT) are the values of the variables for a single observation. Executive routine REGXA (p. 304), which is used when the entire data array is in core, expects a matrix X, with X(1,J), X(2,J), ..., X(NVT,J) representing the J-th observation. Pictorially:

$$X = \begin{vmatrix} X(1,1) \\ \cdot \cdot \\ \cdot \cdot \\ \cdot \cdot \\ X(NVT,1) \\ \cdot \cdot \\ \cdot \cdot \\ \cdot \cdot \\ X(KDIM,1) \end{vmatrix} \quad \begin{vmatrix} X(1,2) \\ \cdot \cdot \\ \cdot \cdot \\ \cdot \cdot \\ X(NVT,2) \\ \cdot \cdot \\ \cdot \cdot \\ \cdot \cdot \\ X(KDIM,2) \end{vmatrix} \quad \cdots \quad \begin{vmatrix} X(1,J) \\ \cdot \cdot \\ \cdot \cdot \\ \cdot \cdot \\ X(NVT,J) \\ \cdot \cdot \\ \cdot \cdot \\ \cdot \cdot \\ X(KDIM,J) \end{vmatrix} \quad \cdots \,,$$

where KDIM is the first dimension of X. Note that this is what usually is considered to be the transpose of the data matrix. FORTRAN stores arrays "column-wise," so it is necessary to use the transpose in order to have elements of observation vectors stored contiguously. Thus the call to REGACC or REGXA1 for the J-th observation could have X(1,J) as its argument.

In addition to its function of storing the basic variables, the data matrix (or vector) can also be used to contain other information pertaining to individual observations (e.g., weights, labels, predicted values, residuals). In general, positions in the observation vector corresponding to variables NVT+1, ..., KDIM are used for this purpose. Information to be passed to or obtained from REGPAK in this manner is requested through a REGPAK service routine REGPAR (p. 310), the arguments of which are a code identifying the information item and the variable to be used for that purpose. For example,

        CALL REGPAR('WGTS',9)

directs REGPAK to use variable 9 as an observation weight and perform weighted least squares (see p. 308).

1.4 Notation and Conventions

In addition to a brief description of the routine, each section of this chapter describing a REGPAK subroutine may contain the following:

   a. Calling sequence - followed by description of arguments. Calling sequences follow the STATLIB-wide conventions described in the PART III Introduction (p. 295).

   b. Optional entry points - additional calling sequences.

   c. Optional printed output - description of printed output, generally printed if first argument is negative, or if specified through OPTION (p. 365). The name of the routine generating the output will be printed at the top of each page. OPAGE provides paging control and contains entry point OPAGEP (p. 363) for further options.

1.5 Ordinary Least Squares

The basic objective of REGPAK is to compute the least squares estimates b_0, b_1, ..., b_k of β_0, β_1, ..., β_k in the model

$$y_j = \beta_0 + x_{j1}\beta_1 + \ldots + x_{jk}\beta_k + \varepsilon_j, \qquad j = 1, \ldots, n,$$

or

$$y_j = \beta_0 + x_j'\beta + \varepsilon_j, \qquad j = 1, \ldots, n,$$

where

$$E(\varepsilon_j) = 0, \quad E(\varepsilon_i\varepsilon_j) = \delta_{ij}\sigma^2.$$

Equations in this chapter are for models with an intercept term β_0. This term may be suppressed through REGPAR (p. 310); the equations differ mostly by setting $\bar{x}$ and $\bar{y}$ to zero and adjusting the degrees of freedom.

The least squares estimates may be obtained by the usual method,

$$\begin{bmatrix} b_0 \\ b \end{bmatrix} = (\widetilde{X}'\widetilde{X})^{-1} \widetilde{X}'y,$$

where

$$\widetilde{X} = \begin{bmatrix} \underline{1} \vdots X \end{bmatrix} = \begin{bmatrix} \underline{1} & x_1 & \cdots & x_n \end{bmatrix},$$

But, for numerical reasons, it is desirable to rescale the X'X matrix into a correlation matrix prior to inversion. Let S be the diagonal matrix of standard deviations of the independent variables (x) and s the standard deviation of the dependent variable (y), i.e.,

$$S = \left[\delta_{ij} \left\{ \frac{1}{n-1} (X'X - n\bar{x}\bar{x}')_{ii} \right\}^{1/2} \right],$$

$$s = \left[\frac{1}{n-1} (y'y - n\bar{y}^2) \right]^{1/2}.$$

Then the correlation matrix may be written

$$C = \frac{1}{n-1} S^{-1}(X'X - n\overline{xx}')S^{-1},$$

and the vector of correlations of x with y

$$g = \frac{1}{n-1} S^{-1}(X'y - n\overline{xy})s^{-1}.$$

The least squares estimates are now

$$b = S^{-1}C^{-1}gs,$$

$$b_0 = \overline{y} - \overline{x}'b,$$

and the estimate of σ^2 is

$$\hat{\sigma}^2 = \frac{n-1}{n-k-1} (s^2 - b'Sgs).$$

1.6 Weighted Least Squares (diagonal weights)

REGPAK performs weighted least squares with diagonal weights, assuming the weight to be one for each observation unless otherwise specified through REGPAR (p. 310) or individual entry points. General (non-diagonal) weighting is also available (Sec. 4.4, p. 322).

As in Section 1.5, we consider the linear model

$$y_j = \beta_0 + x_j'\beta + \varepsilon_j, \qquad j = 1,\ldots,n,$$

with

$$E(\varepsilon_j) = 0,$$

but now assuming

$$E(\varepsilon_i \varepsilon_j) = \delta_{ij} v_j \sigma^2$$

or

$$E(\varepsilon\varepsilon') = V\sigma^2, \quad V \text{ diagonal.}$$

Without loss of generality we may also assume that

$$\sum_{1}^{n} \frac{1}{v_j} = n.$$

Ordinary least squares, of course, is a special case with $v_1 = v_2 = \ldots = v_n = 1$.

Letting W be proportional to V^{-1} and multiplying each term in the model for the j-th observation by

$$\left[w_j \middle/ \left[\frac{1}{n} \sum_i w_i \right] \right]^{1/2}$$

we obtain a linear model for which the errors have mean zero and covariance matrix $I\sigma^2$. The quantity

$$w_j \middle/ \left[\frac{1}{n} \sum_i w_i \right] = w_j / \overline{w}$$

is the (normalized) weight associated with the j-th observation.

As before, REGPAK rescales the X'WX matrix into a weighted correlation matrix prior to inversion. The vector of weighted averages is

$$\overline{x} = \frac{\Sigma w_j x_j}{\Sigma w_j} = \frac{\Sigma w_j x_j}{n\overline{w}} \, ,$$

and the standard deviations

$$S = \left[\delta_{ij} \left\{ \frac{1}{(n-1)\overline{w}} (X'WX - n\overline{w}\,\overline{x}\overline{x}')_{ii} \right\}^{1/2} \right]$$

$$s = \left[\frac{1}{(n-1)\overline{w}} (y'Wy - n\overline{w}\overline{y}^2) \right]^{1/2} .$$

The weighted correlation matrix is then

$$C = \frac{1}{(n-1)\overline{w}} S^{-1} (X'WX - n\overline{w}\,\overline{x}\overline{x}') S^{-1}$$

and the vector of weighted correlations of x with y

$$g = \frac{1}{(n-1)\overline{w}} \; S^{-1}(X'Wy - n\overline{wxy})s^{-1}.$$

As before,

$$b = S^{-1}C^{-1}gs,$$

$$b_0 = \overline{y} - \overline{x}'b,$$

and

$$\hat{\sigma}^2 = \frac{n-1}{n-k-1} \; (s^2 - b'Sgs).$$

2. EXECUTIVE SUBROUTINES FOR BASIC REGRESSION

The REGPAK executive subroutines perform regression analyses by calling other REGPAK subroutines. This section contains all information necessary for their use, while Section 3 (p. 308) describes options the user may wish to incorporate and Section 4 (p. 315) describes auxiliary executive routines.

The regression problem, as described in Section 1.6, may be divided into three phases:

(a) Accumulation (REGXA, p. 304)

(b) Regression (REGXR, p. 305)

(c) Prediction and residuals (REGXP, p. 306)

After performing any phase, the succeeding phases may be executed one or more times (e.g., several regressions on subsets of the accumulated variables, or predictions for several sets of data). Multiphase routines (REGX, REGXAR, REGXRP, p. 307) permit one to perform more than one phase with one call. REGX (or REGXAR) is the only REGPAK subroutine needed for many applications.

The executive subroutines dynamically allocate all storage required by the REGPAK subroutines by calling CORGET (p. 356). There is no fixed limit to the number of variables that these routines can handle. The arrays and variables are available to the programmer through REGGET (p. 311). Storage layouts are described in Section 3.10, p. 312.

Errors detected by executive routines result in error messages from REGERR; OPTION (p. 365) may be called to control REGERR printing.

2.1 REGXA - Accumulation Phase

This subroutine has two entry points: REGXA is used when all the data are stored in core, REGXA1 when the data are available one observation at a time. Both call subroutine REGACC (p. 323) to perform the accumulation.

Calling Sequence (REGXA):

        CALL REGXA(NVT,KDIM,KOBS,X)

        |NVT| = total number of variables to be accumulated.
                If NVT is negative, the data will be printed.
        KDIM = first dimension of X in calling program.
        KOBS = number of observations to be accumulated.
        X   = matrix of observations, dimensioned (KDIM,m),
                m ≥ KOBS. Here X(1,J), ..., X(NVT,J) are the
                values of the variables for the J-th

observation.

REGXA will normally re-initialize each time called. To accumulate more than one set of data, issue

            CALL REGXA2

before each additional call to REGXA.

Calling Sequence (REGXA1):

            CALL REGXA1(NVT,INIT,X)

            |NVT| = (Same as REGXA)
            INIT = variable set to zero before first call to
                    cause initialization (its value will be set
                    to 1 by REGXA1)
            X   = vector of variables for one observation

REGXA1 must be called once for each observation.

2.2 REGXR - Regression Phase

REGXR calls subroutines which calculate and print the means, variances (REGMSD, p. 323), and correlation matrix (REGCOR, p. 324) if necessary, and the regression coefficients (REGSEL, REGINV, REGRES and REGANL, p. 324 - p. 326). A constant term will be included in the model unless suppressed through REGPAR (p. 310).

Calling Sequence (REGXR):

            CALL REGXR(NV,KVAR)

            NV   = number of variables to be included in the
                   regression (i.e., number of independent
                   variables, excluding the constant term, plus
                   one). NV must not be greater than NVT was in
                   the accumulation phase. If NV = 0, the means,
                   standard deviations, and correlation matrix may
                   be computed, but no regression will occur.
            KVAR = vector of indices of variables to be included in
                   the regression. The index of the dependent
                   variable is taken as KVAR(NV). If the constant
                   zero is given as the argument (or KVAR(1) = 0),
                   REGXR will assume KVAR(J) = J, J = 1 to NV.

Additional Regression:

REGXR has a second entry point which causes an additional regression to be performed, changing only the dependent variable.

Calling Sequence (REGXR2):

```
CALL REGXR2(KDEP)
```

KDEP = index of new dependent variable.

Analysis Only:

Subroutine REGXRA may be used to perform the statistical analysis of regression (using REGANL, p. 326) only. This can be used to obtain a reprint of the last analysis or to print the results of updating (i.e., called after REGXU, p. 321).

Calling Sequence (REGXRA):

```
CALL REGXRA
```

Printed Output:

Means, variances, standard deviations (from REGMSD, p. 323), correlation matrix (REGCOR, p. 324), deleted variables (REGINV, p. 325), s^2, multiple R^2, coefficients and their standard errors, t-statistics, and an ANOVA table (REGANL, p. 326) are printed. TRIDIS (p. 349) is called to generate a character display of the correlation matrix, but with printing normally off. OPTION (p. 365) may be called to turn TRIDIS printing on or to suppress printing from the other routines.

2.3 REGXP - Prediction and Residuals Phase

REGXP calculates predicted values and residuals for the data used for regression or for additional data. It has two principal entry points: REGXP, when all the data are stored in core, REGXP1 when the data are available one observation at a time. Both call subroutines REGPRE (p. 327) and REGRSD (p. 327) to perform the actual computations.

Calling Sequences:

```
CALL REGXP(KDIM,KOBS,X)

CALL REGXP1(INIT,X)
```

where the arguments are the same as those of REGXA and REGXA1, respectively (p. 304). To process multiple sets of data using REGXP, issue

```
CALL REGXP2
```

before each additional call to REGXP to suppress initialization.

Predicted Values and Residuals:

The predicted values of the dependent variable and/or the residuals (observed minus prediction) may be obtained through REGPAR (p. 310):

```
CALL REGPAR('PRDN',IPRD)
CALL REGPAR('RSID',IRSD)
```

Then the predicted values will be stored in X(IPRD,J) or X(IPRD) and residuals in X(IRSD,J) or X(IRSD) in succeeding calls to REGXP or REGXP1, respectively. This feature is cancelled by:

```
CALL REGPAR('PRDN',0)
CALL REGPAR('RSID',0)
```

Printed Output:

The weight, dependent variable, estimate, residual, residual as a percentage of the dependent variable, cumulative percentage, and cumulative average-square-residual are printed by REGRSD (p. 327). Output may be suppressed by calling OPTION (p. 365).

2.4 REGXAR, REGXRP, REGX - Multiphase Routines

These multiple-entry subroutines are used to perform two or more phases of the regression analysis. The entry points, with calling sequences, are:

Accumulation, Regression (REGXAR):

```
CALL REGXAR(NVT,KDIM,KOBS,X,NV,KVAR)
```

Regression, Prediction (REGXRP):

```
CALL REGXRP(NV,KVAR,KDIM,KOBS,X)
```

Accumulation, Regression, Prediction (REGX):

```
CALL REGX(NVT,KDIM,KOBS,S,NV,KVAR)
```

The arguments in each case are the same as the arguments for the corresponding single-phase routines.

3. SERVICE ROUTINES

3.1 Suppression of Constant Term

The constant term β_0 in the regression model (Sec. 1.5, p. 300) may be suppressed by

        CALL REGPAR('CON ','OFF') .

Suppression will remain in effect until cancelled by

        CALL REGPAR('CON ','ON') .

3.2 Variable Names

An array of alphanumeric variable names may be defined to be printed along with the variable numbers by OPTLBV (p. 366):

        CALL OPTLBV(XNAME)   ,

where XNAME is an array of titles, XNAME(I) being the name of the I-th variable. The feature is cancelled by

        CALL OPTLBV(0) .

3.3 Observation Labels

An alphameric label may be printed with each observation by storing the desired name as a variable in the observation vector X. The number of the variable to be used is defined to REGPAK through OPTLBO (p. 366):

        CALL OPTLBO(KLBL)

indicates that X(KLBL) contains the label for the observation. In a two-dimensional data matrix, X(KLBL,J) would be the label for the J-th observation. The value of KLBL should be greater than the number of variables used by REGPAK; a good rule is to set it equal to the first dimension of X.

Printing of the observation labels may be discontinued by:

        CALL OPTLBO(0) .

3.4 Weighted Least Squares (diagonal weights)

Weighted least squares (with diagonal weights) is described in

Section 1.6, p. 301. The relative weights w may be contained as variable KWGT in the data matrix, and defined to REGPAK by

       CALL REGPAR('WGTS',KWGT)   .

A subsequent call with an argument of zero will reinstate unweighted least squares.

Weights may also be defined through entry points in individual routines (e.g., REGACW in REGACC, p. 323). If more than one weight is specified for a given observation, the product of the weights will be used.

Negative weights cause the observation to be removed rather than added (Sec. 3.5, below). Observations with zero weight may be printed but will be ignored.

3.5 Removal of Observations

Observations may be removed by assigning them a negative weight (Sec. 3.4, above) and "re-accumulating" or updating them (see Sec. 4.3, p. 317). This is particularly useful when the coefficient vector is assumed to be changing with time (Sec. 3.6, below).

3.6 Exponential Weighting

If the coefficient vector β is changing slowly with time, its estimate should be based mainly on recent observations. One method for doing this is to drop off an old observation and add a new one as each point is obtained. In order to do this, the n-th past observation must be available at each step.

An alternative approach, which requires no memory, is to forget the past exponentially by multiplying the j-th past observation by ρ^j, $\rho < 1$. Thus the X'WX matrix would be

$$(X'WX)_n = \sum_{j=0}^{n-1} \rho^j w_{n-j} x_{n-j} x'_{n-j} .$$

Variance estimates obtained assume that $\rho^j w_{n-j}$ is the correct weight; i.e., that

$$E\left[\varepsilon_{n-j}^2\right] = \frac{\sigma^2}{\rho^j w_{n-j}} .$$

This emphasizes that exponential weighting, which tends to cause the proper type of correction, is usually only an approximation to the true situation. One hypothesizes that the coefficient vector is changing with time, not that the variance of past errors is increasing. An alternative approach to the problem is the more general filter described by Kalman [6], in which the coefficients are allowed to change with time.

Nevertheless, exponential weighting provides a satisfactory solution in many situations, and can easily be implemented in the weighted least squares framework. It is particularly suited to the case in which the coefficients are being updated as each observation is obtained (see Sec. 4.3, p. 317).

The exponential weighting factor may be changed to RHO by

        CALL REGPAR('EXW',RHO)   .

The default value (no exponential weighting) is RHO = 1.

3.7 Automatic Variable Deletion

Variables will be deleted automatically (by REGINV, p. 325) if the square of their multiple correlation with preceding variables exceeds a collinearity threshold, which is initially set to .9999. This value may be changed to RHOSQ by:

        CALL REGPAR('CTHR',RHOSQ)   .

3.8 REGPAR - Regresson Parameter Settings

REGPAR sets parameters for REGPAK subroutines.

        CALL REGPAR(code,VALUE)   .

        code = parameter identifier
        VALUE = new parameter setting

code VALUE	Description
CON ON	constant term included
OFF	constant term suppressed
CTHR X	collinearity threshold = X
CVAR X	coef of var'n threshold = X
EXW X	exponential weight factor = X
FSTD K	forecast std dev in vbl K
PRDN K	predictions in variable K
PSTD K	prediction std dev in vbl K
RSID K	residuals in variable K
RSTD K	residual std dev in vbl K
STOR STD	standard storage mode
COM	compressed storage mode
EXP	expanded storage mode
WGTS K	weights in variable K

Codes CON, CTHR, EXW and WGTS are described in earlier parts of this section. Code CVAR sets the value of the coefficient of variation below which REGMSD will consider a variable to have zero variance (see REGMSD, p. 323). Codes PRDN through RSTD request the executive routines (only) to store results back in the data matrix, and are described in Sections 2 and 4.

Code STOR sets the mode of storage for new blocks created for REGPAK executive routines and for high-level package regression routines. With standard (the default) and compressed modes, some arrays share the same storage locations, causing some restrictions on order of operations (e.g., with compressed mode additional regressions may not be performed without reaccumulation). See Section 3.10 below for further information on storage management.

Default values are CON ON, CTHR .9999, CVAR .000001, EXW 1.0, STOR STD, and all others 0.

Example:

```
        CALL REGPAR('WGTS',3)
        CALL REGPAR('RSID',9)
```

instructs REGPAK to use variable 3 as weights and to store residuals as variable 9.

3.9 REGGET - Retrieving Regression Results

REGGET retrieves results from REGPAK executive routines and high-level package regression routines.

```
        CALL REGGET(code,N1,N2,X)
```

```
        code  = results identifier
        N1,N2 = beginning and ending element numbers (for
                arrays)
        X     = real or integer array receiving data
```

In ISX, up to 100 single-precision, 50 double-precision, words are stored in the "X" array (see Ch. 4, Sec. 2.3, p. 60). If a single item is being retrieved (N1=N2), that item is also defined as variable $XXX.

All high-level STATLIB regression routines use REGPAK elementary routines to perform their calculations. Many REGPAK variables can be retrieved through REGGET; the table below indicates the retrieval codes (correpording to the names used throughout this chapter) and the results.

code N1 N2 X	Description
AVG 1 NVT X	averages
B 1 NV-1 X	regression coefficients
BU 1 NVT X	regression coefficients (unscrambled)
BZERO 1 1 X	regression constant
C 1 f(NVT) X	correlation matrix
DF 1 1 K	degrees of freedom
KVAR 1 NV K	vector of variable indices
NOBS 1 1 K	number of observations
NV 1 1 K	number of variables in regression
NVT 1 1 K	number of variables accumulated
R2 1 1 X	R-squared
SSE 1 1 X	sum of squared errors
SST 1 1 X	sum of squares - dependent vbl
STD 1 NVT X	standard deviations
SUM 1 NVT X	sums
SWGT 1 1 X	sum of weights
S2 1 1 X	estimate of sigma-squared
V 1 f(NV-1) X	correlation matrix inverse
XNAM 1 NVT X	vector of variable names
XPX 1 f(NVT) X	cross products matrix

$$f(I) = I(I+1)/2$$

3.10 REGXWK - Storage Management

REGXWK performs storage management services for REGPAK executive routines and for regression routines in the high-level packages (STREG, TSREG, TABREG). The high-level packages provide storage in DYNCOR blocks with type REG. The REGPAK executive routines normally obtain storage from the operating system through CORGET (p. 356), but the user may, through REGXWK, provide his own storage. This block of core may then be saved externally and used in a later session to continue the analysis (after calling REGXWK to assure that the block is complete prior to dumping).

Calling Sequence:

        CALL REGXWK(code,NVTMAX,NW,W,JW,&ERR)

        code   = 3-character code (NEW, OLD or FIN - see below)

NVTMAX = maximum number of variables to be used
NW   = total number of real words in block
W   = reference array
JW   = pointer subscript
&ERR   = error return (invalid code or insufficient core)

The action taken by REGXWK for each value of code is as follows:

a. If code=NEW, a new (empty) block of length NW real words is accepted and initialized for REGPAK use with up to NVTMAX variables. The block consists of words W(JW) through W(JW+NW-1).

b. If code=OLD, a block of core from a previous regression is accepted for use by REGPAK. The maximum number of variables and the length of the block are returned in NVTMAX and NW respectively. The block consists of NW words beginning at W(JW). REGPAK parameter settings (REGPAR, Sec. 3.8 above) are reset to their value at the time the block was completed (code=FIN, below).

c. If code=FIN, the regression block currently in use is completed by copying appropriate information into it from common blocks REG001 and REG002. The other arguments are ignored.

REGPAK will operate in three modes of storage utilization: expanded (EXP), standard (STD) and compressed (COM) (see REGPAR, Sec. 3.8 above). The number of words (NW) required as a function of the maximum number of variables to be used (NVTMAX) for each mode is as follows:

EXP: NW = 20 + (N1+35)/k + 9*N1 + 2*N1**2
STD: NW = 20 + (N1+35)/k + 7*N1 + N1**2
COM: NW = 20 + (N1+35)/k + 6*N1 + (N1**2 + N1)/2

where k is the number of integers that occupy the same amount of storage as a real number (e.g., 2 on IBM 370).

With standard storage, the vector of variable means over-writes the variable sums and the correlation matrix over-writes the cross-products matrix, so further accumulations cannot be made after reduction to correlation matrix has occurred. If the constant has been turned off (p. 308), it cannot be turned back on without re-accumulation. Also, the regression coefficient correlation matrix, if computed, over-writes the inverse correlation matrix, preventing further regressions without re-inversion.

With compressed storage, the inverse correlation matrix over-writes the correlation matrix, so the dependent variable must follow the independent variables in the input matrix, the independent variables must be specified in the same order they occur in the input matrix, and additional regressions with different independent variables cannot be performed without reaccumulation.

Examples:

```
      DIMENSION W(1200)
      CALL REGXWK('NEW',30,1200,W,1,&88)
```

defines array W as regression workspace for up to 30 variables.

```
      CALL REGX(NVT,20,NOBS,X)
      CALL REGXWK('FIN',0,0,0,0)
      WRITE(17)W
```

performs a regression, then "completes" W and writes it to FORTRAN unit 17.

```
      DIMENSION W(1200)
      READ(17)W
      CALL REGXWK('OLD',NVT,NW,W,1,&88)
      CALL REGXP(20,NOBS,XX)
```

reads W into core, defines it as an "old" regression block, and calls REGXP to compute predictions for a new matrix XX.

4. EXTENDED FUNCTION EXECUTIVE ROUTINES

REGPAK will perform other functions in addition to basic least squares. Some of these may be performed by themselves; others are generally done in conjunction with other regression procedures. This section describes these features and their executive subroutines; users should also be aware of the options and special features described in Section 3. The REGPAK subroutines which are used by these executive routines are described in Section 5, p. 323.

4.1 Regression Coefficient Covariance/Correlation Matrices

4.1.1 REGXV - Executive Subroutine

REGXV computes and prints the covariance matrix or correlation matrix of the regression coefficients from the preceding regression by calling REGRCV (p. 328) or REGRCC (p. 329), respectively. TRIDIS (p. 349) is called to generate a character display of the correlation matrix, but with printing normally off. OPTION (p. 365) may be called to turn TRIDIS printing on or to suppress printing from the other routines.

Calling Sequence:

        CALL REGXV(KCV)

        KCV = 1 covariance matrix.
            = 2 correlation matrix.

4.2 Forecast Variance

The predicted dependent variable, $\hat{y} = x'b$, may be considered as an estimate (a) of the expected value of y given x (i.e., the true regression line at x), and (b) of y, a future observation at x. The error variances for these cases are called the prediction variance and forecast variance, respectively, and are given by

$$\text{(a)} \qquad E(\hat{y} - E(y|x))^2 = x'(X'X)^{-1}x\sigma^2$$

$$\text{(b)} \qquad E(y-\hat{y})^2 = (x'(X'X)^{-1}x + \frac{\bar{w}}{w})\sigma^2$$

where w is the weight associated with the observation, and $\bar{w}$ is the average of the weights used in regression. For example, if the regression was unweighted and w = 2, this will correspond to the mean of 2 observations at x. In the notation of Section 1.6 (p. 301), (a) becomes

$$E(\hat{y} - E(y|x))^2 = \left[\frac{(x-\bar{x})'S^{-1}C^{-1}S^{-1}(x-\bar{x})}{n-1} + \frac{1}{n}\right]\sigma^2.$$

The residual variance is given by

$$E(y-\hat{y})^2 = (\frac{\bar{w}}{w} - x'(X'X)^{-1}x)\sigma^2 \quad .$$

4.2.1 REGXF - Forecasts and Forecast Variances

REGXF calculates and prints forecasts (predictions) and forecast and prediction variances for a set of data by calling REGPRE (p. 327) and REGFOV (p. 329). The coefficients and parameters used are from the preceding regression. The data matrix (or vectors) used may be a different array than that used for regression. Only the independent variables need be included, but they must be in the same position in the matrix as in REGXA (p. 304). The subroutine has two principal entry points: REGXF when all the data are stored in core, REGXF1 when the data are available one observation at a time. Weights may be entered in the usual way or through entry point REGFOW in REGFOV, and are assumed to be on the same scale as those used for the regression.

Calling Sequence (REGXF):

        CALL REGXF(KDIM,KOBS,X)

        KDIM = first dimension of X.
        KOBS = number of observations.
        X   = matrix of observations, dimensioned (KDIM,m), m
               ≥ KOBS. Here X(1,J), ..., X(NVT,J) are the
               values of the variables for the Jth observation.

To process multiple sets of data, issue

        CALL REGXF2

before each additional call to REGXF to suppress initialization.

Calling Sequence (REGXF1):

        CALL REGXF1(INIT,X)

        INIT = variable to be set to zero before first call to
               cause initialization
        X   = vector of variables for one observation

REGXF1 must be called once for each observation.

Predicted Values:

As in REGXP (p. 306), the predicted values of the dependent variable may be obtained through REGPAR (p. 310):

CALL REGPAR('PRDN',IPRD)

Then the predicted values will be stored in X(IPRD,J) or X(IPRD) in succeeding calls to REGXF or REGXF1, respectively. Cancel by

CALL REGPAR('PRDN',0)   .

Standard Errors:

The prediction, forecast and residual standard errors (see Sec. 4.2 above) may be stored in X(ISTD,J) or X(ISTD) by:

CALL REGPAR('PSTD',ISTD)
CALL REGPAR('FSTD',ISTD)
CALL REGPAR('RSTD',ISTD)   ,

respectively. Cancel by calling REGPAR with the appropriate code and ISTD=0.

Optional Printed Output:

Output may be obtained by calling OPTION (p. 365) to force printing. REGFOV (p. 329) will print the estimated dependent variable and the prediction and forecast variances and standard deviations.

4.3 Recursive Estimation (Updating)

Given the linear model

$$y = \widetilde{X}\widetilde{\beta} + \varepsilon,$$

with $\widetilde{X} = [1|X]$, $\widetilde{\beta}' = (\beta_0,\beta')$, $E(\varepsilon\varepsilon') = I\sigma^2$, least squares estimates

$$\widetilde{b}_{n-1} = (\widetilde{X}'\widetilde{X})^{-1}\widetilde{X}'y$$

$$\hat{\sigma}^2_{n-1} = y'y - \widetilde{b}'_{n-1}\widetilde{X}'y$$

of $\widetilde{\beta}$ and σ^2, respectively, based on n - 1 observations, and the n-th observation (x_n,y_n), one wishes to obtain estimates based on n observations. One possibility is to reapply the above equations; a computationally more efficient technique is a recursive one based on the work of Plackett [7] and Bartlett [8], which also has the advantage of not requiring that the X'X matrix or the past data itself be accessible. This section summarizes the algorithms for recursive estimation.

Given the n-th observation, the model becomes

$$\begin{bmatrix} y \\ \\ y_n \end{bmatrix} = \begin{bmatrix} \widetilde{X} \\ \\ \widetilde{x}'_n \end{bmatrix} \widetilde{\beta} + \begin{bmatrix} \varepsilon \\ \\ \varepsilon_n \end{bmatrix},$$

where

$$\widetilde{x}_n = \begin{bmatrix} 1 \\ x_n \end{bmatrix},$$

and the least squares estimate

$$\widetilde{b}_n = \left\{ [\widetilde{X}' \ \ \widetilde{x}_n] \begin{bmatrix} \widetilde{X} \\ \widetilde{x}'_n \end{bmatrix} \right\}^{-1} [\widetilde{X}' \ \ \widetilde{x}_n] \begin{bmatrix} y \\ y_n \end{bmatrix} = (\widetilde{X}'\widetilde{X} + \widetilde{x}_n\widetilde{x}'_n)^{-1}(\widetilde{X}'y + \widetilde{x}_n y_n).$$

If $\widetilde{X}'\widetilde{X}$ is nonsingular,

$$(\widetilde{X}'\widetilde{X} + \widetilde{x}_n\widetilde{x}'_n)^{-1} = (\widetilde{X}'\widetilde{X})^{-1} - \frac{(\widetilde{X}'\widetilde{X})^{-1}\widetilde{x}_n\widetilde{x}'_n(\widetilde{X}'\widetilde{X})^{-1}}{\widetilde{x}'_n(\widetilde{X}'\widetilde{X})^{-1}\widetilde{x}_n + 1}.$$

This may be verified by multiplication. Then

$$\widetilde{b}_n = \left[(\widetilde{X}'\widetilde{X})^{-1} - \frac{(\widetilde{X}'\widetilde{X})^{-1}\widetilde{x}_n\widetilde{x}'_n(\widetilde{X}'\widetilde{X})^{-1}}{\widetilde{x}'_n(\widetilde{X}'\widetilde{X})^{-1}\widetilde{x}_n + 1} \right] (\widetilde{X}'y + \widetilde{x}_n y_n)$$

$$= \widetilde{b}_{n-1} + \frac{(\widetilde{X}'\widetilde{X})^{-1}\widetilde{x}_n(y_n - \widetilde{x}'_n\widetilde{b}_{n-1})}{\widetilde{x}'_n(\widetilde{X}'\widetilde{X})^{-1}\widetilde{x}_n + 1}.$$

Thus the correction made to the estimated regression coefficient is proportional to the residual obtained from predicting y_n using $\widetilde{b}_{n-1}$.

These equations provide the recurrence relations necessary to update regression coefficients to incorporate new observations. In a similar fashion the estimate of the error variance may be updated:

$$(n-k-1)\hat{\sigma}^2_n = (y' \ y_n) \begin{bmatrix} y - \widetilde{X}\widetilde{b}_n \\ y_n - \widetilde{x}'_n\widetilde{b}_n \end{bmatrix} = \dots = (n-k-2)\hat{\sigma}^2_{n-1} + \frac{(y_n - \widetilde{x}'_n\widetilde{b}_{n-1})^2}{\widetilde{x}'_n(\widetilde{X}'\widetilde{X})^{-1}\widetilde{x}_n + 1}.$$

In the weighted least squares case (Sec. 1.6, p. 301), ε has a covariance matrix $V\sigma^2$, where V is diagonal and

$$\sum_{1}^{n} \frac{1}{v_j} = n.$$

Setting $W \propto V^{-1}$, the least squares estimate of β based on m observations is

$$\tilde{b}_m = (\tilde{X}'W\tilde{X})^{-1}\tilde{X}'Wy \ .$$

Given an observation (w_n, x_n, y_n), we again wish to obtain a new estimate $\tilde{b}_n$ of $\tilde{\beta}$, where $|w_n|$ is the weight for this observation, with $w_n > 0$ indicating that the observation is to be added (n = m +1), and $w_n < 0$ indicating that the observation is to be removed (n = m - 1: Sec. 3.5, p. 309). In the latter case the observation is assumed to be one of the m observations presently included in the regression.

Following steps analogous to those above, we have

$$(\tilde{X}'W\tilde{X} + w_n \tilde{x}_n \tilde{x}_n')^{-1} = (\tilde{X}'W\tilde{X})^{-1} - \frac{(\tilde{X}'W\tilde{X})^{-1}\tilde{x}_n \tilde{x}_n'(\tilde{X}'W\tilde{X})^{-1}}{\tilde{x}_n'(\tilde{X}'W\tilde{X})^{-1}\tilde{x}_n + w_n^{-1}}$$

$$\tilde{b}_n = \tilde{b}_m + \frac{(\tilde{X}'W\tilde{X})^{-1}\tilde{x}_n(y_n - \tilde{x}_n'\tilde{b}_m)}{\tilde{x}_n'(\tilde{X}'W\tilde{X})^{-1}\tilde{x}_n + w_n^{-1}} \ ,$$

$$(n-k-1)\hat{\sigma}_n^2 = (m-k-1)\hat{\sigma}_m^2 + \frac{(y_n - \tilde{x}_n'\tilde{b}_m)^2}{\tilde{x}_n'(\tilde{X}'W\tilde{X})^{-1}\tilde{x}_n + w_n^{-1}} \ .$$

Equations for updating in the usual REGPAK framework (Secs. 1.5, 1.6) are listed below (for ease of notation the subscript n is dropped from the new observation; i.e., (x_n, y_n, w_n) becomes (x,y,w)):

$$\bar{w}_n = \frac{m\bar{w}_m + w}{n}$$

$$\bar{x}_n = \frac{m\bar{w}_m \bar{x}_m + wx}{n\bar{w}_n}$$

$$[S_{ii}]_n^2 = \frac{\bar{w}_m}{\bar{w}_n}\left[\frac{m-1}{n-1}[S_{ii}]_m^2 + \frac{m}{n(n-1)}\frac{w}{\bar{w}_n}(x-\bar{x}_m)^2\right]$$

$$C_n^{-1} = \frac{\bar{w}_n}{\bar{w}_m} \left[\frac{n-1}{m-1} RC_m^{-1}R - \frac{n-1}{m} \frac{\frac{m}{m-1} RC_m^{-1}zz'C_m^{-1}R \frac{m}{m-1}}{\frac{m}{m-1} z'C_m^{-1}z + \frac{n\bar{w}_n}{w}} \right]$$

$$b_n = b_m + \frac{m}{m-1} \frac{S_n^{-1}RC_m^{-1}z(y-\hat{y})}{\frac{m}{m-1} z'C_m^{-1}z + \frac{n\bar{w}_n}{w}}$$

$$b_{0n} = \bar{y}_n - \bar{x}_n'b_n$$

$$\hat{\sigma}_n^2 = \frac{1}{n-1} \frac{\bar{w}_m}{\bar{w}_n} \left[(m-k-1)\hat{\sigma}_m^2 + \frac{m(y-\hat{y})^2}{\frac{m}{m-1} z'C_m^{-1}z + \frac{n\bar{w}_n}{w}} \right]$$

where

$$R = S_n S_m^{-1}$$

$$z = S_m^{-1}(x-\bar{x}_m)$$

and

$$\hat{y} = b_{0m} + x'b_m.$$

The equations for $\bar{x}$ and S_{ii} are also used to update the mean and standard deviation of y (in practice y and x are contained in one vector).

When exponential weighting (Sec. 3.6, p. 309) is used, the recurrence relations become

$$(\rho\tilde{X}'\tilde{X}+\tilde{x}_n\tilde{x}_n')^{-1} = \rho^{-1}\left[(\tilde{X}'\tilde{X})^{-1} - \frac{(\tilde{X}'\tilde{X})^{-1}\tilde{x}_n\tilde{x}_n'(\tilde{X}'\tilde{X})^{-1}}{\tilde{x}_n'(\tilde{X}'\tilde{X})^{-1}\tilde{x}_n + \rho} \right]$$

and

$$\tilde{b}_n = \tilde{b}_{n-1} + \frac{(\tilde{X}'\tilde{X})^{-1}\tilde{x}_n(y_n-\tilde{x}_n'\tilde{b}_{n-1})}{\tilde{x}'(\tilde{X}'\tilde{X})^{-1}\tilde{x} + \rho}$$

In the computing framework the change is even simpler. The average weight becomes

$$w_m = \frac{\rho m \overline{w}_m + w}{n} ,$$

which is equal to

$$\frac{1}{n}\left[\frac{1-\rho^n}{1-\rho}\right]$$

if $w_j = 1$ for all j. No further modifications to the recursion formulae are required.

4.3.1 REGXU - Updating

REGXU can be called after REGXR (p. 305) to update regression estimates. It has two entry points: REGXU to update through more than one point using a data matrix stored in core, and REGXU1 to update for one observation only. After updating, entry point REGXRA in REGXR may be called to print the results.

Calling Sequence (REGXU):

        CALL REGXU(KDIM,KOBS,X)

        KDIM = 1st dimension of X
        KOBS = number of observations to be updated
        X   = data matrix

Calling Sequence (REGXU1):

        CALL REGXU1(X)

        X = vector of observations.

4.3.2 REGXPU - Prediction/Residuals and Updating

REGXPU generates predictions and residuals and updates regression estimates by calling REGXP1 (p. 306) and REGXU1 (p. 321) for each observation in the data matrix.

Calling Sequence:

        CALL REGXPU(KDIM,KOBS,X)

where the arguments are identical to those of REGXU (p. 321).

4.4 Weighted Least Squares (non-diagonal weights)

Weighted least squares with a diagonal weight matrix (i.e., a weight for each observation) is handled directly by REGPAK subroutines through entry point REGPAR (p. 310). If the weight matrix is not diagonal several changes are required. The averages in Section 1.6 (p. 301) become

$$\overline{w} = \frac{1}{n}\, \underset{\sim}{1}' W \underset{\sim}{1}$$

and

$$\overline{x} = \frac{X' W \underset{\sim}{1}}{n\overline{w}} \,,$$

where $\underset{\sim}{1}$ is a vector of 1's. The data matrix and the weight matrix must be stored in core and used with a special weighted accumulation routine, REGWAC (p. 331). Executive weighted accumulation routine REGXAW is described in the following section.

4.4.1 REGXAW - Weighted Accumulation

REGXAW is used in place of REGXA for weighted accumulation with a non-diagonal weight matrix.

<u>Calling Sequence:</u>

        CALL REGXAW(NVT,KDIM,KOBS,X,W)

        |NVT| = total number of variables to be accumulated.
                 If NVT is negative, the data will be printed
                 (by REGACC).
        KDIM   = first dimension of X in calling program
        KOBS   = number of observations to be accumulated
        X   = matrix of observations, dimensioned (KDIM,m),
                 m ≥ KOBS. Here X(1,J), ..., X(NVT,J) are the
                 values of the variables for the J-th
                 observation.
        W   = weight matrix (dim ≥ KOBS(KOBS+1)/2). W must
                 be a linearly stored triangular matrix
                 (Chapter 12, p. 343).

REGXAW will normally re-initialize each time called. To accumulate more than one set of data, issue

        CALL REGXA2

before each additional call to REGXAW.

5. ELEMENTARY SUBROUTINES

5.1 REGACC - Accumulator

REGACC accumulates the number of observations, sums, and sums of cross-products of the data. It must be called once for each observation.

Calling Sequence:

CALL REGACC(NVT,NOBS,SUM,XPX,X,SWGT)

|NVT| = number of variables. If NVT is negative, the
        data will be printed.
NOBS = number of observations (must be set to zero
        before first call; it will be incremented for
        each observation).
SUM   = accumulated vector of sums (dim ≥ NVT).
XPX   = accumulated matrix of cross-products
        (dim ≥ NVT(NVT+1)/2).
X   = vector of variables to be accumulated
        (dim ≥ NVT).
SWGT = accumulated sum of weights.

Note:

If the observations are stored in core in a doubly-dimensioned array, where X(1,J), ..., X(NVT,J) are the values for the J-th observation, then the call to REGACC for the J-th observation may be:

CALL REGACC(NV,NOBS,SUM,XPX,X(1,J),SWGT)

Entry to Define Weight for Next Observation:

CALL REGACW(WGT)

5.2 REGMSD - Means and Standard Deviations

REGMSD calculates the mean and standard deviation of each variable.

Calling Sequence:

CALL REGMSD(NVT,NOBS,SUM,XPX,AVG,STD,SWGT)

|NVT| = number of variables. If NVT is negative, the
        sample size, means, variances, and standard
        deviations will be printed.
NOBS = number of observations (from REGACC, above).
SUM   = vector of sums (from REGACC).
XPX   = matrix of cross-products (from REGACC).
AVG   = vector of means (may be same array as SUM)

                          (dim $\geq$ NVT).
           STD   = vector of standard deviations (dim $\geq$ NVT).
           SWGT = sum of weights (from REGACC).

Zero Variance Test:

Round-off error may cause the variance for a variable which has a constant value to be computed as nonzero. To prevent this from affecting later calculations (correlations, etc.), the variance (and standard deviation) of a variable is set to zero by REGMSD if its coefficient of variation is less than a critical value, i.e., if

$$STD(I)/|AVG(I)| < CCV.$$

With double precision on the IBM 370, CCV is set equal to .000001. This value may be changed by:

           CALL REGPAR('CVAR',CCV)

5.3 REGCOR - Correlation Matrix

REGCOR calculates the sample correlation matrix. All correlations involving a variable with zero variance are set to zero.

If the intercept term β_0 is being suppressed (REGPAR, p. 310), forcing the regression line through the origin, REGCOR calculates a normalized cross products matrix in place of the correlation matrix, adjusts the standard deviations, and sets the means to zero.

Calling Sequence:

           CALL REGCOR(NVT,NOBS,XPX,AVG,STD,C,SWGT)

           |NVT| = number of variables. If NVT is negative, the
                    correlation matrix (or cross-products matrix)
                    will be printed.
           NOBS   = number of observations (from REGACC, p. 323).
           XPX   = matrix of cross-products (from REGACC).
           AVG   = vector of means (from REGMSD, above).
           STD   = vector of standard deviations (from REGMSD).
           C   = correlation matrix (may be same array as XPX)
                    (dim $\geq$ NVT(NVT+1)/2).
           SWGT   = sum of weights (from REGACC)

5.4 REGSEL - Independent Variable Selector

REGSEL extracts the elements of the correlation matrix corresponding to the independent variables (regressors) to be used in the regression. The variables are selected as specified by KVAR, a vector of indices. The output arrays from this and all following routines will contain only elements corresponding to selected

variables.   For   example,   B(K)   will   be   the   regression   coefficient
corresponding to variable number KVAR(K).

Calling Sequence:

> CALL REGSEL(NV,C,KVAR,V)
>
> |NV| = number of variables to be included in regression
>   (i.e., number of independent variables,
>   excluding constant term, plus 1).
> C   = correlation matrix (from REGCOR, above).
> KVAR = vector of indices of variables to be included
>   (subsequent routines will consider KVAR(NV) to
>   be the index of the dependent variable). If
>   KVAR(1) = 0, REGSEL will set KVAR(J) = J, J = 1
>   to NV. Note: elements of KVAR will be changed if
>   variables are deleted by subsequent routines.
> V   = subset of original correlation matrix (may be
>   same array as C if KVAR is nondecreasing)
>   (dim $\geq$ NV(NV-1)/2).

5.5 REGINV - Matrix Inversion

REGINV calls TRIPAK subroutine SYMINV (p. 346),   which   inverts   the
correlation   matrix   by Choleski decomposition [9].   If the matrix is
near-singular (Sec. 3.7, p. 310), REGINV   can   delete   the   offending
variable   by   removing   the   corresponding elements of KVAR and V and
reducing NV by one, and continue the inversion.

Calling Sequence:

> CALL REGINV(NV,KVAR,V,MODE)
>
> |NV| = number of variables (from REGSEL, above). NV
>   must be a variable, rather han a constant or an
>   expression, since it will be changed if
>   variables are deleted. If NV is negative, the
>   deleted variables are listed.
> KVAR = vector of indices (from REGSEL).
> V   = correlation matrix (from REGSEL). It will be
>   replaced by its inverse.
> MODE = -1 delete linearly dependent variables and
>   continue.
>   = 1 delete and continue, but suppress printed
>   output.
>   = 0 terminate inversion if linearly dependent
>   variable is encountered. In this case, REGINV
>   sets V(1) equal to 0.0 and V(2) equal to the
>   number of the offending variable (if V(2) = K,
>   KVAR(K) is the index of the offending variable).

5.6 REGRES - Regression Coefficients

REGRES calculates regression coefficients. The index of the dependent variable is taken as KVAR(NV).

Calling Sequence:

CALL REGRES(NV,NOBS,C,AVG,STD,KVAR,V,BZERO,B,S2,
                XPY)

|NV| = number of variables in regression (from REGINV, above).
NOBS   = number of observations (from REGACC, p. 323).
C   = correlation matrix (from REGCOR, p. 324).
AVG   = vector of means (from REGMSD, p. 323).
STD   = vector of standard deviations (from REGMSD).
KVAR   = vector of indices (KVAR(J), J = 1 to NV-1 from REGSEL, p. 324, KVAR(NV) = index of dependent variable).
V   = inverted correlation matrix (from REGINV)
BZERO = regression coefficient corresponding to mean (intercept). If this term has been suppressed (see REGPAR, p. 310), BZERO will be set to zero.
B   = vector of regression coefficients (dim $\geq$ NV-1).
S2   = estimate of σ^2 (variance of ε_j in Sec. 1.5, p. 300).
XPY   = vector for temporary internal use (dim $\geq$ NV-1).

5.7 REGANL - Statistical Analysis

REGANL performs a statistical analysis of the regression (see below for list of printed output).

Calling Sequence:

CALL REGANL(NV,NOBS,AVG,STD,KVAR,V,BZERO,B,S2,STDB,
                SWGT)

|NV| = number of variables in regression (from REGINV, p. 325). If NV is negative, printed output (see below) is generated
NOBS   = number of observations (from REGACC, p. 323).
AVG   = vector of means (from REGMSD, p. 323).
STD   = vector of standard deviations (from REGMSD).
KVAR   = vector of indices (from REGRES, above).
V   = inverted correlation matrix (from REGINV)
BZERO = intercept coefficient (from REGRES).
B   = vector of regression coefficients (from REGRES).
S2   = estimate of σ^2 (from REGRES).
STDB   = vector of standard errors of regression

                              coefficients (dim $\geq$ NV-1).
                    SWGT = sum of weights (from REGACC)

Optional Printed Output:

Sample size, estimate of σ^2, square of multiple correlation
coefficient, regression coefficients, standard deviations of
regression coefficients, t-statistics, analysis of variance table.

5.8 REGPRE - Prediction

REGPRE calculates the estimated value of the dependent variable for a
single observation, for use in prediction or residual analysis. The
linear model

$$y_i = b_0 + x_i'b$$

is assumed unless a different function is specified through REGPRF.

Calling Sequence:

        CALL REGPRE(NV,KVAR,X,BZERO,B,Y,YEST)

        NV   = number of variables in regression (from REGINV,
                  p. 325).
        KVAR = vector of indices (from REGRES. p. 326).
        X   = vector of variables for one observation.
        BZERO = intercept coefficient (from REGRES).
        B   = vector of regression coefficients (from
                  REGRES).
        Y   = dependent variable (will be set equal to
                  X(KVAR(NV)).
        YEST = estimate of dependent variable.

Nonlinear Prediction Function:

A user-supplied function subprogram may be used in place of the usual
linear model. The statement

        CALL REGPRF(.TRUE.,FN,ARG)

(FN must be declared EXTERNAL in the calling program) will result in
subroutine FN being called with the same argument list as REGPRE plus
the additional argument ARG. To reset for linear prediction,

        CALL REGPRF(.FALSE.,FN,ARG)

5.9 REGRSD - Residual Analysis

REGRSD performs an analysis of residuals from regression or from prediction. The true and estimated values of the dependent variable must be supplied (they may be obtained from REGPRE). Weights may be used in calculating the cumulative average squared residual, and will be assumed to be on the same scale as the weights used for regression.

Calling Sequence:

        CALL REGRSD(MODE,Y,YEST,X,TEMP,NOBS,SWGT)

        MODE = -1 print
             = 1 suppress printing
        Y   = dependent variable (from REGPRE, above) (or
               0.0 if dependent variable not available).
        YEST = estimate of dependent variable (from REGPRE or
               other estimation routine).
        X   = vector of variables for one observation.
        TEMP = temporary storage array for internal use
               (dim = 6). Set TEMP(1) = 0.0 before first call.
               TEMP(1) = number of observations accumulated.
               TMEP(2) = sum of squares of residuals.
               TEMP(3) = sum of residuals.
               TEMP(4) = sum of dependent variables.
               TEMP(5), (6) = (not presently used).
        NOBS = number of observations (from REGACC, p. 323).
        SWGT = sum of weights (from REGACC).

REGRSD must be called once for each observation. TEMP(1) must be set to zero before the first call to cause initialization.

Entry to Define Weight for Next Observation:

        CALL REGRSW(WGT)

Optional Printed Output:

Weight, dependent variable, estimate, residual, residual as percentage of dependent variable, cumulative percentage, square root of cumulative average square residual.

5.10 REGRCV - Regression Coefficient Covariance Matrix

This subroutine calculates the covariance matrix of the regression coefficients,

$$R = (\widetilde{X}'\widetilde{X})^{-1}\hat{\sigma}^2$$

or, in the notation of Section 1.2 (p. 298),

$$R = \frac{S^{-1}V^{-1}S^{-1}\hat{\sigma}^2}{n-1}$$

Calling Sequence:

> CALL REGRCV(NV,NOBS,STD,KVAR,V,S2,R)
>
> |NV| = number of variables in regression (from REGINV,
>   p. 325). If NV is negative, the covariance
>   matrix is printed.
> NOBS = number of observations (from REGACC, p. 323).
> STD = vector of standard deviations (from REGMSD,
>   p. 323).
> KVAR = vector of indices (from REGRES, p. 326).
> V   = inverted correlation matrix (from REGINV).
> S2   = estimate of σ^2 (from REGRES)
> R   = regression coefficient covariance matrix (may be
>   same array as V) (dim $\geq$ NV(NV-1)/2).

5.11 REGRCC - Regression Coefficient Correlation Matrix

REGRCC calculates the correlation matrix of the regression coefficients.

Calling Sequence:

> CALL REGRCC(NV,KVAR,V,R)
>
> |NV| = number of variables in regression (from REGINV,
>   p. 325). If NV is negative, the correlation
>   matrix is printed.
> KVAR = vector of indices (from REGRES, p. 326).
> V   = inverted correlation matrix (from REGINV) or
>   regression coefficient covariance matrix (from
>   REGRCV, p. 328).
> R   = correlation matrix (may be same array as V)
>   (dim $\geq$ NV(NV-1)/2).

5.12 REGFOV - Forecast Variance

REGFOV calculates forecast and prediction variances as described in Section 4.2, p. 315. A relative weight, which will be considered to be on the same scale as the weights used for regression, may be defined in the usual way (through REGPAR, p. 310) or through entry point REGFOW described below.

Calling Sequence:

> CALL REGFOV(NV,NOBS,AVG,STD,KVAR,V,S2,NOB,X,YEST,PV,
>   FV,Z,SWGT)
>
> |NV| = number of variables in regression (from REGINV,
>   p. 325). If NV is negative, an estimate of the
>   dependent variable and the prediction and

forecast variances and standard deviations are
printed.

NOBS = number of observations (from REGACC, p. 323).
AVG = vector of means (from REGMSD, p. 323).
STD = vector of standard deviations (from REGMSD).
KVAR = vector of indices (from REGSEL, p. 324).
V   = inverted correlation matrix (from REGINV,
       p. 325).
S2   = estimate of σ^2 (from REGRES, p. 326).
NOB = observation counter variable. Must be set to
       zero before first call.
X   = vector of (independent) variables for one
       observation.
YEST = estimate of dependent variable (from REGPRE,
       p. 327, or other estimation routine).
PV   = prediction variance
FV   = forecast variance
Z   = scratch array (dim $\geq$ NV-1).
SWGT = sum of weights (from REGACC).

Entry Point to Define Weight for Next Observation:

CALL REGFOW(WGT)

Optional Printed Output:

Estimate of dependent variable, prediction and forecast variances and
standard deviations.

5.13 REGUPD - Recursive Estimation (Updating)

REGUPD adds or deletes an observation from regression as described in
Section 4.3, p. 317. It is compatible with other REGPAK routines and
will handle weighted or unweighted least squares with or without a
constant term.

Calling Sequence:

CALL REGUPD(NVT,NOBS,AVG,STD,NV,KVAR,V,BZERO,B,S2,X,
            SWGT,T1,T2)

where X is the new observation vector, T1 and T2 are scratch vectors
of length NV-1 and the other arguments are as described for other
REGPAK routines (Sec. 6, p. 332).

Entry to Update for an Additional Dependent Variable:

CALL REGUPB(KDEP,BZERO,B,S2)

where KDEP is the number of the dependent variable and BZERO, B, and
S2 are corresponding coefficients and variance.

Entry for Estimated y on Next Call:

        CALL REGUPE(YEST)

where YEST is to be used as y on the next call. Otherwise y will be
obtained from REGPRE.

<u>Entry to Define Weight for Next Call:</u>

        CALL REGUPW(WGT)

where WGT is the weight for the next observation (weights may also be
defined through REGPAR, p. 310).

5.14 REGWAC - Weighted Accumulation

REGWAC performs weighted accumulation, as described in Section 4.4,
p. 322.

<u>Calling Sequence:</u>

        CALL REGWAC(NVT,KDIM,NOBS,X,W,SUM,XPX,SWGT)

        |NVT| = number of variables.
        KDIM   = first dimension of X in calling program.
        NOBS   = number of observations to be accumulated.
        X   = matrix of observations, dimensioned (KDIM,m),
                 m ≥ NOBS. Here X(1,J), ..., X(NVT,J) are the
                 values of the variables for the J-th
                 observation.
        W   = weight matrix (dim ≥ NOBS(NOBS+1)/2). W must be
                 a compressed triangular matrix (Chapter 12,
                 p. 343).
        SUM   = accumulated vector of sums (dim ≥ NVT).
        XPX   = accumulated cross-products matrix (dim ≥
                 NVT(NVT+1)/2).
        SWGT   = accumulated sum of weights.

<u>Entry for Additional Accumulation:</u>

        CALL REGWA2

suppresses re-initialization on the next call to REGWAC.

6. SAMPLE PROGRAMS

The sample programs are taken from a paper by Longley [10] which considers the relative merits of several least squares programs. The independent variables in the model are highly correlated, with squared multiple correlation coefficients as high as 0.998. The IBM 370 (double precision) version of REGPAK gives coefficients agreeing with Longley's hand-calculated values to at least eight significant figures.

The data consist of 16 observations on 7 variables. The problem considered by Longley was the regression of the seventh variable on the first six.

Two sample programs are given. The first gives the simplest program sufficient to compute the means, variances and correlations of the variables and perform the regression mentioned above. The second includes two regression models and makes use of Service and Extended Function subroutines.

The complete input streams are shown for running the programs on an IBM VS/370 system; the resulting output appears afterward. The job control statements here are for Bell Laboratories, where the library data set is named STAT.FORTLIB. See Chapter 15, Section 3 (p. 394), for information on accessing STATLIB subroutines in FORTRAN.

6.1 Example 1

Job Input Stream:

```
//jobname JOB (acctg info),parameters
// EXEC FORTGCG
//FORT.SYSIN DD *
      IMPLICIT REAL*8(A-H,P-Z),LOGICAL(O)
      DIMENSION X(10,20)
      READ(5,91) ((X(I,J),I=1,7),J=1,16)
      CALL REGXAR(7,10,16,X,7,0)
      STOP
   91 FORMAT(F4.1,F7.0,2F5.0,F7.0,F5.0,F7.0)
      END
//GO.SYSLIB DD
// DD DSN=STAT.FORTLIB,DISP=SHR
//GO.SYSIN DD *
  830 234289 2356 1590 107608 1947  60323
  885 259426 2325 1456 108632 1948  61122
  882 258054 3682 1616 109773 1949  60171
  895 284599 3351 1650 110929 1950  61187
  962 328975 2099 3099 112075 1951  63221
  981 346999 1932 3594 113270 1952  63639
  990 365385 1870 3547 115094 1953  64989
 1000 363112 3578 3350 116219 1954  63761
 1012 397469 2904 3048 117388 1955  66019
```

```
1046 419180 2822 2857 118734 1956  67857
1084 442769 2936 2798 120445 1957  68169
1108 444546 4681 2637 121950 1958  66513
1126 482704 3813 2552 123366 1959  68655
1142 502601 3931 2514 125368 1960  69564
1157 518173 4806 2572 127852 1961  69331
1169 554894 4007 2827 130081 1962  70551
```

Description:

The data are read into the two-way array X. REGXAR (p. 307) is called to perform the accumulation and regression.

Output:

REGPAK / REGMSD   07/09/80   PAGE 1


```
     SAMPLE SIZE  . . . .    16
     SUM OF WEIGHTS . . .   1.6000D+01
     AVERAGE WEIGHT . . .   1.0000D+00
```

VARIABLE	MEAN	VARIANCE	STD DEV
1	1.0168D+02	1.1646D+02	1.0792D+01
2	3.8770D+05	9.8794D+09	9.9395D+04
3	3.1933D+03	8.7322D+05	9.3446D+02
4	2.6067D+03	4.8430D+05	6.9592D+02
5	1.1742D+05	4.8387D+07	6.9561D+03
6	1.9545D+03	2.2667D+01	4.7610D+00
7	6.5317D+04	1.2334D+07	3.5120D+03

REGPAK / REGCOR   07/09/80   PAGE 2

CORRELATION MATRIX:

1	1.0000				
2	0.9916	1.0000			
3	0.6206	0.6043	1.0000		
4	0.4647	0.4464	-0.1774	1.0000	
5	0.9792	0.9911	0.6866	0.3644	1.0000
6	0.9911	0.9953	0.6683	0.4172	0.9940
	1.0000				
7	0.9709	0.9836	0.5025	0.4573	0.9604
	0.9731	1.0000			

REGPAK / REGANL   07/09/80   PAGE 3

SAMPLE SIZE   16
SUM OF WEIGHTS . . . .   1.6000D+01
ESTIMATED STD DEV . . . . .   3.0485D+02
R SQUARED 0.9955

VARIABLE	COEFFICIENT	ESTD STD DEV	T
0	-3.4823D+06	8.9042D+05	-3.9108
1	1.5062D+01	8.4915D+01	0.1774
2	-3.5819D-02	3.3491D-02	-1.0695
3	-2.0202D+00	4.8840D-01	-4.1364
4	-1.0332D+00	2.1427D-01	-4.8220
5	-5.1104D-02	2.2607D-01	-0.2261
6	1.8292D+03	4.5548D+02	4.0159

7   DEPENDENT VARIABLE

ANALYSIS OF VARIANCE

SOURCE	DF	SS	MS	F
REGRESSION	6	1.8417D+08	3.0695D+07	330.285
ERROR	9	8.3642D+05	9.2936D+04	
TOTAL	15	1.8501D+08		

6.2 Example 2

<u>Job Input Stream:</u>

```
//jobname JOB (acctg info),parameters
// EXEC FORTGCG
//FORT.SYSIN DD *
      IMPLICIT REAL*8(A-H,P-Z),LOGICAL(O)
      DIMENSION X(10,20),XNAME(8),KVAR(6),KDVAR(2)
      DATA NVT/7/,KOBS/16/,KDIM/10/,NV/6/,KVAR/3,1,4,2,5,7/,KDVAR/7,9
      CALL OPTION('*      ','PA',65)
      CALL OPTION('REGRSD','PRINT','OFF')
      CALL OPAGEP(0,'T','REGTEST ')
      CALL OPTLBO(KDIM)
      CALL REGPAR('PRDN',9)
      READ(5,90) XNAME
      CALL OPTLBV(XNAME)
      READ(5,91) ((X(I,J),I=1,NVT),X(KDIM,J),J=1,KOBS)
      CALL REGXAR(NVT,KDIM,KOBS,X,NV,KVAR)
      CALL REGXRP(7,0,KDIM,KOBS,X)
      CALL REGXV(2)
      CALL PPLOTP('LINES',24)
      CALL PPLOT(KDIM,X,0,2,KDVAR,0,KOBS)
      STOP
   90 FORMAT(8A8)
   91 FORMAT(F4.1,F7.0,2F5.0,F7.0,F5.0,F7.0,1XA4)
      END
//GO.SYSLIB DD
// DD DSN=STAT.FORTLIB,DISP=SHR
//GO.SYSIN DD *
```

GNP	IPD GNP		UNEMPLOY	SIZE	AF POPN	>13	TIME	TOTAL	PREDICTD
830	234289	2356	1590	107608	1947	60323	1947		
885	259426	2325	1456	108632	1948	61122	1948		
882	258054	3682	1616	109773	1949	60171	1949		
895	284599	3351	1650	110929	1950	61187	1950		
962	328975	2099	3099	112075	1951	63221	1951		
981	346999	1932	3594	113270	1952	63639	1952		
990	365385	1870	3547	115094	1953	64989	1953		
1000	363112	3578	3350	116219	1954	63761	1954		
1012	397469	2904	3048	117388	1955	66019	1955		
1046	419180	2822	2857	118734	1956	67857	1956		
1084	442769	2936	2798	120445	1957	68169	1957		
1108	444546	4681	2637	121950	1958	66513	1958		
1126	482704	3813	2552	123366	1959	68655	1959		
1142	502601	3931	2514	125368	1960	69564	1960		
1157	518173	4806	2572	127852	1961	69331	1961		
1169	554894	4007	2827	130081	1962	70551	1962		

<u>Description:</u>

Before the program reads the labels and data, several setup routines
are called. OPTION (p. 365) turns printing off for REGRSD, OPAGEP
(p. 363) defines the page title, OPTLBV (p. 308) defines XNAME to be

the array containing variable names, OPTLBO (p. 308) defines the observation labels to be variable KDIM, and REGPAR (p. 310) specifies that predicted values are to be stored in variable 9. REGXAR (p. 307) accumulates and regresses variable 7 on variables 3, 1, 4, 2, and 5. REGXRP (p. 307) regresses variable 7 on variables 1 through 6 and calculates predicted values and residuals. Next, REGXV (p. 315) computes the regression coefficient correlation matrix. Finally, PPLOT (p. 358) is called to print a plot of predicted and observed values.

Output:

REGPAK / REGMSD   REGTEST   07/09/80 PAGE 1

     SAMPLE SIZE   16
     SUM OF WEIGHTS . . .   1.6000D+01
     AVERAGE WEIGHT . . .   1.0000D+00

         VARIABLE   MEAN   VARIANCE   STD DEV

         1 GNP IPD   1.0168D+02   1.1646D+02   1.0792D+01
         2 GNP   3.8770D+05   9.8794D+09   9.9395D+04
         3 UNEMPLOY   3.1933D+03   8.7322D+05   9.3446D+02
         4 SIZE AF   2.6067D+03   4.8430D+05   6.9592D+02
         5 POPN >13   1.1742D+05   4.8387D+07   6.9561D+03
         6 TIME   1.9545D+03   2.2667D+01   4.7610D+00
         7 TOTAL   6.5317D+04   1.2334D+07   3.5120D+03

REGPAK / REGCOR   REGTEST   07/09/80   PAGE 2

     CORRELATION MATRIX:

     1 GNP IPD   1.0000

     2 GNP   0.9916   1.0000

     3 UNEMPLOY   0.6206   0.6043   1.0000

     4 SIZE AF   0.4647   0.4464   -0.1774   1.0000

     5 POPN >13   0.9792   0.9911   0.6866   0.3644   1.0000

     6 TIME   0.9911   0.9953   0.6683   0.4172   0.9940
                   1.0000

     7 TOTAL   0.9709   0.9836   0.5025   0.4573   0.9604
                   0.9731   1.0000

REGPAK / REGANL   REGTEST   07/09/80   PAGE 3

    SAMPLE SIZE   16
    SUM OF WEIGHTS . . . . . .   1.6000D+01
    ESTIMATED STD DEV . . . . .   4.8324D+02
    R SQUARED 0.9874

    VARIABLE   COEFFICIENT   ESTD STD DEV   T

    0   9.2461D+04   3.5169D+04   2.6290
    3 UNEMPLOY   -4.0387D-01   4.3854D-01   -0.9210
    1 GNP IPD   -4.8463D+01   1.3225D+02   -0.3665
    4 SIZE AF   -5.6050D-01   2.8381D-01   -1.9749
    2 GNP   7.2004D-02   3.1734D-02   2.2690
    5 POPN >13   -4.0351D-01   3.3026D-01   -1.2218

    7 TOTAL   DEPENDENT VARIABLE

ANALYSIS OF VARIANCE

    SOURCE   DF   SS   MS   F

    REGRESSION   5   1.8267D+08   3.6535D+07   156.450
    ERROR   10   2.3352D+06   2.3352D+05

    TOTAL   15   1.8501D+08

REGPAK / REGANL   REGTEST   07/09/80   PAGE 4

SAMPLE SIZE   16
SUM OF WEIGHTS . . . .   1.6000D+01
ESTIMATED STD DEV . . . . .   3.0485D+02
R SQUARED 0.9955

VARIABLE	COEFFICIENT	ESTD STD DEV	T
0	-3.4823D+06	8.9042D+05	-3.9108
1 GNP IPD	1.5062D+01	8.4915D+01	0.1774
2 GNP	-3.5819D-02	3.3491D-02	-1.0695
3 UNEMPLOY	-2.0202D+00	4.8840D-01	-4.1364
4 SIZE AF	-1.0332D+00	2.1427D-01	-4.8220
5 POPN >13	-5.1104D-02	2.2607D-01	-0.2261
6 TIME	1.8292D+03	4.5548D+02	4.0159

7 TOTAL   DEPENDENT VARIABLE

ANALYSIS OF VARIANCE

SOURCE	DF	SS	MS	F
REGRESSION	6	1.8417D+08	3.0695D+07	330.285
ERROR	9	8.3642D+05	9.2936D+04	
TOTAL	15	1.8501D+08		

REGPAK / REGRCC   REGTEST   07/09/80   PAGE 5

	1	2	3	4	5
1 GNP IPD	1.0000				
2 GNP	-0.6494	1.0000			
3 UNEMPLOY	-0.5550	0.9456	1.0000		
4 SIZE AF	-0.3488	0.4686	0.6186	1.0000	
5 POPN >13	0.6592	-0.8332	-0.7583	-0.1889	1.0000
6 TIME	0.1863	-0.8017	-0.8241	-0.5494	0.3882
	1.0000				

PPLOT   REGTEST   07/09/80   PAGE 6

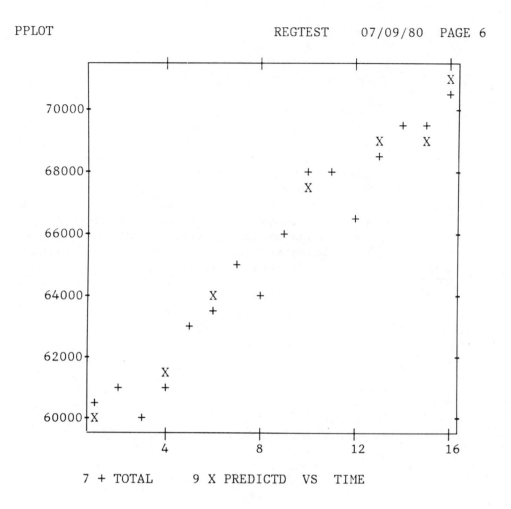

7 + TOTAL   9 X PREDICTD   VS   TIME

7. SUBJECT INDEX

8. GLOSSARY OF VARIABLES AND ENTRY POINTS

8.1 Executive and Service Subroutines

Variable	Dimension	Description
INIT		initialization variable, set to 0 before first call
KDIM		first dimension of X
KOBS		number of observations
KVAR	$\geq$ NV	vector of indices of variables for regression
|NV|		number of variables in regression
|NVT|		total number of variables accumulated
X	KDIM or KDIM,m	observation vector or data matrix
XNAME	$\geq$ NVT	vector of names of variables

8.2 Elementary Subroutines

Variable	Number of Elements	First Used	Description
AVG	NVT	REGMSD	averages
B	NV-1	REGRES	regression coefficients
BZERO		REGRES	intercept coefficient
C	NVT(NVT+1)/2	REGCOR	correlation matrix
KVAR	NV	REGSEL	vector of indices of variables
NOBS		REGACC	number of observations
|NV|		REGSEL	number of variables in regression
|NVT|		REGACC	number of variables accumulated
R	NV(NV-1)/2	REGRCV, REGRCC	regression coefficient covariance or correlation matrix
STD	NVT	REGMSD	standard deviations
STDB	NV-1	REGANL	standard errors of regression coefficients
SUM	NVT	REGACC	sums
SWGT		REGACC	sum of weights
S2		REGRES	estimate of σ^2
V	NV(NV-1)/2	REGSEL	correlation matrix (or inverse)
XPX	NVT(NVT+1)/2	REGACC	cross products matrix
Y		REGPRE	dependent variable
YEST		REGPRE	estimate of dependent variable

8.3 Glossary of Subroutine Calls (FTN)

CHAPTER 12

TRIPAK - TRIANGULAR MATRIX PACKAGE

1. INTRODUCTION

Symmetric and triangular matrices are often used in statistical and mathematical computing. Let

$$
A = \begin{vmatrix}
a(1,1) & a(1,2) & \dots & a(1,n) \\
a(2,1) & a(2,2) & \dots & a(2,n) \\
\cdot & \cdot & \dots & \cdot \\
\cdot & \cdot & \dots & \cdot \\
\cdot & \cdot & \dots & \cdot \\
a(n,1) & a(n,2) & \dots & a(n,n)
\end{vmatrix}
$$

The matrix A is symmetric if $a(i,j)=a(j,i)$ and (lower) triangular if $a(i,j)=0$ for $j>i$. Storing such matrices as two-dimensional nxn arrays is inefficient, since the upper triangular portion $[a(i,j), j>i]$ is redundant. An alternative is to store the lower triangular portion in a linear array:

$$A = (a(1,1), a(2,1), a(2,2), a(3,1), \dots).$$

Thus the storage space required is reduced from n^2 to $n(n+1)/2$ locations, a reduction of almost one-half. The disadvantage is that one must do one's own indexing; element $a(i,j)$, $j \le i$, is the $(i(i-1)/2+j)$-th element of A. This is not a serious problem, however, since most operations on such matrices can be done sequentially.

TRIPAK is a package of subroutines which perform operations on these compressed triangular matrices. Operations provided include addition, multiplication, inversion, dot product, and evaluation of quadratic forms. Utility routines are also included which provide printing, character display, and compatibility with two-dimensional arrays.

The package consists of the following routines:

(A)	ISYMLO	Location function
	SYMCHL	Choleski reduction (square root)
	SYMDOT	Dot product
	SYMINV	Symmetric matrix inversion
	TRIINV	Triangular matrix inversion
	TRITSQ	Multiplication by transpose
(B)	SYMQFM	Quadratic form
	SYMRCM	Row/column scalar multiplication
	TRIADD	Addition
	TRICPY	Matrix copy
	TRIDIS	Display
	TRIMAT	Matrix compatability
	TRIMLT	Multiplication
	TRIPRT	Printing
	TRISCM	Scalar multiplication
	TRISTI	Store identity matrix
	TRISTZ	Store null matrix
	TRISUB	Subtraction

The subroutines in (A) are used directly by REGPAK, Chapter 11 (p. 297), the STATLIB regression package. Those in (B) perform auxiliary operations. Subroutines which generally operate on symmetric matrices have the prefix "SYM"; most other TRIPAK routines have the prefix "TRI".

Sections 2 and 3 describe TRIPAK subroutines in (A) and (B), respectively, and provide calling sequence descriptions; calling sequences follow the STATLIB-wide conventions of the Part III Introduction (p. 295). Section 4 is a subject index. Section 5 is a one-page summary of TRIPAK calling sequences.

2. TRIPAK SUBROUTINES

2.1 ISYMLO - Location Function

ISYMLO calculates the location of any element in a a TRIPAK matrix. The matrix is considered to be symmetric, i.e., ISYMLO(I,J) = ISYMLO(J,I).

Calling Sequence:

        ...ISYMLO(I,J)...

        I = row (or column) number
        J = column (or row) number

A(ISYMLO(I,J)) is the (I,J)-th element of A.

2.2 SYMCHL - Choleski Reduction (Square Root)

SYMCHL reduces a symmetric positive definite matrix A to a lower triangular matrix B such that BB' = A. The method was developed by Choleski and is described in [9].

SYMCHL is primarily intended for use with correlation matrices and will consider the matrix to be nonpositive definite if a diagonal element becomes less than $(1-\rho^2)$; i.e., if the square of the multiple correlation of a variable with preceding variables exceeds ρ^2 (the constant ρ^2 is initially set to .9999D0 and may be modified through entry point SYMCHC, described below). If this condition occurs, the variable I is set equal to the number of the offending row, and control is returned to the calling program. If desired, that row and column may be deleted by the calling program (and N reduced by 1), and the reduction continued beginning with row I. For the first call, I must be set to zero or one.

Calling Sequence (SYMCHL):

        CALL SYMCHL(A,N,I)

        A = symmetric triangular matrix to be reduced
        N = number of rows (columns)
        I = row number to begin (or continue) reduction (zero
            or one on first call)

SYMCHL returns I = 0 if the reduction is successfully completed, I = J if the J-th row causes a near-singularity.

Calling Sequence (SYMCHC):

```
CALL SYMCHC(K,RHOSQ)
```

K = 1 - changes ρ^2 to RHOSQ
K = 0 - sets RHOSQ equal to current value of ρ^2

In regression analysis, subroutine REGPAR (p. 310), callable from FORTRAN or ISX, may also be used to reset the threshold.

2.3 SYMDOT - Dot Product

SYMDOT calculates dot (scalar) products of rows/columns of symmetric triangular matrices and/or vectors. The first and last elements to be included are selected by the user, so the routine may also be used with strictly triangular matrices.

Calling Sequence:

```
...SYMDOT(NS,NE,X,I,Y,J)...
```

NS = position in row/column of first element to be included
NE = position in row/column of last element to be included
X,Y = triangular arrays or vectors
I,J = row indices for X and Y, respectively. This index must be zero if the corresponding array is a vector.

2.4 SYMINV - Symmetric Matrix Inversion

SYMINV inverts symmetric positive definite triangular matrices. The inversion is performed by calling three other TRIPAK routines which (a) reduce the matrix to a lower triangular matrix (SYMCHL, p. 345), (b) invert the lower triangular matrix (TRIINV, below), and (c) multiply the inverted matrix by its transpose (TRITSQ, p. 347). If the matrix is not positive definite (see SYMCHL, TRIINV), control is returned to the calling program with the corresponding error indication.

Calling Sequence:

```
CALL SYMINV(A,N,I)
```

A = symmetric triangular matrix to be inverted
N = number of rows (columns)
I = row number to be passed to SYMCHL (zero or one on first call)

SYMINV returns I = 0 if the inversion is successfully completed, I = J if the J-th row causes a near-singularity in SYMCHL, or I = -J if the J-th row causes a near-singularity in TRIINV.

2.5 TRIINV - Triangular Matrix Inversion

TRIINV performs a matrix inversion of a positive definite triangular matrix. The inversion is carried out by a pivotal method which pivots on the main diagonal element at each stage. This program is primarily intended for use with reduced correlation matrices and will consider the matrix to be singular if a diagonal element becomes zero or negative. This should not happen if the matrix was reduced from a symmetric matrix by SYMCHL, since that routine detects singularities.

Calling Sequence:

        CALL TRIINV(A,N,I)

        A = positive definite triangular matrix to be inverted
        N = number of rows (columns)
        I = return code

TRIINV returns with I = 0 if the inversion is successfully completed, I = -J if the Jth row causes a near-singularity.

2.6 TRITSQ - Multiplication by Transpose

TRITSQ multiplies a (lower) triangular matrix by its transpose, obtaining a symmetric triangular matrix.

Calling Sequence:

        CALL TRITSQ(A,N)

        A = triangular matrix to be replaced by $A'A$
        N = number of rows (or columns)

3. TRIPAK AUXILIARY SUBROUTINES

3.1 SYMQFM - Quadratic Form

SYMQFM calculates the value of the quadratic form x'Ay, where A is symmetric.

Calling Sequence:

        ...SYMQFM(N,X,A,Y)...

        N = number of rows/columns in A,
            number of elements in X,Y
        X = vector of length N
        A = symmetric triangular matrix
        Y = vector of length N

3.2 SYMRCM - Row/Column Scalar Multiplication

SYMRCM multiplies rows and/or columns of triangular matrices by a constant. The first and last elements to be multiplied are selected by the user (see Usage below).

Calling Sequence:

        CALL SYMRCM(NS,NE,A,I,C)

        NS = position in row/column of first element to be
             multiplied
        NE = position in row/column of last element to be
             multiplied
        A = triangular array
        I = row/column to be multiplied
        C = multiplier

Usage:

type	row/column	NS	NE
symmetric	both	1	N
triangular	row	1	I
triangular	column	I	N

3.3 TRIADD, TRISUB - Addition/Subtraction

TRIADD adds and TRISUB subtracts triangular matrices.

Calling Sequence:

```
          CALL TRIADD(N,A,B,C)
          CALL TRISUB(N,A,B,C)
```

N   = number of rows/columns in A,B,C
A,B = triangular matrices to be added/subtracted
C   = A +/- B (may be same array as A or B)

3.4 TRICPY - Matrix Copy

TRICPY sets triangular matrix B equal to triangular matrix A.

Calling Sequence:

```
          CALL TRICPY(A,B,N)
```

A = triangular matrix to be copied
B = new triangular matrix
N = number of rows/columns

3.5 TRIDIS - Display

It is often easier to interpret numbers expressed in terms of ranges than to analyze the numbers themselves. Subroutine TRIDIS enables the user to display a triangular matrix of real numbers as a matrix of character symbols, each symbol designating the portion of the overall range in which the corresponding element lies. TRIDIS is called by regression executive routines REGXR (p. 305) and REGXV (p. 315) and by regression routines of STATLIB's high-level packages (Part II), but always with printing turned off. TRIDIS printing may be turned on by calling subroutine OPTION (p. 365).

Calling Sequence:

```
          CALL TRIDIS(NV,C,OCOR)
```

NV   = number of rows/columns
C   = input triangular matrix
OCOR   = .TRUE. if C is a correlation matrix,
           .FALSE. otherwise

The scaling limits are [-1,1] if C is a correlation matrix, the minimum and maximum elements of C otherwise.

3.6 TRIMAT - Matrix Compatibility

TRIMAT copies a triangular matrix A to or from a lower triangular two-dimensional matrix B, depending on the value of MODE.

Calling Sequence:

```
CALL TRIMAT(A,N,B,M,MODE)
```

A   = triangular matrix
N   = number of rows/columns in A
B   = lower triangular doubly-dimensioned matrix,
         i.e., uses B(I,J), I≤J
M   = actual row dimension of B in calling program
         [i.e., B dimensioned (M,K)]
MODE = 1: A is copied into B
      = 2: A is copied from B

3.7 TRIMLT - Multiplication

Calling Sequence:

```
CALL TRIMLT(N,A,B,C)
```

N   = number of rows/columns in A,B,C
A,B   = two linearly stored lower triangular matrices
C   = product of A and B (may be same array as A)

3.8 TRIPRT - Printing

Subroutine TRIPRT prints a triangular matrix according to the format specified by the user. Printing may be controlled through use of subroutine OPTION (p. 365).

Calling Sequence:

```
CALL TRIPRT(A,N,fmtcod)
```

A   = triangular matrix to be printed
N   = number of rows/columns
fmtcod = format code for each element to be printed
          (e.g., 'F10.3   ', 'E13.6   '). It must be
          eight characters long, right-padded with
          blanks if necessary.

3.9 TRISCM - Scalar Multiplication

Calling Sequence:

```
CALL TRISCM(N,A,S,B)
```

N = number of rows/columns in A,B
A = triangular matrix to be multiplied by a scalar
S = scalar multiplier
B = result, i.e., SA (may be same array as A)

3.10 TRISTI/TRISTZ - Store Identity/Null Matrix

TRISTI   generates an identity matrix.   TRISTZ generates a null (zero)
matrix.

<u>Calling Sequence:</u>

```
        CALL TRISTI(N,A)
        CALL TRISTZ(N,A)

        N = number of rows/columns
        A = identity/null triangular matrix
```

4. SUBJECT INDEX

5. GLOSSARY OF SUBROUTINE CALLS (FTN)

CHAPTER 13

UTILITY ROUTINES

1. INTRODUCTION

This chapter contains miscellaneous FORTRAN subroutines. Some of them supplement the SERVICE routine descriptions of Chapter 10, appearing here because they contain entry points callable from FORTRAN only; in such cases, they are documented in their entirety. The chapter also describes routines for plotting and display, routines for controlling the execution and printing of most of STATLIB, routines for calculating probability distribution functions, and routines for character string manipulation.

Sections 2 through 5 contain subroutine documentation. Wherever possible, interrelated subroutines are grouped into common sections and subsections; otherwise, the listings are alphabetical. Calling sequences follow the STATLIB-wide conventions described in the Part III Introduction (p. 295). Section 6 is a subject index. Section 7 is a summary of UTILITY routines and their calling sequences.

2. MISCELLANEOUS

2.1 CORGET, CORFRE - Dynamic Core Storage Allocation

CORGET gets and CORFRE frees main storage by calling operating system storage allocation routines. DYNCOR (Ch. 9, p. 257), which performs more extensive core management services, uses CORGET to obtain core storage. CORLEF and CORREM (p. 282) may be called to obtain information on amount of storage available.

Calling Sequences:

```
        CALL CORGET(NWDS,L,J,&ERR)
        CALL CORFRE(NWDS,L,J)

        NWDS = number of words (single precision)
        L    = reference array
        J    = pointer subscript
        &ERR = error return (core not available)
```

The pointer subscript J is computed such that L(J), ..., L(J+NWDS-1) are the NWDS words. (See DYNCOR for further discussion of reference arrays and pointer subscripts.)

2.2 DSPLAY - Plotting Display

DSPLAY, called by some of STATLIB's high-level packages, generates low-resolution time plots, allowing several such plots to be stacked on a page. Entry point DSPPAR resets DSPLAY parameters; it is also callable from ISX (see p. 282).

Calling Sequence:

```
        CALL DSPLAY(KROW,NCOL,X,NR,KV)

        KROW = row dimension of X
        NCOL = number of columns
        X    = data matrix, dimensioned (KROW,m), m ≥ NCOL
        NR   = number of rows to be plotted
        KV   = vector of indices of rows to be plotted.
               If KV(1)=0, DSPLAY will set KV(I)=I, I=1,...,NR.
```

DSPLAY produces many plots on a page, individually scaled. The attached example (and the one in STPAK, p. 129) illustrate the technique. The data matrix contains six years of Bell System inward movement data, each row corresponding to one month. Turned sideways, the display shows twelve (one per month) low-resolution "time" plots; i.e., variables plotted one observation per column against observation indices. For clarity, the plotted points are connected to their variable's minimum value; a set of axis "labels" also provides values of points to greater precision than can be obtained from the number of asterisks alone.

Example:

```
KV(1)=0
CALL OPTLBV('JANUARY FEBRUARYMARCH   ...   DECEMBER')
CALL OPTLBO(13)
CALL DSPLAY(13,6,BSMI,12,KV)
```

sets up row and column labels, then displays the first 12 rows of Bell System inward movement data.

MISC / DSPLAY   07/09/80   PAGE 1

VBL:	1 JANUARY	2 FEBRUARY	3 MARCH	4 APRIL
MIN:	684418.00	643274.00	754978.00	689162.00
MAX:	865972.00	841846.00	979926.00	926128.00

1961	0 *	0 *	2 *	0 *
1962	29 ***	17 **	8 *	28 ***
1963	37 ****	25 ***	0 *	46 *****
1964	58 ******	61 ********	35 ****	69 *******
1965	56 ******	71 *********	72 *********	78 *********
1966	99 ***********	99 ***********	99 ***********	99 ***********

VBL:	5 MAY	6 JUNE	7 JULY	8 AUGUST
MIN:	773371.00	893521.00	794136.00	919291.00
MAX:	938801.00	1207102.00	1078439.00	1222488.00

1961	0 *	0 *	0 *	0 *
1962	14 **	9 *	33 ****	22 ***
1963	30 ****	6 *	55 *******	25 ***
1964	42 *****	51 ******	74 *********	33 ****
1965	54 ******	74 *********	91 ***********	59 ******
1966	99 ***********	99 ***********	99 ***********	99 ***********

VBL:	9 SEPTEMBR	10 OCTOBER	11 NOVEMBER	12 DECEMBER
MIN:	975007.00	879541.00	791770.00	678332.00
MAX:	1334681.00	1090884.00	984492.00	883662.00

1961	0 *	0 *	0 *	0 *
1962	5 *	29 ***	14 **	3 *
1963	24 ***	42 *****	4 *	35 ****
1964	60 *******	64 *******	29 ***	78 ********
1965	83 **********	77 *********	88 **********	99 ***********
1966	99 ***********	99 ***********	99 ***********	87 **********

OPTION (p. 365) may be used to set certain DSPLAY parameters, as follows: PAGSIZ (default = 132), PRINT (ON), and UNIT (6). Variable names and observation labels may be provided through OPTLBV and OPTLBO (p. 366). Other DSPLAY parameters are set through entry point DSPPAR.

Calling Sequence (DSPPAR):

        CALL DSPPAR(code,VALUE)

sets DSPLAY parameters, according to the table below.

code VALUE	Description
AXIS X	draws an axis at X for each variable
BAR OFF	turns off the BAR option for each variable. Normally, each point will connected to the axis or its variable's minimum by a line.
LABEL K	sets number of digits comprising axis label to K (default = 2)
LIN K	sets number of columns per display to K (default = 10)
VMIN X VMAX X	sets the corresponding limits to X. Values outside the limits will not be displayed.

2.3 PPLOT - Plotting

PPLOT generates printer plots. Called by all STATLIB high-level plot routines, it provides automatic scaling and titling, draws axes, etc.; numerous examples of its output appear in Part I of this manual. Entry point PPLOTP resets PPLOT parameters; it is also callable from ISX (see p. 287).

Calling Sequence:

        CALL PPLOT(KROW,X,IX,NY,IY,N1,N2)

        KROW   = row (first) dimension of X
        X   = data matrix, dimensioned (KROW,m)
        IX   = row index of horizontal variable
                = 0 for time plot
        NY   = number of vertical axis variables
        IY   = vector of row indices of vertical variables
        N1,N2 = vector of beginning and ending columns
                  (observations) for vertical axis variables.
                  Setting N1(K) = 0 indicates that variables K
                  through NY are to be plotted for observations
                  1 through N2(K).

Example:

        CALL PPLOT(13,X,0,12,KV,0,6)

plots the twelve (monthly) rows (variables) of the Bell System inward movement matrix (Sec. 2.2, above) against time (years).

OPTION (p. 365) may be used to set certain PPLOT parameters, as follows: PAGSIZ (default = 132), PRINT (ON), UNIT (6), VLINEC ("|"),

and DEVICE (PRTR). When DEVICE is PRTR, the plot is enclosed in a
box.   Variable names and observation labels may be provided through
OPTLBV and OPTLBO (p. 366). Other PPLOT parameters are set through
entry point PPLOTP.

Calling Sequence (PPLOTP):

          CALL PPLOTP(code,A1,A2)

sets PPLOT parameters, according to the table below.

code A1 A2	Description
MODE COMIC	causes subsequent time plots (not scatter plots) to be printed in "comic mode", i.e., down the page
CINE	resets PPLOT to "cine mode" (across the page)
LINES K	limits the number of plot lines for scatter plots and "cine" time plots to K (default=45, maximum=45).
CHAR K [cstrng]	changes the first K plot characters to those in cstrng (default = +XO*#12...) or, if K<0, returns the first K plot characters in the cstrng argument. In ISX, the "X" array is used for the last argument if cstrng is omitted.
CHAR M	indicates that the characters to be plotted are stored in the data matrix. The last vertical variable will not be plotted, but will contain the plotting characters (one character per variable). Reset by CHAR 0.
VMIN X VMAX X HMIN X HMAX X	sets the corresponding limits to X. Values falling outside the limits will not be plotted.
VAXIS X cc HAXIS X cc	draws axes at X. The second argument contains the characters to be used: the first character for scatter and "cine" time plots, second for "comic" time plots.
TITLE NC tstrng	prints the NC-character (NC<25) title in tstrng at the top of the plot
BAR K X	turns on the BAR option for the K-th variable plotted. Each point will then be connected to the point X by a vertical line.
BARV K1 K2	turns on the BAR option for the K1-th variable plotted. Each point will then be connected by a vertical line to the K2-th variable.
VGRID HGRID	turns on the vertical and horizontal grid options
VTIC X HTIC X	sets the tick-mark spacing to X
TIME XO XI	defines the time origin and time increment for time plots
TNAM timevbl	specifies the name for the time variable in time plots (default = TIME)
OBL	uses observation labels on time axis for cine time plots
RESET *	resets all parameters (except MODE, LINES, CHAR) if resetting is off
OFF	causes all parameters to not be reset after succeeding plots. Normally all parameters except MODE, LINES, and CHAR are reset
ON	resets all parameters (except MODE, LINES, CHAR) and turns re-setting back on

Note: Twice the number of bars (BAR,BARV) plus the number of axes (HAXIS,VAXIS) may not exceed 16.

When more than one plotting character falls in the same print position, priority is as follows: (1) variables in the order given, (2) axes in reverse order, (3) horizontal grid lines, (4) vertical grid lines, (5) bars in reverse order.

Examples:

```
CALL PPLOTP('LINES',25)
CALL PPLOTP('HMAX',6D0)
CALL PPLOTP('VAXIS',2D0,'I-')
CALL PPLOTP('VMIN',0D0)
CALL PPLOTP('TITLE',23,'INWD DATA & PREDICTIONS')
CALL PPLOT(7,X,3,1,2,0,130)
```

sets the plot depth to 25 lines, calls for a horizontal maximum of 6, a vertical axis at 2, a vertical minimum of 0, a 23 character title, and plots row 2 of matrix X (dimensioned 7 by 130) against row 3.

2.4 SIMPSN - Simpson's Rule Integration

SIMPSN integrates a given FORTRAN function by Simpson's rule, successively using shorter and shorter intervals until convergence is achieved. Entry point SIMPAR allows the convergence criteria to be reset.

Calling Sequence:

```
...SIMPSN(A,B,FN[,A1,A2])...
```

A,B   = limits of integration
FN   = function (declared EXTERNAL in calling program)
A1,A2 = function parameters

SIMPSN selects an interval size, computes the area under FN using Simpson's Rule, bisects these intervals, computes the areas again with the smaller intervals, and continues until one of the convergence criteria (see below) is satisfied.

Calling Sequence (SIMPAR):

```
CALL SIMPAR(code,VALUE)
```

sets SIMPSN convergence parameters, according to the table below.

code	VALUE	Description
NBIS	K	allows up to K bisections (default = 10)
THR	X	terminates iterations when the function changes less than X (default = .000001)

2.5 SORTC - Sorting

Calling Sequence:

        CALL SORTC(KROW,NCOL,X,IR,code)

        KROW = row dimension of X
        NCOL = number of columns
        X   = data matrix, dimensioned (KROW,m), m ≥ NCOL
        IR   = index of row determining sort
        code = A for ascending, D for descending

SORTC sorts columns of X according to row IR. The hollerith code
determines whether row IR is to be arranged in ascending or
descending order. Workspace of length 2*KROW+NCOL is obtained from
CORGET (p. 356).

2.6 XORDST, XMEDN - Order Statistics, Medians

Calling Sequences:

        ...XORDST(KROW,NCOL,X,P)...
        ...XMEDN(KROW,NCOL,X)...

        KROW = row dimension of X
        NCOL = number of columns
        X   = data matrix, dimensioned (KROW,m), m ≥ NCOL
        P   = fractional order statistic

XORDST returns the P-th order statistic, XMEDN the median, of the
first row of X. The P-th order statistic is the i-th ordered
observation, where i = P*NCOL+(1+P)/3. Interpolation between
adjacent values is performed when necessary. To perform the
compuations efficiently, a histogram of 100 cells is constructed and
the cell containing the P-th order statistic determined (P = .5 for
median). If too many values are in the cell, the histogram is
successively regenerated on the narrower interval until the order
statistic is found.

Execution times are comparable to sorting for NCOL < 20, but about 50
times faster for NCOL = 1000. The procedure runs fastest on random
samples from a uniform distribution, slower on distributions lacking
low order moments.

Examples:

        X1=XMEDN(NROW,NCOL,X(K,1))
        X2=XMEDN(1,NROW,X(1,J))
        X3=XORDST(1,N,V,.25D0)

compute the medians of the K-th row and J-th column of X and the .25
order statistic of the N elements in V, respectively.

3. CONTROL OPTIONS

This section describes subroutines which control page numbering, execution and printing, and the labelling of rows and columns in two-way arrays. Selected options are obtained by "interested" STATLIB routines; e.g., prior to printing, a subroutine might check for additional instructions specified for it, its package, or the entire library, regarding whether to print and on which unit.

3.1 OPAGE - Automatic Page Control

OPAGE, used extensively by STATLIB subroutines, provides automatic page control, and prints the date, page number, and an optional title at the top of each page. OPAGEH provides the same service and, in addition, prints a heading as each new page is started. Parameter settings are controlled through OPAGEP. A final entry point OPAGES instructs OPAGE to call a user-supplied subroutine prior to beginning each page. OPAGE and OPAGEP are both callable from ISX (see p. 284).

Calling Sequence:

>   ...OPAGE(M,K)...
>
>   M = FORTRAN unit on which output will occur
>   K > 0 adds K to line count (i.e., K lines will be
>   written on unit M by subsequent WRITE
>   statements in calling program). If fewer than K
>   lines remain on the current page, a new page will
>   be started.
>   K = 0 sets to start a new page on next call to
>   OPAGE regardless of line count
>   K < 0 starts a new page immediately and sets the
>   line count for unit M to |K|

With each call, the user tells OPAGE how many lines he intends to write with a subsequent WRITE statement. If insufficient lines remain on the current page (OPAGE maintains an internal line count), a new page will be started. OPAGE is a logical function that returns a value of .TRUE. if a new page has been started; the user may use this information to print page headings, etc. Page control is provided for up to 10 unit numbers.

Calling Sequence (OPAGEH):

>   ...OPAGEH(M,K,KC,H,NH)...
>
>   M,K = as above
>   KC = number of lines to be written by the calling
>   program if a new page is started
>   H   = character string heading
>   NH = number of characters in heading (<43)

OPAGEH = .TRUE. if a new page has been started.

Example:

      IF(OPAGEH(6,1,3,'SUMMARY',7)) WRITE(6,90)LBLS

Calling Sequence (OPAGEP):

      CALL OPAGEP(M,code,VALUE)

sets parameter options for unit M (M=0 means all), according to the table below.

code VALUE	Description
C x	sets new-page carriage control character to x (default="1")
L K	sets lines per page to K (default=55)
N K	sets number for next page to K
P ON|OFF	turns pause on or off
T tstrng	prints tstrng, an eight-character title, at the top of each page

If the pause feature is ON, OPAGE pauses before starting each page by reading a line from unit 5.

Example:

      CALL OPAGEP(6,'T','UPSTATE ')

Calling Sequence (OPAGES):

      CALL OPAGES(SUBNAM[,IA1,IA2])

instructs OPAGE to call a user-supplied subroutine prior to beginning each page.

SUBNAM must be declared EXTERNAL; IA1 and IA2 are optional arguments to be passed to it. SUBNAM is called as follows by OPAGE:

      CALL SUBNAM(M,NPAGE,IA1,IA2,&ERR)

where M is the unit number and NPAGE is the next page number. An error return causes OPAGE to return without starting a new page or printing a page heading.

Example:

      EXTERNAL TIMER
      CALL OPAGES(TIMER)

3.2 OPTION, OPTGET - Execution, Print Options

OPTION allows the user to control printing and subroutine execution for STATLIB. Selected options (e.g., print/no print, output unit number, page size, device type) are stored in a table; the subroutines themselves retrieve this information during execution through entry point OPTGET. OPTION and OPTGET are both callable from ISX (see p. 285).

<u>Calling Sequence:</u>

> CALL OPTION(idname,code,VALUE)

> idname = 6-character identifier, padded on the right with blanks. Generally, it is a subroutine name or a package prefix followed by the universal character "*".
>
> code = character string code for the option type; only two characters are required. Standard values are shown in table below.
>
> VALUE = value to be entered in option table (see below), or "*" indicating remove last matching (idname,code) entry from the table.

code VALUE	Description
PRINT ON	forces printing
OFF	suppresses printing
UNIT K	sets output unit number (e.g., 8)
PAGSIZ K	sets page size to K (e.g., 72)
DEVICE TERM	format for terminal
PRTR	format for high-speed printer
ERRLIM K	terminate execution after K errors (default = 32)
VLINEC v	sets vertical line character (default = "|")

In retrieving option values, the most recent entry with matching idname will be used. A match occurs if the user entered (a) the actual subroutine name, (b) the first k characters of the subroutine name followed by the universal character ("*"), (c) the universal character followed by the last k characters of the subroutine name, or (d) the universal character by itself. Since packages generally have all subroutines beginning with the same characters, calling OPTION with the package prefix and the universal character matches every subroutine in the package. Message and error routines, which all end with the characters MSG and ERR, can easily be controlled as well.

OPTION should be called with VALUE=* to remove old entries rather than specifying the previous value, since the table can hold only 20 entries and will ignore further calls once full. For example, a subroutine should specify "PRINT *" rather than "PRINT ON" to remove the effect of an earlier "PRINT OFF" call.

Examples:

```
CALL OPTION('REG*  ','PRINT','OFF')
CALL OPTION('REGANL','PRINT','ON')
CALL OPTION('*MSG  ','UNIT',8)
CALL OPTION('*ERR  ','UNIT',8)
CALL OPTION('*     ','PAGSIZ',80)
CALL OPTION('TS*   ','PRINT','*')
```

turns off printing by all REGxxx (i.e., REGPAK) routines except REGANL, directs all message and error routines to print on FORTRAN unit 8, sets the page size for the entire library to 80 columns, and removes a previous print entry for TSxxxx (i.e., TSPAK) routines.

Calling Sequence (OPTGET):

```
CALL OPTGET(idname,code,IVALX,IVAL)
```

idname = 6-character identifier, padded on the right
         with blanks; generally a subroutine name
code   = character string code for the option type,
         as above
IVALX = single-word value to be returned if no
         (idname,code) match occurs
IVAL   = single-word value returned

Example:

```
CALL OPTGET('TSREG ','UNIT',6,M)
WRITE(M,1) INFO
```

3.3 OPTLBO, OPTLBV - Observation, Variable Labels

Observation (column) and variable (row) labels are defined for use by STATLIB routines which accept two-way matrices as arguments; e.g., DSPLAY (p. 356), REGPAK (Ch. 11, p. 297). OPTLBO and OPTLBV specify these labels; OPTLGO and OPTLGV may be used to retrieve them.

Calling Sequences:

```
CALL OPTLBO(IR)
CALL OPTLBV(VLBL)
```

IR   = matrix row containing observation labels
VLBL = vector of variable labels

Observation labels are assumed to occupy row IR of the data matrix; variable (row) labels are in vector VLBL, VLBL(I) being the name of the Ith variable. Calling either routine with an integer zero argument cancels the effect of a previous call.

Example:

```
          CALL OPTLBO(5)
          CALL OPTLBV('INWARD  OUTWARD NET GAIN')
```

Calling Sequences (OPTLGO, OPTLGV):

```
          CALL OPTLGO(OBL,IR)
          CALL OPTLGV(KV,VNAME)
```

```
          OBL   = .TRUE. if observation labels are in effect
          IR    = row containing observation labels
          KV    = row for which variable label is desired
          VNAME = variable label (blank if variable labels not in
                  effect)
```

4. PROBABILITY FUNCTIONS

Routines of this section calculate probabilities, quantiles, and random numbers for various standard distributions. Conventions are that the first letter of the name identifies the operation to be performed, the second through sixth letters point to the distribution involved. P, Q, and R routines return cumulative probabilities, quantiles, random numbers respectively. Available routines are:

	P	Q	R
Beta	*	*	
Binomial			*
F	*	*	
Gamma	*	*	
Multinomial			*
Normal	*	*	*
t	*	*	
Uniform			*
2-dimensional normal	*		*

4.1 PBETA - Beta Distribution Probabilities

Calling Sequence:

        ...PBETA(X,A,B)...

PBETA computes the probability that a beta random variable with shape parameters (A,B) is less than X:

$$PBETA = \frac{\Gamma(A+B)}{\Gamma(A)\,\Gamma(B)} \int_0^X t^{A-1}(1-t)^{B-1}dt.$$

The method uses a recurrence formula found in [11] to express the function as the sum of a power series in X/(1-X) and the probability that a beta random variable with shape parameters (A+[B],B-[B]) is less than X. The former series is summed in a way that avoids machine overflows and underflows: the index of the largest term is found, and summation is carried out by working forwards and backwards from there. The latter integral is obtained by expanding (1-t)**(B-[B]-1) in its Taylor series about t = 0 and integrating term-by-term. The algorithm has been extensively tested and compared with Karl Pearson's Incomplete Beta Function tables.

Precision (PBETAS):

        CALL PBETAS(NS)

resets the convergence threshold for relative absolute error to 10**-NS. NS is initialized to 7.

4.2 PFDIST - F Distribution Probabilities

Calling Sequence:

$$...PFDIST(X,A,B)...$$

PFDIST computes the probability that an F random variable with (A,B) degrees of freedom is less than X:

$$PFDIST = \frac{\Gamma\left[\frac{A+B}{2}\right]}{\Gamma\left[\frac{A}{2}\right]\Gamma\left[\frac{B}{2}\right]} A^{\frac{A}{2}} B^{\frac{B}{2}} \int_{0}^{X} \frac{t^{\frac{A}{2}-1}}{(B+At)^{\frac{A+B}{2}}} dt.$$

PFDIST calls PBETA, utilizing the fact that if Z has an F distribution with (A,B) degrees of freedom, AZ/(B+AZ) has a beta distribution with shape parameters (A/2,B/2).

4.3 PGAMMA - Gamma Distribution Probabilities

Calling Sequence:

$$...PGAMMA(X,A)...$$

PGAMMA computes the probability that a gamma random variable with shape parameter A is less than X:

$$PGAMMA = \frac{1}{\Gamma(A)} \int_{0}^{X} t^{A-1} e^{-t} dt.$$

The method uses a series approximation obtained by expanding the exponential function in its power series about zero and then integrating term-by-term [12]. The series is summed in a way that avoids machine overflows and underflows: the index of the largest term is found, and summation is carried out by working forwards and backwards from there. The algorithm has been extensively tested and compared with Karl Pearson's Incomplete Gamma Function tables.

Precision (PGAMMS):

        CALL PGAMMS(NS)

resets the convergence threshold for relative absolute error to 10**-NS. NS is initialized to 7.

4.4 PNORM - Normal Distribution Probabilities

Calling Sequence:

...PNORM(X)...

PNORM uses DERF [13], the IBM "error function", to compute the probability that a standard normal random variable is less than X:

$$PNORM = \frac{1}{\sqrt{2\pi}} \int_{-\infty}^{X} e^{-t^2/2} dt.$$

4.5 PTDIST - t Distribution Probabilities

Calling Sequence:

...PTDIST(X,A)...

PTDIST computes the probability that a Student-t random variable with A degrees of freedom is less than X:

$$PTDIST = \frac{\Gamma\left[\frac{A+1}{2}\right]}{\Gamma\left[\frac{A}{2}\right]\Gamma\left[\frac{1}{2}\right]} A^{-\frac{1}{2}} \int_{-\infty}^{X} \left[\frac{1}{1 + t^2/A}\right]^{\frac{A+1}{2}} dt.$$

PTDIST calls PBETA, utilizing the fact that if T has a Student-t distribution with A degrees of freedom, T/(A+T) has a beta distribution with shape parameters (1/2,A/2).

4.6 P2NORM - Bivariate Normal Probabilities

Calling Sequence:

...P2NORM(X1,X2,RHO)...

P2NORM computes the probability that a bivariate normal random vector with unit variances and correlation rho is less than (X1,X2):

$$P2NORM = \int_{-\infty}^{X_1} \int_{-\infty}^{X_2} \frac{1}{2\pi(1-rho^2)^{1/2}} \exp -\frac{1}{2}\left[\frac{t_1^2 - 2t_1 t_2\ rho + t_2^2}{1 - rho^2}\right] dt_2 dt_1$$

The bivariate integral is obtained by performing a one dimensional Simpson's rule integration of the appropriate function of the cumulative normal distribution. Subroutines PNORM (p. 369) and SIMPSN (p. 361) are used.

4.7 QBETA - Beta Distribution Quantiles

Calling Sequence:

        ...QBETA(P,A,B)...

QBETA finds the quantile associated with probability P for a beta random variable with shape parameters (A,B); i.e., QBETA satisfies

$$\frac{\Gamma(A+B)}{\Gamma(A)\Gamma(B)} \int_0^{QBETA} t^{A-1}(1-t)^{B-1} dt = P.$$

The bisection method is used in solving

        PBETA(QBETA,A,B) = P.

QBETA remembers the shape parameters and the quantile and probability from the previous call; thus, if shape parameters stay the same, it begins with a smaller (possibly much smaller) interval than [0,1].

Precision (QBETAS):

        CALL QBETAS(NS)

resets the convergence threshold for relative absolute error to 10**-NS. NS is initialized to 7.

4.8 QFDIST - F Distribution Quantiles

Calling Sequence:

        ...QFDIST(P,A,B)...

QFDIST finds the quantile associated with probability P for an F random variable with (A,B) degrees of freedom; i.e., QFDIST satisfies

$$\frac{\Gamma\left[\frac{A+B}{2}\right]}{\Gamma\left[\frac{A}{2}\right]\Gamma\left[\frac{B}{2}\right]} A^{\frac{A}{2}} B^{\frac{B}{2}} \int_0^{QFDIST} \frac{t^{\frac{A}{2}-1}}{(B+At)^{\frac{A+B}{2}}} dt = P.$$

QFDIST calls QBETA, utilizing the fact that if Z has an F distribution with (A,B) degrees of freedom, AZ/(B+AZ) has a beta distribution with shape parameters (A/2,B/2).

4.9 QGAMMA - Gamma Distribution Quantiles

Calling Sequence:

...QGAMMA(P,A)...

QGAMMA finds the quantile associated with probability P for a gamma random variable with shape parameter A; i.e., QGAMMA satisfies

$$\frac{1}{\Gamma(A)} \int_0^{QGAMMA} t^{A-1} e^{-t} dt = P.$$

The bisection method is used in solving

PGAMMA(QGAMMA,A,B) = P.

QGAMMA remembers the shape parameter and the quantile and probability from the previous call; thus, if the shape parameter stays the same, the initial interval is shorter (possibly much shorter) than otherwise.

Precision (QGAMMS):

        CALL QGAMMS(NS)

resets the convergence threshold for relative absolute error to 10**-NS. NS is initialized to 7.

4.10 QNORM - Normal Distribution Quantiles

Calling Sequence:

        ...QNORM(P)...

QNORM finds the quantile associated with probability P for a standard normal random variable; i.e., QNORM satisfies

$$\frac{1}{\sqrt{2\pi}} \int_{-\infty}^{QNORM} e^{-t^2/2} dt = P.$$

The rational function approximation of Hastings [14] is used.

4.11 QTDIST - t Distribution Quantiles

Calling Sequence:

        ...QTDIST(P,A)...

QTDIST finds the quantile associated with probability P for a Student-t random variable with A degrees of freedom: i.e., QTDIST satisfies

$$\frac{\Gamma\left[\frac{A+1}{2}\right]}{\Gamma\left[\frac{A}{2}\right]\Gamma\left[\frac{1}{2}\right]} A^{-\frac{1}{2}} \int_{-\infty}^{QTDIST} \left[\frac{1}{1 + t^2/A}\right]^{\frac{A+1}{2}} dt = P.$$

QTDIST calls QBETA, utilizing the fact that if T has a Student-t distribution with A degrees of freedom, T/(A+T) has a beta distribution with shape parameters (1/2,A/2).

4.12 RBINOM - Binomial Random Numbers

<u>Calling Sequence:</u>

        ...RBINOM(N,P)...

    N,P = Binomial parameters

RBINOM generates a binomial(N,P) random variable. The method, designed for efficiency when N is large, involves looking at medians in Uniform(0,1) samples of size N/2**i, i=1, ... , log N, each of which is generated in a single step via approximation techniques [15]. Execution times grow only logarithmically with N.

4.13 RMLTN - Multinomial Random Numbers

<u>Calling Sequence:</u>

        CALL RMLTN(N,NP,P,X)

    N = number of trials
    NP = number of cell probabilities
    P = vector of cell probabilities, summing to 1
    X = vector of cell counts

RMLTN returns a vector X of counts with a multinomial(N,P) distribution. The well-known relation is exploited between the multinomial and binomial distributions; RBINOM is called.

4.14 RNORM - Normal Random Numbers

<u>Calling Sequence:</u>

        ...RNORM(K)...

    K = a dummy argument (not used)

RNORM generates N(0,1) (standard normal) random numbers. The Box-Muller transform [16] is used on alternate calls to generate

independent N(0,1) variables from two uniform random numbers obtained
from RUNIF (see below).

4.15 RPERM - Random Permuations

Calling Sequence:

          CALL RPERM(N,KV)

          N = number of elements in vector
          KV = vector of integers

The vector KV(1), KV(2),..., KV(N) is randomly permuted. If N<0, KV
is first filled with the integers 1,2,...,|N|.

Example:

          CALL RPERM(-100,KV)

generates a random permutation of the first 100 integers.

4.16 RUNIF - Uniform Random Numbers

Calling Sequence:

          ...RUNIF(K)...

          K = 0 on first call get starting value from clock;
                 otherwise, cycle
          K < 0 get starting value from clock and set
                 K = starting value
          K > 0 use K as starting value

RUNIF uses a combination congruential and Tausworthe algorithm to
generate uniform random numbers on (0,1). RUNIF provides uniform
random numbers for sampling and function routines in STATLIB's
high-level packages; starting values may be set through ISX (see
p. 291).

RUNIF(0) should be used, except to start (or restart) the generator,
either specifying a starting value (K > 0) or retrieving the starting
value supplied (K < 0).

Examples:

          X=RUNIF(57385)

starts (or re-starts) RUNIF, using starting value 57385.

          K=-1
          X=RUNIF(K)

starts (or re-starts) RUNIF, using a starting value obtained from the system clock; the starting value is returned in K.

... RUNIF(0) ...

generates a random number as part of an arithmetic expression. If RUNIF has been called before, the next value in the sequence is generated; otherwise, a starting value is obtained from the system clock.

4.17 R2NORM - Bivariate Normal Random Numbers

Calling Sequence:

CALL R2NORM(X,Y,RHO)

X,Y = random normal deviates
RHO = correlation

R2NORM generates bivariate N(0,1) (standard normal) random numbers with specified correlation rho by transforming independent N(0,1) variables obtained via the Box-Muller transform [16].

5. CHARACTER STRING MANIPULATION

Subroutines of this section perform character (or byte) string functions. BSCANW scans byte strings for occurrences of a given word. GETPUT and OEQUAL are assembly language routines for fast moving and comparing. QREAD and QWRITE perform quick reading and writing of character strings, bypassing the standard FORTRAN format interpreter. VALUED and VALUEI convert real and integer numbers to character strings; DVALUE and IVALUE translate these back to numbers.

5.1 BSCANW - Scan String for Words

Calling Sequence:

        CALL BSCANW(NCW,WORD,IW,STRING,N1,N2,N3,K,&ERR)

The character (byte) string STRING is searched for the first occurence of the NCW characters beginning at the IW-th position of WORD. THE NCW-character substrings of STRING considered are those beginning at position N1 through those beginning at N2, in steps of N3. The number of the successful comparison is returned in K; if the search fails, K is set to zero and the error return taken.

Examples:

        CALL BSCANW(3,WORD,1,'EXPLOGSQR',1,9,3,K,&88)

determines whether WORD contains EXP, LOG, or SQR.

        CALL BSCANW(7,'STATLIB',1,LINE,1,74,1,K,&88)

searches for the first occurence of the word STATLIB in the 80-character array LINE.

5.2 DVALUE, IVALUE - Conversion from Character String

Calling Sequences:

        ...DVALUE(STRING,N1,N2)...
        ...IVALUE(STRING,N1,N2)...

DVALUE converts bytes N1 through N2 of STRING to floating point real; the indicated byte locations must contain a valid real or integer constant. IVALUE converts these to integer; a valid integer constant must be supplied here (a non-numeric character, other than a leading sign or blank(s), will terminate the conversion; e.g., 123D8 becomes 123).

5.3 GETPUT - Move Character String

Calling Sequence:

        CALL GETPUT(NC,X,IX,Y,IY)

GETPUT moves NC characters from X, starting at character IX, to Y, starting at character IY.

5.4 OEQUAL - Compare Character Strings

        ...OEQUAL(NC,X,IX,Y,IY)...

OEQUAL is a logical function which returns the value .TRUE. if the NC characters starting at character IX of X equal those starting at character IY of Y.

5.5 QREAD, QWRITE - Quick Reading and Writing

Calling Sequences:

        CALL QREAD(NUNIT,X,NC,&EOF,&ERR)
        CALL QWRITE(NUNIT,X,NC,&EOF,&ERR)

        NUNIT = read/write unit
        X   = array receiving (QREAD) or containing (QWRITE)
                data
        NC   = number of characters to be transmitted
        &EOF = end-of-file return
        &ERR = transmission error return

NC characters (bytes) are read into X (QREAD) or written from X (QWRITE); the data set control block may specify either formatted or unformatted records. In either case, format interpreting is bypassed, resulting in substantial time improvements for long logical records.

5.6 VALUED, VALUEI - Conversion to Character String

Calling Sequences:

        CALL VALUED(D,STRING,N1,N2)
        CALL VALUEI(I,STRING,N1,N2)

VALUED returns the character string representation of the real number D; the result is left-justified and stored between characters N1 and N2 of STRING. VALUEI returns the character string representation (also left-justified) of the integer I. The substring generated by

VALUED has the form of a real or integer constant, with or without a
decimal exponent depending upon which has more significant digits.
In either case, if the resulting character string requires more than
the N2-N1+1 bytes available, asterisks are returned.

6. SUBJECT INDEX

7. GLOSSARY OF SUBROUTINE CALLS (FTN)

PART IV

IMPLEMENTATIONS

This part of the manual discusses how to access STATLIB routines and describes its implementations on several IBM operating systems. In all cases, the software is available in FORTRAN and ISX modes. On most systems, ISX may be run interactively in a time-sharing environment as well as in batch mode.

Specific implementation details, such as data set names and the availability of supplementary documentation, may vary between installations and over time. Check with local distribution sources for current information.

Chapter 14 contains general implementation information, including a discussion of potential problems in converting the software to run on non-IBM systems. Chapter 15 discusses procedures for using STATLIB on IBM VS/TSO installations. Chapter 16 discusses procedures for IBM VM/CMS and VP/CSS systems.

CHAPTER 14

GENERAL PROCEDURES

1. INTRODUCTION

This chapter discusses general information for using STATLIB on any system. Section 2 describes ISX, the library's interactive command system. Section 3 contains information on calling STATLIB subroutines directly from FORTRAN. Section 4 discusses portability considerations that would surface in attempting to transport the library to new installations.

2. GENERAL ISX INFORMATION

ISX programs are load modules made up of STATLIB's FORTRAN subroutines and the ISX driver program. Because of ISX's facility for easily including or excluding entire packages of programs, several different versions of ISX may easily be created. Two standard versions of ISX exist at most installations: a "complete" version containing all packages from Part II (STPAK, TSPAK, SPPAK, TABLE, DYNCOR and SERVICE), and an "STPAK" version containing just STPAK, DYNCOR, and SERVICE.

The complete version of ISX is generally overlaid to economize on core storage. ISX (Ch. 4) and most DYNCOR (Ch. 9) and SERVICE (Ch. 10) routines are included in the root segment, whereas each of the other packages are included in overlay segments. Users of overlaid programs should try to minimize the amount of switching between overlay segments: excessive switching taxes the system's resources and, depending on the charging algorithm, can result in significantly higher direct program charges.

The STPAK version is generally not overlaid, and runs in about 250K bytes of core on IBM VS systems. It exists separate from the overlaid version because IBM offers a facility for easily combining FORTRAN subroutines with non-overlaid load modules. Thus programs which combine FORTRAN and ISX statements are easy to write and run. For additional details, see Chapter 15, Section 2.2 (p. 392). A heavy demand exists for programs which primarily analyze two-way matrices. For such analyses, the STPAK version of ISX (or the complete version) may be viewed as an alternative to SPSS, SAS, BMDP and others.

ISX is intended for batch as well as interactive (time-sharing) use. ISX is preferred to FORTRAN for batch use because it avoids the compilation and link-editing (loading) costs of FORTRAN and because it provides vastly simpler syntactic calling sequences.

On systems offering both batch and interactive programming, the choice between batch and interactive use of ISX is not always clear. Interactive use provides better response time and true interactive data analysis. But batch operation may on some systems be cheaper for the user and easier on the system. Furthermore, because many systems provide flexible and powerful online remote job entry and fetching capabilities (such as WYLBUR at Rand), remote entry jobs may often be submitted and retrieved within minutes. For programs with heavy computational and/or printing requirements, this may provide adequate response time.

Because ISX reads statements free-form, one must be careful when submitting programs via remote entry editors to enter them "unnumbered", since the line numbers (which normally appear in columns 73 through 80) will be read as part of the command. Alternatively, /ISXIO (p. 71) may be called to limit the card size to 72 (or fewer) columns:

        /ISXIO * * 72

3. GENERAL FORTRAN INFORMATION

STATLIB may be accessed from FORTRAN programs by instructing the system loader to search the STATLIB library as well as the system library (or libraries). The remaining chapters of Part IV describe how this is done on different systems.

In writing programs that use subroutines from STATLIB and other private libraries, it is important to avoid external name clashes. Most of STATLIB's routines have distinctive prefixes (the first two or three characters of the package name), and all STATLIB common blocks end with the characters 00i, i = 1-9, so if the user is careful, the chances of encountering such problems should be small. A list of STATLIB's functions, subroutines, and entry points follows.

ADDRFNS	BSCANF	BSCANW	CLOCK	CORFRE	CORFRM
CORGET	CORGTFR	CORGTM	CORLEF	CORREM	DATE
DSPCMN	DSPLAY	DSPLBO	DSPPAR	DVALUE	DYNAPD
DYNCMN	DYNCON	DYNCPY	DYNDEF	DYNDEL	DYNDMP
DYNENL	DYNERR	DYNEXT	DYNFNB	DYNFN1	DYNFN2
DYNGBG	DYNGET	DYNINB	DYNINL	DYNINP	DYNIN1
DYNLOC	DYNLST	DYNMAP	DYNMSA	DYNNAM	DYNNEW
DYNOLD	DYNOUE	DYNOUT	DYNPTD	DYNPTR	DYNPUT
DYNXXD	DYNXXN	DYNXXP	FFT	FMTCRD	FMTGEN
FTNFUN	FTNSUB	FUNM	FUN12V	GETPUT	GTPTOEQL
HSHCMN	HSHDEL	HSHNEW	HSHOLD	HSHPAR	IADDR
IDATE	ISXABD	ISXCLP	ISXCMD	ISXCMN	ISXCMX
ISXCNV	ISXCTL	ISXDAT	ISXDTX	ISXDUM	ISXDYN
ISXERR	ISXMIS	ISXPRC	ISXRDL	ISXSP	ISXSPA
ISXSPM	ISXST	ISXSVC	ISXTAB	ISXTS	ISYMLO

IVALUE	KADDR	LOCATM	LOGDSK	LSTRNG	LVALUE
MSG	MSGPRT	OEQUAL	OPAGE	OPAGEH	OPAGEP
OPAGES	OPTCMN	OPTERR	OPTGET	OPTION	OPTLBO
OPTLBV	OPTLGO	OPTLGV	OPTPRT	OSDATE	PBETA
PFDIST	PGAMMA	PNORM	PPLCMN	PPLOT	PPLOTP
PTDIST	P2NORM	QBETA	QFDIST	QGAMMA	QNORM
QREAD	QTDIST	QWRITE	RBINOM	READ	REALTR
REGACC	REGACW	REGANL	REGANX	REGCMN	REGCON
REGCOR	REGERR	REGEXW	REGFOV	REGFOW	REGGET
REGINV	REGMSD	REGPAR	REGPRE	REGPRF	REGPUT
REGRCC	REGRCV	REGRES	REGRSD	REGRSW	REGSEL
REGUPB	REGUPD	REGUPE	REGUPW	REGWAC	REGWA2
REGWGT	REGX	REGXA	REGXAR	REGXAW	REGXA1
REGXA2	REGXD	REGXF	REGXF1	REGXF2	REGXP
REGXPU	REGXP1	REGXP2	REGXR	REGXRA	REGXRP
REGXR2	REGXU	REGXU1	REGXV	REGXWG	REGXWK
REGXWN	REGX0	RMLTN	RNNR	RNORM	RPERM
RUNIF	RUNIFS	R2NORM	SIMPAR	SIMPSN	SORTC
SPACOR	SPACOV	SPADD	SPADD1	SPARC1	SPARC2
SPARF1	SPARF2	SPAR1	SPAR2	SPBXCX	SPBXTR
SPCFT	SPCMLT	SPCML1	SPCMN	SPCNVL	SPCOHE
SPCONC	SPCONJ	SPCONV	SPCPZN	SPCUTL	SPDANL
SPDF1T	SPDF2T	SPDIF	SPECT	SPECTM	SPECTN
SPECTX	SPFCS1	SPFCS2	SPFIT1	SPFIT2	SPFTI
SPFTIN	SPFTMU	SPFTSQ	SPGAIN	SPIFEV	SPINV2
SPMCNV	SPMLT	SPMLT1	SPMODL	SPPARM	SPPHAS
SPPRZN	SPREG	SPREGN	SPREG1	SPRFT	SPRFT2
SPRPZN	SPRVBD	SPSD1	SPSD2	SPSFT	SPSMTH
SPTFN	SPTRCJ	SPTRND	SPTR2	SPWIND	SPWINW
SPXAMP	SPXCOR	SPXCOV	SPXTRA	STCMN	STCODE
STCPY	STDIM	STDSP	STENL	STENLX	STERR
STEXT	STFITD	STFNC	STFNOB	STFN0	STFN1
STFN2	STGET	STGETC	STGETW	STGETX	STGETY
STLINK	STLOGS	STLOGT	STLOGW	STMSG	STNAM
STPLT	STPRT	STPUT	STRCDK	STRCOD	STREAD
STREG	STREGA	STREGP	STREGW	STSAMP	STSORT
STSRTX	STTSFN	STUINP	STUINS	STUSER	STWRIT
STXRGN	STXTAB	STXTB0	SYMCHC	SYMCHL	SYMDOT
SYMINV	SYMQFM	SYMRCM	SYSALF	SYSCMD	SYSERS
SYSLOG	SYSWRT	TABAOV	TABAVP	TABAVX	TABCON
TABDFN	TABDIM	TABDSP	TABENL	TABERR	TABEXT
TABFND	TABFN1	TABFN2	TABFT1	TABFT2	TABMSG
TABNEW	TABOLD	TABPLT	TABPRJ	TABPRM	TABPRP
TABPRS	TABPRT	TABREG	TABRSD	TABTRN	TABXCO
TABXEX	TABXFD	TABXF1	TABXF2	TABXS1	TABXS2
TABXTR	TABXXC	TABXXI	TABXXM	TABXXN	TIME
TIMEDATE	TIMEOD	TIMER	TIMSET	TIMZER	TRIADD
TRICPY	TRIDIS	TRIINV	TRIMAT	TRIMLT	TRIPRT
TRISCM	TRISTI	TRISTZ	TRISUB	TRITSQ	TSACOR
TSARFS	TSCLIM	TSCMN	TSCSUM	TSDETR	TSDIFF
TSERR	TSEXT	TSFNM	TSFNS	TSFNTS	TSFN0
TSFN1	TSFN2	TSGET	TSHARM	TSLBL	TSLBLS
TSMAVG	TSMED3	TSMED4	TSMODL	TSMODR	TSMSG
TSNEW	TSNEWZ	TSNHAN	TSNLSM	TSNLS2	TSNLS3
TSNLS4	TSNL3R	TSNMOD	TSNORM	TSN3RC	TSOLD

TSOLDZ	TSOUTL	TSPACF	TSPLIT	TSPLT	TSPLTH
TSPLTR	TSPOLO	TSPOLY	TSPRDN	TSPRT	TSPRTX
TSPT	TSPTG	TSPTGH	TSPTH	TSPUT	TSREG
TSREGA	TSRFSD	TSRSDA	TSTAB	TSTABK	TSTAPR
TSTIME	TSTORG	TSTYPE	TSUNDF	TSXCOR	TS3RSH
UREAD	VALUED	VALUEI	VREAD	WRITE	XFMAXM
XFMINM	XFSSQM	XFSUMM	XMEDN	XORDST	

In all cases, object modules with these external names will take
precedence over STATLIB routines. Link-edited subroutines on other
libraries will take precedence if their library appears first in the
SYSLIB list; otherwise, the STATLIB routines will be loaded.

Nonstandard applications may require that certain STATLIB subroutines
be modified. STATLIB's modular coding should simplify that task
considerably. For example, if one preferred a different matrix
inversion algorithm in regression analysis, only subroutine REGINV
(p. 325) may need to be replaced, not the regression driver program
itself.

4. PORTABILITY

Nearly all of STATLIB is written in the IBM FORTRAN IV language. The
exceptions are some nine routines written in IBM ASSEMBLY language
which issue macro instuctions to get and free core storage, to
retrieve the time and date, to obtain the base addresses of arrays,
etc. Problems should not occur in transferring object modules or VS
load modules between IBM installations; standard IBM utilities may be
used to dump and reload them. Recompiling source code at different
IBM installations may encounter problems due to differences between
compilers or local compiler parameter settings. Generally, one might
expect a few routines to not pass successfully through a given
FORTRAN compiler.

STATLIB has been installed on Xerox and UNIVAC computers, but with
considerable difficulty. At this time we recommend implementation of
STATLIB on IBM (or Amdahl) systems only.

CHAPTER 15

IBM VS/TSO PROCEDURES

1. INTRODUCTION

This chapter discusses the use of STATLIB on IBM systems running under VS (or OS) in batch or time-sharing (TSO). Sections 2 and 3 discuss procedures for using ISX in batch and TSO, respectively. Section 4 describes procedures for using STATLIB subroutines directly in FORTRAN.

2. ISX USAGE - BATCH

2.1 Running ISX Without FORTRAN

ISX may be executed in batch via the ISX catalogued procedure, listed below.

```
              ISX Catalogued Procedure

//ISX          PROC VER=isxver,DSN=isxlib
//GO      EXEC PGM=ISX,REGION=350K
//STEPLIB  DD  DSNAME=&DSN&VER,DISP=SHR
//SYSPRINT DD  SYSOUT=A
//FT05F001 DD  DDNAME=SYSIN
//FT06F001 DD  SYSOUT=A

   isxlib = name of the default ISX data set
   isxver = default ISX version suffix
```

The arguments isxlib and isxver are locally set, depending on the installation's data set naming conventions and the particular mix of work at the site. Check with local distribution sources for actual names. Regardless of naming conventions, however, the complete version of ISX will be stored as member ISX on isxlib, whereas the STPAK version is stored on isxlibST (for a discussion of versions, see Ch. 14, Sec. 2, p. 387). According to IBM job control language procedures, calling the catalogued procedure will execute the default version if VER is omitted, the complete version if VER=(null), and the STPAK version if VER=ST.

Additional special-purpose versions of ISX may be available at various installations. Furthermore, the DSN parameter allows the user to specify a data set other than the standard ISX data set. Note, however, that VER, if not null, will be concatenated to the data set name.

The ISX catalogued procedure will normally be available on the system library. It may vary from installation to installation and from time to time, so use of the supplied catalogued procedure is recommended.

<u>Examples:</u>

```
//jobname JOB (acctg info),parameters
// EXEC ISX,VER=ST
//GO.FT10F001 DD DSN=DATA,DISP=SHR
//GO.SYSIN DD *
STDIM DATA 2 WAGES EXPER
STREAD DATA 10 (2F6.0) 100
STENL DATA 2 PRDN RSID
STREG DATA WAGES 1 EXPER
STPLT DATA PRDN 1 RSID
```

executes the STPAK version of ISX, fitting a wages versus experience regression model and plotting the residuals.

```
//jobname JOB (acctg info),parameters
// EXEC ISX,VER=
//GO.FT10F001 DD DSN=DATA,DISP=SHR
//GO.SYSIN DD *
DYNINL 29 .... BSMI
TSMODL AREG BSMI 3 1 12 13 INDV
TSMODL AREG BSMI 1 0 DEPV
TSREG AREG 1958 1 1967 12
TSREGA AREG BSMI
TSPLT 1 RSID BSMI 1958 1 1967 12
DYNNAM RSID BSMI DATA BSMI
STDIM BSMI 1 RSID
STFITD BSMI RSID NORMAL
STPLT BSMI NORMAL 1 RSID
```

executes the complete version of ISX, fitting an autoregressive model and plotting the residuals via TSPAK, then producing a normal probability plot via STPAK.

2.2 Running ISX With FORTRAN

Truly flexible statistical analysis requires at times that one combine FORTRAN subroutines in with the analysis. Routines of STATLIB have been written with several readily accessible FORTRAN links. For example, STUSER (p. 121) passes data matrices directly to FORTRAN subroutine FTNSUB, DYNFN1 and DYNFN2 (p. 263) call FTNFUN, STSAMP (p. 119) calls STUINP, etc. The loader enables one to easily and inexpensively mix new subroutines with ISX. It picks up the FORTRAN compiler output from the primary input stream (SYSLIN), replaces whatever duplicate names it finds in the ISX load module,

then transfers control to ISX. The loader may be used only with ISX
programs that are not overlaid; the standard catalogued procedure
references the STPAK version of ISX (see Ch. 14, Sec. 2, p. 387).

```
┌─────────────────────────────────────────────────────────────────┐
│              ISX Load and Go Catalogued Procedure                 │
├─────────────────────────────────────────────────────────────────┤
│  //ISXG         PROC VER=ST,DSN=isxlib                            │
│  //GO     EXEC  PGM=LOADER,REGION=350K,                          │
│  //             PARM='LET,NOMAP,EP=MAIN'                          │
│  //SYSLIB   DD  DSNAME=fortlib,DISP=SHR                           │
│  //         DD  DSNAME=statlib,DISP=SHR                           │
│  //SYSLIN   DD  DSNAME=compout,DISP=(OLD,PASS)                    │
│  //         DD  DSNAME=&DSN&VER(ISX),DISP=SHR                     │
│  //SYSLOUT  DD  SYSOUT=A                                          │
│  //SYSPRINT DD  SYSOUT=A                                          │
│  //FT05F001 DD  DDNAME=SYSIN                                      │
│  //FT06F001 DD  SYSOUT=A                                          │
├─────────────────────────────────────────────────────────────────┤
│   fortlib = name of the standard IBM FORTRAN                      │
│             library (normally SYS1.FORTLIB)                       │
│   statlib = name of the STATLIB FORTRAN library                   │
│   compout = name of the FORTRAN compiler output                   │
│             data set (normally &&LOADSET)                         │
│   isxlib = name of the default ISX data set                      │
└─────────────────────────────────────────────────────────────────┘
```

The arguments fortlib, statlib, compout, and isxlib are locally set,
depending on the installation's data set naming conventions. Check
with local distribution sources for actual names. The IBM FORTRAN
library must have the extended error handling routines on it as well
as the standard routines.

Example:

```
        //jobname JOB (acctg info),parameters
        // EXEC FORTGC
        //FORT.SYSIN DD *
              FUNCTION FTNFUN(X)
              IMPLICIT REAL*8(A-H,P-Z),LOGICAL(O)
              FTNFUN=DATAN(DLGAMA(X**5)-DSQRT(X+7))
              RETURN
              END
        // EXEC ISXG
        //GO.FT10F001 DD DSN=DATA,DISP=SHR
        //GO.SYSIN DD *
        STDIM DATA 2 WAGES EXPER
        STREAD DATA 10 (2F6.0) 100
        STENL DATA 2 PRDN RSID
        STFN1 DATA WAGES FTN WAGES
        STREG DATA WAGES 1 EXPER
        STPLT DATA PRDN 1 RSID
```

fits a transformed wages versus experience regression model and plots
the residuals. The dependent variable is transformed according to

the FORTRAN function FTNFUN.

3. ISX USAGE - TSO

ISX may be invoked in TSO via the ISX CLIST, listed below.

```
                              ISX CLIST

   10 PROC 0 VER(isxver) DSN(isxlib)
   20 FREE FILE(SYSPRINT,FT05F001,FT06F001)
   30 ALLOC FILE(FT05F001) DATASET(*)
   40 ALLOC FILE(FT06F001) DATASET(*)
   50 ALLOC FILE(SYSPRINT) DATASET('NULLFILE')
   60 CALL '&DSN.&VER.(ISX)'
   70 FREE FILE(SYSPRINT,FT30F001) DATASET('&DSN.&VER.')
   80 ALLOC FILE(SYSPRINT) DATASET(*)

          isxlib = name of the default ISX data set
          isxver = default ISX version suffix
```

The arguments isxlib and isxver are locally set, depending on the
installation's data set naming conventions and the particular mix of
work at the site. At most installations isxver will be null; check
with local distribution sources for actual names. When the CLIST is
invoked with VER('') (or no VER parameter if isxver is null), the
complete version of ISX will be used, while VER(ST) causes the STPAK
version to be used.

Additional special-purpose versions of ISX may be available at
various installations. Furthermore, the DSN parameter allows the
user to specify a data set other than the standard ISX data set.
Note, however, that the fully qualified data set name must be used
and that VER, if not null, will be concatenated to it.

The ISX CLIST will normally be available in the system library or in
a library which may be concatenated to the system library. The CLIST
may vary from installation to installation and from time to time, so
use of the supplied CLIST is recommended. The TSO command "HELP ISX"
or local distribution sources may be able to provide further
information on setting up a TSO userid for ISX use.

A minimum region size of about 350K is required for ISX.

Examples:

        ISX

invokes the default version of ISX.

        ISX VER(X)

invokes version X of ISX.

      ISX DSN(ABC.ISXLIB)

invokes the ISX module stored as member ISX on library ABC.ISXLIB.

4. FORTRAN USAGE

STATLIB subroutines are stored as individually link-edited load modules on a library data set. To use the library in batch, one concatenates it to the standard IBM FORTRAN library:

```
//stepnam.SYSLIB DD DSN=fortlib,DISP=SHR
// DD DSN=statlib,DISP=SHR   ,
```

where

      fortlib = IBM FORTRAN library
      statlib = STATLIB library name

The arguments fortlib and statlib are locally set, depending on the installation's data set naming conventions. The operands "DSN=fortlib,DISP=SHR" are not required on some systems. Check with local distribution sources for actual names. The IBM FORTRAN library must have the extended error handling routines on it as well as the standard routines.

For catalogued procedures using the linkage editor (e.g., FORTHCLG, FORTHLG), stepnam is "LKED", whereas for procedures using the loader, stepnam is "GO". Of course, the placement of these DD statements with respect to other job control statements should follow IBM conventions of occuring in the same order as in the catalogued procedure. On most systems this statement may follow any "FORT DD" statements (if any) and precede all other "LKED DD" or "GO DD" statements (if any).

The SYSLIB job control statements provide access to all routines in STATLIB, the high-level routines of Part II as well as the low-level ones of Part III. Program link editing or loading costs, however, may be unacceptably large if many high-level routines are being called. For example, the first program below would cause about 200 routines to be loaded, including most of DYNCOR (Ch. 9) and REGPAK (Ch. 11); the second program would construct a load module of some 300 routines. If ISX can perform the same job, and it usually can, the ISX user will avoid this overhead completely, whereas if ISX augmented with a few FORTRAN subroutines is sufficient, at least 80 percent of the overhead will be avoided by concatenating the ISX main program to the FORTRAN compilation output (see Sec. 2.2, above).

Local enhancements to the FORTRAN catalogued procedures may permit a simpler method for including STATLIB: e.g., at Bell Laboratories,

```
        // EXEC FORTxx,FORTLB2='STAT.FORTLIB'
```

were FORTxx is one of the FORTRAN catalogued procedures FORTGCG, FORTHCL, etc.

<u>Examples</u>:

```
        //jobname JOB (acctg info),parameters
        // EXEC FORTGCG
        //FORT.SYSIN DD *
              CALL STDIM('DATA',2,'WAGES   EXPER   ')
              CALL STREAD('DATA',5,'(2F6.0)',100)
              CALL STENL('DATA',2,'RSID    PRDN    ')
              CALL STREG('DATA','WAGES   ',1,'EXPER   ')
              CALL STPLT('DATA','PRDN    ',1,'RSID    ')
              STOP
              END
        //GO.SYSLIB DD DSN=SYS1.FORTERR,DISP=SHR
        // DD DSN=SYS1.STATLIB,DISP=SHR
        //GO.SYSIN DD *
           325    20
           210    11
              ...
```

(at Rand) compiles, loads, and executes a simple FORTRAN program which regresses wages on experience and plots the residuals. The main program calls on STPAK routines (Ch. 5), which in turn use DYNCOR (Ch. 9) for data management and REGPAK (Ch. 11) for the actual computations.

```
        //jobname JOB (acctg info),parameters
        // EXEC FORTHCL,FORTLB2='STAT.FORTLIB'
        //FORT.SYSIN DD *
              EXTERNAL ISXDUM,ISXDYN,ISXSVC,ISXST
              CALL ISXCTL(ISXSVC,ISXTS,ISXDYN,ISXDUM,
            . ISXDUM,ISXDUM,ISXDUM,ISXDUM)
              STOP
              END
        //LKED.SYSLMOD DD DSN=YOURLIB(ISX),DISP=OLD
```

(at Bell Laboratories) compiles and link-edits a FORTRAN program which calls the ISX control program ISXCTL.

CHAPTER 16

IBM VM/CMS AND VP/CSS PROCEDURES

1. INTRODUCTION

This chapter discusses use of STATLIB on IBM systems running under VM/CMS or VP/CSS in time sharing (or batch) mode. Section 2 discusses procedures for using ISX and Section 3 discusses procedures for using STATLIB subroutines directly in FORTRAN.

In order to use STATLIB, one must first attach the STATLIB disk. On most systems, the CMS (or CSS) command

        ATTACH STATLIB BTL

is used to do this. After attaching STATLIB, the CMS command

        STATNEWS

will direct the user to further information regarding use of STATLIB on the particular system.

2. ISX USAGE

ISX is invoked via the ISX EXEC. The minimum virtual machine size required is about 448K on VM/CMS and 384K on VP/CSS. The complete version of ISX is used, with the various high-level packages in overlay segments. The ISX EXEC accepts as optional arguments filenames of files (with filetype ISX) containing ISX statements, such as procedure definitions, to be executed (see /XEQF, p. 74), in reverse order, upon entering ISX.

Examples:

        ISX

invokes ISX.

        ISX MYPROCS IPTREG

invokes ISX and executes files IPTREG ISX and MYPROCS ISX.

3. FORTRAN USAGE

STATLIB subroutines are stored as individual members of one or two TXTLIB files. To use the library, one concatenates it to the system library by executing the command

        STATLIB

Additional TXTLIB files to be searched may be specified as arguments to the STATLIB command.

Example:

        STATLIB MYLIB
        RUN MYPROG

loads and executes the TEXT file MYPROG, searching libraries MYLIB and STATLIB, as well as the system library, to resolve references.

REFERENCES

1. Anderson, R., R. McL. Greenley, J. Kravits, and O. W. Anderson, Health Service Use: National Trends and Variations, U.S. Department of Health, Education, and Welfare, DHEW Publication No. (HSM) 73-30004, October 1972.

2. Brown, R. G., Smoothing, Forecasting and Prediction of Discrete Time Series, Prentice-Hall, New Jersey, 1962.

3. Box, G. E. P., and G. Jenkins, Time Series Analysis: Forecasting and Control, Holden-Day, San Francisco, 1970, p. 300.

4. Efron, B., "The Efficiency of Logistic Regression Compared to Normal Discriminant Analysis," Journal of the American Statistical Association, Vol. 70, Number 352, December 1975, pp. 892-898.

5. Singleton, R. C., "An Algorithm for Computing the Mixed Radix Fast Fourier Transform," IEEE Transactions on Audio and Electroacoustics, Vol. AU-17, pp. 93-103.

6. Kalman, R. E., "A New Approach to Linear Filtering and Prediction Problems," ASME Journal of Basic Engineering, Vol. 82D, 1960, pp. 35-45.

7. Plackett, R. L., "Some Theorems in Least Squares," Biometrika, Vol. 37, 1950, 149-157.

8. Bartlett, M. S., "An Inverse Matrix Adjustment Arising in Discriminant Analysis," Annals of Mathematical Statistics, Vol. 22, 1951, pp. 107-111.

9. Bodewig, E., Matrix Calculus, North Holland Publishing Co., New York, p. 110.

10. Longley, J. S., "An Appraisal of Least Squares Programs for the Electronic Computer from the Point of View of the User," Journal of the American Statistical Association, Vol. 62, 1967, pp. 819-841.

11. Handbook of Mathematical Functions, National Bureau of Standards Applied Mathematics Series .55 U. S. Government Printing Office, Washington D. C., 1964, p. 945.

12. Wilk, M. B., R. Gnanadesikan, and M. J. Huyett, "Probability Plots for the Gamma Distribution," Technometrics, Vol. 4, 1962, pp. 1-21.

13. IBM System/370 FORTRAN IV Library - Mathematical and Service
    Subprograms.

14. Hastings, C., Approximations for Digital Computers, Princeton
    University Press, Princeton, N. J., 1955.

15. Relles, D. A., "A Simple Algorithm for Generating Binomial
    Random Variables when N is Large," Journal of the American
    Statistical Association, Vol. 66, 1972, pp. 724-728.

16. Box, G. E. P., and M. E. Muller, "A Note on the Generation of
    Random Normal Deviates," Annals of Mathematical Statistics,
    Vol. 29, 1958, pp. 610-611.

PART II (ISX) SUBROUTINE SUBJECT INDEX

PART III (FTN) SUBROUTINE SUBJECT INDEX

PART II (ISX) GLOSSARY OF SUBROUTINE CALLS

PART III (FTN) GLOSSARY OF SUBROUTINE CALLS

SELECTED BELL LABORATORIES BOOKS

1. Aho, A. V., *Principles of Compiler Design,* Reading, Mass.: Addison-Wesley, 1977.

2. Bawa, V. S., S. J. Brown, and R. W. Klein, *Estimation Risk and Optimal Portfolio Choice,* New York: North-Holland, 1979.

3. Carroll, J. D., *Analyzing Multivariate Data,* New York: The Dryden Press, 1978.

4. Chambers, J. M., *Computational Methods for Data Analysis,* New York: Wiley, 1977.

5. Garey, M. R., and D. S. Johnson, *Computers and Intractability: A Guide to the Theory of NP-Completeness,* San Francisco: W. H. Freeman, 1978.

6. Gnanadesikan, R., *Methods for Statistical Data Analysis of Multivariate Observations,* New York: Wiley, 1976.

7. Hamming, R. W., *Digital Filters,* Englewood Cliffs, N.J.: Prentice-Hall, 1977.

8. Helms, H. D., J. F. Kaiser, and L. R. Rabiner (eds.), *Literature in Digital Signal Processing,* New York: IEEE Press, 1976.

9. Kernighan, B. W., *Software Tools,* Reading, Mass: Addison-Wesley, 1976.

10. Kernighan, B. W., *The C Programming Language*, Englewood Cliffs, N.J.: Prentice-Hall, 1977.

11. Kernighan, B. W., and P. J. Plauger, *Elements of Programming Style* (2nd ed.), New York: McGraw-Hill, 1978.

12. Kruskal, J. B., and M. Wish, *Multidimensional Scaling,* Beverly Hills, Calif.: Sage, 1977.

13. MacWilliams, F. J., and N. J. A. Sloane, *Theory of Error-Correcting Codes,* New York: North-Holland, 1977.

14. Roberto, J. T., and L. E. Heindel, *LANG-PAK—A Language Design System,* New York: Elsevier, 1975.

15. Tukey, J. W., *Data Analysis and Regression, A Second Course in Statistics,* Reading, Mass.: Addison-Wesley, 1977.

16. Tukey, J. W., *Exploratory Data Analysis,* Reading, Mass.: Addision-Wesley, 1977.

17. Williams, W. H., *A Sampler on Sampling,* New York: Wiley, 1978.

18. Zajac, E. E., *Fairness or Efficiency: An Introduction to Public Utility Pricing,* Cambridge, Mass.: Ballinger Press, 1979.

SELECTED RAND BOOKS

1. Aumann, R. J., and L. S. Shapley, *Values of Non-Atomic Games,* Princeton, N.J.: Princeton University Press, 1974.

2. Baer, W. S., *Cable Television: A Handbook for Decisionmaking,* New York: Crane, Russak & Company, 1974.

3. Bellman, R. E., *Dynamic Programming,* Princeton, N.J.: Princeton University Press, 1957.

4. Coleman, J. S., and N. L. Karweit, *Information Systems and Performance Measures in Schools,* Englewood Cliffs, N.J.: Educational Technology Publications, 1972.

5. Dalkey, N. C., *Studies in the Quality of Life: Delphi and Decision-Making,* Lexington, Mass.: Heath, 1972.

6. Dantzig, G. B., *Linear Programming and Extensions,* Princeton, N.J.: Princeton University Press, 1963.

7. Fishman, G. S., *Spectral Methods in Econometrics,* Cambridge, Mass.: Harvard University Press, 1969.

8. Harman, A. J., *The International Computer Industry: Innovation and Comparative Advantage,* Cambridge, Mass.: Harvard University Press, 1971.

9. Hastings, C., *Approximations for Digital Computers,* Princeton, N.J.: Princeton University Press, 1955.

10. Kiviat, P. J., R. Villanueva, and H. M. Markowitz, *The SIMSCRIPT II Programming Language,* Englewood Cliffs, N.J.: Prentice-Hall, 1969.

11. Markowitz, H. M., B. Hausner, and H. W. Karr, *SIMSCRIPT: A Simulation Programming Language,* Englewood Cliffs, N.J.: Prentice-Hall, 1963.

12. McKinsey, J. C. C., *Introduction to the Theory of Games,* New York: McGraw-Hill, 1952.

13. Mitchell, B. M., W. G. Manning, and J. P. Acton, *Peak-Load Pricing: European Lessons for U.S. Energy Policy,* Cambridge, Mass.: Ballinger Publishing Company, 1978.

14. Newhouse, J. P., and A. J. Alexander, *An Economic Analysis of Public Library Services,* Lexington, Mass.: Heath, 1972.

15. Smith, J. P. (ed.), *Female Labor Supply: Theory and Estimation,* Princeton, N.J.: Princeton University Press, 1980.

16. Sharpe, W. F., *The Economics of Computers,* New York: Columbia University Press, 1969.

17. Turn, R., *Computers in the 1980s,* New York: Columbia University Press, 1974.

18. Walker, W. E., J. M. Chaiken, and E. J. Ignall (eds.), *Fire Department Deployment Analysis, A Public Policy Analysis Case Study: The Rand Fire Project,* New York: Elsevier North-Holland, 1979.